Judging under Uncertainty

Judging under Uncertainty

An Institutional Theory
of Legal Interpretation

Adrian Vermeule

Harvard University Press
Cambridge, Massachusetts
London, England
2006

Library of Congress Cataloging-in-Publication Data

Vermeule, Adrian, 1968–
Judging under uncertainty : an institutional theory of
legal interpretation / Adrian Vermeule.
p. cm.
Includes bibliographical references and index.
ISBN 0-674-02210-6 (alk. paper)
1. Judicial review—United States.
2. Law—United States—Interpretation and construction.
3. Judicial process—United States. I. Title.
KF4575.V47 2006
337.73'12—dc22   2005055117

For my family

Acknowledgments

Thanks are due, above all, to my extended family, including Kun Ja Lim; Blakey Vermeule; Cornelius Vermeule; Emily Vermeule, who will always be a vital presence; my wife Yun Soo, whose capacities for support and tolerance are seemingly infinite; and my children, Emily and Spencer, the best playmates ever.

Special thanks are also due to several friends and colleagues. Eric Posner is a model of academic rigor whose work on contract interpretation has indirectly inspired much of what follows. Antonin Scalia kindled my interest in the subject, both in person and through his superb academic and judicial writings. David Strauss has provided a model of collegiality and thoughtfulness; his work on common-law constitutionalism informs the whole book (sometimes as a clear and powerful statement of views I reject, but that sort of help is often the most helpful of all). Cass Sunstein has been an invaluable colleague and intellectual companion over the past seven years. One of the articles that form the backbone of the book was co-authored with him. Although I am not sure whose ideas were whose, there are good grounds to suspect that the original and incisive ones were his. I also draw upon his independent work throughout; special mention should be made of his work on the empirical determinants of formalism and on agencies as common-law courts. Fred Schauer has also provided inspiration for the ideas here. I should particularly mention his work on rules, formalism, and interpretive absurdity, all of which appears within. His clearminded contributions frequently shine through the dense clouds of my argument. Any errors are my own.

Helpful comments on the whole manuscript came from Matthew Adler, Will Baude, Adam Cox, John Donohue, Carolyn Frantz, Jack Goldsmith, Don Herzog, Eric Posner, Fred Schauer, David Strauss, Cass Sunstein, and two anonymous reviewers. Justin Rubin and Sean Heikkila provided superb research assistance, showing great patience with my foibles and passing humors. In writing what follows, I have drawn upon several previously published articles, although in each case with heavy revisions and in many cases radical surgery. The articles include the following: "Legislative History and the Limits of Judicial Competence: The Untold Story of *Holy Trinity Church*," 50 *Stanford Law Review* 1833 (1998); "Interpretive Choice," 75 *New York University Law Review* 74 (2000); "Hercules, Herbert, and Amar: The Trouble with Intratextualism," 111 *Harvard Law Review* 730 (2000) (with Ernest A. Young); "Institutional Design of a Thayerian Congress," 50 *Duke Law Journal* 1277 (2001) (with Elizabeth Garrett); "Judicial Review and Institutional Choice," 43 *William and Mary Law Review* 1557 (2002); "Interpretation and Institutions," 101 *Michigan Law Review* 885 (2003) (with Cass R. Sunstein); "The Judiciary Is a They, Not an It: Interpretation and the Fallacy of Division," 14 *Journal of Contemporary Legal Issues* 549 (2005); "Three Strategies of Interpretation," 42 *San Diego Law Review* 607 (2005); and "Constitutional Amendments and the Constitutional Common Law," forthcoming in *Legislatures and Constitutionalism: The Role of the Legislature in the Constitutional State* (T. Kahana and R. Bauman, eds.) (Cambridge University Press). I thank the many colleagues, too numerous to list, who provided comments on these works.

Contents

Introduction   1

I. Critique

1 Interpretation without Institutions   15

2 Dynamism and Pragmatism: A Tale of Two Nirvanas   40

II. Reconstruction

3 The Institutional Turn   63

4 Judicial Capacities: A Case Study   86

5 Systemic Effects and Judicial Coordination   118

III. Applications

6 Judges, Uncertainty, and Bounded Rationality   153

7 Statutory Interpretation   183

8 Judicial Review and Constitutional Interpretation   230

Conclusion: Interim Interpretive Theory   289

Notes   293

Index   323

Judging under Uncertainty

Introduction

In this book I advance an institutional argument for a version of formalism in legal interpretation, principally the interpretation of statutes and the Constitution. I define "formalism" at length in later chapters. In the version of formalism offered here, judges should (1) follow the clear and specific meaning of legal texts, where those texts have clear and specific meanings; and (2) defer to the interpretations offered by legislatures and agencies, where legal texts lack clear and specific meanings. These positions run contrary to the mainstream of American legal theory, which favors flexible, policy-saturated judicial interpretation of statutes and the Constitution, is often suspicious of deference to administrative agencies in statutory interpretation, and generally rejects deference to legislatures in matters of constitutional interpretation.

Institutions and Legal Interpretation

By offering an institutional argument for legal formalism, I mean to advance two distinct theses, one methodological, the other substantive. These two theses are partially independent as a logical matter. One can adopt an institutional approach to legal interpretation without subscribing to formalist conclusions, although the version of formalism I offer presupposes and derives from the institutional approach.

The methodological thesis is that institutional analysis is indispensable to any account of legal interpretation. The question in law is never "How should this text be interpreted?" The question is always "What decision-procedures should particular institutions, with their particular capacities, use to interpret this text?" Put negatively, legal theory cannot reach any

1

operational conclusions about how judges, legislators, or administrative agencies should interpret texts unless it takes account, empirically, of the capacities of interpreters and of the systemic effects of interpretive approaches.

My target here is *first-best conceptualism:* the attempt to deduce operating-level rules of interpretation directly from high-level conceptual commitments—for example, commitments to democracy, or the rule of law, or constitutionalism, or an account of law's authority or of the nature of legal language. All such deductions fail, because intermediate premises about the capacities and interaction of legal institutions are necessary to translate principles into operational conclusions. An inescapable problem for first-best conceptualism is the possibility of *second-best effects.* Interpreters situated in particular institutions make mistakes when implementing any first-best account, and the rate of mistakes will vary with changes in the decision-procedures the interpreters use, as will the cost of reaching decisions. There is no decision-procedure for implementing any high-level interpretive commitment that is best a priori, or that can be deduced from conceptual commitments. The best decision-procedure will vary with the facts about institutional capacities and systemic effects. The upshot is that conceptualism can never provide a full account of the operating-level interpretive procedures that judges should use. The normative theory of legal interpretation turns upon empirical questions and factual findings.

Sometimes we can go further. Given some empirical findings about institutional capacities and systemic effects, interpreters may bracket their high-level commitments, agreeing to disagree or even remaining resolutely agnostic about first principles. Such bracketing or agnosticism is possible where, and because, empirical findings would point proponents of any (plausible) first-best account to the use of particular interpretive procedures. Disagreement at the level of first principles proves irrelevant to the extent that proponents of different views reach converging agreement upon decision-procedures at the operating level of the legal system.

I shall suggest, for example, that both interpreters who hold that the aim of statutory interpretation is to recapture legislators' intentions and interpreters who deny that thesis should be able to agree that judges should not read internal legislative documents for evidence of legislators' intentions. This is a second-best claim: fallible judges are less likely to recapture legislators' intentions successfully by using such documents than by refusing to use them. In domains such as this one, an old debate at the level of political theory—do legislators' intentions make the law?— turns out to be irrelevant to the question what interpretive procedures judges should use, for strictly empirical reasons.

Overall, the methodological thesis suggests that the marginal value of further conceptual work in legal theory is much less than the marginal value of new empirical work. Ever-more-refined conceptual analysis has long dominated legal theory, even though the principal first-best positions are well understood, while empirical work on the institutional determinants of interpretation is still in its infancy. The former, I suggest, has passed well beyond the point of diminishing marginal returns, while the latter now promises large intellectual dividends.

The Institutionalist Dilemma

If all this is right, what exactly are judges to do? Academics can afford to wait until empirical findings emerge. Judges, however, must interpret legal texts now. Which procedures they should follow will vary with findings about institutional capacities and systemic effects. Such findings, however, do not currently exist, for the most part. The sheer complexity of the legal system means that the empirical questions at issue are often "transscientific": although they are empirical in principle, they are unresolvable at acceptable cost within any reasonable time frame. Worse, judges are boundedly rational: their capacity to process the information they can obtain is limited, in part because of cognitive failings. While those failings are shared by all decisionmakers, they are exacerbated by the case-by-case decisionmaking procedure that defines adjudication—a procedure that emphasises the salience of particulars and hampers judges in discerning the systemic effects of the interpretive approaches they adopt. The overall picture, then, is that boundedly rational judges must necessarily adopt some interpretive decision-procedure or other, on empirical grounds, but without the necessary information. This is the *institutionalist dilemma:* judges cannot escape the enterprise of choosing interpretive decision-procedures under conditions of uncertainty and bounded rationality.

In emphasizing this dilemma, I hope above all to push legal theory beyond *the stalemate of empirical intuitions.* To the extent that legal theory takes account of empirical and institutional issues, theorists often record their intuitions about the facts of the matter and then move on. Where A's empirical intuitions diverge from B's, and no findings are available to settle the matter, conventions of academic discourse often suggest that the issue be dropped with the shrug "It's empirical." This is a reasonable course for academics, but not for decisionmakers in the legal system (like judges) who face some category of decisions that can neither be postponed nor avoided.

Judges should, I suggest, choose interpretive decision-procedures through a repertoire of tools for choice under conditions of limited information and bounded rationality. The repertoire is drawn from a variety of disciplines. It includes the allocation of burdens of proof; cost-benefit analysis, supplemented by the principle of insufficient reason; the maximin criterion for choice under uncertainty; satisficing; arbitrary picking, as opposed to choosing; and the use of fast and frugal heuristics. The repertoire is eclectic, and many of the tools are fallback counsels for situations where fully rational decisionmaking is impossible. I claim only that judges using these tools will act reasonably, whether or not they act rationally in any strong sense.

Formalism, Consequentialism, and Rules

What decision-procedures do these tools for interpretive choice select? My substantive thesis is that when the analysis is done, the best decision-making strategy for judges in America, given their current circumstances and the current state of empirical knowledge, is a version of formalism. The tools I have described all suggest that judges should stick close to the surface-level or literal meaning of clear and specific texts, resolutely refusing to adjust those texts by reference to the judges' conceptions of statutory purposes, legislators' or framers' intentions or understandings, public values and norms, or general equity. Where texts are intrinsically ambiguous, the legal system does best if judges assign the authority to interpret those texts to other institutions—administrative agencies in the case of statutes, legislatures in the case of the Constitution. Overall, judges should sharply limit their interpretive ambitions, in part by limiting themselves to a small set of interpretive sources and a restricted range of relatively wooden decision-rules.

This set of prescriptions amounts to "formalism" in a particular sense of the term. Following existing work by legal philosopher Fred Schauer and others, we may distinguish two senses of formalism. In the first, formalism refers to the attempt to deduce legal rules from intelligible essences, such as "the nature of contracts" or "the rule of law," while excluding considerations of morality and policy. This is emphatically not the sense in which my proposals are formalist. Indeed, formalism in this sense is a species of first-best conceptualism, and as such is one of my principal targets. I shall claim, for example, that the essentialist version of formalism is alive and well in recent attempts to derive rules of interpretation directly from the Constitution's text and structure.

In another sense, however, formalism refers to a rule-bound decision-making strategy. Crucially, formalism in this sense itself can be justified only on empirical grounds, indeed consequentialist grounds; the argument for decisional formalism must be that it will produce better consequences for the legal system than will alternative decisionmaking strategies. In this sense my conclusions are formalist indeed. The basic idea, only apparently paradoxical, is that judges acting under conditions of grave uncertainty and bounded rationality should restrict the range of information they attempt to collect and reduce the complexity of their behavioral repertoire, on the ground that further increments of information, complexity, and flexibility produce definite costs for only speculative gains. So judges should follow simplistic, even wooden decision-rules. Such rules may produce poor results in particular cases. Their justification is that they produce the best results overall—with "best" defined according to a converging agreement, at the operational level, among interpretive approaches that differ at the level of first principles.

My premises are thus firmly consequentialist. Indeed they are rule-consequentialist: judges should interpret legal texts in accordance with rules whose observance produces the best consequences overall. One contrast here is with an act-consequentialist account of interpretation, which counsels judges directly to choose whichever interpretation produces the best consequences in the case at hand. Throughout Part I, I critique this sort of act-consequentialist approach to judging, on the ground that judges' limited information and bounded rationality cause them to go badly wrong when they attempt to assess the consequences of decisions in particular cases. The best decisionmaking approach proceeds by indirection: rather than attempting to assess consequences in each particular case, judges should adopt the interpretive rules that, if followed, produce the best possible consequences for the interpretive system overall. There is no paradox in this counsel. Judges can know the limits of their own knowledge, and when they do, they can make a second-order decision to follow the rules that are best in light of their limited competence as first-order decisionmakers.

Rule-consequentialism also entails that interpretive approaches should be evaluated over a whole array of outcomes, not merely over particular decisions. Where rule-consequentialism makes sense, it is because imperfect decisionmakers will do better overall with rules. Even if those rules are best overall, it will always be possible to point to particular cases in which a perfect decisionmaker would produce a better outcome in that very case than would an imperfect decisionmaker applying the best overall rules to an array of cases that includes the case at hand. This kind of perfectionist reasoning from particular cases is a mistake, however. Throughout the chapters that follow, I suggest that judges' intuitions misfire under *the distorting force of particulars,* in part because the vivid facts of particular cases trigger cognitive distortions.

As for analysts of legal interpretation, we ought to get clear about the best decision-procedures and then let the chips fall where they may in particular cases. The consequence is that I construct a top-down argument that moves from decision-procedures to applications, rather than a bottom-up argument rich with concrete cases and examples. Because the concrete so often misleads, I regard this as an intellectual virtue, though others will not.

Consequentialism and Pragmatism

In principle, these consequentialist premises exclude a domain of (wholly or partially) nonconsequentialist approaches to interpretation. It turns out, however, that this is not a very large loss of generality, because few people hold views of that sort. Interpretive consequentialism is an extremely broad rubric, as we shall see. It includes, for example, the interpretive jurisprudence of legal philosopher Ronald Dworkin, who is an avowed consequentialist (contrary to a widespread but mysterious assumption). Perhaps surprisingly, a view that does not come under the capacious umbrella of consequentialism is "pragmatism," at least in the form of "everyday pragmatism" that Judge Richard Posner has recently championed. Posner wants to say that a pragmatic interpretation is one that produces better consequences than the alternatives, but Posner resolutely refuses to say what, in his view, counts as a good consequence. This is a puzzling stance (or so I argue in Chapters 2 and 3). As Dworkin argues, interpretive consequentialism requires a value theory that specifies what consequences are good.

Dworkin in turn goes wrong, however, to the extent he suggests that consequentialism requires the interpreter to adopt some particular value theory. A central aim of my project is to suggest, and to show, that consequentialists can make progress on interpretive theory by bracketing high-level disagreements about competing value theories. For empirical and institutional reasons, a range of value theories converge at the operational level, yielding similar recommendations about the decision-procedures judges should use. One can do consequentialist interpretation without settling all questions at the level of first principles, not because competing value theories are themselves dispensable in principle, but because the differences between them turn out to make little difference on the ground.

Values and Facts

Another premise is that we can, throughout the domain covered by this book, fruitfully use the distinction between value theories, on the one hand, and facts, on the other. This distinction drives the argument in several places, most conspicuously in the claim (laid out in Part I and substantiated in Parts II and III) that competing interpretive value theories converge at the operational level, given certain factual premises. Of course, the distinction between fact and value is contentious at the philosophical level and has spawned large literatures. On one view, all "facts" are theory-laden constructs; a simple appeal to "what the facts show" is a nonstarter.

I do not contest that view, nor need I do so, for the view is more limited than some of its most zealous proponents seem to understand. Take the question whether an increase in the minimum wage would increase unemployment. Of course both "minimum wage" and "unemployment" are thick concepts whose very meaning is intertwined with ethical and legal theories. (What, for example, is the baseline from which unemployment is measured?) To make sense of the factual question, we need background assumptions of value. But those background assumptions need not be contentious or sectarian. To the extent that they are widely shared within a given community, asking what the facts show, relative to the shared assumptions, is perfectly coherent and often useful. It is the routine stuff of policy debates to distinguish the question (1) how much an increase in the minimum wage will increase unemployment from the question (2) whether it would be good to increase the minimum wage by $X at the price of an increase of Y percent in the unemployment rate.

Sophisticated critics of the fact/value distinction thus confine their criticism to the conceptual level, and willingly acknowledge that distinctions between fact and value are useful at other levels of inquiry.[1] Legal interpretation, I am suggesting, is the type of inquiry in which the distinction between facts and values can be used without too much philosophical anxiety. To prefigure a later example, what the legislative history of a given statute shows about the median legislator's intention is a factual question, in much the same way that the effect of minimum wages on unemployment is factual. The objection to such a question, if there is one, is that it is not a good question for judges to ask, given certain facts about judicial capacities (a topic I take up throughout, especially in Chapters 5 and 7). The crucial problems that surround questions of this sort are institutional, not philosophical.

A Note on Scope

Throughout, my emphasis is on three classes of interpretive problems: statutory interpretation by courts, statutory interpretation by agencies, and constitutional interpretation by courts. This is, in one sense, an arbitrary limitation of the project's natural scope. Straightforward extensions of the institutional approach to interpretation could encompass treaty interpretation and the interpretation of regulations by agencies. The justifications for not examining these contexts are, first, that different institutional variables doubtless matter in those settings, just as there are important differences between the variables relevant to statutory and constitutional interpretation; and second, that my expertise is too limited to permit a confident treatment of these areas.

For the same reasons I do not treat the common law per se, although I discuss the problem of judicial coordination on rules of precedent in Chapter 5, treat the problem of statutory precedent extensively in Chapter 7, and discuss "common-law" approaches to constitutional interpretation in Chapter 8. Again, the extension to areas of the common-law would be a natural one, were I competent to make it. Judicial precedents are texts too; in deciding what a precedent means, a common-law court should pay close attention to institutional considerations. This point is increasingly well understood in the common-law context, especially in the institutionally sophisticated literature on contract interpretation.[2]

Finally, my inquiry is limited to the question what interpretive decision-procedures judges, agencies, and other actors should use, *given* the institutions we currently have. I therefore do not consider changes to institutional rules, such as the Supreme Court's voting rules, nor do I consider such problems as interpretation in parliamentary systems. I do, however, draw upon comparisons to other legal systems where such comparisons can illuminate interpretation in our system, constituted as it actually is.

Critique, Reconstruction, and Applications

I begin in Part I with a brisk critique of Anglo-American interpretive theory. Chapter 1 moves from Blackstone and Bentham to H. L. A. Hart, the American legal process school of the 1950s, and current theorists. I make no pretense of doing justice to the accounts and theorists I review; certainly I make no effort to place these theorists in historical context or even to provide a full jurisprudential treatment of their views. My aim is instead to document a chronic condition of institutional blindness in Anglo-American interpretive theory. To that end I contrast legal theory with the intentionalist movement in literary theory, whose leading figures, Steven Knapp, Walter Benn Michaels, and Stanley Fish, freely acknowledge that their high-level commitments have no methodological implications for interpretive practice in literature or law.

In its most virulent form, institutional blindness in legal theory manifests as out-and-out philosophizing, a style of interpretive theory that attempts to move directly from first principles to operational conclusions, skipping over the intermediate institutional terrain. I attempt to show, not merely say, that no such leap is possible; on any first-best account, intermediate institutional premises will determine the operational conclusions. In less virulent forms, the condition manifests either as stylized institutionalism, which proceeds on the basis of stereotyped visions of the essence of courts and legislatures, or else as asymmetrical institutionalism, which juxtaposes a romantic picture of one institution (usually the judiciary) with a jaundiced picture of others (usually legislatures). This is the "nirvana fallacy." Chapter 2, which focuses on the views of two especially prominent recent theorists—William Eskridge's dynamism and Richard Posner's pragmatism—is thus "A Tale of Two Nirvanas." Both theorists, I suggest, overestimate the judiciary's capacity to succeed at dynamic updating and flexible interpretation, especially relative to administrative agencies. Throughout this part I argue for an institutionalism that is evenhandedly empirical, proceeding by reference to the actual capacities and interactions of judges, legislatures, and agencies.

My aim is to move quickly from critique to constructive work. Part II begins the work of reconstruction. Chapter 3 urges that interpretive theory should take an institutional turn. I emphasize two points. The first is that no interpretive value theory—no high-level principle for sorting good interpretive outcomes from bad ones—can, all by itself, dictate decision procedures at the operational level. First-best accounts of interpretation are thus necessarily incomplete. The second is that interpretive value theories may converge on particular decision-procedures, in which case high-level disagreement makes no difference on the ground. In light of these points I attempt to indicate the empirical conditions under which, given any plausible value theory, formalism would produce the best consequences for a legal system—using formalism in the operational rather than the essentialist sense. The empirical considerations are multifaceted, involving relative rates of error, relative decision costs, the choice between rules and standards, and other features of alternative legal regimes. For simplicity I herd these considerations into two broad classes of institutional variables: institutional capacities and systemic effects.

Chapters 4 and 5 focus on these two principal (classes of) institutional variables. Chapter 4 is a case study of judicial capacities. Here I aim to illustrate the inevitability of second-best effects and the potential for institutional analysis to pretermit high-level disagreements. Analyzing one of the Supreme Court's most famous statutory decisions—the *Holy Trinity* case of 1892—I suggest that the modern controversy over legislative history has proceeded on the wrong grounds. The decisive questions about legislative history do not involve the authority of statutory text, background norms derived from constitutional structure, or other high-level considerations. The questions that turn out to be decisive at the operational level are instead thoroughly empirical and institutional. A principal issue involves judicial capacities and second-best effects. I suggest that relative to any value theory, even the view that good interpretation should track legislators' intentions or purposes, fallible judges will do better by ignoring legislative history than by using it.

Chapter 5 is concerned with systemic effects. Here my target is a congeries of "democracy-forcing" accounts of interpretation, under which courts should choose interpretive rules with a view to forcing or encouraging a certain quantity and quality of legislative deliberation over policy issues and constitutional values. Such accounts laudably emphasize the systemic interactions between courts and legislatures, but they overlook systemic problems within the judiciary itself. I suggest that there are high costs of coordination across judges and over time, produced by the distributive effect of interpretive rules, and that judges will often prove unable to coordinate on a democracy-forcing regime for any sustained period. This implies another second-best effect: even if democracy-forcing is a laudable ideal, uncoordinated attempts at democracy-forcing, conducted by less than a critical mass of judges, will prove at best futile and at worst perverse.

Part III turns to applications. Chapter 6 addresses the problems of judging under empirical uncertainty. I describe the stalemate of empirical intuitions, articulate the dilemma that institutionalist judges face, and canvass techniques for decisionmaking and choice under conditions of uncertainty and bounded rationality. Chapters 7 and 8 provide concrete applications of the institutional approach. In Chapter 7 I focus on statutory interpretation. Drawing upon the techniques laid out in Chapter 6, I advance the following claims: When the particular statutory text directly at hand is clear and specific, judges should stick close to its surface or literal meaning, forswearing the use of legislative history and other collateral sources to enrich their sense of meaning, intentions, or purposes. When the statutory text at hand is ambiguous or vague, judges should defer to the interpretations of administrative agencies or executive agents. And judges should apply a strong doctrine of statutory precedent, subject however to defeasance by later administrative interpretations.

Chapter 8 turns to judicial review of statutes for constitutionality and to the problems of constitutional interpretation. I claim that the considerations developed in Parts I and II and applied in Chapters 6 and 7 generalize fully from the statutory to the constitutional setting. The institutional turn is fully appropriate, indeed necessary, for constitutional as well as statutory interpretation. Judicial review of statutes for constitutionality and judicial decision-procedures for constitutional interpretation must be assessed in light of institutional capacities and systemic effects. The problem of interpretive choice under uncertainty thus arises in the constitutional setting and must be resolved with the tools developed in Chapter 6.

Applying those tools yields surprising conclusions. Judges should choose a rule-bound decision-procedure for constitutional cases, enforcing clear and specific constitutional texts, but deferring to legislatures on the interpretation of constitutional texts that are vague or ambiguous, that can be read at multiple levels of generality, or that embody aspirational norms whose content changes over time with shifting public values. The category of provisions to be remitted to legislative enforcement includes the principal provisions of the Bill of Rights and the Fourteenth Amendment, especially the guarantees of free speech, due process, and equal protection.

This is a contrarian view, at least in today's judge-besotted constitutional culture. It rests in part on a *rule-consequentialist critique of ambitious judicial review.* The idea is that judicial review always produces a set or package of outcomes over an array of cases, that some of those outcomes will be good and others bad, and that proponents of ambitious judicial review fantasize that they can have the good without the bad. In fact there is no mechanism for unbundling the outcomes, which means that judicial review must be evaluated by reference to its worst possible outcomes as well as its best. In espousing this skeptical view of constitutional adjudication, I take comfort in the intellectual companionship of nineteenth-century legal scholar James Bradley Thayer and his disciples Judge Learned Hand and Justice Felix Frankfurter. I have also profited from the work of current scholars such as Larry Kramer, Mark Tushnet, and Jeremy Waldron—although I eschew the historical, populist, and jurisprudential grounds these scholars sometimes offer for their views in favor of a resolutely institutional account.

— I —

Critique

We shall begin in a critical register, though with a view to laying foundations for more constructive work in Parts II and III. My central claim in Part I is that interpretive theory suffers from lack of attention to institutional and empirical questions. This is not merely a wish that the emphasis of interpretive theory should be more empirical, although it is true that in the current state of affairs the marginal value of additional empirical work is certainly higher than the marginal value of further conceptual analysis of interpretive approaches (a point to which I return later). Rather, I mean to advance a stronger claim: *first-best conceptualism cannot, even in principle, yield any conclusions about the design of interpretive decision-procedures.* A typical slippage in interpretive theory is the attempt to move directly from high-level concepts or political and moral premises—premises such as a commitment to democracy, or to constitutionalism, or to some jurisprudential theory of law's authority—to conclusions about institutional arrangements or about interpretive approaches. No such move is possible. Empirical questions always and necessarily intervene between high-level premises, on the one hand, and conclusions about the decision-procedures that should be used at the operating level of the legal system, on the other. The intervening questions can be roughly grouped into two categories: questions about the interpretive capacities of institutions and questions about the system effects of interaction between or among institutions.

Part II advances this central claim at the level of theory. This Part lays the foundation by sketching an overview of the history of interpretive theory in Chapter 1 and by focusing in detail on the work of two currently prominent theorists, William Eskridge and Richard Posner, in Chapter 2.

— 1 —

Interpretation without Institutions

In this chapter I attempt a panoramic tour of interpretive theory and influential theorists. The sights of interest are the English debate over common-law approaches to statutory interpretation, modern interpretive work in legal theory, and an important strand of literary theory. Chapter 2 focuses on the work of two current theorists, William Eskridge and Richard Posner. Throughout these two chapters my emphasis is on statutory interpretation, in part because most Anglo-American interpretive theory before World War II itself focused on statutes. I touch on constitutional examples as well, however, and Chapter 8 supplies a full guided tour of approaches to constitutional interpretation.

The overall objective is to document a certain blindness or insensitivity to institutional considerations that pervades the canonical works of interpretive theory. There are two qualifications to this claim that must be made clearly, right off the bat. First, I make no pretense here of supplying a complete and adequately nuanced intellectual history. Indeed, the catalogue will have the flavor of Whig history, praising theorists who anticipate the institutional turn I advocate in Chapter 3 and (far more often) condemning those who do not. But the goal is not merely critical. Rather the hope is to make some movement toward the task, ventured in Part II, of isolating the issues that must be faced by an approach to interpretation that is concerned with institutional capacities and systemic effects.

Second, I shall claim that the theorists I survey in this chapter and the next are all to some extent insufficiently sensitive to the institutional dimensions of interpretation. But this is not at all to denigrate their accomplishments. In many cases we might see these theorists as solely interested in, and speaking about, the ideal or first-best considerations that bear on interpretive theory. There is nothing objectionable about such a project, so far as it goes. My point is just that all first-best theorizing is incomplete without institutional premises, because first principles by themselves cannot yield conclusions about what real-world interpreters ought to do. Despite the great accomplishments of first-best interpretive theorizing, especially since World War II, an indispensable dimension of interpretive theory remains to be understood.

Three Types of Institutional Blindness

Throughout this part I shall identify three types of institutional blindness that in one form or another pervade the canonical works of interpretive theory. Of course, much interpretive theorizing has discussed institutions. Although some interpretive theory is resolutely noninstitutional, more typically accounts of interpretation embody claims about the behavior of legislatures, agencies, courts, litigants, and citizens—especially in the "legal process" approach that dominated American law after World War II. As we shall see, however, such claims are often stylized abstractions and often commit the nirvana fallacy: they juxtapose rosy accounts of some institutions with jaundiced accounts of others and fail to compare the real-world capacities of all relevant actors.

We may usefully arrange the three types of institutional blindness from most to least extreme:

Out-and-out philosophizing. Some theorists attempt to derive an account of interpretation from resolutely noninstitutional premises, particularly high-level political concepts like "democracy," "authority," or "integrity," or abstractions about the character of legal language. Philosopher-lawyers like Ronald Dworkin are the paradigm here. To be sure, these philosopher-lawyers do not purport to address all relevant questions about interpretation all at once; in their better moments they limit their attentions to what we may call first-best questions, leaving institutional considerations for other scholars. Although this sort of partial analysis is valuable as far as it goes, I shall claim that it is not possible to use first-best analysis to derive conclusions about specific interpretive doctrines and outcomes, absent any account of the institutional considerations that always intervene between abstract premises and concrete conclusions. Although this form of institutional blindness is important and, remarkably, still widespread, there are also other ways in which interpretive theories take inadequate account of institutions.

Stylized institutionalism. Here the interpretive theorist talks about comparative institutional competence, but in a stylized or stereotyped way, on the basis of abstract visions of "legislatures," "agencies," and "courts." As we shall see later, this is a charge that may fairly be lodged against the 1950s legal process account of Henry Hart and Albert Sacks: their talk is of institutions, but the institutions are pictured in stereotyped, stylized, and excessively laudatory ways that correspond only hazily to the facts of American government. In these and other versions, stylized institutionalism proceeds by reference to conceptual claims about the essential features of legislatures, courts, and agencies, rather than by reference to empirical claims about institutions in particular legal systems.

Asymmetrical institutionalism. A distinct but related mistake is to take a cynical or pessimistic view of some institutions and an unjustifiably rosy view of others. In constitutional law, John Hart Ely's "representation-reinforcing" version of legal process theory, in which farsighted and politically responsible courts police invidious stereotyping and other process failures on the part of dysfunctional legislatures, is an exemplar. Ely's theory is attractive to many; but what if courts are unwilling to do what Ely urges, and what if courts would fail to do the task well if they tried? Much of public choice theory is similar, albeit with a different diagnosis of process failure, one that sees inefficient "rent-seeking" by legislators and interest groups, rather than racial discrimination, as the principal danger that the process-policing judiciary is to prevent.

   The danger here is the nirvana fallacy:[1] a pseudo-institutional analysis that compares a worst-case picture of one institution to a best-case picture of another. In Chapter 2 I suggest that William Eskridge and Richard Posner both fall prey to the seductions of nirvana, in both cases by juxtaposing a cynical picture of legislatures to an idealized view of courts, and especially by taking too little account of the central interpretive role of agencies. Although this is by far the most common species of asymmetrical institutionalism, it is also possible to juxtapose a rosy picture of legislative capacities to a jaundiced view of courts. Political philosopher Jeremy Waldron does this explicitly as a deliberate debiasing exercise for the pervasively judge-centered culture of the legal academy.[2]

Aside from Waldron's important enterprise, asymmetrical accounts are by now intellectually bankrupt, although they have a tenacious hold on the legal academic mind. As I emphasize in Chapter 2 and foreshadow in this chapter, important treatments of interpretation and adjudication by lawyer-economists such as Neil Komesar and Einer Elhauge have demonstrated the inability of asymmetrical institutionalism to underwrite plausible conclusions about constitutional and statutory interpretation. The alternative, one that I will argue for throughout, is *an institutionalism that is evenhandedly empirical*—an institutional account that is realistic about the capacities of all relevant actors.

Common-Law Interpretation and Bentham's Mistake

I begin the historical overview with Blackstone and Bentham, the foremost proponent and critic, respectively, of the common-law approach to statutory interpretation. This approach has many shades and variants that license varying degrees of judicial freedom in interpretation, but a defining idea is that judges appropriately sensitive to legislative purposes and to the surrounding fabric of law should mold and shape statutes with the sensitivity and flexibility accorded to judicial precedents. In these respects the common-law approach is a precursor of the legal process school that came to dominate American interpretive theory after World War II.[3]

I shall suggest that the common-law style of interpretation presupposes a fanciful, even romantic account of judicial capacities and also fails to ask questions about likely legislative responses to different judicial approaches. There is, however, a major historical irony: Blackstone, the archetypal common-law interpreter, came far closer to recognizing the suppressed institutional questions and the institutional case for formalist statutory interpretation than did Bentham, the common law's principal critic. We shall also see that later theorists, such as H. L. A. Hart, followed Bentham rather than Blackstone and hence repeated Bentham's mistake.

Blackstone. William Blackstone's brief account of statutory interpretation in Book I of the *Commentaries* is easily the most famous description of the common-law style of statutory interpretation;[4] Hart and Sacks featured it prominently in the legal process materials that influenced a generation of leading academic theorists.[5] The object of interpretation, for Blackstone, is to uncover the "will of the legislator" by "exploring his intentions," as manifested in "signs the most natural and probable."[6] Despite this ceremonial bow to legislative supremacy, however, the discussion quickly turns from the words of the statute to surrounding statutes, the subject matter, and a potpourri of more fluid interpretive sources, particularly the "reason and spirit" of the law and the Aristotelian principle of "equity"—the latter being the power "of excepting those circumstances, which (had they been foreseen) the legislator himself would have excepted."[7] Interpretive equity, on this view, "depend[s], essentially, upon the particular circumstances of each individual case."[8]

Here are all the hallmarks of the common-law interpretive style: flexible treatment of statutory text, based on a nuanced sensitivity to legislative intentions or purposes and to the surrounding fabric of the common law. Especially striking is the stylized assumption that interpretation according to the "reason" or "equity" of the statute will capture the legislature's true intentions, or the intentions that rational legislators would have had if informed about the particular application at bar, as well as the accompanying insistence that equity is necessarily a particularistic or case-specific consideration.

Under certain assumptions about institutional capacities, the common-law style might be best. But Blackstone says little in defense of those assumptions and does not acknowledge them as such. The discussion, almost until the very end, shows little awareness of several relevant possibilities. Judges might mistake legislative purposes. They might do better by deferring to legislators' expressed judgments about equity than by enforcing their own. They might, by treating statutes flexibly, be purchasing case-specific benefits at the price of increased uncertainty, imposing resulting burdens on the interpretive system as a whole. Legislators, confronted with judges refusing to invoke purposes to make sense of text, might be more careful in advance and might make corrections as the need arises.

Consider, as one example among many, Blackstone's casual embrace of the absurd-results canon: the idea, in Blackstone's words, that "where words bear either none, or a very absurd signification, we must a little deviate from the received sense of them. Therefore the Bolognian law, mentioned by Puffendorf, which enacted 'that whoever drew blood in the streets should be punished with the utmost severity,' was held after long debate not to extend to the surgeon, who opened the vein of a person that fell down in the street with a fit."[9]

There is much to be said, pro and con, about interpretation to avoid absurd results. The relevant institutional variables are complex, and I shall discuss them at greater length in Chapters 2 and 3. What is important for present purposes is Blackstone's institutional blindness—his failure to identify those variables or to find them even relevant. It may well be true that if apprised of the surgeon's case, the legislature would have provided a relevant exception. But it does not follow that the legislature would necessarily wish the judges to provide the exception themselves, given the legislature's failure to do so. For many reasons, good and bad, the legislature might want to reserve to itself the authority to correct poorly drafted statutes. Perhaps the legislature would not trust the judges' views about whether a result would be absurd; perhaps the legislature would be willing to tolerate occasional absurdity for the sake of clarity and predictability. Nor does it follow that, apart from the question of legislative preferences about judicial interpretation, the best overall interpretive system would be one in which the judges possessed this case-specific power to modify seemingly absurd statutory applications in light of purpose, reason, and equity. To know whether that is true would require judgments about a range of matters Blackstone fails to consider, such as the rate of mistaken identification of absurd results, the added decisional burdens of absurd-results claims, and the ex ante effects of such a power on legislative drafting.

All this said, the end of Blackstone's discussion offers an incisive afterthought that, although barely sketched, anticipates the role of *second-best considerations* in interpretive theory: "[L]aw, without equity, tho' hard and disagreeable, is much more desirable for the public good, than equity without law; which would make every judge a legislator, and introduce most infinite confusion [by producing] as many different rules of action laid down in our courts, as there are differences of capacity and sentiment in the human mind."[10] In this passage "law," cast in opposition to equity, seems to connote a formalist style of interpretation that enforces rules apparent on the face of statutory texts, rather than molding those texts to background legal principles or attributed legislative purposes. The first-best, Blackstone is suggesting, would be law and equity in an appropriate mix, distributed appropriately across cases. But if the mix is unstable, if judges must choose between enforcing law in all cases or doing equity in all cases, then resolute enforcement of statutory text is preferable on second-best grounds.

On Blackstone's account, equity without law is defective on two counts:

it "makes every judge a legislator" and introduces an unacceptable amount of uncertainty ("most infinite confusion") into the interpretive system. The first point is a gesture toward the separation of lawmaking power from adjudicative power; I shall subsequently argue that this sort of appeal is unhelpful, because it is too abstract to supply valid reasons for or against interpretive formalism. Far more impressive and significant is the second point, an early attempt to introduce institutional considerations and ex ante effects into interpretive theory. We shall see, however, that Blackstone's passing insight proved infertile. Later theorists largely ignored the significance of second-best considerations.

Bentham. Given this picture of Blackstone, there is an illuminating contrast with the interpretive views of Jeremy Bentham, an imposing critic of common-law adjudication in general and of Blackstone in particular. Bentham's brilliant critique of Blackstone's *Commentaries* develops the claim that common-law adjudication is both incoherent and inconsistent with a rational, meaning utilitarian, legal order. The positive side of Bentham's program was the codification of utilitarian legal principles and, more generally, a consolidation and expansion of legislation's domain that would bring clarity, certainty, and order to the law. Increasingly precise and comprehensive codification would ultimately cause adjudication itself to wither away, because citizens and officials could simply consult the code to ascertain their legal rights and duties. In the interim, however, Bentham was intermittently aware that statutes would contain gaps, ambiguities, and generalities ill adapted to specific cases—the usual sources of difficult interpretive questions. Bentham thus discussed interpretation on several occasions, most prominently in his account of adjudication under his "Pannomion" or comprehensive code,[11] and in *A Comment on the Commentaries,* which contains two substantial chapters titled "Interpretation of Laws" and "Construction of Statutes."[12]

For present purposes, the significance of Bentham's work on interpretation lies in his imperfect consequentialism—in his neglect of institutional variables in his discussion of the judicial role. Despite his piercing depiction of the sponginess of common-law adjudication, which he equated with arbitrary judicial tyranny, Bentham failed to transpose his critique of judicial capacities to interpretive theory in any consistent way. The chapters on interpretation and construction in *A Comment on the Commentaries* manage both to approve flexible, purposivist interpretation devoted to forwarding legislative "ends," on one hand, and on the other to mock the pretensions of common-law interpretation by emphasizing what Bentham saw as the arbitrariness of judicial claims about "reason" and "equity." Thus Bentham both supports the absurd-results canon on purposive grounds, in Blackstone's example of the surgeon prosecuted for "drawing blood" in the streets, and also denies that the common-law judge's appeal to reason or reasonableness is anything other than a statement of personal "opinion." On the one hand, "reasonableness or unreasonableness is nothing but conformity or nonconformity to . . . opinion." On the other hand, "[t]he words of a legislator are no otherwise to be regarded than inasmuch as they are expressive of his will."[13]

But these two positions are in tension with each other. Recall that Blackstone's argument for purposive, equitable interpretation assumed that reasonable legislators would have recognized the need for an exception if they had been aware of the application at hand. Purposivism usually attributes goals or aims by envisioning reasonable legislators acting reasonably; certainly that is the premise for purposivism in the later legal process account of interpretation, as we shall see later. This may even be a necessary feature of purposivism. It may be conceptually impossible for judges to proceed by imagining what unreasonable legislators would do. So to deny that the judges can assess the reasonableness or equity of some particular statutory application is also to deny purposivism. Bentham cannot have it both ways.

Conversely, Blackstone's second-best argument for interpretive formalism was precisely that judicial disagreement about what is equitable would make interpretation unacceptably subjective and uncertain (because of "differences of capacity and sentiment" across judges). Bentham fails to appreciate that the rapier he uses to skewer the common-law judges might be turned against the purposivist statutory interpretation he also embraces. If even Bentham—the greatest critic of the common law and the greatest advocate of legal utilitarianism—overlooks the significance of judicial capacities and the systemic effects of flexible interpretation, the institutional blindness in interpretive theory runs very deep indeed.

Why might Bentham, in his critique of common-law method, have neglected the institutional critique of flexible interpretation? There may be a clue in his most focused treatment of the relationship between interpretation and judicial discretion, a short discussion in his great unpublished work on legislation, *Of Laws in General*. There Bentham argues that legislative mistakes—the enactment of statutes that are overinclusive or underinclusive relative to their purposes, due to inadvertence, lack of foresight, or changed circumstances—require that judges possess the power to "mould[] statutes into form."[14] Yet this power in turn created the possibility that informational deficits or bad motives on the part of judges would pervert the legislative product and increase legal uncertainty: "How difficult to distinguish what the legislator would have adopted had he adverted to it, from what he actually did advert to and reject. How easy to establish the one under pretence of looking for the other. . . . And thus sprang up by degrees another branch of customary law, which striking its roots into the substance of the statute law, infected it with its own characteristic obscurity, uncertainty, and confusion."[15] This is a powerful indictment of purposivism and imaginative reconstruction. On the score of institutional sophistication, Bentham here outdoes his jurisprudential successors of the next century, including both H. L. A. Hart and the legal process scholars; we shall see that the later accounts fail even to see the problem that Bentham poses.

Yet for this Bentham himself must take a great deal of blame. The prescriptions he offered to cure the problems of purposivism rest on the same sort of idealized or stylized view of institutional capacities that infects most of Blackstone's treatment, and that Bentham might have been expected to transcend. Bentham first suggests that "the necessity of discretionary interpretation" can be "supersede[d]" by the development of a sufficiently perspicacious legislative code (doubtless the Pannomion or comprehensive code developed in Bentham's own extensive proposals for law reform).[16] But this idealizes legislative capacities, thus reversing the characteristic error of common-law interpretation. Bentham himself recognizes, both here and elsewhere, that institutional limitations on legislatures make the project of a fully specified code fantastic. So Bentham abashedly sketches a fallback plan, never fully developed, whereby judges would "declare openly" the need for judicial "alteration" of a statute in appropriate cases and certify a proposed emendation to the legislature; the emendation would have legal force unless "negatived" or vetoed by the legislature within a certain time.[17] Absent from the proposal is any explanation why the judges, whose information and motivations Bentham has so powerfully impeached, will be able to distinguish alterations from permissible interpretations or be willing to comply with the plan even where alterations are identifiable as such.

If Blackstone and Bentham are taken together, the striking irony is that the common-law jurist more nearly appreciates and anticipates the second-best justifications for formalist, rule-bound statutory interpretation than does the great critic of the common law. Bentham's idealized picture of legislative capacities did little more than create a target for subsequent critics, such as H. L. A. Hart, who could justify antiformalist interpretation by pointing to the limits of legislative foresight, while overlooking the countervailing limits on the capacities of antiformalist interpreters.

The Modern Era: Positivism, Purposivism, Integrity, and Textualism

We now turn to a succession of accounts that cover the period of modern interpretive theory, roughly from World War II to the present.[18] For present purposes I focus on the arguments for and against formalism, and on the institutional blindness that afflicts all sides of that debate. My ambition here is not to show that formalism is best (a task taken up in Parts II and III), but instead to identify the issues on which its acceptance or rejection might turn.

We must be very clear that the theorists surveyed here are more alert to institutional problems than were some of their predecessors. After World War II institutional blindness took more subtle forms. One of the most striking features of this period is the dominant place of the "legal process" school, whose central mission was to focus attention on institutional considerations. Indeed, the legal process materials do talk a great deal about comparative institutional competence[19] and do discuss the relevance of agency interpretations of law.[20] But even in those materials, I shall suggest, the question of interpretation is typically addressed in stylized fashion, by discussing stereotyped features of stereotyped institutions. Even more often, interpretation is discussed in an asymmetrical fashion, by asking how ideal judges would proceed rather than how real judges should proceed.

Hart. The best place to begin is with H. L. A. Hart's canonical treatment of legal interpretation. In his treatment of mechanical jurisprudence and rule-skepticism, Hart offers a highly influential account of the failures of formalism—an account that, remarkably, says not a word about institutional issues.[21] A chief contribution is an influential account of why Bentham was wrong to hope that a rule-bound legislative code could sensibly resolve all cases that might arise under it. What is absent is a serious treatment of how institutions should respond to the inevitability that unexpected cases will confound the expectations of rulemakers.

Hart's principal submission is that in hard cases interpretive problems arise from legislators' "inability to anticipate."[22] In his view, a "feature of the human predicament (and so the legislative one) is that we labour under two connected handicaps whenever we seek to regulate, unambiguously and in advance, some sphere of conduct by means of general standards to be used without further official direction on particular occasions."[23] These handicaps are "our relative ignorance of fact" and "our relative indeterminacy of aim."[24] Mechanical jurisprudence or formalism, involving simple application of law to fact, would be possible only if "the world in which we live were characterized only by a finite number of features, and these together with all the modes in which they combine could be known to us."[25] But "[p]lainly this world is not our world."[26]

Hart claims that the "vice known to legal theory as formalism or conceptualism consists in an attitude to verbally formulated rules which both seeks to disguise and to minimize the need for . . . choice, once the general rule has been laid down."[27] This is sometimes done by freezing "the meaning of the rule so that its general terms must have the same meaning in every case where its application is in question."[28] What is wrong with that freezing? Hart has a simple answer. He urges that this approach secures "a measure of certainty or predictability at the cost of blindly prejudging what is to be done in a range of future cases, about whose composition we are ignorant. We shall thus indeed succeed in settling in advance, but also in the dark, issues which can only reasonably be settled when they arise and are identified."[29] What is wrong with decision in the dark? Hart urges that this kind of decision forces us "to include in the scope of a rule cases which we would wish to exclude in order to give effect to reasonable social aims."[30]

Hart is entirely right to urge that legislative foresight is necessarily limited, and that this can create serious problems for interpretation. But notice Hart's apparently unself-conscious use of the word "we" to identify the interpreting authority. Of course, Hart's readers do not constitute a community of "we's" who have the power to adopt a mutually agreeable approach to interpretation. And once it is seen that a system of interpretation must be established that some "they" must apply—"they" being judges, agencies, and other officials—the assessment of "reasonable social aims" will appear in a very different light. In institutional terms, Hart is neglecting two points. The first involves the risk that interpreters will blunder under one or another approach; the second involves the dynamic effects of one or another approach to interpretation.

Suppose, for example, that judges will err if they attempt to discern "reasonable social aims." It is quite conceivable, in light of human fallibility, that some or all judges will do better at determining legislators' reasonable aims if the judges refuse to inquire into reasonable aims. In addition, a sensible system of interpretation is based on an understanding that dynamic effects are highly likely; it sees that the judges' approach will not be limited, in its effects, to the immediate parties. Hart seems oblivious to these points. Suppose that courts, deciding the issue in the light of reasonable social aims, will introduce new decisional burdens and inject a high degree of uncertainty into the law, making it harder for people to plan their affairs. Suppose too that if they proceed in the dark, they will create strong incentives for the legislature, which will promptly correct the problems that arise. In these circumstances, might not formalism be the most sensible path? What is most remarkable is that Hart appears not to see the problem at all.

Hart and Sacks. For two generations of American lawyers after World War II, the most influential treatment of legal interpretation was that offered by Henry Hart and Albert Sacks in their legal process materials.[31] In a "note on the rudiments of statutory interpretation," Hart and Sacks urge that the task of interpretation requires courts, first and foremost, to "decide what purpose ought to be attributed to the statute and to any subordinate provision of it which may be involved," and to "interpret the words of the statute immediately in question so as to carry out the purpose as best it can."[32] Hart and Sacks caution that courts should not give words a meaning that their text will not bear, but they also urge that courts should require Congress to speak clearly if it wishes to accomplish certain ends, including "a departure from a generally prevailing principle or policy of the law."[33] These are the building blocks for a complex system of interpretation in which judges treat legislators as "reasonable people proceeding reasonably," make "purposes" crucial to interpretation, and push statutory language, where fairly possible, in the direction of sense and consistency with the rest of the law's fabric. Legal coherence, both in the thin sense of consistency and the thick sense of rich integration of statutory purposes, is perhaps the paramount value for the legal process interpreter.

In the abstract, this approach seems appealing to many; purposive coherence has seemed an indisputable value for law. But legal philosopher Andrei Marmor has raised important questions about whether legislative coherence is a value, even in principle, for a thoroughly pluralistic society.[34] Marmor's conceptual point has an institutional parallel. I shall suggest in Chapter 8 that the search for interpretive coherence is a first-best aspiration that may go badly awry in the hands of second-best judges. Fallible judges may produce a bad coherence that is far worse, on a range of value theories, than is a mixed picture of partial incoherence. An interpretive patchwork gives all views a partial victory and thus lowers the stakes, and the risks, of the interpretive system.

To evaluate the legal process approach, then, we need to know how well judges are able to execute it, and how other persons and institutions will react. The fact that Hart and Sacks do little to explore these issues is extremely revealing, for a primary contribution of the legal process materials was to put the spotlight on institutional issues, and indeed to assess much of law in a pragmatic spirit. With respect to legal interpretation, Hart and Sacks did not keep the institutional project in mind, perhaps because of the tenacity of the common-law framework with which they began. The evaluation of purposive interpretation must depend in large part on an assessment of the relevant institutions and of the effects of that approach over time. It is ludicrous to suggest that purposive interpretation is best in the abstract, for the simple reason that no approach to interpretation is best in the abstract. Here, as elsewhere, Hart and Sacks's elaborate talk about institutional competence is undercut by their stylized, nonempirical treatment of actual institutions and their capacities, and by their crude treatment of the systemic effects of competing interpretive approaches.

Dworkin. Ronald Dworkin is often taken to be H. L. A. Hart's antagonist, urging an approach that Dworkin calls "integrity," meant to be an alternative to Hart's form of positivism.[35] But Dworkin shares the institutional blindness common to both Hart, on the one hand, and legal process, on the other. On Dworkin's account, judges who seek "integrity" attempt to put existing legal materials in "the best light possible."[36] They owe a duty of fidelity to those materials; but they are also authorized to attempt to understand the materials by reference to what they see as the most appealing principle that organizes them. "Law as integrity asks judges to assume, as far as this is possible, that the law is structured by a coherent set of principles about justice and fairness and procedural due process, and it asks them to enforce these in the fresh cases that come before them, so that each person's situation is fair and just according to the same standards."[37] In arguing for this understanding of adjudication, Dworkin says far too little about the virtues and the imperfections of judges and the systemic effects of one or another approach to interpretation.

Dworkin usually discusses law in the abstract, but he does offer a conclusion about the appropriate resolution of *TVA v. Hill*,[38] the famous snail darter case. The question was whether the Endangered Species Act should be taken to block the completion of an important dam because of the late discovery on the land of an ecologically uninteresting fish. Does this application of the act violate reasonable social aims? There is no general agreement about the answer to that question. Dworkin supposes that his idealized judge, Hercules, "shares the substantive opinion that seemed dominant on the [Supreme] Court, that the wiser course would be to sacrifice the fish to the dam."[39] If so, Dworkin urges, it is "not difficult" to see how Hercules will vote, because he "thinks reading the statute to save the dam would make it better from the point of view of sound policy." Given that judgment, Hercules will vote to allow the dam to be completed.

But to know how to vote in *TVA v. Hill*, is it really enough to consult "sound policy"? And if real judges are not as competent as Hercules, is it best for the legal system if they ask the same questions a godlike judge would ask? Here Dworkin sounds very much like Hart, urging that statutory language should not be taken to conflict with reasonable social purposes. Other things being equal, the claim is surely correct. But it is important to ask whether Congress would overturn a literal interpretation of the Endangered Species Act if the consequence was indeed to violate sound policy. Subsequent events showed that Congress was entirely willing to do that.[40] It is also important to ask about the systemic effects of a ruling that would allow the dam to be completed. If that were the ruling, what would the Endangered Species Act actually mean? Would subsequent cases become hard too? If this question is in turn difficult to answer, then the consequences of the ruling, in itself sensible, might in their way conflict with "sound policy" as well. And in cases of this sort, do we have good reason to trust judges' views about sound policy? These points suggest that it is hardly enough to ask, as Dworkin urges, which interpretation of the Endangered Species Act would best complete the story that Congress has begun. If institutional considerations are taken into account, we might conclude that judges should ask themselves a very different set of questions.

Where statutes are entirely ambiguous, it is impossible to decide cases simply by reference to their words. But in *TVA v. Hill* the words were far more easily taken to ban the completion of the dam; and in conflicts between environmental and economic goals, judicial unreliability might well be taken to argue in favor of formalism. What is striking about Dworkin's analysis is that it is undertaken without any thought at all about judicial capacities and about the effects over time of one or another approach to interpretation. Like Hart, Dworkin proceeds as if the question is how an idealized judge Hercules deals with interpretive problems—not how a real-world judge, operating under conditions of limited information, expertise, and even rationality, should proceed.

Manning. Among contemporary writers the chief formalist voice is John Manning, whose work details an important account of interpretation rooted in constitutional law. Manning is a "textualist" who urges that courts interpret statutes according to the ordinary meaning of their texts, and who takes a correspondingly narrow view of the doctrine of absurd results. So Manning is a formalist in the sense that he favors rule-bound interpretation according to the surface meaning of statutory texts, where those texts are unambiguous.

Crucially, however, Manning does not derive his formalist prescriptions at the operating level of the legal system from empirical assessments of institutional capacities and the systemic effects of formalism. Rather, he derives his formalism principally from constitutional text and structure. These two types of justification for operating-level formalism are crucially different, a point I touched upon in the Introduction and amplify in Chapter 3. Here and in what follows, I shall also claim that formalism cannot be justified on the constitutional grounds, themselves conceptualistic, that Manning favors; it can be justified, if at all, solely on grounds that take into account institutional capacities and systemic effects.

Manning's work shows that insufficient attention to institutional capacities is an equal-opportunity hazard that afflicts nonformalists and formalists alike. Manning's contribution is to have provided the most rigorous attempt to justify formalist modes of interpretation by reference to formal sources of law, principally the Constitution. But the project is an impossible one; it is doomed to failure despite Manning's unsurpassed skill at deductive reasoning from abstract constitutional premises. Interpretive formalism at the operational level—formalism in the jurisprudentially modest sense of rule-bound interpretation that sticks close to the surface of statutory texts, where it is possible to do so—cannot itself be justified by conceptual deduction from constitutional premises. Supplemental institutional and empirical premises are needed, premises about the comparative capacities of institutional actors, about the costs of decisionmaking under alternative decision-procedures, and about formalism's ex ante effects.

Consider Manning's influential critique of judicial resort to legislative history.[41] The argument suggests that the Constitution, particularly Article I's procedure of statutory enactment, should be read to embody an implicit norm against legislative self-delegation. That constitutional norm forbids courts to afford "authoritative" weight to legislative history in statutory interpretation, but allows consultation of legislative history as a persuasive or confirmatory source.[42] But this deduction, even if it is valid, leaves open the most important questions about legislative history at the operative level, the level of the interpretive procedures that judges should use.

Few if any people think that the legislative history is "authoritative" in the sense that it is itself a source of law that is hierarchically superior even to unambiguous text. The usual argument is that the history is relevant to ascertaining meaning, and even self-described textualists have acknowledged that legislative history might in principle be useful to illuminate the text.[43] Manning's claim, then, does not tell judges what they need to know. His position forbids the judges to afford legislative history authoritative weight, but nothing in the analysis suggests that the Constitution either requires or forbids the judges to consult legislative history strictly for its persuasive or confirmatory value. The judges presumably retain constitutional discretion to use it or to eschew its use on other grounds.

That question, the crucial one, cannot be resolved through Manning's methods; its resolution depends on institutional issues. Whether judges should consult legislative history as persuasive information is a function of the consequences of the various alternative rules about legislative history that the judges might adopt. Those consequences will turn on institutional facts about judges' capacities as interpreters of legislative history, about the decisional burdens of legislative history for courts and litigants, and about the ex ante effects of legislative history on legislative drafting.

The general point here is that the formal constitutional premises that Manning marshals, such as the textual separation of powers and its original understanding, mandate neither formalist interpretive methods nor nonformalist interpretive methods.[44] The Constitution cannot plausibly be read to say a great deal about the contested issues of statutory interpretation; what it does say is often so minimal and so abstract as to leave open all the reasonably contested questions of interpretive choice. Article I of the Constitution, for example, specifies the conditions for the enactment of valid statutes, and the Supremacy Clause mandates that constitutionally valid statutes are supreme law, so all major interpretive approaches agree that judges should in some general sense take account of the statutory text. But no provision sets out explicit instructions to judges about the limits of interpretive flexibility or about what other sources or considerations are admissible and relevant to help interpret the text.

Textually, provisions like the vesting clauses of Articles I and III seem to deny judges the power to "legislate," but textualists, intentionalists, purposivists, and other schools can all validly claim that their preferred method respects this weak constraint. All concerned can plausibly claim to respect legislative supremacy in statutory interpretation, which shows only that legislative supremacy is an essentially contested concept that is compatible with a wide range of conceptions. At least at the level of express commands, then, the Constitution simply does not take sides in the competition between first-best interpretive approaches that characterizes modern legal theory.

Beyond express text, any supplemental instructions that can be elicited from the Constitution through structural and historical analysis prove compatible with most plausible positions on the contested problems of statutory interpretation. To see this, we must contrast Manning's theory with that of his chief adversary, William Eskridge, who has advanced a resolutely antitextualist, "dynamic" account of legal interpretation. In

Chapter 2 I offer a full critique of Eskridge's work; suffice it to say here that Eskridge argues for flexible judicial treatment of statutory text, the incorporation of a broad range of "public values" into statutory interpretation, and expansive judicial authority to update "obsolete" statutes and even constitutional provisions.

Thus Manning and Eskridge have engaged in an important debate over the role of equitable, Blackstonian considerations in legal interpretation. In large part Manning and Eskridge debate the relationship between Blackstonian equity, on the one hand, and the original meaning of the grant of "judicial Power" to the federal courts in Article III of the Constitution.[45] Manning says that the grant of judicial power, understood both historically and in light of structural inferences from other provisions, bars "equitable" interpretation of the Blackstonian sort and thus commands federal courts to follow a "faithful-agent" account of interpretation. Eskridge says that the Blackstonian appeal to statutes' equity and spirit has a better historical pedigree than faithful-agent approaches, and that courts interpreting equitably are helpful partners in the process of lawmaking—and thus better agents, even on Manning's own terms, than are courts enslaved to a hierarchical vision of legislative supremacy.

On the score of institutionalism, however, the common ground between Eskridge and Manning is more important than their differences; both are afflicted by institutional blindness. Strikingly, despite their spirited debate, Eskridge and Manning largely share the crucial and mistaken premise that the important questions about interpretive theory are first-best questions, rather than second-best questions about institutional performance and systemic effects. But the first-best argument is a fight that ends only in stalemate. As for the history, there are respectable bits of originalist evidence on both sides, and no agreed-upon originalist criterion or metaprocedure exists for adjudicating between them. As for the structural inferences, constitutional premises about equity, agency, and legislative supremacy are pitched at too high a level of generality to cut between competing views about, say, the interpretive value of internal legislative documents or the idea that statutes should be interpreted to avoid absurd results. Both sides can claim, with equal warrant, that their approach respects the principle that courts should be faithful agents of legislatures in areas where legislatures are supreme. It is just that Manning and Eskridge have different conceptions of what a faithful agent would do.

Most important, the debate between Manning and Eskridge rests on an assumption, common to both parties, that the contest of interpretive theories must take place on constitutional terrain. But the best reading of the Constitution is that interpretive formalism and interpretive anti-formalism are constitutionally optional for judges. On this view, Manning's project fails (as does Eskridge's constitutional critique of it), not by virtue of any failure in execution, but by virtue of its intrinsic limitations: the tools of constitutional conceptualism are too weak to produce closure, by themselves, on the contested questions of interpretive doctrine. Those questions require empirical and institutional analysis in addition to first-best theorizing from constitutional premises.

These points are legally contingent. We might imagine a specific constitutional clause instructing the judges to consult or not to consult legislative history, or to embrace or eschew a doctrine of absurd results. In that sense, it might have been true in our legal system that many operating-level questions about statutory interpretation could be settled on the basis of constitutional interpretation. Although this might have been true, it actually is not. The first point I am making here is just that our Constitution cannot plausibly be read to take a stand one way or another on the operating-level issues. Because the Constitution does not speak to interpretive method, the decisive considerations are institutional.

There is also a second point: although constitutional instructions might settle operating-level issues about statutory interpretation, such instructions could not, even in principle, prescribe decision-procedures for interpreting the Constitution itself. A clause stating that "all constitutional texts are to be interpreted literally" could not, without circularity, control the interpretation of the clause itself; and if read nonliterally, the clause might then be understood to instruct an interpretive approach other than the one its surface-level or literal meaning indicates. As I emphasize in Chapter 8, the decisive considerations in choosing methods of constitutional interpretation are necessarily institutional, rather than high-level claims about constitutionalism, democracy, or the nature of law. None of this is to deny that there are easy constitutional cases. If courts should enforce clear and specific constitutional texts according to their surface meaning, however, it is precisely because that decision-procedure will produce the best ground-level consequences for legal institutions, rather than because some higher source of law or higher-level principle mandates it.

Breyer. We will touch briefly upon the interpretive theory of Justice Stephen Breyer, both here and in Chapter 8. Breyer is an exponent of legal process purposivism, and his account suffers from the same problems that afflicted Hart and Sacks. Breyer contrasts textualism with legal process purposivism, and suggests that purposivist interpretation follows from the Constitution's commitments to legislative supremacy and representative democracy.[46] It does not, not directly anyway. As we have seen, given certain findings about judicial capacities and the systemic effects of purposivism, textualism would itself be the best means of discerning legislators' purposes across a set of cases. Although Breyer emphasizes the role of consequences in choosing between interpretive approaches, he shows little interest in facts about interpreters' capacities and systemic consequences. Absent those facts, Breyer's premises do not connect to his conclusions.

The Literary Intentionalists

Let us finish our catalogue by briefly contrasting interpretive theory in law with the theory of literary interpretation. I shall merely glance at a crucial strand of literary theory, one that instructively avoids the flawed assumption that first-best principles directly dictate interpretive methods. I refer to the strand of intentionalism urged by Steven Knapp and Walter Benn Michaels,[47] and later endorsed by Stanley Fish.[48] We shall see that Knapp, Michaels, and Fish propose a particular first-best account of the aims of interpretation, one covering both literature and law; but they also understand that their account, or any other, has no implications at all for methods of interpretation in literature or law.

Knapp, Michaels, and Fish are interpretive intentionalists. On this view, the only *interpretive* question one can ask about a literary or legal text is the question "What did the text's author intend to say?" (bracketing for the time being the possibility of collective authorship). For these theorists, intentionalism is the precondition for having genuine disagreements about textual meaning. Suppose that the purely linguistic meaning of a text is ambiguous, relative to the conventions of language used in a particular community; for example, "I went to the bank by the river" might mean either that "I went to the financial institution by the river" or that "I went to the terrain at the river's edge." To ask, "What does it mean?" is necessarily to ask what the author intended. Any other question

fails to produce real disagreement, fails to produce a joinder of the interpretive issue. Where linguistic conventions are ambiguous, reader A
can understand the text to say one thing, while reader B can understand
it to say something else. Unless there is some fact of the matter that can
arbitrate their dispute, the two readings are fully compatible, and the
disagreement is merely an ersatz one. The author's historical intentions
supply the only possible candidate for a factual benchmark against which
an interpretive dispute can be framed. Of course, there are many things
readers might wish to do with a text beside interpreting it; it might be
construed, or performed, or manipulated. But a reader who wishes to
interpret the text must look to historical intentions.

The intentionalist thesis is controversial. What is crucial for our purposes, however, is the intentionalists' further view that nothing of methodological consequence follows from a commitment to, or against, intentionalism. As Knapp and Michaels put it, "[I]f recognizing that
interpretation is always historical gives no help in deciding what counts
as the best historical evidence, it also gives no help in deciding between
competing interpretations of any text. Intentionalism, as we understand
it, is therefore methodologically useless."[49] The reason is that there is
always a separate question what interpretive decision-procedure, what set
of rules about admissible sources and operations on those sources, will
best conduce to capturing intention. As Fish argues, one who believes
that the original understandings of the Constitution's framers are the
touchstone of constitutional meaning might nonetheless reject the view
that legal interpreters should consult the framers' writings. This rejection
"doesn't mean that [originalists] have forsaken intention but that they
have a different notion as to where evidence of that intention is to be
sought. They may think, for example, that the text provides the best
evidence for the author's (or authors') intention (formalism and intentionalism are not necessarily opposed)."[50]

Fish's insight is crucial. In both literature and law, it does not follow
from originalism or intentionalism that the interpreter does best by simplemindedly collecting and reviewing all possible evidence of original understandings or intentions. On second-best grounds, some other decision-
procedure might yield better interpretations over a set of texts or cases,
defining better according to the intentionalist's own criterion. If, for example, the interpreter's capacities are poor, the nontextual evidence is
confusing, and the textual evidence often captures authorial intentions,

then restricting the range of admissible evidence of intentions might produce better interpretations. In Chapter 4, accordingly, I suggest that intentionalist judges interpreting statutes will do better, by their own intentionalist lights, if they reject legislative history than if they consult it. Overall, the literary intentionalists are laudably alert to the problem that first-best criteria of interpretation cannot translate straightforwardly into conclusions about methodology at the operating level. The theory of legal interpretation, I am suggesting, can profit from their insight.

Some Mechanisms of Institutional Blindness

We have surveyed a range of legal theorists from a range of periods, concluding that intellects of the highest caliber have explored interpretive strategies without attending to the fact that such strategies will inevitably be used by fallible institutions, with likely systemic effects extending far beyond the case at hand. To make a claim of this sort plausible, we need not only to demonstrate institutional blindness, but to explain its genesis. Why have interpretive theories neglected institutional issues? I offer here a sketch of some mechanisms that conduce to neglect of institutional capacities and of systemic effects.

Role confusion. Because of their own role, judges themselves naturally ask a particular question ("How should I interpret this text?"), and that question naturally diverts attention from the issue of institutional capacities. Legal education, and the legal culture more generally, follow suit by asking theorists, students, and others the following role-assuming question: "How would you interpret this text?" If the question is posed in that way, institutional issues drop out. The very form of the question makes them irrelevant.

Built into the role-assuming question, then, is a crucial mistake. The right question is not "How, in principle, should a legal text be interpreted?" The question instead is "How should certain institutions, with their distinctive abilities and limitations, interpret certain texts?" The key consideration, one I have emphasized throughout, is that the relevant interpretive rules are to be used by judges rather than theorists. Theorists should design their proposals in light of the capacities of the implementing institutions, rather than by imagining that the institutions are just like the theorists themselves.

Specialization (academic but not judicial). Academic observers, usually specialists in the subject at hand, often deplore judicial decisions as "wooden" or "formalistic" without appreciating the risk that generalist judges, unmoored from the text, might do even worse. Indeed, it is possible that specialized interpreters should reject formalism but that non-specialists should embrace it; and academic specialists are unlikely to appreciate this point. Law professors, who are usually highly specialized in some particular field or other, often overlook the limited competence of generalist judges. It is very common to see a law professor complaining that some generalist court has blundered in its latest interpretation of the specialized statute that the professor has made a career of studying; usually the blunder occurs because the court, in the critic's view, has interpreted "woodenly," "mechanically," or "formalistically," with insufficient attention to history, policy, and nuance.

In such cases there is a kind of selection bias in play. By interpreting woodenly, sticking close to apparent meaning, the court increases the risk of one sort of error (the sort the critic castigates). But the court decreases the risk of another, opposite sort of error—the error that an intellectually ambitious antiformalist court would make by misreading statutory purposes, misidentifying sensible text as absurd, or mispredicting the consequences of its rulings. Where courts are more often formalist than not, the law professor rarely sees that kind of error and rarely complains about it. The overall point is that specialists, such as legal academics, criticize the insufficiently nuanced opinions issued by generalist judges in particular cases, overlooking that the same judges might well have done far worse, over a series of cases, by attempting to emulate the specialists' approach.

An ethical analogy and the distorting force of particulars. An analogy to ethics is useful here. The choice between interpretive formalism and antiformalism has some of the same logical and cognitive structure as the choice between rule-consequentialism, which counsels that ethical subjects act in accordance with rules whose general observance will maximize best consequences overall, and act-consequentialism, which counsels ethical subjects directly to choose whichever action maximizes best consequences in the case at hand.[51] The rule-consequentialist acknowledges that the globally maximizing rules may sometimes call for actions that, when viewed in isolation, are suboptimal from the act-consequentialist point of view. The rule-consequentialist, then, will sometimes be placed in the awkward position of defending acts whose immediate effect is, when viewed in isolation, socially detrimental. So too, it is the easiest thing in the world for specialized law professors to recall and emphasize specific cases in which formalism produces blunders, relative to a nuanced anti-formalism that is sensitive to the particulars of cases.

In both legal and ethical settings, however, the second-order, rule-based decisionmaking strategies of rule-consequentialism and operating-level formalism show their virtues when the decisionmaker cannot be trusted to identify socially beneficial acts or appealing conceptions of statutory purpose in particular cases. I shall amplify this point in Part II, suggesting that a type of second-best formalism is most attractive in law when decisionmakers cannot be trusted to identify legislators' intentions or statutory purposes in particular cases, and when entrusting the decisionmaker with that authority would produce debilitating legal uncertainty or other systemic costs. For now, the point is that second-order decisionmaking strategies attempt to avoid *the distorting force of particulars.* The concern here is that vivid costs in particular cases may trigger cognitive failings in both theorists and judges, causing them to overreact to the specifics of particular cases while ignoring the overall systemic effects of the interpretive rules they defend or adopt.[52]

One crucial mechanism here is *salience,* a heuristic that causes decisionmakers to overweight the importance of vivid, concrete foreground information and to underweight the importance of abstract, aggregated background information.[53] In the general case of public policy, officials, citizens, and other publics may often underestimate the relatively abstract social benefits that result from governmental infliction of vivid social harms on particular parties. Consider, as possible examples, public opposition to the use of shaming penalties in criminal law and to certain forms of land-use or environmental regulation.

So too in the case of interpretive theory and practice. The vivid harms that wooden, rule-bound interpretive strategies produce in particular cases tend to drive the absurdity doctrine—the idea, which we saw in discussing Blackstone, that judges may interpret statutes flexibly to avoid "absurd results." The benefits of absurdity to the parties in the case at hand are highly visible to theorists and to judges. The costs, however, are relatively pallid and abstract. As I shall discuss at greater length in Chapter 2, the principal costs of absurdity are the risk of error—judges may mistakenly believe that statutory applications are absurd merely because the judges do not understand the relevant policies or legislative purposes—and the decision costs and legal uncertainty that the very existence of a doctrine of absurdity generates. Such costs, however, fall in a diffused way upon the whole legal system and upon citizens generally. The focused and highly visible costs of rule-bound decisionmaking always have the psychological upper hand.

In light of these mechanisms, interpretive theory tends to institutional blindness of the types we examined at the outset of this chapter. Let us now turn to a crucial testing ground for these claims: the work of the arch antiformalist currently on the scene, William Eskridge, and the work of the self-described pragmatist Judge Richard Posner. As we shall see, the mechanisms we have sketched, especially the distorting force of particulars, operate with full force upon these leading theorists.

— 2 —

Dynamism and Pragmatism

A Tale of Two Nirvanas

This chapter pursues the theme of institutional blindness through a closer critique of two of the most prominent interpretive theorists on the current scene: Yale law professor William Eskridge and Judge (and former Chicago law professor) Richard Posner. Chapter 1 suggested that some canonical interpretive theorists, especially Dworkin, are systematically insensitive to institutional considerations altogether. This chapter features more subtle forms of institutional blindness. In terms of the typology offered at the beginning of Chapter 1, the categories of stylized institutionalism and asymmetrical institutionalism come to the fore.

A familiar shorthand for asymmetrical institutionalism is the nirvana fallacy, in which an excessively optimistic account of one institution is compared with an excessively pessimistic account of another. I shall suggest that both Eskridge and Posner urge us toward a false nirvana based on a romantic appraisal of judicial capacities and a jaundiced appraisal or even neglect of administrative interpretation. To be sure, the two theorists say that nirvana lies in different directions: "dynamic" interpretation for Eskridge and "pragmatic" interpretation for Posner. But the common theme is that both theorists rest their arguments on excessively stylized accounts of legislative, judicial, and administrative institutions, and both pay insufficient attention to the systemic effects of their approaches. Most critically, both theorists work with an excessively optimistic account of judicial capacities and (therefore) a one-sided accounting of the risks or costs of freewheeling judicial interpretation.

The Nirvana of Dynamism

William Eskridge's incisive critique of the "new textualism"[1] and advocacy of "dynamic statutory interpretation"[2] redefined the theory of statutory interpretation in the late 1980s and early 1990s. The nub of dynamic interpretation is that judges need not, and in some cases cannot, stick closely to original legislative intentions and purposes. Rather, judges should or must interpret statutes in nonintentionalist or even counter-intentionalist fashion. The dynamic interpreter updates obsolete statutes over time as legal and social circumstances change.

I begin with Eskridge's critique of formalism, especially in the textualist variant seen in the work of John Manning (in turn partially inspired by the opinions of Antonin Scalia). There is great value in this critique, but Eskridge fails to see that he has knocked out only a certain type of justification for formalism, not the position itself. I then turn to the possibility that formalism may be justified anew on different grounds, namely institutional ones. Eskridge largely ignores this possibility; a neglect of institutional factors undercuts Eskridge's conclusions just as it did his predecessors'. Dynamic interpretation, it turns out, embodies the nirvana fallacy—the juxtaposition of an idealized picture of judicial capacities with a grudging picture of the capacities of other actors in the interpretive system.

Eskridge's critique of formalism is transitional work in the history of interpretation scholarship. Eskridge's work presages and made possible the explosion of interpretive theorizing in the 1990s, but itself is still entangled with various sterile problematics—in particular the idea that the principal justifications for interpretive formalism are either formalist constitutional constraints like the separation of legislative and judicial powers or political-theory abstractions like the "countermajoritarian difficulty." By contrast, my concern here and throughout Part II will be to suggest a new direction for interpretation scholarship: an *institutional turn* that puts into play new consequentialist justifications for formalist interpretive practices.

Eskridge is a grandmaster of intellectual critique, and it is educative to see him jousting with his formalist opponents. His work demolishes the twin claims, central pillars of the older noninstitutional formalism, that dynamic interpretation either violates the separation of legislative and judicial power or creates a "countermajoritarian difficulty." The separation of powers is commonly taken to establish that judges must be faithful agents of the legislature. But dynamism, Eskridge emphasizes, might itself be a perfectly acceptable commitment for a faithful judicial agent respectful of the legislature's supremacy in nonconstitutional matters. Sensible legislators might have a higher-order preference that judges be not only faithful agents but also intelligent ones, updating primary legislative instructions over time to accomplish legislative purposes. So far as the ideal of faithful agency goes, there is no answer to this argument. And as we discussed in Chapter 1, the text, structure, and history of the Constitution simply contain no real instructions about interpretive method. Formalism cannot be justified on formalist grounds.

So far so good. But Eskridge appends a further set of jurisprudential objections to formalism that are far less successful. First, "the drafter's context, or intent, can never be perfectly discoverable in hard cases, [so that] the formalist claim to determinacy and objectivity is undermined." Second, as emphasized in the "hermeneutic" theory associated with Hans-Georg Gadamer, "meaning is constructed by the interaction of readers and text." Accordingly, legal interpretation must recognize "the critical importance of the interpreter's context."[3]

Such principles, however, are too abstract, too thin, to get any purchase on the institutional questions that drive legal interpretation. Here and elsewhere, jurisprudential argument is too general to cut between the alternative interpretive approaches that are available to judges at the mundane level of statutory interpretation. There is an unbridgeable chasm between high-level abstractions of this sort and any concrete conclusions about the interpretive questions that divide formalists and antiformalists—questions about whether and when judges should consult legislative history, for example, or about the utility of policy-based canons. A warning sign here is that some of the most prominent "legal realists" of the 1920s and 1930s, who subscribed to something like Eskridge's general claim about legal determinacy, were also interpretive textualists.[4] Likewise, Gadamerian theory neither compels nor even justifies any particular view about, say, the interpretive value of committee reports. Eskridge is right that formalism cannot be justified on formalist grounds, but by the same token it cannot be opposed on jurisprudential ones.

Eskridge occasionally tries to cash out his critique by arguing that (1) dynamic interpretation by judges is inevitable and that (2) formalist interpretation that sticks close to the surface meaning of clear texts is in some sense impossible. The first claim is a merely partial truth. Perhaps it is inevitable that a judge will sometimes (perhaps rarely) find herself unavoidably engaging in dynamic interpretation. But as John Nagle emphasizes,[5] there are many cases in which judges can and do stick close to the surface meaning of text or to legislators' original intentions and purposes, or both. Eskridge almost always discusses hard cases in which texts are ambiguous and judges do actually engage in updating, but this is the law professor's occupational hazard of focusing to excess on the rare and intriguing cases at the expense of the more numerous and more mundane cases. The claim that dynamism is inevitable rests on a methodological mistake, a form of selection bias.

The point that dynamic interpretation by judges is inevitable is akin to the point that crime is inevitable: it is true in a statistical sense, at the aggregate level, but false as to any individual judge, who is usually free to decide whether or not to engage in aggressive statutory or constitutional updating. Even at the aggregate level, moreover, judicial dynamism is the product of other institutional choices. Eskridge emphasizes that the legal system is under constant pressure to adjust old statutes to new circumstances, but it does not follow that *judges* must do any adjusting. As I shall discuss shortly, agencies may be entrusted with initial or even exclusive authority to update legal policies (a point Eskridge acknowledges). Agency updating relieves the pressure on judges and thus ensures a lower aggregate level of judicial dynamism. Far from being inevitable, the level of judicial dynamism is an endogenous product of institutional arrangements.

Eskridge's second claim, that formalism is inconsistent with the contextual character of language, holds only as against a trivial and erroneous conception of text-based interpretation, a conception that holds that texts are self-interpreting and invariant across contexts—a view that, to my knowledge, no interpretive formalist currently holds (and maybe has ever held). Eskridge's repeated accusation that textualists like Manning are insensitive to interpretive context just sets up a particularly unimpressive straw man. Having drunk the heady Gadamerian wine, we may reel around declaiming that no text is "clear" except by reference to the interpreter's horizon of assumptions or by reference to the practices of some linguistic community, but, as Posner says, that does not mean that no text is clear.[6] Formalism, when justified on consequentialist grounds, is merely the claim that the legal system will work best if judges stick to (contextually and socially constituted) clear meanings in that modest sense. The formalist argument cannot be knocked out of court on the basis of claims about the nature of language; the only relevant objections are empirical and institutional.

So the formalist view is not that all texts are self-interpreting; it is that for good consequentialist reasons judges might do best to choose (most of the time) to stick pretty close to the surface meaning of texts (as constituted by social contexts, assumptions, and practices) instead of constantly impeaching them by reference to all sorts of other considerations, like legislative history or public values or whatnot. Once it is granted that there are easy cases in the pool as well as hard cases, that, as Nagle says, there is a domain of cases in which neither countertextual readings nor dynamic updating are inevitable, then the question just becomes which interpretive method will produce the best mix of results across a total pool that contains both Nagle-type cases and Eskridge-type cases. As I suggest later, that question reduces to a question about the incidence of two different types of judicial error, about the costs of decisionmaking, and about the systemic effects of dynamism.

Similar things can be said about Eskridge's treatment of a second major objection to dynamic interpretation, the "countermajoritarian difficulty," often expressed as a view that dynamism is "undemocratic" and not a proper activity for "unelected judges." Eskridge says that the countermajoritarian difficulty is not worrisome because the original majority that enacted the statute will often have dissipated by the time of interpretation, and because the lawmaking system is, by originalist design, only imperfectly majoritarian in the first place. This is absolutely right as far as it goes: the critical objection to dynamic interpretation is not that dynamic interpretation is "undemocratic" or "nonmajoritarian."

As with the separation-of-powers or faithful-agency objection to dynamic interpretation and the hermeneutic defense of it, concepts like democracy and majoritarianism are pitched at too high a level of generality to cut between interpretive formalism and its competitors. Democracy and majoritarianism are essentially contested concepts that can be cashed out in a range of plausible ways;[7] any colorable approach to interpretation can claim their mantle. As we shall see in Chapter 8, even aggressive judicial review in constitutional law can and often has been justified as democracy-promoting, either on Alexander Hamilton's argument that judicial review merely enforces the will of "the people" as against their governmental agents, on John Hart Ely's argument that judicial review can be tailored to the procedural preconditions of democracy, or on Dworkin's argument that judicial review implements principles that reflect the best substantive understanding of democracy. It follows a fortiori that a commitment to democracy or majoritarianism is too abstract to tell us how to interpret statutes, given that statutory decisions are at least subject to legislative override.

Here too, knocking out the democratic underpinnings of formalist interpretation or impeaching its claim to majoritarian legitimacy does not entail accepting nonformalist interpretation; that is a false dichotomy. A third option is to discard the appeal to democracy or majoritarianism while subscribing to formalist interpretive practices on the ground discussed in Part II: formalist interpretation will produce better consequences relative to a wide range of value theories than will nonformalist interpretation. So the whole debate about countermajoritarianism and dynamic interpretation itself looks like an obsolete issue. It should be replaced by the less grand but more useful question whether dynamic interpretation puts excessive strain on the judges' institutional capacities. Eskridge's work, then, opens up the possibility that interpretive formalism might find an institutional justification, one that cannot, even in principle, be rejected by appeals to hermeneutic theory and to a countermajoritarian conception of constitutional democracy.

From the institutional perspective, Eskridge is at his best in refuting abstract or conceptual justifications for formalist interpretive practices; by doing so he cleared away distracting conceptual underbrush. But Eskridge's work does not refute or even speak to the possibility, opened up by the institutional turn, that formalist interpretive practices might be justified anew on functionalist and consequentialist grounds. Those new justifications depend upon largely empirical answers to various institutional-choice questions about the allocation of interpretive authority between courts and agencies and to various institutional-design questions about the relative costs of formalist interpretive strategies and their antiformalist competitors. So Eskridge's work corrects the false belief that we can move directly from the separation of powers or from political theory to formalist interpretive practices, yet it does not exclude the possibility that we can still get to formalist interpretive practices through intermediate institutional and empirical premises.

Dynamism and Institutions

Let us now turn away from Eskridge's valuable demolition of noninsti-
tutionalist formalism to examine the institutional gaps in Eskridge's own
dynamic account. As we have seen, Eskridge's principal target is the formalist approach that emphasizes the original meaning of statutory text.
His principal criticism is that this approach stumbles on the problem of
statutory obsolescence—statutes that have fallen out of step with the
public values prevailing in the surrounding context of the legal system.
Dynamic interpretation is the answer to the problem of obsolescence.
Rather than adhering to ordinary meaning at the time of enactment or
even to legislative intent conceived in strictly originalist terms, courts
should "update" statutes by intelligent adaptation of original purposes to
new social circumstances and by taking account of changes in the overall
fabric of public law. (Sometimes Eskridge cautions that these principles
are merely "clear statement" rules: judges should treat contemporary
public values as something like an interpretive principle or canon, defeasible by clear contrary instructions from legislatures.)[8]

At first glance this position is attractive, even compelling. Eskridge
often derides textualism as embodying a "wooden" or "mechanical" account of interpretation, and the charge seems devastating. How could
"wooden" or "mechanical" enforcement of obsolete statutes possibly be
the best course of action for judges to take? Moreover, Eskridge's claims
certainly have descriptive power. American courts, including or especially
federal courts interpreting federal laws, do sometimes claim or implicitly
assume some sort of power to update statutes, molding them to fit the
contemporary legal landscape. And as I shall discuss later, we may even
acknowledge that on certain factual assumptions, Eskridge's position
could be justified on institutional grounds.

Yet Eskridge fails to systematically discuss those assumptions or those
grounds. He never systematically considers how the case for dynamic
interpretation fares once we recognize the possibility that judges will make
serious mistakes in updating, or that the ex ante effects of dynamism on
legislative behavior might prove pernicious. We may agree with Eskridge
that judicial updating of obsolete statutes is a good thing in the abstract.
The key question, however, is whether the institutional costs of licensing
judges to exercise updating authority are worth the benefits. The possibility of judicial mistakes or of deleterious system effects makes Eskridge's

defense of dynamism incomplete. Dynamic interpretation might or might not prove justified, given adequate information on these variables; I postpone that further question to Part II. For present purposes, what matters is to get clear on the critical questions, whatever the answers turn out to be.

Start with the question of judicial error. The linchpin of dynamism is the claim that "when societal conditions change in ways not anticipated by Congress and, especially, when the legal and constitutional context of the statute decisively shifts as well, this current perspective should, and will, affect the statute's interpretation."[9] This is essentially a recommendation to minimize what statisticians call a false negative: the possibility that nondynamic approaches will erroneously fail to update obsolete statutes, given some stipulated theory about which statutes count as "obsolete." But Eskridge says little about the converse possibility, the false positive: the risk that judges might err in the other direction, reinterpreting statutes that are not in fact obsolete, because the judges fail to comprehend those statutes' current social utility. If judicial updating is frequently erroneous because statutes have sensible and fully up-to-date justifications that the judges have simply failed to understand, then dynamism may cause more institutional failure than would a rule that denies judges the authority to update.

The net incidence—the frequency and gravity—of the false positives may well swamp the net incidence of the false negatives for institutional reasons. Neil Komesar has emphasized a basic tradeoff arising from judicial independence: although the judiciary's institutional insulation from quotidian politics may promote a certain type of impartiality, it also produces an informational deficit. Judges insulated from politics are often also remote from people, from the very political and social wellsprings of current public values upon which Eskridge would have interpretation draw. Moreover, federal judges are a type of gerontocrat, often serving long careers on the bench while embodying the public values and policy commitments of a bygone era. Although we shall see that Judge Posner celebrates this fact, for Eskridge it should be a concern; there is no reason to expect judges to be systematically au courant with shifts in public values and policies.

Put differently, if the legal system should contain an institution charged with issuing dynamic, updating interpretations of obsolete legislation, it is hardly clear that the judiciary should be that institution. Cass Sunstein suggests that agencies have become the legal system's "common-law courts." The idea, in part, is that agencies' superior capacities qualify them as the best dynamic updaters; Eskridge's interpretive methods might, on Eskridge's own premises, be better applied by administrative agencies than by courts.[10] Sunstein argues that "dynamic interpretation is—simply as a matter of actual practice—an administrative task, not a judicial one,"[11] an allocation that is normatively appealing because of agencies' relatively greater information about current conditions, superior technocratic expertise, and heightened political responsiveness. If so, courts should support interpretive rules that channel the responsibility for updating away from courts and toward agencies such as the canon of deference to administrative agencies' interpretation of ambiguous statutes. On this view, even signing on to Eskridge's largely pessimistic picture of legislative capacities would not necessarily yield the conclusion that judges should aggressively fill in statutory gaps and ambiguities or aggressively move to update statutes in light of social, political, and policy change. Perhaps such activities should be left strictly to agencies. We shall examine agency interpretation at length in Chapter 7; suffice it to say here that the question is one dynamic interpreters must reckon with.

In some of his most recent work on interpretation, Eskridge acknowledges these points, suggesting that most updating should be done by agencies rather than courts. On this revised view, the courts' role is, above all, to serve as "the guarantor of the rule of law," protecting citizens' and officials' reasonable expectations and reliance interests against "excessive" updating by agencies.[12] This represents a shift away from Eskridge's earlier emphasis on judicial dynamism and updating. Unfortunately, however, the new view, like the old, rests on a stylized and asymmetrical institutionalism. Eskridge says that "[j]udges are well-situated to enforce the values of predictability and continuity embedded in the rule of law, because they are partly insulated from the political process and because they are highly regarded lawyers who are skilled in the interpretation of legal texts."[13] We have already seen that this view ignores the crucial tradeoffs identified by Komesar: the insulation of generalist judges deprives them of information relevant to interpretation, which on Eskridge's own account requires more than the reading of lawyerly texts. Moreover, insulation from politics does nothing to guarantee that judges will use their freedom to promote the rule-of-law values Eskridge now praises, as opposed to other values: perhaps distributive justice, or economic efficiency, or the interests of the American Bar Association or the Republican Party, or any other aims the judges may happen to favor. I return to these questions in more detail in Part III and elsewhere.

Dynamism and Systemic Effects

Eskridge also underplays the possibility that the systemic effects of non-dynamic interpretive approaches would prove better, on Eskridge's own criteria, than would the systemic effects of dynamism. Eskridge supports his case for dynamism by drawing upon process theory and public choice theory, arguing that "the legislature acting alone will be subject to . . . biases,"[14] and that "given the biases of the political process, the fact that judges are not elected may enable them to be better 'representatives' of the people than their elected legislators are (in some instances)."[15] It may be true that interest-group pressure and institutional failures will cause Congress to update statutes with insufficient frequency, relative to some optimal rate of policy change. But this is to compare an imperfect legislature with a judiciary that is implicitly assumed to be unerring. As we have seen, this is the nirvana of dynamic interpretation, and it is an inadequate picture of legal interpretation, because judges may not only correct legislative failures to update; they may also update erroneously. Recall from Chapter 1 that a genuinely institutional account of legal interpretation must not only discuss institutions, but must do so even-handedly, with due attention to the relative capacities and shortcomings of institutions in various settings.

The legislative failings that dynamic interpreters condemn might themselves be, at least in part, an endogenous consequence of the interpretive theory the judges use. Some textualists argue that their methods will spur legislatures to update at an optimal rate. The aftermath of *TVA v. Hill,* discussed in Chapter 1, suggests some evidence of updating in response to textualism. To his credit, Eskridge has attempted to study how Congress responds to judicial approaches to statutory interpretation. As I discuss at length in Chapter 6, however, the attempt founders on the standard problem of omitted variables. Given more solid empirical findings, in other words, it might turn out that textualism produces the amount of updating Eskridge thinks best, in which case textualism would itself just be the dynamic approach to interpretation. On certain empirical premises about institutional capacities, Eskridge ought to support the very textualism that he spends so much time excoriating.

Here we must disentangle two different questions: whether Eskridgean

dynamism or textualism rests on the right type of institutional justification, on the one hand, from the substantive merits of the possible justifications, on the other. In Chapter 5 I shall suggest that pervasive coordination problems within judicial institutions undercut the textualist case
for dynamism as well. That is consistent with my point here, which is
just that dynamic interpretive theory can be justified, if at all, only on
institutional grounds.

In later work Eskridge discusses some institutional considerations in
the limited context of the debate over whether judges should consult the
internal legislative history of statutes. Eskridge acknowledges that the desirability of judicial resort to legislative history turns importantly on a
cost-benefit calculus that examines judicial performance, litigation costs,
and legal certainty in competing legislative-history regimes.[16] In even
more recent work, however, Eskridge reverses his ground, arguing both
that empiricism is conceptually meaningless without normative premises
(a question I address in Chapter 3) and that the relevant empirical and
institutional variables are costly to measure[17]—certainly true, but hardly
a sufficient argument for nonempirical interpretive theory. All told, as
with some of the other theorists we shall consider, Eskridge notes the
critical institutional considerations in passing, but fails to incorporate
them into his normative account of interpretation in any systematic way.

It is worth emphasizing that none of these considerations necessarily
refutes Eskridge's dynamic conclusions. If judges update successfully more
often than not, and if textualist interpretation causes legislatures to spend
most of their time correcting mistaken (because wooden or mechanical)
judicial interpretations, then textualism would prove inferior to dynamic
interpretation, and Eskridge's methods would push the courts closer to
the optimal rate of updating. But there is no valid path to that conclusion
from Eskridge's institutionally insensitive premises.

A Note on Positive and Normative Institutionalism

We must look briefly at another important strand of Eskridge's work, a
strand with much richer institutional content. Eskridge helped pioneer,
at least among academic lawyers, the positive political-theory analysis of
interpretation, cast broadly as an ongoing game between legislatures,
courts, the president, and agencies,[18] or cast more narrowly as positive
analysis of particular subprocesses in that game, like the generation of
legislative history.[19]

Eskridge, however, does little to link such work with the normative side of his project, and it would not be very easy to forge such links. We need not hold some jejune view of the distinction between positive and normative analysis to think that this work has little obvious payoff for normative interpretive theory (the specification of the aims that interpreters should pursue) or even for prescriptive and instrumental interpretive theory (the selection of institutional means for pursuing those aims). The problem with the positive political analysis is that it presupposes that the judges' "ideal points" (the location of their preferences on the standard one-dimensional spatial model that positive theorists use) are exogenously fixed. But the entire thrust of interpretive theory is to make normative arguments about where those ideal points should lie. What Eskridge calls "The Article I, Section 7 game"—the interaction between legislatures, the executive, and courts that produces equilibrium interpretations of statutes—is an external analysis from the Archimedean standpoint of a legal anthropologist surveying the system, while normative interpretive theory is an internal analysis from the standpoint of participants. (Imagine a positive political theorist who is hired to give an oral argument before the Supreme Court. The Justices ask, "What is the applicable law here?" The theorist answers, "The law is whatever equilibrium position emerges from your interaction with other institutions.").[20] Positive political theory and normative or prescriptive interpretive theory never come to grips with one another.

At one point, other strands of positive political theorizing looked like they might have greater cash value for interpretive theory. Theorists like McNollgast, for example, have tried to provide strictly positive rules of inference that would allow judges to make use of legislative history. Fortified by the complex methods of Bayesian decision theory, judges would be enabled to gauge the probability that items of legislative history reflect a consensus among the enacting coalition.[21] As I discuss in Chapter 4, however, McNollgast offers judges a decision-procedure that is too demanding, given the judges' limited information and information-processing capacities.[22] The problem is general: the more sophisticated the positive theory, the more strain it puts on judicial capacities and the more serious become the suppressed concerns about mistakes, the costs of decision, and systemic effects.

The consequence of all this is that the positive political strand of Eskridge's work cannot repair the broken links between Eskridge's jurisprudential premises and his dynamic conclusions. There is no magical methodological technique, no new body of theory that can be arbitraged over from other university departments, that will enable us to avoid institutional questions about judicial capacities and the systemic effects of competing approaches. Nor will a self-consciously antitheoretical stance help, as we shall see in the next section with respect to the "pragmatic" interpretive theorizing of Judge Richard Posner.

The Nirvana of Pragmatism

I turn now to Judge Richard Posner, who urges that legal interpretation should be a "pragmatic" enterprise. The substance and especially the atmosphere of Posner's work are very different from Eskridge's. Posner is a hardheaded debunker of high theory and high aspirations in law, and his favorite epithet for his nonpragmatic opponents is "highfalutin'." But we shall see that Posner is at heart a romantic about the capacities of his fellow judges. His pragmatic account of interpretation, although a long step in the right direction, ultimately shares the insensitivity to systemic effects and the nirvana-like assessment of judicial capacities that undermine Eskridge's dynamism.

Imaginative Reconstruction: A False Start

In his early writing Posner endorsed an "imaginative-reconstruction" approach to interpretation, asking judges to reconstruct the views of the enacting legislature and to do what the legislature would have done had it been presented with the case at hand.[23] This approach, adapted in part from Judge Learned Hand, is an expanded version of Blackstone's idea that judges should make exceptions to overbroad statutes in "those circumstances, which (had they been foreseen) the legislator himself would have excepted."[24]

Like Blackstone's approach, however, imaginative reconstruction is blind to institutional considerations of the sort that we have been emphasizing throughout. That the legislature, if informed of the application at hand, would have adopted a particular statutory amendment does not mean that it would want the judges to do so on their own initiative. The premise entails the conclusion only if we assume arbitrarily that the allocation of tasks across institutions is irrelevant. Moreover, the possibility of judicial error undermines imaginative reconstruction just as it undermines Eskridge's dynamism. If judges frequently err in their counterfactual suppositions about what the legislature would have done, then imaginative reconstruction may, even on its own terms, push the judges even further away from the legislature's intentions than unimaginative textualism would have.

Pragmatism and Systemic Effects

More recently Posner has endorsed a pragmatic account of adjudication generally, one that subsumes a pragmatic account of statutory interpretation.[25] The pragmatic account should be fertile soil for the sort of institutional analysis needed in interpretive theory. Pragmatism, as Posner uses the term, pays a great deal of attention to the consequences of the possible interpretations judges might adopt—seemingly hospitable territory for the approach urged here. (We shall see in Chapter 3, however, that Posner is at pains to deny that pragmatism is a form of "consequentialism" in the philosophical sense.) The major theme of this part is precisely that interpretive rules cannot sensibly be chosen without consideration of institutional consequences. Indeed, Posner does recognize the possibility that the pragmatic judge might, on certain empirical premises about the institutional capacities of judges and legislatures, decide that interpretive formalism at the operational level would itself be the pragmatically best course of action.

Yet this possibility remains an abstraction. As soon as possible Posner falls back upon a distinction between consequences for the "case at hand" and the "systemic" consequences of decisions. On this view the pragmatist attempts to do what is best in the case at hand, subject to a side constraint: that case-specific adjudication not produce unacceptable systemic costs in legal uncertainty and other undesirable consequences: "The pragmatist thinks that what the judge is doing in deciding the non-routine case is trying to come up with the most reasonable result in the circumstances, with due regard for such systemic constraints on the freewheeling employment of 'reason' as the need to maintain continuity with previous decisions and respect the limitations that the language and discernible purposes of constitutional and statutory texts impose on the interpreter."[26] The point of all this is to preserve some domain of policymaking discretion for judges, some field in which pragmatic judges can run free, bringing their all-things-considered consequentialist judgments to bear on the parties before them. Posner is quite candid about this: "[A]t their best American appellate courts are councils of wise elders and it is not completely insane to entrust them with responsibility for deciding cases in a way that will produce the best results in the circumstances rather than just deciding cases in accordance with rules created by other organs of government or in accordance with their own previous decisions, although that is what they will be doing most of the time."[27]

But the distinction between case-specific consequences and systemic consequences, between the pragmatist's aim and the pragmatic side constraint, is illusory. The decision to license judges, in some domain, to interpret statutes so as to maximize beneficial consequences in the case at hand is itself a system-level choice of a particular kind, a choice that will have system-level effects on the legislatures, agencies, and litigants who must anticipate the judges' efforts to sort cases from one domain to the other. Depending on the values to be attached to the relevant institutional variables, the legal uncertainty, including decision and litigation costs, that the distinction creates might overwhelm the social benefits attainable in the class of cases that Posner would leave to freewheeling judicial discretion. So the questions are systemic all the way down, and the distinction collapses on itself.

If the distinction is illusory, it nonetheless has harmful effects. The very making of the distinction has real and unfortunate consequences for the pragmatic account of adjudication generally and interpretation in particular. The insistence, amounting to a faith, that there just has to be some domain of entirely carefree discretion left to the wise elders of the bench produces a one-sided view of the empirical and institutional variables that a pragmatist would consider if genuinely open to the possibility that interpretive formalism is pragmatically best for judges. The point here is not, of course, that all discretion can be squeezed out of interpretation or adjudication, even in cases of real statutory or constitutional ambiguity; I take up decision-procedures for cases of ambiguity in Chapters 7 and 8. The point is that judicial discretion always has system-level effects that judges should consider. There just is no domain of wholly discretionary decisionmaking whose effects are confined entirely to the case at hand.

This neglect of systemic effects undercuts Posner's claim that American judges have no choice but to assume the burdens of rulemaking and policymaking. On Posner's view, because American legislatures (in contrast to the United Kingdom's Parliament and to continental legislatures) do not exercise sufficient oversight of the statutory system, they do not correct gaps and resolve ambiguities at a sufficient rate and thus leave the judges with no option but to amend statutes and fill statutory gaps through interpretation.[28] The institutional analysis here is incomplete, and perhaps mistaken. Posner offers no systematic analysis of the behavior of American legislatures; he does not show that the legislative failure is as pervasive as he suggests that it is. But even if it is that pervasive, the supposed irresponsibility of American legislatures might be at least in part the result, not (as Posner assumes) the cause, of the relatively independent, policy-oriented approach to interpretation taken by American courts. Perhaps American legislatures opt for ambiguity and passivity, to the extent that they do, partly because the correctivist stance of American courts ensures that underspecified or ill-considered legislation will in effect be supplemented or amended by judicial decisions. To know which of these stories is true, we would have to know the systemic effects on legislatures of judicial formalism (or antiformalism); as a result, we cannot rule out formalism as a strategy for American courts. Posner's claim that American judges cannot be formalist turns out to rest not on evidence, but on an ungrounded and highly contestable causal intuition about the systemic interaction of legislatures and courts. The point here is not that when all of the relevant variables are considered, the pragmatic judge should be an interpretive formalist; I take up that question in Part II. The point is that Posner's attempt to treat systemic consequences as merely a side constraint on interpretation, despite its appearance of institutional sensitivity, is just one more attempt to wall off institutional considerations from interpretive theory.

Pragmatism and Judicial Capacities

In the typology of institutional blindness introduced at the beginning of Chapter 1, Posner falls squarely into the third category, that of asymmetrical institutionalism. Posner holds a persistently jaundiced picture of legislative and administrative capacities that is heavily influenced by the public choice idea that legislators merely supply law to organized interest groups.[29] As to judges, Posner is clearminded, as when he speculates on the components of the judicial utility function.[30] Sometimes, however, Posner holds a celebratory view of other appellate judges. Consider again his vision of "American appellate courts" as "councils of wise elders." (Does this apply to state appellate courts, say, the Rhode Island intermediate courts, as well as to the Seventh Circuit?) Posner says that this vision rests on "institutional factors." So it does, but only in part: the only factors Posner's analysis considers are those characteristics of judges that happen to support a benign view of judicial capacities. Here is Posner's discussion:

> Judges of the higher American courts are generally picked from the upper tail of the population distribution in terms of age, education, intelligence, disinterest, and sobriety. They are not tops in all these departments but they are well above average, at least in the federal courts because of the elaborate preappointment screening of candidates for federal judgeships. Judges are schooled in a profession that sets a high value on listening to both sides of an issue before making up one's mind, on sifting truth from falsehood, and on exercising a detached judgment. Their decisions are anchored in the facts of concrete disputes between real people. Members of the legal profession have played a central role in the political history of the United States, and the profession's institutions and usages are reflectors of the fundamental political values that have emerged from that history. Appellate judges in nonroutine cases are expected to express as best they can the reasons for their decisions in signed, public documents (the published decisions of these courts) and this practice creates accountability and fosters a certain reflectiveness and self-discipline.[31]

Absent from this account, however, is the requisite comparison of these factors to the characteristics of legislators (or, for that matter, agency officials). Legislators are also picked from the upper tail of the population distribution on all the measures Posner mentions, and if they are not as detached as judges, they have much better information about real-world consequences than judges do, due to their greater institutional resources and their contact with affected citizens. A whiff of guild interest hangs about Posner's discussion when he says that "[m]embers of the legal profession have played a central role in the political history of the United States, and the profession's institutions and usages are reflectors of the fundamental political values that have emerged from that history." Do lawyers, as a class, really have privileged insight into the nation's fundamental political and moral values? In any event, many legislators are lawyers as well.

The point is not to dispute Posner's assessment of institutional capacities on the merits. The point of disagreement is that Posner's assessment fails, not because it is substantively erroneous (a question I am bracketing in this part), but instead because it fails to provide a full consideration of the relevant institutional factors. Absent a systematic, empirically informed comparison of institutional capacities, celebratory optimism about judges is unsupported.

Statutory Absurdity and Pragmatic Judging

Posner gives a glimpse of his judge-centered premises when he discusses the idea that statutes should or even must be interpreted to avoid absurd results. Drawing upon Blackstone's famous example discussed in Chapter 1—a statute providing that "whoever drew blood in the streets should be punished"—Posner agrees with Blackstone's conclusion, saying that "the law should not be interpreted to make punishable a surgeon 'who opened the vein of a person that fell down in the street with a fit.' " Posner thinks that this example knocks out any thoroughgoing interpretive formalism or textualism. Is it really conceivable that the surgeon should be held liable or guilty? What exactly should judges do, Posner asks, with statutes like the French provision that forbade passengers to get on or off a train that was *not* moving?[32]

It might be that a well-designed interpretive system should lodge absurdity-avoiding power in judges; I mean to bracket that question for now. But Posner has not elicited the systemic considerations that would bear upon the question. For one thing, as Harvard legal scholar Fred Schauer has emphasized, a judicial power to avoid absurd results is also a judicial power to avoid results that the judges mistakenly think are absurd merely because, as ill-informed generalists, they have misunderstood the statutory scheme.[33] An absurdity doctrine minimizes the former type of error, but the absence of an absurdity doctrine minimizes the latter type of error. The systemic question about the absurdity doctrine— a question pitched at the level of rules, not a question about particular outcomes—is which type of error will be more frequent and more costly in a given legal system. This is the problem of false negatives and false positives again. All this shows the mechanisms of institutional blindness in action, as discussed at the end of Chapter 1. Habituation to the case-by-case, fact-specific decisionmaking practices of the courts may diminish a judge's capacity to think at the level of systemic tradeoffs rather than at the level of ensuring "sensible" results in particular cases.

Posner's defense of the absurdity doctrine is excessively judge-centered. The dilemma upon which Posner wants to impale formalists—either permit a discretionary judicial power to avoid absurdity or endorse crazy results—exists only on the further, implicit premise that only *judicial* decisions can avoid absurdity. But any plausible institutional system con-tains many institutions that exercise power to weed out absurd cases, of which the judiciary is only one, and not at all the most important. Con-sider the role of private-bill legislation that provides relief from general laws in unusual cases; prosecutorial discretion, both in charging and sen-tencing, that channels resources toward serious rather than silly cases; jury discretion and nullification with respect to both liability and sen-tencing; executive clemency and pardons; and administrative waivers or other case-specific relief. Furthermore, as we have seen in discussing Es-kridge, there is the role of administrative agencies as common-law courts. Agencies exercise a hybrid kind of prosecutorial or judicial discretion in initiating and adjudicating cases, and even in rulemaking, and plausibly have better information than judges about which applications are genuinely absurd in light of statutory policies. It is striking that Posner rarely discusses agencies; I return to the role of agencies at length in Chapter 7.

So the crucial questions about absurdity are institutional. First, will judges avoid more absurdity than they create, or vice versa? Second, is judicial power to correct absurdity beneficial in net effect, given that some fraction (perhaps a very high fraction) of genuine absurdities will be weeded out by other institutions in the legal system? Finally, Manning makes the important point that a doctrine of absurdity can undo legis-lative bargains, making it harder for legislators to strike bargains in the future.[34] Posner does not really engage these issues. Instead, he deploys absurd cases for rhetorical effect, trading on the distorting force of par-ticulars discussed in Chapter 1.

At the deepest level the problem with Posner's "pragmatic" account of interpretation is that it is too focused on the viewpoint of judges rather than on the overall design of the interpretive system, in which judges are only one actor, and in the administrative state not clearly the most important actor. Chicago law professor Richard Epstein hits the mark dead center when he observes: "The deep flaw in Posner's pragmatism is that it cares too much about the mental processes of the judge and not enough about the merits of the legal rules created by the judicial process."[35] The judge-centered view produces a chronic, systematic tendency to overestimate judicial capacities, to underestimate the capacities of legislatures and agencies, and to ignore the systemic costs of judicial discretion for other institutions. As with Eskridge, Posner's nirvana of judge-dominated interpretation begs the critical questions.

— II —

Reconstruction

So far we have criticized extant accounts of legal interpretation, charging them with one or another form of institutional blindness. But critique is easy; it is time to begin to build an affirmative account of the institutionalist view of legal interpretation. In this part I begin the work of reconstruction. Chapter 3 is the core theoretical chapter of this Part. I suggest that the theory of legal interpretation should be recast along resolutely institutional and empirical lines, outline an empirical research program for institutionalists, and consider important objections to institutionalism. Chapters 4 and 5 provide extended case studies of two considerations or variables that are central to institutional analysis: interpretive rules must be chosen in light of *institutional capacities* and the *systemic effects* of interpretive approaches.

Subsequently, Part III returns to the theoretical plane, taking up crucial issues of the relationship between empiricism and judicial decision-making. There I suggest that where judges must choose interpretive rules under conditions of profound uncertainty and bounded rationality, a modest brand of interpretive formalism is the best response in both the statutory and constitutional arenas.

— 3 —

The Institutional Turn

In this chapter my basic suggestion is that interpretive theory in law should take an *institutional turn.* In some respects the institutional turn began some time ago, even as early as the legal process school. But we saw that legal process institutionalism was incomplete or unsuccessful in many respects, especially its tendencies toward stylized abstraction and toward one-sided praise of judicial capacities. Much more work remains to bring the institutional turn to fruition. Part of my task here will be to supply a theoretical account that buttresses the emerging institutionalist position.

From another perspective, such an account is antitheoretical. One of my central claims will be that the high-level premises commonly brought to bear on interpretation, as we saw in Part I—premises about democracy, or constitutionalism, or the nature of law, of statutes, or of language—are fatally abstract. Such claims are pitched too high; they typically lack the cutting power to resolve operational controversies at the ground level about what interpretive rules judges ought to follow. It follows, I shall suggest, that high-level premises are incomplete unless they are supplemented by lower-level institutional analysis. Indeed, I shall also claim, more ambitiously, that in some domains the high-level controversies may be bracketed as irrelevant to the operational problems and thus dispensed with altogether.

Turning Away from Nirvana

We have seen in Chapter 2 that Eskridge's work performed a valuable service by clearing away a range of conceptual and essentialist justifications for formalist interpretive practices. After Eskridge, interpretive theory has, in some quarters, turned to an exploration of institutional and empirical considerations bearing on interpretive method—an exploration that moves well beyond the stylized, abstract institutionalism of Hart and Sacks in the 1950s. The new interest in institutionalism has been fed by many streams, including transaction-cost economics, the rise of behavioral economics, the widening scope and ambitions of positive political theory, and the increasing flow into the legal academy of scholars skilled in empirical methods of one sort or another. And the effects of the institutional turn on interpretive theory have been direct and important. The new institutionalism, I shall argue, provides powerful intellectual resources for those who both reject conceptual defenses of formalism, such as Manning's, and yet also reject Eskridge's (and Posner's) antiformalist conclusions. I will not attempt to sketch the overall intellectual history of interpretive theory in recent years, leaving that task for competent historians. Instead, I will merely emphasize those strands of the institutional turn that bear most directly on my theme, omitting mention of a great deal of important work.

Institutional Choice

We may start with *institutional choice:* the insight that specifying a criterion for a successful interpretive outcome (for example, the Eskridgean ideal that statutory law should reflect changes in surrounding legal and social context) says nothing at all about which institution is best situated to implement the chosen aim. Important work of the 1990s drew upon increasingly sophisticated methodological tools to cash out the implications of this insight for public law. In constitutional law, lawyer-economists like Neil Komesar[1] and Einer Elhauge[2] drew upon transaction-cost economics and interest-group theory to refute simple arguments for an aggressive judicial posture in constitutional cases—what we have called asymmetrical or nirvana-like arguments that fail to compare all relevant costs and benefits of the available institutional alternatives. Consider the standard line that judges should intervene to correct failures of the democratic process—a line formulated in a traditional legal process vocabulary by John Hart Ely and translated into the vocabulary of public choice by libertarians and free-marketeers in the 1980s. After Komesar's and

Elhauge's work, defending that line is at least a far more complicated business.[3] Process failures in the form of rent-seeking activity and differential interest-group access afflict the courts as well as legislatures (Elhauge), and whatever relative insulation judges enjoy comes at the price of severe informational deficits (Komesar). These points make the premise of comparative judicial advantage underlying the standard line questionable at best.

The Komesar/Elhauge refutation of crude arguments for judicial intervention in constitutional adjudication spilled over onto, and collaterally damaged, Eskridge's and Posner's accounts of statutory interpretation as well. In Chapter 2, we saw Eskridge arguing that "the legislature acting alone will be subject to . . . biases," and that "given the biases of the political process, the fact that judges are not elected may enable them to be better 'representatives' of the people than their elected legislators are (in some instances)."[4] Posner likewise tends to describe legislatures as forums for interest-group dealmaking. After the institutional-choice groundswell, these views look like a pretty severe case of single-institutionalism.

It may be true that institutional failures will cause Congress to enact "rent-seeking" legislation that grants socially inefficient benefits to interest groups, or to update statutes with insufficient frequency. But from an institutional-choice perspective we still need to ask whether the judges' relative insulation and the resulting informational deficits might not cause them to err in other directions. Judges might well, for example, misidentify statutes as thoroughly inefficient interest-group handouts because they fail to understand the relevant public policies, or simply because a well-motivated legislature was pursuing its aims under conditions of disagreement and thus was subject to compromises and political constraints. Likewise, Chapter 2 emphasized the possibility that judges may update statutes that are not obsolete on any account, simply because the judges fail to comprehend the statute's current social utility, and because the judges mistakenly believe that a current electoral or legislative majority does not favor the statute's retention. On this sort of comparative institutional ground we might want judges to behave formalistically even if it means that they will fail to update in cases of genuine obsolescence, simply because the costs of a regime that permits erroneous judicial updating would be even greater than the costs of a regime that leaves all updating to imperfect legislatures.

Interpretive Choice

Rules of interpretation are decision-rules for statutory and constitutional cases. To propose an interpretive methodology is to specify what will count as an admissible input into cases and what operations the judges will perform on those inputs. As in the institutional-choice setting, the analysis proceeds by considering the relative costs and benefits of alternatives. Here, however, the alternatives are not institutions to which a given task might be allocated. They are alternative rules and doctrines that structure the interpretive process—for example, a rule that judges should never consult legislative history, or should always consult legislative history, or should consult it only when text is ambiguous. The choice between these alternative regimes of interpretation might be called *interpretive choice,* as a shorthand analogue to institutional choice.

Important examples of this sort of analysis emerged during the 1990s, examples that recast old interpretive debates in fundamental ways. We have mentioned Fred Schauer's argument that doctrines licensing nontextual or antitextual flexibility, such as the absurd-results canon, should be analyzed by ascertaining the relative frequency and gravity of judicial errors in a regime that contains those doctrines and in a regime that excludes them. As we saw in Chapter 2, the question is whether a judge licensed to identify absurd results will err more frequently and more seriously by correcting nonexistent absurdities than a judge not so licensed will err by failing to correct real absurdities. A parallel analysis applies to legislative history, as I will emphasize in Chapter 4. There a key question is whether interpretive rules that license recourse to internal legislative materials will increase or decrease the net total of judicial mistakes (where mistake may be defined by reference to any aim specified by the interpretive theory, such as ascertaining legislative intent or producing the best overall consequences). Other work in the institutionalist vein expands this sort of interpretive-choice analysis to ask about not only the error costs of competing regimes but their relative decision costs, their relative effects on the interaction between courts, legislatures, and agencies, the costs of transition from one regime to another, their stability, and other effects.[5]

The significance of interpretive-choice analysis is that it cuts the links between high-level premises—such as jurisprudential commitments, claims about the nature of language, and accounts of democracy or constitutionalism—and the operational, ground-level rules that judges are to follow. Suppose that, following Eskridge, we reject essentialist or constitutional justifications for formalist interpretive practices. Nonetheless, antiformalist conclusions about those practices hold only if we suppose certain answers to the interpretive-choice questions. The bite of interpretive-choice problems, like the bite of institutional choice problems, is that no fully specified account of interpretation can avoid taking a stand on them one way or another. On the institutional-choice side, no amount of insistence on a social goal answers the question which institution is best positioned to attain that goal and should therefore be allocated that task. So too with interpretive choice: no specification of a criterion for interpretive success, for deciding what outcomes count as erroneous, will tell us what interpretive rules and doctrines to use until we have decided how all of the candidate rules or doctrines (within the feasible set) compare along the relevant dimensions (the frequency and gravity of mistakes, the costs of decision, and other effects).

So, for example, return to Eskridge's argument that "when societal conditions change in ways not anticipated by Congress and, especially, when the legal and constitutional context of the statute decisively shifts as well, this current perspective should, and will, affect the statute's interpretation."[6] We may agree in an all-else-equal sense that judicial updating is a good thing. Yet so long as we reject the overblown claim that updating is inevitable, we should also worry that judicial updating will produce erroneous rewriting of statutes whose sensible and fully up-to-date justifications the judges have simply failed to comprehend, and will thus cause more institutional failure than would a rule denying judges that authority. No amount of repeating the arguments for updating, no amount of clever debunking of the constitutional premises on which interpretive formalism is usually justified, will answer or even address that question.

The Inescapability of Interpretive Choice

As the last example shows, interpretive-choice problems are inescapable. Such questions always intervene between high-level jurisprudential, political, and linguistic commitments, on the one hand, and the operational level of interpretive rules, on the other. Eskridge is concerned that statutes be au courant in light of changing public values; but he cannot simply assume that *therefore* judges should be given authority to update statutes. There is an intervening issue, about judicial capacities, that cannot be assumed away. Conclusions about what judges should do at the operational level—what I have called interpretive choice—require considerations of at least the following sort:

Rules and standards. The anatomy and behavior of rules and standards are fairly well understood, at least in the abstract, as are the connections and distinctions that link these concepts to such other concepts as error costs and decision costs and the allocation of institutional authority between principals and agents or delegates.[7] Rules economize on information and thus often reduce legal uncertainty and judicial decision costs, at least in the short term. Yet rules bar direct recourse to an all-things-considered determination about whether the background justifications for a legal norm apply to particular facts. This means that rules inevitably prove both over- and underinclusive relative to their justifications. Rules may thus raise error costs relative to the performance of a fully informed and fully competent decisionmaker using a standard, although in some circumstances a mediocre decisionmaker using a rule may prove more accurate than a mediocre decisionmaker using a standard, as when some of the information excluded by a rule has inflammatory or distortive effects on the decisionmaking process.

Implementing an interpretive goal thus requires a choice among a whole menagerie of forms (for example, rule, standard, presumption, and rule-with-exceptions) in which the legal norm or directive suggested by that aim may be embodied. That choice will itself require empirical assessments of the competence of the judges or decisionmakers who will apply the chosen legal doctrine, the relative decision costs of rules and standards and their variants, and the effects of the choice of form on the legislative and administrative institutions that create law and on the private firms and individuals who live under it.

Institutional capacities and decisionmaking authority. The choice of legal form has important effects on the allocation of decisionmaking authority. Rules and standards allocate decisionmaking authority in different ways within an institution over time, between different levels of a hierarchical institution, and among institutions. Standards in effect delegate decisionmaking authority to the decisionmaker at the point of application, as when a standard instructs a judge to decide whether a driver was proceeding at a "reasonable speed." Rules vest authority in the rule-formulators rather than in those who apply the rule in particular cases at a later time. Rules thus require more information and decisional competence ex ante, at the time the rule-formulators decide what the content of the rule should be. Standards require more information and decisional competence ex post, at the time of application. It follows that one important consideration in the choice between rules and standards is whether the rule-creators or the rule-appliers have better information and superior competence to translate information into sound legal policy.

Incentives, motivations, and agency. The institution that applies a legal directive (rule, standard, or variant) may be the same institution that created it (as when the Supreme Court creates a standard to govern its own certiorari jurisdiction), may be a subordinate official within that institution (as when the lower federal courts apply a directive announced by the Supreme Court), or may be a different institution altogether (as when legislators enact a rule or standard for subsequent judicial application). Each possibility introduces further complexities, heavily empirical in character, into the choice of legal form. One critical problem involves the trustworthiness of agents and delegates: even if creating a standard might otherwise be beneficial in order to vest discretion in competent, well-informed agents at the point of application, will those agents act to promote the principal's interests or their own? Agency slippage between principals and agents creates costs; monitoring of agents by principals can reduce this slippage, but monitoring is costly in turn. Where agency costs are high, principals might be wise to create rules even if standards would be a better choice for more trustworthy agents.[8] The rigidity of rules can lower the costs that principals must incur to monitor the behavior of suspect agents.

These principal-agent problems are closely linked to the question of the proper scope of a rule or standard. Both rules and standards can be broad or narrow; "do the good" is a broad standard, while "trucks may stand in loading zones for fifteen minutes except between 7 and 9 A.M." is a narrow rule. The scope of a rule or standard will increase or diminish the effects of the choice of legal form. A broad rule reduces decision costs dramatically at the point of application by bringing more cases within its scope and reduces the discretion of the possibly incompetent or untrustworthy agents who apply it. Yet for precisely those reasons a broad rule formulated by an ill-informed or incompetent principal will prove more damaging than a narrow rule would have been.

Systemic effects: Legislative, administrative, and private reactions. Another important theme involves a difficult set of systemic questions about the likely reaction of other institutions to the rules or standards chosen by a decisionmaker engaged in interpretive choice. Those institutions may stand in the relationship of either principal or agent to the institution that chooses an interpretive rule. Positive political theory emphasizes that judges choose doctrines in the context of anticipated reaction from other lawmaking institutions.[9] Whether the models suggested by positive political theory accurately describe the interactions between courts, legislatures, and agencies involves a morass of empirical questions of great complexity.

Take the question whether a rule excluding legislative history would have significant effects on legislative output. The nineteenth-century commentator Francis Leiber suggested that English statutes became absurdly complex and detailed because the judges pursued a literalist approach to interpretation,[10] including a refusal to consult parliamentary instructions found in the recorded debates.[11] At the federal level, it is possible that some such effect would take place if the courts excluded all legislative history. A different view, pressed by textualist judges and commentators, argues that flexible statutory interpretation and frequent judicial recourse to legislative history give legislators incentives to enact ambiguous, vague, or excessively general statutes. On this view, excluding legislative history will cause Congress to legislate more clearly, thus providing a beneficial increase in authoritative information about legislative intent. There is a third possibility: both Lieber's view and the textualist view may overestimate the effects of judicially developed interpretive doctrine on legislators' behavior, specifically legislators' production of statutory text and legislative history. This will be so if, as I will argue in Chapter 5, judges have a great deal of difficulty coordinating on interpretive approaches that would systematically push legislative behavior in one direction or another. For now, the important point is that this is just another answer to a question about systemic effects, a question that no account of interpretation can ignore.

Institutions, Formalism, and Consequences

Let us step back to assess what has been said so far. The significance of these claims about institutional choice and interpretive choice is twofold. First, institutional questions are inescapable. It is impossible to move directly from high-level commitments—about democracy, language, or the nature of law—to the operational level of interpretive rules judges use. Problems of interpretive choice always intervene between high-level premises and ground-level conclusions. I shall return to this point later.

Second, formalism need not be justified on high-level conceptual, theoretical, or constitutional grounds. The institutional turn raises the possibility that formalism as a strategy for adjudicating statutory and constitutional cases might be justified on the basis of formalism's consequences, rather than by claims about language, democracy, or the Constitution's text and structure. The claim would be that formalism, as a mode of adjudication, produces better consequences for the legal system than do the nonformalist alternatives. Of course, "better" must be defined by reference to some theory of value, some account of what makes consequences good or bad. Importantly, however, we shall see that the consequentialist justification for formalism need not assume any *particular* value theory. One of my principal claims will be that formalism might produce the best consequences on a wide range of value theories. Proponents of different conceptions of value might converge to an agreement on formalism, so that formalism would represent something like an overlapping consensus among various camps.

Nothing in Eskridge's high-level, Gadamer-influenced jurisprudential commitments precludes this sort of consequentialist justification for formalism. And formalism of this variety, a formalism justified by reference to its consequences, would not be pragmatic either. Posner specifically distinguishes pragmatism from consequentialism, the view that actions are to be judged by their consequences. There is an important issue here that I shall merely identify for later discussion: consequentialism requires some value theory—some account of what makes the consequences of decisions good or bad. This means that formalism cannot be pragmatic in Posner's sense, because his version of pragmatism—what he calls "everyday pragmatism"—quite self-consciously lacks any value theory of the sort that consequentialism must provide. Posner quite explicitly acknowledges that everyday pragmatism has no general account of what makes some judicial decisions good and some bad. Although Posner seems to think that this is a virtue, I agree with Dworkin that it is an incorrigible vice.

Two Senses of Formalism (Revisited)

My central claim, so far, is that formalism might be justified on the basis that it produces better consequences (relative to a wide range of value theories) than its nonformalist competitors. There are many suppressed issues and questions here; we must unpack this central claim one step at a time.

A good beginning is to reemphasize the two different senses of the protean word "formalism" to which the Introduction referred. In one sense, formalism refers to a type of justification for legal rulings or doctrines, namely a conceptualistic or essentialist justification that excludes considerations of morality and policy. Consider the Supreme Court's occasional embrace of conceptualistic jurisprudence in constitutional law, such as the essentialist distinction between "manufacturing" and "commerce"[12] or between "legislative" and "executive" power.[13] This is the sense in which, I said in Chapters 1 and 2, theorists like Manning are "formalists." Eskridge's contribution, on this view, is to knock out formalist justifications for interpretive practices of the sort that Manning defends. My suggestion is that neither Eskridge nor Manning is correct. Manning has the wrong sort of justification for his preferred practices, but Eskridge does not see that we might give a different sort of justification—namely, a consequentialist one—for the practice that he dislikes and that Manning favors.

In the second and very different sense of formalism, explicated by Schauer, among others,[14] formalism refers to a consequentialist decision-making strategy that courts might follow at the operational level. Here courts make a second-order decision[15] to decide cases, where possible, according to rules rather than standards, sticking close to the apparent or surface meaning of legal texts and placing great emphasis upon the value of legal certainty and the value of adhering to common understandings of constitutional and statutory commands. On this account, a judicial preference for formalist decisionmaking need not and cannot rest upon a deduction from any superior source of principles, such as the Constitution or some definition of law's essence. Formalism is justified, if at all, by reference to a claim that formalism will have better consequences than will alternative decisionmaking strategies. Here the claim is that formalism will improve the legal system in relevant respects, with improvement defined by reference to a value theory that points to social goods exterior to law itself.

After the institutional turn, formalism in the second sense can be seen as a potentially sensible decisionmaking strategy for courts interpreting statutes. Formalism in this sense counsels courts to stick close to the surface meaning of texts, where possible, and to promote, ex ante, the clarity of legal commands and the intelligibility of the default rules against which legislatures must draft statutes in the first instance. The formalist judge would decline to attempt to mold statutes to fit apparent purposes or intentions, would decline to declare the apparent import of statutory text "absurd," and would narrow the range of outside sources admissible to impeach textual meanings. Again, it is no objection to formalism, so conceived, to insist that texts are "clear" only by reference to the practices of some linguistic community. Courts might choose to be formalists, not by pretending that all texts are self-interpreting in some context-free sense, but on good consequentialist grounds, thinking that things will be better if courts emphasize the surface or apparent meaning of texts (as constituted by relevant assumptions and practices in the linguistic community) rather than impeaching them by reference to other sources and considerations.

The significance of the institutional turn, on this view, is just to make clear that formalism in the second, operational sense is entirely independent of formalism in the first, justificatory sense. Formalism in the operational sense cannot be justified or opposed by an appeal to self-evident constitutional principles, by an appeal to the nature of democracy or language, or by an appeal to a definition of law. Conversely, however, formalism as a decisionmaking strategy in statutory or constitutional interpretation, or for that matter in any other setting, can be justified or opposed (solely) on the basis of a forward-looking assessment of the consequences of the competing alternatives. Just as Manning errs by arguing for formalism by reference to formal sources, so Eskridge errs by engaging Manning on the same terrain in order to oppose formalism.

The only correct ground for opposing formalism, on this view, is that antiformalism will produce better consequences for public law than formalism would.

The General Conditions for Formalism

Why might it be true (or false) that formalism in the second, operational sense would be the best interpretive method for courts to follow? What would we have to know about the consequences of the competing alternatives to know whether courts should subscribe to formalism? The variables are numerous, but can be herded into two large categories: the capacities of the interpreting judges, and the systemic effects of the judges' interpretive rules on other actors. The former category subsumes the costs of mistaken rulings—what I have called false positives and false negatives—and also the costs of decisionmaking itself. The latter category subsumes a range of questions, including the effect of the judiciary's interpretive rules on legislative and administrative behavior; the possibility that different judges might not coordinate on interpretive rules and the costs of coordination; and the effect of judicial practices on citizens' and agencies' compliance with law and on the behavior of other courts, including both lower courts and future courts at the same level of the legal hierarchy.

A commitment to interpretive formalism, in the operational sense, would follow from particular views about the values of these two (classes of) variables. On a dim assessment of the performance of interpreting judges, for example, interpretive formalism will appear more attractive than antiformalism. Relevant here are many questions I shall discuss at length in later chapters, questions about the manageability of alternative interpretive sources, such as legislative history and canons of construction, and about the limits of judicial information. A court interpreting under tight constraints of time and information may do better to ignore or subordinate interpretive sources, like legislative history, whose large volume and unfamiliar components could often provoke judicial error, and whose marginal informational payoff is low. For similar reasons a court staffed by generalist judges might do better, all else equal, by sticking to the apparent or common meaning of texts and by eschewing empirically ambitious innovations in statutory policy. A specialized court, by contrast, would often do better with antiformalist interpretive techniques that give free play to the court's superior appreciation of legislative intentions, interest-group deals, statutory policies, and social and economic consequences. In later discussion I shall suggest, along the same lines, that specialist administrative agencies might often wield nontextualist interpretive techniques more successfully than generalist courts; specialized courts are an intermediate case.

So too, interpretive formalism will look more attractive on certain empirical assumptions about feedback effects on legislative behavior or system effects more generally. Suppose that judicial formalism would produce more careful legislative drafting ex ante and would encourage the development of corrective mechanisms ex post, such as the "Corrections Day" procedure instituted in 1996 by the House of Representatives.[16] These possibilities are overlooked by Posner in his claim that the sloppiness of American legislatures requires American courts to adopt an antiformalist stance. It is possible that the effects run in the other direction; to the extent that they do, formalism should be preferred as the approach that will push the interpretive system, taken as a whole, in desirable directions. In Chapter 5, however, I introduce the complication that judges may not be able to coordinate on the rulings necessary to produce beneficial system-level effects.

The Empirical and Legal Contingency of Formalism

An important corollary of all this is that the case for (or against) formalism is emphatically contingent upon the values that the empirical variables take at a given time and in a given legal system. I emphasized in the Introduction that the inquiry here is limited to our legal system, constituted as it currently is and with the institutions it actually has. As institutional arrangements vary, formalism in the institutional sense will look more or less attractive. In Chapters 7 and 8 I will urge the view that institutional formalism is indeed best, given our institutional circumstances, although it might not be best for other times and places. Here the theoretical point is just that the attractiveness (or not) of operating-level formalism is not a conceptual issue. It is a contingent and empirical issue that can only be assessed relative to the facts about our legal institutions, given their actual capacities and systemic interactions.

The case for formalism at the operating level is legally contingent as well as empirically contingent, as I emphasized in the discussion of Manning's work in Chapter 1. We might imagine a legal system in which the constitution indisputably prescribed rules of statutory interpretation other than those operating-level formalism would recommend—for example, a specific clause instructing courts to construe statutes to avoid absurd results. In such a system legal considerations might be taken to preclude operating-level formalism even if formalism were best overall from a consequentialist point of view. The relevant constitutional rules would then be bad ones, but still valid (let us assume).

This point is correct, but it is not helpful, for two reasons. The first is that our actual legal system is not like the imaginary one. Our sketchy Constitution, I have argued, cannot plausibly be read, on any interpretive approach, to dictate rules of statutory interpretation, either through express text or through structural inference. Validly enacted statutes are "law," the Constitution tells us, but none of the relevant approaches deny that premise. The fighting questions are how best to figure out what the law says, whether legislative intentions or purposes are relevant to figuring out what the law says, and whether legislative history may be consulted in figuring out what the law says.

Second, no constitution could, even in principle, dictate rules for its own interpretation; the meaning of the relevant clauses would always pose an interpretive question of a higher order. So even under a constitution that contains instructions for statutory interpretation, institutional considerations are decisive at the level of constitutional interpretation. Those considerations might or might not suggest that judges or other officials should follow the apparent or surface-level meaning of the constitution's directives for statutory interpretation. At most, then, the significance of legal contingency would be to push the questions about operating-level formalism back one step, or up one step, to the level of constitutional interpretation itself.

Institutional Variables

The possibility of operating-level formalism, then, is an empirically contingent one within our legal system. Upon what contingencies does that possibility depend? Let us consider a more systematic list of the institutional variables that must be explored in order to assess the appeal of formalism as a decisionmaking strategy at the operational level of statutory and constitutional interpretation, given the institutions of our legal system. Of course, the domains of statutory interpretation and constitutional interpretation are different in important respects; in Chapter 8 I offer a more detailed account of constitutional interpretation. But we must distinguish the character of variables from their actual values. Although the differences between the constitutional and statutory domains may yield different values for particular variables, the institutional considerations fall into similar classes of variables in the two settings, or so I shall claim. Moreover, the critical questions are empirical, and this is a major feature of the institutional turn. By emphasizing the central place of institutional variables in the choice among competing interpretive approaches, it yields a research agenda for interpretive theory that is far more empirical than the accounts we canvassed in Chapters 1 and 2. I explore the connection between formalism and empiricism at greater length in Chapter 6.

Formalism, antiformalism, and error. The first question involves judicial capacities: will a formalist or nonformalist judiciary, in one or another domain, produce more mistakes and injustices? Of course, people might dispute the content of these categories. One person's error might be another's fidelity to law. But the extent of social disagreement should not be overstated here. It is easy to imagine cases in which courts have used background purposes not to make sense of the law, but to impose their own views about sound policy. We could know far more than we now do about whether state or federal courts have done well or poorly when they have consulted purposes, attempted to avoid absurdities, or invoked background principles within the legal system. One empirical project would involve comparisons among the courts of different states to see if large differences can be found in interpretive behavior. Another such project would involve comparisons over time to see if courts have changed from formalist to nonformalist approaches, or vice versa, and to see the antecedents and consequences of such shifts.

Cognition, motivation, and agency costs. The general rubric of interpreters' capacities can be broken down into motivational and cognitive components. Well-motivated interpreters might make mistakes because of limited information, limited capacity to process information, and bounded rationality, including vulnerability to cognitive errors. Even cognitively perfect interpreters, however, might make mistakes because they are not trying to avoid them. An important case here is agency slack, in which judges or other interpreters charged with implementing some interpretive approach pursue other goals. Principals, such as legislators, can reduce agency slack by monitoring their agents, such as judges, but monitoring is costly and thus inevitably imperfect.

Two important empirical issues, then, involve the cognition and motivation of interpreters. Are judges, agencies, and other interpreters boundedly informed and boundedly rational? How much slack do interpreting agents possess? Here the connections to formalism are obvious and important. If some judges are untrustworthy, formalism may appear valuable, in part as a means of constraining judges' discretion and reducing the costs of monitoring by superior judges, legislators, and citizens. If judges are well motivated but ill informed and prone to cognitive blunders, formalism may also appear valuable, in part because more ambitious and information-intensive approaches to interpretation will increase the frequency and gravity of mistakes.

Systemic effects: Mistakes and their correction. A crucial systemic question is whether and when formalist decisions that produce clear mistakes will be corrected by the legislature and whether the corrections have low or high costs. Undoubtedly this question will have different answers in different circumstances. We know far too little to know how to answer it in the United States. Is the New York legislature, for example, different on this count from the legislatures of California and Missouri? It would be highly desirable to know much more about the interpretive practices of courts in different states and to make some evaluation of the different solutions. We might be able, for example, to find state courts that are especially unwilling to make exceptions in cases of evident absurdity— and we might be able to see whether courts of this kind have produced outcomes that have remained legislatively uncorrected. We might also ask whether legislatures are more likely or less likely to oversee and to fix judicial decisions that attempt to follow statutory text.

A similar inquiry might proceed by comparing judicial and legislative behavior in different domains of substantive law. Perhaps Congress is unlikely to police judicial decisions interpreting the Administrative Procedure Act and the Sherman Act; perhaps Congress is entirely willing to oversee judicial decisions in the areas of tax and bankruptcy. If so, different judicial approaches might be sensible in the different areas. Where

Congress is inattentive and appears to rely on courts for long periods of time, an irreverent judicial approach to statutory text might be defensible. Where Congress will correct judicial errors fairly costlessly, formalism is easier to justify. People with different first-best theories might well accept these suggestions. Does our practice, in various domains, suggest that courts are less formal where Congress is less attentive? It would be highly desirable to know. Here there is a large set of empirical projects.

Systemic effects: Decision costs and uncertainty. A final question is whether a nonformalist judiciary will greatly increase the costs of decision for courts, litigants, and those seeking legal advice. A large issue here involves planning; nonformalist approaches might so increase uncertainty as to make planning costly or impossible.[17] Some areas have a greater demand for planning than others, and hence it might be predicted that courts will perceive themselves as most constrained when planning is necessary. We might expect that the basic rules governing disposition of estates will require a good deal of clarity, and that in view of considerations of fair notice, many courts will be reluctant to interpret criminal statutes flexibly to cover criminal defendants.

Formalism, Consequentialism, and Value Theory: An Objection

Let us review the argument thus far in order to identify and assess an important objection. Part I criticized a wide range of theorists for their failure to engage institutional issues. Turning in this part from critique to reconstruction, I have suggested the need for an institutional turn in interpretive theory. Institutional issues—both institutional choice and interpretive choice—are inescapable; such issues always intervene between higher-level commitments and judicial practice. In light of the institutional turn, I have also suggested, there is a possible case for formalism at the operational level, a case that is not dependent on high-level claims about democracy, the nature of law, the nature of language, or the deep premises of the Constitution's text and structure. The case for formalism might instead be resolutely low-level, institutional, and consequentialist: my central claim in Chapter 6 will be that formalism as a mode of decisionmaking in constitutional and statutory cases produces better consequences, in light of institutional capacities and systemic effects, than do its nonformalist competitors.

But there is an important objection to the emphasis on the institutional turn and on the consequences of operational-level formalism or antiformalism. The objection takes this form: Is it useful, or even possible, to evaluate institutional variables without agreeing on a value theory—on an account of what makes (the consequences of) particular interpretive approaches good or bad? Without such a theory, we will be unable to know what counts as interpretive "error." For some textualists, adherence to the text is simply the definition of a correct judgment; there is no independent measure of whether a judge has blundered. It is easy to imagine an advocate of purposive interpretation or of intentionalism as offering a like claim. Perhaps a judge proceeds correctly if and only if she captures legislative purposes or intentions. If this is so, how can the idea of institutional turn be valuable or even coherent? Perhaps an institutional turn would be rudderless or useful only as an adjunct to the underlying value theory.

I suggest two responses to these questions. Less ambitiously, institutional and second-best considerations are always a necessary complement to high-level value theories, even where second-best considerations are not sufficient, in and of themselves, to indicate what the operating-level rules of interpretation should be. More ambitiously, institutional considerations may themselves be sufficient to select operating-level rules of interpretation in many domains, because different high-level value theories converge upon similar operating-level prescriptions. In those domains high-level disagreements may be bracketed and ignored altogether.

First-best and second-best. A simple response is to distinguish between first-best and second-best accounts of interpretation. A first-best account specifies a value theory that makes some interpretive regimes good, some bad. But first-best accounts are necessarily incomplete. The problem for first-best accounts is that those accounts may be implemented by a range of institutional arrangements and interpretive regimes. Some of these arrangements may produce worse outcomes, according to the very criteria of value specified by the first-best account, than others. There is no escaping the question of how the first-best account is to be implemented at the operational level.

Put differently, my minimal submission is that without institutional analysis, first-best accounts cannot yield any sensible conclusions about interpretive rules. It is impossible to derive interpretive rules directly from first-best principles without answering second-best questions about institutional performance. Consider an analogy. In economics, the idea of second-best demonstrates that if perfect efficiency cannot be obtained, efficiency is not necessarily maximized by approximating the first-best efficiency conditions as closely as possible. The second-best outcome might, in principle, be obtained by departing from the first-best conditions in other respects as well.[18] So too, if an imperfect judge knows that he will fall short of the standard of perfection defined by the reigning first-best account of interpretation, it is by no means clear that he should attempt to approximate or approach that standard as closely as possible.

Suppose, for example, that we believe that the meaning of a statute should in principle, as a matter of political theory, be established by ascertaining the subjective intentions of those who enacted it. This is legal intentionalism, as opposed to the literary intentionalism we encountered in Chapter 1. As we emphasized there, it may turn out that fallible judges ought not simplemindedly to collect and examine as much evidence of subjective intentions as they can find. If the text supplies reliable evidence of intention, perhaps the best evidence, and if judges will mishandle other types of evidence, such as legislative history, perhaps restricting judges solely to the text will increase the likelihood that the judges will accurately ascertain the legislators' intentions. Or suppose that an ideal interpreter would not read statutory texts to produce absurd results, results not possibly intended by a rational legislator. As we discussed in Chapters 1 and 2, it does not follow from this premise that the interpretive rules should license real judges to prevent unintended absurdity. If judges will often see absurdity when it is not really present, simply because they misunderstand the substantive policies in play, then allowing them to attempt to correct absurdity might do more harm than good; perhaps they should not make that inquiry at all.

These examples illustrate that at the very least, institutional analysis is necessary, even if not sufficient, for an adequate evaluation of interpretive methods. It is of course true in these examples that some first-best account is needed in order to define judicial error. The minimal point is that the first-best account, taken by itself, is necessarily incomplete. It is impossible to derive interpretive rules directly from the first-best account because institutional considerations always intervene. An intentionalist account of statutes' authority by itself tells us nothing about whether real judges should consult or not consult legislative history; a theoretical injunction to avoid absurd outcomes by itself tells us nothing about whether real judges should be licensed to use an absurd-results doctrine. In any of these settings, certain findings about institutional capacities might cause the proponent of the first-best account either to adopt or reject the interpretive doctrine in question. Theory without institutional analysis spins its wheels, unable to gain traction on the question of what interpretive rules real-world judges should use.

Incompletely theorized agreements on interpretive practice. There is also another, more ambitious response. In some cases a second-best assessment of institutional issues might be not only necessary but indeed sufficient to resolve conflicts over interpretive theories, simply because the assessment might lead people with different views on the theoretical issues to agree on the appropriate practices. For example, at a high level of abstraction, intentionalists disagree with textualists, who believe that the ordinary meaning of statutory texts counts as law, rather than the intentions of statutes' enacters. But the two camps agree on a great deal, and most of the time, their disagreements are quite irrelevant to the choice of interpretive rules or even to the decision of particular cases. Both agree that the statutory text is the starting point for interpretation, and both accept the view that courts should not lightly depart from the text, which most intentionalists see as strong evidence of intentions. On the current Supreme Court, textualists are often able to join opinions written by intentionalists, and vice versa.

Given certain empirical and institutional assumptions, moreover, both the intentionalist and the textualist might even be able to agree upon a rule excluding legislative history. The intentionalist would agree because, on particular empirical premises, the rule would minimize both erroneous determinations of legislative intent and the costs of litigation. The textualist would agree because, on the same premises, the rule would minimize erroneous determinations of ordinary textual meaning and litigation costs. This consensus would be in the nature of what Cass Sunstein calls an "incompletely theorized agreement":[19] interpreters holding different theories of authority might be enabled in this way to converge on particular doctrines.

The last example shows that value theories may be bracketed and thus ignored where incompletely theorized agreements at the operational level are possible. Institutional analysis might even enable interpreters to choose particular doctrines before, or in place of, choosing a value theory that specifies what counts as a good or bad consequence of interpretive practices. If, on certain empirical findings, it turned out that legislative history should be excluded on any high-level theory specifying what counts as good or bad interpretation, then as far as that interpretive question goes, there would be no need to choose a fundamental theory.

So it is uncontroversial, even banal, to point out that institutional analysis presupposes some underlying, first-best account of interpretation. But the point does not cut very deeply, nor does it contravene any of the claims I have made. What modern interpretive theory has largely overlooked is that institutional analysis is a necessary condition for choosing interpretive rules, even if it is not a sufficient condition. And in some domains it may indeed be a sufficient condition. Even if institutional analysis must be underpinned by value theory, it does not follow that interpreters must agree upon some *particular* value theory in order to agree upon interpretive doctrines; to suppose otherwise is a simple logical blunder. Where an overlapping consensus or incompletely theorized agreement is possible, interpreters may choose rules while bracketing and remaining agnostic about first-best accounts.

Of course, the scope or size of the domain in which such agreement is possible remains uncertain. The scope of convergence cannot be established in the abstract; it can only be established by inspection, through detailed consideration of various interpretive areas and problems. Later chapters offer ground-level analysis of operational convergence. Here I emphasize that the size of the domain in which that convergence occurs is just one more factual question for institutional analysis to answer.

Pragmatism, Consequentialism, and Value Theory: Posner versus Dworkin

The puzzles of pragmatism. The foregoing enables us to take a fresh look at an important criticism of Judge Posner's pragmatism by Ronald Dworkin. We can understand the force of Dworkin's criticism if we ask: Is pragmatism the same thing as, or a version of, consequentialism—the view that actions (or rules for action) are to be judged by the goodness or badness of their consequences? If pragmatism is consequentialism, then pragmatism requires a value theory; it requires an account of which consequences are good or bad.

Posner, however, repeatedly denies that pragmatism is consequentialism, in part because he wants to defend something he calls "everyday pragmatism" as opposed to "philosophic pragmatism." Although he claims that pragmatic judging is "forward-looking," he also says that "pragmatic adjudication is not consequentialist, at least not consistently so. That is why I prefer 'reasonableness' to 'best consequences' as the standard for evaluating judicial decisions pragmatically."[20] On this view, the everyday pragmatist can pronounce that particular judicial decisions or legal rules are "reasonable," or "sensible," or "work" or "don't work."

But such words are intellectual bubbles that burst and disappear at the slightest touch. Dworkin, himself an avowed consequentialist,[21] says that it is empty to advise judges to do what "works" unless the pragmatist specifies some criterion—what I have called a value theory—by which judges may know what "working" means. Suppose (to pick an example that postdates Dworkin's critique) that the judges face the choice of intervening or not intervening to decide a presidential election; suppose also that intervening will produce a kind of short-term political stability at the price of a reduction in the legitimacy of the presidential contender the judges install. To advise the judges to intervene because doing so "works" or is "sensible" or "pragmatically best" is vacuous counsel. What the judges need to know is whether the goods the decision produces are more valuable than the bads, and to know that, some account of what makes consequences good or bad is necessary. Here and elsewhere, Dworkin's criticism is unanswerable. Pragmatism, at least in its everyday as opposed to philosophic variant, is just consequentialism with no value theory. Everyday pragmatism is a stunted form of consequentialism, one that is coy about the good and refuses to commit to any substantive criteria for evaluating consequences.

The limits of value theory. There is a flip side to the coin, however. That consequentialism requires a value theory—and that everyday pragmatism fails for lack of one—does not entail either of two further claims. It does not entail either that (1) a value theory is, all by itself, enough to yield operational conclusions about what judges ought to do or that (2) a commitment to any particular value theory is required in order to do institutional analysis at the operational level. The first claim overlooks that second-best institutional analysis is inescapable if a value theory is to be implemented at the operational level. The second claim overlooks the possibility of an incompletely theorized agreement in which various value theories converge on operational conclusions. These two points, of course, just repeat the two responses to the value-theory objection that I gave in the preceding section.

Dworkin, then, goes wrong in turn to the extent that he suggests either that a value theory can directly dictate legal rules at the operational level or that consequentialists must commit to some particular value theory before any institutional analysis can be done. In a charitable spirit we might also construe Posner's everyday pragmatism as a form of consequentialism that rests upon a suppressed, implicit, but indispensable appeal to convergence on particulars across a range of value theories. If this is what Posner means, then everyday pragmatism is a perfectly valid version of consequentialism; indeed, it is the version I am suggesting here.

Institutionalism as a Theory of the Middle Range

The larger point is that the sort of institutional analysis I mean to advocate here occupies a middle position between two extremes. At one extreme lies the sort of hollow pragmatism that refuses to acknowledge the need for criteria of good and bad outcomes. At the other extreme lies Dworkin and the other theorists canvassed in Part I, many of whom seem to think that high-level value theory is all that is necessary. Institutional analysis rejects both views and thus aspires to provide a "theory of the middle range."[22] Institutionalism acknowledges the place of value theories in constructing accounts of interpretation, but insists both that such theories are necessarily incomplete without second-best analysis and that where value theories converge at the operational level, those theories may be bracketed and ignored in certain domains and for certain purposes. When such bracketing is possible, I have tried to suggest, the remaining questions are empirical ones about a range of institutional variables, not conceptual or philosophical puzzles about language, constitutionalism, political morality, or the nature of law.

— 4 —

Judicial Capacities

A Case Study

It is time to turn from discussing institutionalism to doing it. The next two chapters flesh out the discussion of the last by providing extended examples of the two principal institutional variables we have discussed—interpretive capacities and systemic effects. In this chapter we shall examine judicial capacities, in relation to the much-debated problem of legislative history: should judges use internal legislative materials as an aid to statutory interpretation? Here I seek to demonstrate a possibility that has second-best implications: judges may do worse, on a range of value theories, by consulting legislative history than by declining to use it. Chapter 5 turns to systemic effects, examining accounts of statutory and constitutional interpretation that urge judges to engage in ambitious *democracy-forcing,* in which judges pick interpretive rules with a view to provoking desired legislative responses. I suggest that serious coordination problems within the judiciary render democracy-forcing interpretation infeasible. Together these two chapters begin to suggest, on institutional grounds, that judges should adopt modest interpretive practices, sticking close to the surface meaning of statutory texts and eschewing ambitious systemic goals. In Part III I provide some underpinnings for these suggestions and examine a range of examples from both statutory and constitutional interpretation.

I will begin the work of fleshing out the institutional program by offering, in this chapter, a case study of what is perhaps the most famous statutory-interpretation decision ever to issue from the Supreme Court: *Holy Trinity v. United States,* decided in 1892 yet still a focus of controversy. Here my basic suggestion is that *Holy Trinity* and the legislative-history debate for which the decision has become a synecdoche are best viewed through the lens of judicial capacities. Judges work under constraints of information, cognitive capacity, and time. Constrained judges seeking for legislative intentions or purposes may often make mistakes, even serious blunders, when they use legislative history as a source of intentions. If this is so, I shall suggest, then on second-best grounds even judges who subscribe to intentionalist principles would want to behave like textualists in practice.

That argument fleshes out the central claims advanced in Chapter 3. First, high-level interpretive premises (here intentionalism) are always subject to second-best problems at the operational level. Second, intentionalists and textualists might be able to reach agreement, starting from different high-level premises, that legislative history is not a cost-justified tool for interpreting judges. If so, it might even be possible to bracket the high-level questions altogether, so far as the problem of legislative history goes. Interpreters who are undecided about, or uncommitted on, the high-level questions might still be able to take an intelligent position on the value of legislative history.

Holy Trinity and the Legislative-History Debate

Recent years have witnessed a debate about whether judges interpreting statutes should consult legislative history—the material generated within legislatures during the process of statutory enactment. On one side of the debate, textualist judges and commentators have presented a manifold argument against legislative history. First, the judicial practice of consulting legislative history as an interpretive source is unconstitutional. Statutes themselves are the law; reliance on legislative history both assumes and encourages the assumption that legislative intent is the law and that statutes are merely evidence of that intent. Second, consulting legislative history produces bad statutory interpretation. Legislative intention is a meaningless concept because intentions cannot coherently be attributed to collective bodies. Even if the concept of legislative intent were coherent, legislative history is unreliable evidence of that intent. Legislators are often unaware of the contents of the legislative history and may not assent to it even if they are aware of it. Moreover, legislative history is systematically manipulated and distorted by legislative factions and private interests.

Intentionalists dispute each of these assertions. First, they claim that the Constitution permits judicial resort to legislative history; the relevant constitutional provisions prescribe conditions for the valid enactment of federal statutes, but those provisions neither require nor forbid judges to use any particular method of statutory interpretation. Second, legislative intent is indeed a coherent concept, just as it is coherent to speak about the intention of other collective bodies. Even the evidentiary unreliability of legislative history is greatly overstated. Conventions that operate within the legislative process, such as deference to committees or sponsors by other legislators, ensure that legislative history reflects positions that can (at least in a conventionalist sense) fairly be attributed to the Congress as a whole.

A leading point of reference in this debate has been the Supreme Court's 1892 decision in *Holy Trinity Church v. United States*.[1] *Holy Trinity* considered the Alien Contract Labor Act of 1885,[2] which made it unlawful to assist the immigration of aliens under contract to perform "labor or service of any kind" in the United States. The government invoked the statute in an action for civil penalties against a church that had assisted an English clergyman to immigrate under contract to become the church's rector. Relying in part on legislative history, the Court held that the statute should not be construed to prohibit the church's conduct even though that conduct fell "within the letter of" the statute—principally because Congress intended the statute to apply only to contracts to import manual laborers and did not intend it to reach "brain toilers." Two features of *Holy Trinity* have made it the leading case in the legislative-history debate. First, *Holy Trinity* elevated legislative history to new prominence by overturning the traditional rule that barred judicial recourse to internal legislative history. Although nineteenth-century decisions sometimes referred to legislative history in its broader sense of "the public history of the times" against which the legislature acted,[3] and a few prior opinions had quietly breached the traditional rule,[4] *Holy Trinity* was the first majority opinion of the Supreme Court to give legislative history sufficient weight to trump contrary statutory text. Second, in later years judges invoked *Holy Trinity* to signal that statutory text would not control the decision at hand. Famous passages from *Holy Trinity* endorsed countertextual interpretive techniques that provided crucial premises for majority and dissenting opinions in many of the Burger and Rehnquist Courts' most prominent statutory cases. Much of the judicial and academic commentary on legislative history and interpretive theory in recent years thus takes *Holy Trinity* as the starting point for discussion.

Overview

Despite *Holy Trinity*'s canonical status, the conventional understanding of the case turns out to be wrong in important respects; and it is wrong in ways that illuminate our institutionalist themes, especially the role of judicial capacities in statutory interpretation. I shall begin at the case-study level by providing a critical reevaluation of *Holy Trinity*. According to the conventional understanding, *Holy Trinity*'s importance stems from the conflict between statutory text and legislative history that the case posed. Faced with statutory text that strongly supported a judgment of liability against the church and legislative history that strongly supported a judgment in the church's favor, the Court held that the legislative history should trump the text, thus provoking a debate over the relative authority of the two sources that persists to this day. Yet scholars have not previously examined this legislative history in any detail, and it turns out that the conventional understanding is misleading. The legislative history at issue in *Holy Trinity* did not support the Court's holding, but rather supported the rule apparent on the face of the statutory text itself. The Court misread the legislative history in *Holy Trinity*.

From one standpoint this surprising feature of *Holy Trinity* makes the case less interesting than previously thought; far from being a case in which the conflict between two types of source poses an important question of relative priority, *Holy Trinity* turns out to be a case in which the relevant sources supported the same result. Yet from another standpoint the Court's mishandling of the legislative history makes the case even more interesting. I trace the causes of the Court's misstep in *Holy Trinity* to defects in the adjudicative process by which the Court evaluated the legislative history at issue. Viewed in that light, *Holy Trinity* suggests that the legislative-history debate has, for the most part, failed adequately to explore the question of judicial capacity to evaluate legislative history. Both textualists and intentionalists base their arguments about judicial use of legislative history largely on descriptive and normative claims about the legislative process. Yet even if those arguments were resolved by accepting intentionalist premises, there would remain the question whether structural features of the judicial process might systematically undermine judicial competence to discern legislative intent from legislative history.

In later sections of this chapter I draw upon the *Holy Trinity* case study to present a second-best thesis about the interaction between legislative history and the adjudicative process. Intentionalists claim that judicial resort to legislative history is constitutional, that legislative intent rather than textual meaning is the ultimate goal of statutory interpretation, and that legislative history reliably embodies that intent in a broad range of cases. Even if one accepts these premises, however, serious second-best problems must be confronted. Judicial fallibility creates a grave risk that judicial resort to legislative history to gauge legislative intent will prove counterproductive, even from the intentionalist point of view. Distinctive features of the adjudicative process—the whole set of institutional and procedural rules that determine when and how litigants try and argue cases and when and how courts decide them—might interact with distinctive features of legislative history in a manner that causes courts systematically to err in their attempts to discern legislative intent from legislative history. Indeed, judicial error in the use of legislative history— with "error" here defined as mistaken attribution of legislative intent— might occur sufficiently often, and with sufficiently serious consequences, that courts restricting themselves to statutory text and other standard sources of interpretation would achieve more accurate approximations of legislative intent over the whole run of future cases than would courts that admit legislative history as an interpretive source.

Holy Trinity: The Decision

I begin with the legal background and describe the Court's opinion. Turning then to the legislative history, I evaluate the Court's claim that the history supported a holding at odds with the apparent meaning of the statutory text.

In September 1887 the Holy Trinity Church of New York City arranged for E. Walpole Warren, an Episcopalian minister living in England, to travel to New York and take a position as its rector.[5] The Alien Contract Labor Act of 1885, however, made it unlawful to assist the immigration of an alien under contract to perform "labor or service of any kind."[6] The statute contained specific exceptions to the labor-or-service prohibition for "professional actors, artists, lecturers or singers," for "private secretaries," and for "persons employed strictly as personal or domestic servants," but not for rectors or clergymen.[7] The United States prosecuted the church in federal court.

The Supreme Court issued its decision in February 1892. In an opinion by Justice David Brewer, who was both an evangelical Christian and the son of a minister,[8] the Court reversed and held the church exempt from penalties. The opinion initially conceded that "the [church's act] is within the letter of this section," yet proceeded on the premise that intent trumps text: "While there is great force to this reasoning, we cannot think congress intended to denounce with penalties a transaction like that in the present case. It is a familiar rule, that a thing may be within the letter of the statute and yet not within the statute, because not within its spirit, nor within the intention of its makers."[9]

The Court, however, gave two alternative grounds for concluding that the transaction before it fell outside the intent of the statute's makers. The first ground was that the critical phrase in section 1, which prohibited immigration under contract to perform "labor or service of any kind," was intended to cover only manual labor rather than professional or intellectual work. The second, narrower ground was that Congress could not have intended to prohibit the immigration under contract of a Christian minister.

The Court relied on several sources to support the first of these two grounds. One source was the title of the act, which referred only to "labor" and not, as in the body of the text, to "labor or service of any kind"; this suggested, in the Court's view, that the statute reached "only to the work of the manual laborer, as distinguished from that of the professional man"—or equivalently "any class whose toil is that of the brain." The Court also argued that the statute should be limited to the scope of the evil that the statute was designed to remedy, as evidenced by "contemporaneous events." It was "common knowledge" that the act's "motive" was to prevent an influx of "cheap, unskilled labor" in the form of "an ignorant and servile class of foreign laborers."

So far the Court's methods were familiar, whatever the merit of its conclusions. The Court's next source for determining congressional intent, however, was internal legislative history, and the opinion gave no explanation for that break from traditional doctrine. The Court relied on two items of legislative history. The first was a report from the Committee on Labor of the House of Representatives, in which the bill had originated. This report stated, in general terms, that the act sought to prohibit the immigration or importation of "[laborers] from the lowest social stratum, [who] live upon the coarsest food . . . and are certainly not a desirable acquisition to the body politic."[10] The second item, which provided the best support for the Court's limitation of the act to manual "labor or service of any kind," was a report of the Senate Committee on Education and Labor—a crucial document in the story of *Holy Trinity*.

The Senate committee report specifically raised the question whether the statute covered only employees performing manual labor or rather covered both professional and manual employees. In a curious passage the report stated that the committee would have preferred to introduce an amendment explicitly limiting the bill to manual employees, but refrained from doing so because (1) it hoped that the bill would pass during "the present session" (presumably referring to the first session of the Forty-eighth Congress, during which the committee reported the bill to the Senate), and (2) the committee believed that even without an amendment the bill would be construed to cover only manual labor or service. In the words of the report:

> The committee report the bill back without amendment, although there are certain features thereof which might well be changed or modified, in the hope that the bill may not fail of passage during the present session. Especially would the committee have otherwise recommended amendments, substituting for the expression "labor and service," whenever it occurs in the body of the bill, the words "manual labor" or "manual service," as sufficiently broad to accomplish the purposes of the bill, and that such amendments would remove objections which a sharp and perhaps unfriendly criticism may urge to the proposed legislation. The committee, however, believing that the bill in its present form will be construed as including only those whose labor or service is manual in character, and being very desirous that the bill become a law before the adjournment, have reported the bill without change.[11]

According to the Court, the Senate committee report relayed a "singular circumstance, throwing light upon the intent of congress." By that remark, the Court implied that it accepted at face value the plea of exigency by which the report explained the committee's failure to introduce the amendment. Moreover, the Senate committee report, taken together with the House committee report, showed that "the intent of Congress was simply to stay the influx of . . . cheap unskilled labor."

In the final portion of the opinion, Brewer shifted to the second, narrower ground of decision, holding that Congress could not have intended to subject a contract with a Christian minister to the statutory prohibition. Drawing not on legislative history but rather on "a mass of organic utterances" attesting that "this is a Christian nation"—including such canonical texts of American law as Ferdinand and Isabella's commission to Christopher Columbus—the Court declared it impossible that Congress "intended to make it a misdemeanor for a church of this country to contract for the services of a Christian minister residing in another nation."[12] Although the addition of this second, narrower ground made *Holy Trinity* notorious in the distinct context of debates about religious liberty,[13] the Court's first ground—the limitation of the statute's coverage to manual labor—is the important one for purposes of *Holy Trinity*'s place in the legislative-history debate.

A Reassessment

The conventional understanding of *Holy Trinity* assumes that the case did present a genuine conflict between the statutory text and the legislative intention revealed in the legislative history, regardless of whether the Court's ultimate decision to give priority to the legislative history was correct.[14] Yet the conflict proves illusory. The legislative history, taken as a whole, cuts strongly against the Court's position. The dominant sentiment of both houses, expressed on several occasions, was that the Alien Contract Labor Act should apply to any employee, manual or professional, except those specifically exempted. The Court's contrary conclusion appears to have been the result of errors of information and evaluation.

In particular, the legislative history undercuts the Court's attempt to constrict the statute's coverage to manual "labor or service of any kind." The Senate committee report's stated reason for refusing to propose an amendment to limit the statute to manual labor was that the committee hoped to ensure the statute's enactment before the close of the first session of the Forty-eighth Congress. Yet it turns out, as I shall detail later, that the Alien Contract Labor Act did not pass the Senate during the first session; it was put over to the second session and then hotly debated. In those debates the statute's principal sponsor, who was both a member of the committee and its spokesman on the floor, abandoned any attempt to obtain an amendment and explicitly conceded that the statute covered both manual and professional employees. The Court thus overlooked or ignored events that made the Senate committee report irrelevant to the statute's subsequent passage.

The conclusion that the Court mishandled the legislative history at issue in *Holy Trinity* has significance beyond the particulars of the case itself. The intentionalist practice of consulting legislative history produced a serious misstep in the very case that first carried out that practice; and it did so even though the legislative history, read as a whole, provides direct and relatively reliable evidence that undermines the Court's interpretation and confirms the evident meaning of the statutory text. These features of *Holy Trinity* highlight a range of concerns about judges' capacity to derive legislative intent from legislative history.

The legislative history: House proceedings. The bill that would eventually become the Alien Contract Labor Act was introduced in the House of Representatives by Congressman Martin A. Foran of Ohio, a member of the Committee on Labor. Foran apparently prepared both the House committee report quoted in the *Holy Trinity* opinion and an amendment, introduced simultaneously with the bill, that excepted "professional actors, lecturers or singers" from the statute.[15] The thrust of the committee report was, as the Court suggested, that the initial draft of the bill aimed to halt the importation of European and Asian manual laborers thought to be a degraded species of immigrants harmful to American labor and institutions.

Yet the bill's legal prohibitions displayed a scope far broader than this objective. First, the amendment introduced with the bill excepted "professional actors, singers and lecturers" from the act's scope. The amendment thus suggested that absent these exceptions, the committee understood the bill to apply to those categories. On the Court's view that only manual laborers, as opposed to "brain toilers," were included within the prohibition's scope, the exception would have been unnecessary, for no professionals—and thus no professional actors, lecturers, or singers—would have fallen within it.

Second, there is no evidence in the House proceedings—or in the Senate proceedings, as we shall see—that the bill was written to be narrowly tailored to its purposes; instead, it was written to enact a broader, categorical rule. When House members discussed the scope of the bill's prohibitions, as opposed to the social evil that had initially inspired the bill, opponents, reluctant supporters, and firm supporters all commented on the bill's breadth.[16] Legislators described the bill as broad precisely because it swept beyond manual labor. For example, Representative William Kelley, a reluctant supporter, stated:

I am quite sure that the first half-dozen lines express what the authors of the bill did not mean to ask us to enact into law, for they contain a provision prohibiting citizens from employing an unnaturalized resident of the country in the performance of any service.

I do not think the exceptions made in its prohibitory clauses are as broad as they ought to be.[17]

A specific example debated in the House record supports Kelley's reading, although it also undercuts Kelley's claim that the breadth of the bill was unintended. John Adams, a congressman from New York, engaged in the following colloquy with John O'Neill of Missouri, a member of the Labor Committee:

Mr. ADAMS of New York. While I favor a bill similar to this there are some things involved in the pending proposition in reference to which I would like to have clearer information than that now before us as to what will be the exact effect of its provisions if enacted into law. I wish to know of the gentleman from Missouri whether under section 3 of this bill [which included the critical language "labor or service of any kind"], if it becomes a law, it would not prohibit Arnold, Constable & Co., or Lord & Taylor, or any of the large retail dealers in the city of New York who may be abroad purchasing goods and who finds there an efficient clerk they would like to transfer to this country, and to whom they would pay a salary, whether this section would not prohibit them from employing any such clerk under penalty of a thousand dollars.

Mr. O'NEILL of Missouri. All I have to say is that if Arnold, Constable & Co. . . . . go to Europe and import this labor for the purpose of breaking down men in their own employ, I hope the law will reach them. That is the intention of the law.[18]

A "clerk" in the nineteenth century meant principally an office employee who worked with the pen; although of low status, clerks performed mental rather than manual labor.[19] The clerk example reveals a publicly expressed intention on the part of a member of the committee and supporter of the bill to reach employees who would qualify as brain toilers. Ultimately the House passed the bill by a lopsided vote.[20]

The legislative history: Senate proceedings. The bill's passage through the Senate is the real locus of controversy over *Holy Trinity* because, on a superficial glance, the report of the Senate Committee on Education and Labor speaks directly to the issues in the case. The timing and content of the Senate proceedings are thus critical to the Court's misunderstanding of the legislative history of the Alien Contract Labor Act.

The Senate committee report stated that the committee "report the bill back without amendment . . . in the hope that the bill may not fail of passage during the present session,"[21] even though substitution of "manual labor" or "manual service" for "labor or service of any kind" would "remove objections which a sharp and perhaps unfriendly criticism may urge to the proposed legislation."[22] Although the committee stated that it believed that the bill would be so interpreted even without the addition, the report's timing was critical to the Court's case. The committee's plea of urgency was necessary to explain why it did not simply propose an amendment inserting the word "manual" into the statute and to rebut any suspicion that the amendment was not introduced because the full Senate would not have agreed to it.

But subsequent events surrounding the passage of the bill undermined the report's explanation. Senator Henry William Blair, a Republican from New Hampshire and a member of the committee, presented the bill to the Senate, submitted the committee report, and served as floor manager for the bill's passage through the Senate.[23] As the committee wished, Blair strove to bring the bill to a vote during the first session of the Forty-eighth Congress, which extended from December 3, 1883, to July 7, 1884. Accordingly, on July 5—two days before the end of the session—Blair moved for consideration of the bill, stating that "I am exceedingly anxious, as is the Committee on Education and Labor, who reported it unanimously, that it be considered and disposed of at this session."[24] In language echoing the committee report, Blair went on to state that he would propose amendments that would "absolutely remove any of the objections which have been raised by an adverse, hostile criticism to the bill."[25]

It quickly became apparent, however, that the rest of the Senate did not want to rush the bill through before the adjournment of the first session. Blair lost an initial voice vote on his motion for consideration of the bill and only obtained consideration after calling the yeas and nays.[26] The first senator other than Blair to speak suggested that the committee "frankly say that the bill does not meet with their approbation,"[27] which prompted Blair to respond that he planned "to move the modifications alluded to in the Senate report," specifically by inserting the word "manual," so that "the provisions of the bill would then be restricted to the evil that exists."[28] That statement squarely and publicly contradicted the assertion in the committee report that the legal scope of the bill was limited to manual labor or service even without formal amendment. Later on the same day the Senate voted, over Blair's protest, to suspend further consideration of the bill until the second session.[29]

With the argument of urgency eliminated by the advent of the new session, there could be only two reasons committee members did not move for the insertion of "manual," as Blair had promised: either (1) they expected that the bill would be so interpreted in any event, making the amendment unnecessary, or (2) senatorial support for the amendment was insufficient. But Blair's statement that without the amendment the bill would sweep more broadly than manual labor had decisively undercut the first possibility. The record of the second session reveals that in all likelihood the amendment was never proposed because it lacked sufficient support.

At the beginning of the second session Blair stated that the committee had "reported the bill without any amendment in the hope that it might be passed during the last session" and finally introduced amendments that, he said, would remove "some objections made to the bill."[30] Yet the manual labor amendment was conspicuously absent. Indeed, Blair proposed, and the Senate adopted, other amendments to the critical sections of the bill, yet the effect of all the amendments was either to broaden the bill or to make further specific exceptions from its scope.

Later discussion shows that Blair had at some point abandoned the manual labor amendment and now conceded that the bill reached both professional and manual employees. A critical colloquy between Blair and Senator John Tyler Morgan of Alabama, an opponent of the bill, illustrates Blair's new position. Morgan protested that the bill was "class legislation" and "vicious" in that "it discriminates in favor of professional actors, lecturers, or singers. It makes an express exception and provision for professional actors, lecturers, and singers, leaving out all the other classes of professional men."[31] Blair's response was not to reassert the claim that the bill covered only manual labor; rather, he simply noted that domestic servants were also exempted.[32] Morgan continued:

[I]f [the alien] happens to be a lawyer, an artist, a painter, an engraver, a sculptor, a great author, or what not, and he comes under employment to write for a newspaper, or to write books, or to paint pictures, . . . he comes under the general provisions of the bill. . . .

. . . . .

I shall propose when we get to it to put an amendment in there. I want to associate with the lecturers and singers and actors, painters, sculptors, engravers, or other artists, farmers, farm laborers, gardeners, orchardists, herders, farriers, druggists and druggists' clerks, shopkeepers, clerks, book-keepers, or any person having special skill in any business, art, trade or profession.[33]

Again, Blair's response confirmed this understanding of the bill's scope:

The Senator will observe that it is only the importation of such people under contract to labor that is prohibited.

. . . .

. . . If that class of people are liable to become the subject-matter of such importation, then the bill applies to them. Perhaps the bill ought to be further amended.[34]

Despite Blair's wistful expression at the end of this passage, the Senate had essentially settled the question of the bill's scope in favor of coverage of both brain toilers and manual laborers. Later in the debate minor tinkering occurred; an exception for artists was inserted, and proposals to remove the exception for singers and create one for artisans were rejected.[35] These amendments show both that the Senate focused on the bill's scope and that the majority was content to pass a bill that would prohibit all alien contract labor except as specifically permitted.

That understanding of the bill was confirmed when, after passage in the Senate, it was returned to the House for consideration as amended. In the only substantive debate on the amended bill, one congressman inquired whether the bill would prohibit the immigration of agricultural laborers under contract. Representative James Hopkins, managing the House's consideration of the amended bill, stated that "[i]t prohibits the importation under contract of all classes with the exceptions named in the bill."[36] The House promptly voted to concur in the amended version, and Congress had passed the bill.

Evaluating the Court's Performance

The legislative history of the Alien Contract Labor Act undermines the Court's suppositions in *Holy Trinity* at every critical point. First, the

Court's reliance on the House committee report to show the statute's general purpose and to interpret the statute's text in accordance with that purpose wrongly assumed that as the bill moved through the legislative process, its legal scope remained only as broad as the perceived social evil that first inspired it. Although members of both houses freely acknowledged that the initial impetus for the bill was the contractual importation of "degraded" manual labor, they also understood the bill's legal scope to extend more broadly. Their motives for approving a statute of such breadth are neither wholly clear nor particularly important. Some members may have feared that a narrower prohibition would be too easy to evade; others appear to have believed, on egalitarian premises, that the contractual importation of any class of employee should be prohibited; still others may have resisted attempts to narrow the bill in the hope that it would be defeated. The important point is that the Court's reliance on the House committee report to support a purposive approach to the case simply overlooked that for a range of reasons the legislative product became, as Blair had specifically noted, broader than the particular evil that provided the initial impetus for legislative action.[37]

Second, the specific intentionalist evidence of the Senate committee report also proved treacherous. To begin with, that report displayed severe internal tension by simultaneously endorsing and rejecting an explicit amendment to limit the bill to manual labor. The report in essence both stated a belief that the broad language of the bill would be construed as implicitly limited to manual labor and endorsed an amendment because it recognized a grave risk that the bill would not be so construed. Even on its face, then, the report shows that the committee had no fixed understanding of what the bill would be read to mean and thus provides only internally inconsistent support for the Court's construction. More important, the timing of the bill's passage wholly undercut the report's plausibility. Because, as the report had feared, the bill did "fail of passage during the present session [i.e., the first session of the Forty-eighth Congress]," the committee's principal reason for failing to move the amendment it recommended—the exigency of the limited time remaining before the session's end—proved irrelevant. The events of the second session suggest that Senator Blair and the committee must also have had some other, unavowed reason for failing to move the limiting amendment; and by far the best candidate for such a reason is that the coalition favoring the bill would have rejected it.

By contrast, the statutory text in *Holy Trinity* provided a more accurate gauge of the legislative intent than did the partial legislative history the Court cited. The plain meaning of the statutory text perfectly tracks the understanding of the act's own sponsors and supporters, such as Senator Blair: Labor or service of any kind—that is, including the labor or service of professionals—fell within the scope of the textual prohibition, save as specifically excepted. Even Justice Brewer evidently thought it necessary to concede that the statutory text could not reasonably be read to cover only manual labor and that "the relation of rector to his church is one of service."[38] Modern commentators who agree on little else, such as Ronald Dworkin and Antonin Scalia, have agreed with Brewer on the textual issue.[39]

To be sure, textual arguments for the Court's holding are not wholly lacking. The church's brief in *Holy Trinity* argued that the ordinary meaning of the phrase "labor or service of any kind" in section 1 of the statute reached no farther than manual labor or service. The church quoted precedents and *Webster's Dictionary* to establish that "labor" denotes manual labor, while "service" denotes "the occupation of a servant; the performance of labor for the benefit of another . . . [or] the attendance of an inferior, or hired helper or slave, etc., on a superior employer, master or the like."[40] On this view, the addendum "of any kind" could reach no more broadly than the meanings of "labor" and "service" themselves.

But the more this argument is considered, the less attractive it becomes; the text, structure, and statutory context of the act combine to make it suspect. As a textual matter, the restricted definition of "service" upon which the church relied was not its only contemporary meaning. Dictionaries and judicial precedent from the period also defined "service" to encompass any employment, position, or duty, whether of a menial or professional character, and that meaning would be captured by the phrase "of any kind."[41] The exemptions in section 5 provide inferential support for reading "service" in the broader sense. That section specifically excluded "personal or domestic servants" from the statute's scope, an exemption that negates much of the area covered by the church's definition of "service" and thus renders that definition implausible.

The church's reading of "labor or service of any kind" thus gave the phrase no more scope than the word "labor" would have standing alone. That reading ran afoul of the basic principle that each statutory word should, if possible, be given independent effect rather than be treated as superfluous. The legislative history confirms that the word "labor" was not the exclusive focus of debate. Members of both houses, including the Senate floor manager, noted the independent word "service" and its effect of broadening the sweep of the critical phrase.[42] The church's reading, then, truncated that phrase without warrant.

Two other structural inferences also undercut the church's view. First, section 4 of the act enacted penalties for masters of vessels who transported any alien "laborer, mechanic or artisan" under contract. The church's reading of "labor or service of any kind" ignored the difference in phrasing between the two prohibitions. The more natural reading is that the restricted coverage of section 4, which is best read to confine itself to manual laborers, confirms the breadth of section 1 by negative implication. That reading is just the standard inference from negative implication—in lawyers' parlance, the "expressio unius" canon.

Second, by restricting "labor or service of any kind" to manual work, the church's reading suffered from a fatal inability to account for the statutory enumeration of specific exceptions for "professional actors, artists, lecturers or singers" and, elsewhere in the same section, for "private secretaries." As the circuit court noted, "the proviso is equivalent to a declaration that contracts to perform professional services . . . are within the prohibition of the preceding sections."[43] The church's brief argued gamely that Congress inserted the exceptions as a deliberate exercise in cautious redundancy; even though the prohibition itself did not cover professionals, Congress inserted the exceptions to make doubly sure that the statute would not be interpreted to cover them.[44] That argument, however, betrayed a self-defeating uncertainty. If the ordinary meaning of the "labor or service" prohibition was so clear, why take extraordinary precautions against misinterpretation? And why take precautions by inserting an incomplete list of particular types of professionals, rather than by simply inserting the word "manual" before the critical phrase or by explicitly exempting all professionals?

Finally, the church's account also failed to explain the statutory landscape surrounding the Alien Contract Labor Act. The most important feature of that landscape was the Chinese Exclusion Act of 1882, which prohibited the immigration of Chinese "laborers."[45] Decisions rendered before the passage of the Alien Contract Labor Act in 1885 interpreted the Chinese Exclusion Act to reach only manual labor[46] and also held that various professionals, such as actors, did not count as laborers.[47] On a textualist approach, this context mandates two inferences. First, Congress must be taken to have known that the simplest way to restrict the coverage of the Alien Contract Labor Act to manual labor would have simply been to say "labor," as it had three years earlier in the Chinese Exclusion Act. In accordance with this inference, the Senate floor manager drew a parallel between the Chinese Exclusion Act and section 4 of the Alien Contract Labor Act—a natural parallel because section 4, unlike section 1, was limited to those who performed manual labor.[48] Second, there was no reason for Congress to fear that a provision reaching only manual labor would be interpreted to reach professionals; courts deciding cases under the Chinese Exclusion Act had avoided that mistake. The first inference undercuts the church's reading of "labor or service of any kind"; the second undercuts its explanation for the specific exceptions to that prohibition.

The lack of any persuasive argument to justify the Court's holding need not bar textual arguments that support the Court's ultimate judgment on other grounds. Laurence Tribe, for example, suggests that a minister might count as a "lecturer" under the express exemption of section 5.[49] Whatever the merits of the suggestion, a ruling on that ground would have yielded a judgment in favor of the minister under an explicit textual exemption. The important question for the legislative-history debate is not whether *Holy Trinity* was correctly decided on its facts, but whether the Court correctly read the legislative history to restrict the statute's coverage to manual labor.

The reading advanced in this section suggests that the Court erred; the legislative history contradicts its holding. The interesting feature of *Holy Trinity* is not, as the conventional understanding has it, that the Court accorded priority to legislative history over contrary statutory text. Rather, the interesting feature of the case is that the Court erroneously found that choice of priorities necessary.

Legislative History and the Adjudicative Process

Let us step back to consider the broader context of the legislative-history debate. Although *Holy Trinity* is canonical, it may also be unusual. Its pathbreaking character makes it both a good and a bad test case for views about legislative history: good because the case has uncritically been taken to present a classic example of divergence between text and intentions, bad because legislative history posed very different problems in 1892 than it poses today. In what follows I will not attempt to generalize a critique of legislative history directly from the (quite possibly) idiosyncratic features of Holy Trinity itself. Rather, the principal value of *Holy Trinity* and its historical setting is just to suggest a larger hypothesis, to be amplified in what follows: that the interaction between distinctive features of legislative history and structural features of the adjudicative process causes legislative history to reduce, rather than increase, judicial accuracy in the determination of legislative intent.

The adjudicative process in Holy Trinity. Curiously, the stock issues of the legislative-history debate—the (in)coherence of legislative intent and the (un)reliability of legislative history as evidence of that intent—are of marginal relevance to *Holy Trinity*. The legislative history in *Holy Trinity*, read as a whole, displays a fairly definite understanding about the statute's meaning on the part of the legislators involved. To be sure, some parts of the legislative history, particularly the Senate report, are fundamentally unreliable when viewed in isolation. Yet it seems unlikely that a reader with information about the whole legislative history, ample time to consider it, and sufficient background expertise would be misled.

Rather, the Court's mistakes in *Holy Trinity* derived from structural and contingent features of the adjudicative process in the case. The causes of the Court's performance will, of course, never fully be known. Yet three possibilities stand out as likely candidates, and all three stem from defects in the Court's adjudicative process rather than from features of the legislative process that produced the statute.

One cause of the Court's misreading seems to have been dependence on the parties—in fact, one of the parties—for information about the legislative history. Only the church briefed the legislative history; its brief stated that it would not "allude to the debates of individual members," but would "submit a portion of" the House and Senate committee reports.[50] The Court seems to have then simply copied into its opinion, without independent scrutiny, those portions of the reports block quoted in the church's brief. In so doing, the Court overlooked the surrounding context of the timing of the reports and the critical floor statements by sponsors of the bill that undercut the church's selectively chosen sources. The government's brief, however, made no arguments on the legislative history beyond reasserting, in passing, the nineteenth-century rule that legislative intent should "be collected from the statute itself." The mis-leading one-sidedness of the parties' presentation may have deprived the Court of valuable information about the legislative history and caused it to view the case as presenting a direct conflict between statutory text and congressional intent.

A second possible cause of the Court's misstep in *Holy Trinity* is a cognitive problem introduced in Chapter 1: the tendency for decision-makers to overweight the most vivid, salient, or readily available infor-mation. Often different sources in the legislative history are pitched at differing levels of generality; some describe the statute's general legal scope, while others specifically address the application of the statute to particular facts. The specificity of a source often bears little relation to its probative value as an indicator of congressional intent. The specific source may have been introduced by an actor of dubious relevance to the leg-islative process or under conditions that make it otherwise unreliable. In many ways the dominant import of sources that demonstrate the general range and structure of the statute may nullify the effect of the single most specific source in the record.

Yet judges may often accord controlling weight to highly specific sources; this is the distorting force of highly salient particulars, discussed in Chapter 1. Federal courts are limited to deciding specific cases and controversies. The particular facts on the judicial record before the court will often occupy the foreground, dominate the debate, and cause the court to emphasize specific sources over general sources. Moreover, as a matter of argument and opinion writing, it is easier to defend a position or justify a decision by a flat reference to a specific source than by elu-cidation and application of more general sources.

The problem of salience provides a plausible account of the *Holy Trinity* episode. The prime attraction of the Senate committee report must have been that its restriction of the bill to manual labor spoke directly to the issue before the Court—not, it is true, by mentioning "ministers," but by suggesting the next most specific limitation that would exempt the minister. Flat, simple, and direct quotation from the Senate committee report seems to have provided such attractive support for the Court's opinion that the background deficiencies of the report and the more diffuse contrary evidence from the rest of the legislative history went unnoticed.

A third factor at work in *Holy Trinity* may have been judicial preconception. The Court's (and Justice Brewer's) internal decisionmaking processes in *Holy Trinity* are opaque. Yet it hardly seems unjust to infer from Justice Brewer's personal commitments, extrajudicial statements, and the tone of the opinion—particularly its fervent and one-sided exegesis of the United States' Christian heritage—that Justice Brewer, at least, did not approach the case in the spirit of judicial detachment. The legislative history of the Alien Contract Labor Act provided ample scope for the operation of such preconceptions. The internal tensions within the Senate committee report and the tensions between that report and subsequent events in the legislative history provided a sufficient variety of material that Justice Brewer's preconceptions could well have filtered out the mass of evidence contradicting his view.

The question of judicial capacities. On this account, the Court's performance in *Holy Trinity* is attributable not to the incoherence of legislative intent or the unreliability of the legislative history of the Alien Contract Labor Act, but rather to structural and contingent features of the adjudicative process that produced the decision. The principal significance of the decision concerns, not legislative history in its own right, but judicial competence to evaluate legislative history. Against that background, *Holy Trinity* suggests that the current legislative-history debate is artificially constricted.

The standard arguments of both textualists and intentionalists about legislative history share a common feature that narrows the field of the debate. Those arguments, by and large, center on the legislative process. They describe the constitutional conditions for valid congressional lawmaking in a system of separation of powers or assess the reliability of legislatively generated materials and, in general, focus chiefly on assertions about how legislatures do or should operate. Accordingly, although the arguments prescribe what judges should (or should not) do with legislative history, those prescriptions flow from prior descriptive or normative claims about the legislative process. Commentators have previously discussed the relationship between legislative history and the judicial process principally by debating the claim that the admission of legislative history as an interpretive source undesirably increases judicial "discretion" in statutory interpretation. However, judicial-process considerations remain an underdeveloped strand of the debate, for discussion of those considerations tends to be intertwined with legislative-process arguments.

For example, the judicial-discretion argument usually appears in conjunction with the separation-of-powers principle that legislatures rather than courts should make law.

As we saw in Chapter 2, the debate's inadequate consideration of judicial competence finds an exemplar in McNollgast's effort to describe a set of principles that will enable judges to draw intentionalist inferences from legislative history.[51] Posing the question "So how can the legislative history of a statute reveal legislative intent?" McNollgast attempts to provide positive rules of inference that would allow judges to gauge the probability that items of legislative history reflect a consensus among the enacting coalition. As a necessary supplement to those rules, McNollgast supplies some statistical decision theory to help judges assess the relevant probabilities. This sort of recommendation makes particularly heroic assumptions about judicial competence. As Yale legal scholar Jerry Mashaw puts it: "[McNollgast's approach] is enormously information demanding. If McNollgast mean to suggest that legislative history is reliable only when it can be deployed in this sophisticated fashion (using Bayesian decision theory in the bargain), they may have offered judges and administrators a tool that they cannot use."[52]

The *Holy Trinity* episode, by contrast, suggests that the debate might profit from a sharper focus on the judiciary's capacity to discern legislative intent from legislative history. Intentionalists claim (1) that judicial resort to legislative history is constitutional; (2) that ascertaining legislative intent is the ultimate object of interpretation; and (3) that legislative history generally provides reliable evidence of intent. But even taken together these claims do not suffice to demonstrate that courts should consider legislative history. Intentionalists must also show (4) that over the run of future cases, courts that consult legislative history will produce more accurate determinations of legislative intent than courts that restrict themselves to statutory text and other standard sources of interpretation.[53] That additional claim does not follow from the premise that legislative history is generally reliable, for (as subsequently discussed) judges labor under constraints that sometimes cause them to mistake or only partially discern the import of reliable evidence.

Holy Trinity sharply poses the question whether intentionalists can establish that legislative history increases the accuracy of judicial determinations of legislative intent. After all, in *Holy Trinity* the Court would have captured the legislative intent more accurately by deciding solely in accordance with the Court's own understanding of the text than it did by also considering (and misreading) the legislative history. This is not to say that the legislative history in *Holy Trinity* proves unreliable or unhelpful when read as a whole, without significant constraints of time or background information. In that sense the legislative history provides valuable confirmation of the legislative intent evidenced by the statutory text. But that valuable confirmation was available only if the Court had gotten the legislative history right. As the case actually developed, the structural and contingent constraints under which the Court did its work caused it to form a less accurate assessment of legislative intent by looking at the legislative history than it would have achieved by not looking at it.

Legislative History: A Second-Best Thesis

Accordingly, one thesis that *Holy Trinity* suggests might be put this way: Imagine a court faced with an indefinite set of statutory-interpretation cases. Assume that in each instance Congress and the president formed a collective intention about the meaning of the statutory text at issue. Also assume that in each case the legislative history, taken as a whole, provides reliable evidence of that intention in the sense that an ideal interpreter who is knowledgeable about the legislative process and who suffers no constraints of time or information would, on reading all of the relevant legislative-history materials, correctly discern that collective intention. In other words, assume away the textualist argument against legislative history, insofar as that argument is based on the legislative process. Is there now any reason to question judicial resort to legislative history?

There is. Unlike an ideal interpreter, courts do operate under significant constraints of time, information, and expertise. In certain circumstances those constraints may cause courts to mistake the import of the legislative history, just as a court presiding in a bench trial might, for various reasons, issue erroneous factual findings even if the evidence reliably reflected the events that are the subject of the suit. Moreover, courts might mishandle legislative history with sufficient frequency and gravity that courts relying principally on statutory text (as well as canons of construction, judicial precedent, and other standard sources of interpretation) might achieve more accurate approximations of the legislature's intent over the whole run of future cases than would courts that admit legislative history as an interpretive source.

This possibility at first seems remote. Intuition suggests that whatever the risks of error in judicial use of legislative history, adding legislative history to the standard sources of text, precedent, and canons of construction would surely move interpreters closer to the genuine legislative intent than would an approach that relied solely on those other sources. After all, legislative history provides courts with additional information about legislative intent, indeed with information that (unlike judicial precedent and most canons of construction) is at least generated within the legislature.

But it is not the case that more information always and necessarily produces more accurate decisionmaking than does less information. A range of legal rules, such as the restrictions on the admissibility of especially lurid or prejudicial evidence in jury trials, rest on the premise that certain special types of additional information may prove particularly distorting, inflammatory, or burdensome when considered by a decisionmaker with limited capacity to absorb and evaluate the information. Such information not only may fail to improve the accuracy of the decision made by the constrained decisionmaker, but may decrease it, relative to a decision made without the distorting information. It is at least possible, then, that distorting features of legislative history might interact with structural constraints of the adjudicative process in a manner that decreases, rather than increases, judicial accuracy in the determination of legislative intent. At this stage, of course, we are merely indicating an empirical possibility; an argument in support of this possibility requires a partly empirical assessment. I take up the vexing problems of empiricism and institutional analysis in Chapter 6. Note, however, that the implicit assumption of intentionalism—that resort to legislative history enhances judicial accuracy—rests on precisely the same sort of empirical assessment.

The following considerations suggest that the interaction between distinctive features of legislative history and structural constraints of the adjudicative process may, on intentionalist premises, cause legislative history to reduce, rather than increase, judicial accuracy.[54] We can sort errors into two categories: errors of information and errors of evaluation. Errors of information occur when the court lacks or fails to seek full information about the materials in the legislative history. Perhaps the court's attempts to generate a complete set of such information have failed, or the court has relied on the parties to bring all relevant information to its attention and they have failed to do so; perhaps some mix of the two possibilities has occurred. Errors of evaluation occur when the court acts with a full set of information, but mistakes the significance of material in the legislative history because of constraints of time, background expertise, or other resources. For example, the court's lack of familiarity with the legislative process, or the press of judicial business, might cause it to overestimate or underestimate the weight due to a particular item of legislative history.

These general considerations do not provide reason to question judicial resort to legislative history in particular unless there is some alternative to its use. Even proof that use of a particular source poses severe risks of adjudicative error is irrelevant if there is no conceivable alternative to that source. In many domains judges must consider and evaluate complex and voluminous information, sources, and arguments and are thought competent to do so. Moreover, any accuracy-related critique of legislative history must provide reason to believe that courts are especially prone to err in their evaluation of legislative history. After all, errors of information and evaluation can occur with respect to many different sources. Litigants may fail to reference, or courts to find through independent research, relevant statutory texts, judicial precedents, or canons of construction; and even if those sources are introduced, the court may misjudge their weight or meaning in any particular case. The possibility of error hardly justifies skepticism of a particular source unless there is some distinctive risk that courts will err in evaluating that source.

Even on these terms, however, there is a plausible case that legislative history indeed warrants skepticism. First, in statutory interpretation, unlike other areas in which a particular source creates risks of adjudicative error, there is a conceivable alternative to the use of legislative history. Because statutory interpretation, on any account, takes into consideration many interpretive sources—statutory text, judicial precedent, and canons of construction, to name a few—it is at least possible to exclude legislative history while leaving in place other sources from which adjudication can proceed, whether or not it is attractive to do so. Second, legislative history is a source with unique characteristics. In particular, as described later, legislative history is distinctively voluminous and heterogeneous in comparison with other interpretive sources. The interaction of those characteristics with structural features of the adjudicative process creates a distinctive risk that judges will mishandle legislative history, even if an unconstrained interpreter would find that the legislative history accurately reflects congressional intent.

Volume. The legislative history of a statute will often be dramatically more voluminous than any other relevant interpretive sources. As Richard Pierce observes, "The legislative history of any major statutory enactment is voluminous, difficult to compile, and difficult to research."[55] For example, the legislative history of the Refugee Act of 1980 runs to 2,112 pages.[56] That legislative history is, however, rather svelte by comparison to others. The legislative history of the Energy Policy Act of 1992 runs to 4,999 pages, while that of the Clean Air Act Amendments of 1990—itself a fraction of the total legislative history of the amended act—runs to no less than 10,878 pages. As for *Holy Trinity,* the legislative history of the Alien Contract Labor Act runs into the hundreds of pages, even though the text of the act fills barely more than a page in the *Statutes at Large.*

It might be said that other sources, such as statutory text and judicial precedents, may be as voluminous as legislative history. Under a textualist approach, for example, the whole *United States Code* is potentially relevant as a source for statutes that use relevant terms in ways that supply information about the statute under review. Yet such observations do not wholly persuade. First, on an intentionalist approach, the legislative histories of statutes related to the statute at hand should also be consulted. To assess comparative volume, then, it does not suffice simply to compare the texts of all relevant statutes with the legislative history of the particular statute under interpretation; rather, the correct omparison is between the texts of all relevant statutes and the legislative histories of all relevant statutes.

Second, whatever the comparative volume of legislative history and text in particular cases, the incentives that operate in the legislative process suggest that the legislative history applicable to the average case will be longer and more discursive than the statutory text relevant to that case. The political costs of inserting language into statutory text greatly outweigh the costs of inserting language into legislative history, making it likely that even if particular statutes outrun their legislative histories, legislative actors will generate a greater amount of relevant legislative history than of statutory text over the aggregate of statutes.[57]

The distinctive volume of legislative history heightens the risk of judicial error in several ways. Initially, litigant error and strategic behavior may distort the presentation of legislative history to the court. Parties labor under constraints of time and other resources that force them to be selective in their study of a massive set of legislative-history material. That selectivity poses the risk that important material will simply be overlooked or that even if its existence is noted, its significance will be misperceived. In either event the material may not be presented to the court, and opposing counsel is unlikely to correct the error and thereby damage his own case. To be sure, only a fraction of the legislative history of a statute will be relevant to particular cases arising under that statute, which will sometimes turn on the interpretation of only one or two provisions. Yet that observation takes an ex post view, whereas parties developing arguments must take an ex ante view. Parties may not know ex ante which portions of the legislative history will be relevant and may overlook some of the relevant portions in the course of their research. And the high proportion of irrelevant information in the legislative record may itself hamper parties' ability to assess the legislative history.

A court whose principal, albeit not exclusive, source of information is the arguments of litigants will often replicate errors of information and evaluation initially committed by litigants themselves. Judges lack full capacity to remedy informational defects caused by the sheer volume of legislative history, for courts are in substantial degree dependent on parties to discover and present relevant legislative history. Judges faced with conflicting demands on their time may often be unable to conduct thorough original research in order to generate legislative-history arguments on behalf of parties who fail to present them, and judges who subscribe to a strict version of the party-presentation model of adjudication, under which courts consider only arguments presented by the parties themselves, may perceive such research as incompatible with their role. Although in recent decades judges have acquired large staffs of law clerks and staff attorneys who may be available to cull the legislative record, those subordinates often lack developed research skills and will usually lack the judge's greater appreciation for the import of relevant items. The adversarial character of the legal process may ameliorate the relevant problems in part, but it may also exacerbate them in others, as I mention later.

The massive volume of legislative history creates especially severe risks of error in particular types of cases and by particular types of parties and courts. An ongoing debate has centered on the inaccessibility of legislative history and the high costs that researching it imposes on the bar. Although that debate is conceptually distinct from the question whether judicial resort to legislative history poses uniquely high risks of adjudicative error, the two issues are intertwined in practice. When the potential gains from investigation of the legislative history are uncertain or the expected value of victory is low, the relative inaccessibility and costliness of legislative-history will cause interested actors to curtail their research, increasing the risk that dispositive material will be overlooked or misevaluated. And the costliness of legislative history research affects different types of parties differently. When the large law firm assigns a half-dozen associates to comb through every committee hearing, counsel retained by contingent fee or by court appointment may well be unable to keep pace. The volume of legislative history may thus tend to skew judicial evaluation in favor of claims about legislative history advanced by affluent parties. Importantly, the argument that "[t]echnology has made an anachronism" of arguments about legislative history's costliness,[58] overlooks that lowering the costs of information affects the supply side as well as the demand side. Although the new information technology makes legislative history easier to research, it also makes it easier to produce, so that there is more of it to be researched; the net effect is indeterminate.

The voluminous character of legislative history relative to other sources also has different effects on different types of courts. A multimember appellate court in which each judge simultaneously examines the same case can give far more comprehensive and knowledgeable scrutiny to the legislative record than, for example, a district court staffed by a single judge and two clerks. Some fraction of the errors made in district court adjudication will survive appellate scrutiny, and even when the appellate court can successfully correct the district courts' mistaken analyses of legislative history, those errors will burden the appellate court's capacity to assess legislative history in other cases.

Heterogeneity. A second distinctive feature of legislative history is that it is far more heterogeneous than other sources. A partial list of materials that might appear in a legislative history includes the original draft bill, subsequent drafts, rejected proposals for amendment, House and Senate committee reports, conference committee reports, transcripts of committee hearings and committee markup sessions, sponsors' statements, drafters' statements, statistical or historical studies inserted into the record by legislative staff, executive staff, or private parties, floor debates, presidential signing statements, and legislative history of other relevant statutes. The generation of legislative history is an open-ended process to which many different actors—legislators and their staffs, executive officials and their staff, private associations and individuals, and others—may contribute. Each of these actors may also contribute in different capacities: as proponents, opponents, or as neutral experts.

The extreme heterogeneity of legislative history is distinctive. Statutes, for example, come in only a single tenor: In principle, every word of the statute is entitled to weight in the interpretive process. Precedents relevant to a particular case display a greater degree of heterogeneity; there may be majority, concurring, and dissenting opinions, dicta and holding may have to be distinguished, and judicial precedents from courts of varying authority may be cited. Yet only one type of actor—judges—may create judicial opinions, and well-established rules govern the relative authority of different opinions. The canons of construction—judge-made interpretive maxims, such as expression unius (negative implication) and the rule of lenity (construe penal statutes against the government)—display the greatest degree of heterogeneity and are most like legislative history in this regard. Nonetheless, the heterogeneity of legislative history is of a different order of magnitude, for it contains an astonishing range of unusual material produced in various ways by various actors.

The heterogeneity of legislative history increases the risks of adjudicative error in at least three ways. First, parties and judges will often be unfamiliar, or only superficially familiar, with the roles, characteristics, and incentives of the actors who have contributed to a legislative record and with the unusual materials it contains. The record will consist of materials offered on different occasions, presented for different purposes, and enjoying different degrees of authority; actors in the judicial process may often simply lack the comprehensive background knowledge of the legislative process necessary to assess the significance and weight of the sources. Similarly, judges deciding legal questions usually interpret texts that are themselves legally operative, such as statutes, regulations, and judicial decisions. Legislative history, however, lacks any legal effect apart from the use that can be made of it in interpreting statutes. The habits and assumptions formed from interpreting authoritative texts may cause judges to accord too much weight to legislative-history documents that are not themselves legally operative.

Second, the heterogeneity of the legislative record provides broad scope for the operation of judicial preconception. The oft-repeated quip that consulting legislative history is like entering a crowded room and looking around for one's friends makes a point about the reliability of the legislative record. Yet it also makes an analytically distinct point about the accuracy of judicial assessment of legislative history. If there is something for everyone in a legislative history, a judge may select the material that suits his preconceptions even if the dominant tenor of the legislative history, taken as a whole, fairly suggests a different result.

Third, heterogeneity also provides broad scope for the operation of salience and other cognitive problems. Legislative history will usually contain multiple sources pitched at varying levels of generality and authority. Judges will be tempted to favor more specific and more pointed legislative-history sources over more general sources even if the specific source is of dubious provenance or weak authority.

Learning effects and the adversary system. Perhaps the foregoing claims do not sufficiently account for two institutional processes: learning over time and the revelation of information by the adversary system. Judges have an individual and collective capacity to learn over time, to do better with legislative history than they did in *Holy Trinity*—a hoary case, after all, and one decided before legislative history came into widespread use. Perhaps familiarity breeds success. In the modern era, moreover, lawyers on all sides are alert to the uses and abuses of legislative history. Perhaps the mutual threat of exposing the abuses will ensure that all useful material and only the useful material comes to the judges' attention.

Yet not all of the difficulties of legislative history tend to diminish as judges gain familiarity with its dangers, or as adversaries attempt to expose each other's weak points. Although long judicial experience with legislative history may obviate some dangers, such as judicial ignorance of the provenance or significance of various types of legislative-history materials, other dangers result from the interaction between legislative history's unique characteristics and permanent structural features of the adjudicative process. The second-best question of judicial competence suggested by *Holy Trinity* cannot be dismissed simply by pointing out that the poor briefing of the legislative history and the lack of independent judicial scrutiny may have occurred in that case because all concerned were relatively unfamiliar with the general dangers of legislative history. Unfamiliarity with background features of the legislative process and legislative history is just one circumstance that causes the structural conditions of the adjudicative process to mislead courts. Others include constraints of time and disparity of resources between the parties; note that the adversary process may exacerbate, rather than ameliorate, the latter problems.

Furthermore, we have seen that judicial error may also arise from cognitive constraints resistant to correction by experience or by lawyers' argumentation. Salience and judicial preconception, two of the most serious problems we have discussed, fall into this category. In general, learning and adversarial process may mitigate the relevant problems, but will not plausibly eliminate them; in some cases it may even exacerbate them.

Volume, heterogeneity, and agencies. A brief note to anticipate later discussion: my remarks here are confined to the problems that legislative history poses for generalist judges. In particular, administrative agencies occupy a very different position with respect to legislative history. Specialized agencies are far more familiar with particular statutes, with the details of their enactment and legislative histories, than are generalist judges. Agencies are generally not in the position of having to absorb and understand the voluminous and heterogeneous legislative history of unfamiliar statutes in every new case; rather, agencies can amortize the costs of comprehending legislative history over a long series of related cases and rulemaking ventures. The hypothesis that generalist judges may do worse by consulting legislative history than by ignoring it, even from an intentionalist standpoint, need not at all apply to agency interpreters. In Chapter 7 I suggest that specialized agencies and generalist judges might quite sensibly choose to follow different interpretive decision-procedures; a formalist rule barring legislative history makes far more sense for judges than for agencies, on institutional grounds.

The Irrelevance of Intentionalism

In all these respects distinctive features of legislative history, particularly its volume and heterogeneity, may increase the risk of erroneous judicial interpretation even if an unbiased interpreter, acting under no constraints of time, information, or expertise, would find that the legislative history reliably reflects a collective intention concerning the relevant interpretive question. There will surely be cases in which text and other sources fail to capture legislative intent while legislative history, correctly read, would provide helpful or even dispositive evidence of that intent. But, on intentionalist premises, such cases should hardly be the norm. Even intentionalist proponents of legislative history posit that statutory text supplies the best evidence of legislative intent across a broad range of cases; intentionalism does not claim that legislative history constitutes the primary source for determining legislative intent. Likewise, intentionalist interpreters premise their selection of supplemental interpretive principles, such as canons of construction, on the ground that those principles provide information about legislative intent. On such premises there is little reason to think that legislative history is an indispensable resource for generating accurate judicial assessments of legislative intent.

More important, it matters little whether a regime that incorporates legislative history would provide an omniscient and infallible decisionmaker with better information about legislative intent than would a regime that does not, for courts are neither omniscient nor infallible. The relevant question is whether legislative history increases the incidence of error, over the run of cases, when considered by judges constrained by the structural limitations of the adjudicative process and corollary effects such as party dependence, salience, and preconception. The foregoing considerations suggest that distinctive features of legislative history, features not shared by statutory text or other standard sources, may interact with these constraints in ways that produce distinctively severe risks of judicial error in the determination of legislative intent. Accordingly, even on intentionalist premises judicial resort to legislative history may prove counterproductive.

This possibility remains unproven, although the contrary intentionalist assumption that legislative history increases judicial accuracy is equally so; I take up the issues of empiricism and uncertainty in Chapter 6. Here the only point I aim to establish is that *Holy Trinity*'s central lesson is squarely institutionalist: given limited judicial capacities, judicial resort to legislative history may often impede, rather than aid, the search for legislative intent. *Holy Trinity* thus proves only that limits on interpretive capacities pose inescapable problems of second-best.

Most important is the possibility that opposing high-level views about legislative intentions might converge on operating-level views about the utility of legislative history. Suppose that it is indeed true that interpreters who consult legislative history often end up further away from, rather than closer to, legislative intentions. To the extent that this is so, textualists and intentionalists can converge on a skeptical assessment of legislative history at the operational level despite their high-level disagreements. Indeed, so far as legislative history is concerned, those high-level disagreements can be bracketed and even ignored altogether. Of course, nothing here shows or claims to show that such value convergence is possible in other areas or with respect to other interpretive problems. As I suggested in Chapter 3, the extent to which high-level value theories converge at the operational level cannot be established in the abstract; it can only be established by inspection, across different areas and problems of interpretation. In Chapters 7 and 8 I will attempt to show, on the ground, that the extent of convergence is indeed large.

— 5 —

Systemic Effects and Judicial Coordination

The last chapter examined judicial capacities; this one turns to the systemic effects of interpretive rules on other actors in the legal system, most importantly legislatures. My principal target here is a suite of views or arguments that I collect under the rubric of *democracy-forcing interpretation*. Roughly, these are arguments that judges should choose interpretive rules with a view to provoking desirable legislative responses. If legislators' preferences are treated as exogenously fixed, then these are what Harvard legal scholar Einer Elhauge calls "preference-eliciting" rules.[1] In other versions, legislators' preferences or values are taken to be endogenous to legislative deliberation, and democracy-forcing interpretation has the aim of producing a certain quantity or quality of legislative deliberation about statutory and constitutional policies.

I shall suggest here that democracy-forcing interpretation is exposed to serious institutional objections. Most important is a second-best problem that arises from the collective character of judicial institutions. If judges cannot coordinate on a particular democracy-forcing regime, then decisions by individual judges in accordance with democracy-forcing precepts will be futile, perhaps even perverse. The problems inherent in democracy-forcing interpretation thus illustrate the basic claim, advanced in Chapter 3, that interpretive theory based on first principles must be supplemented by second-best or nonideal interpretive theory. Any account of constitutional and statutory interpretation should address the institutional conditions of judicial decisionmaking, chief among them the collective character of judicial institutions.

Democracy-Forcing Interpretation

Part I criticized extant accounts of legal interpretation for failure to take adequate account of institutional variables, including judicial capacities and systemic effects. Yet we saw in Chapter 2 and elsewhere a strand of systemic argument that I am calling democracy-forcing interpretation. Consider the following views and arguments:

- Judges should adopt textualism because it has a disciplining effect, ex ante, on legislatures and other drafters of legal texts.
- Judges should adopt canons of statutory interpretation that require a clear legislative statement—for example, the canon that statutes should be construed to avoid serious constitutional questions—in order to promote beneficial legislative deliberation about constitutional values or important policy questions.
- Judges should adopt constitutional rules that enforce "due process of lawmaking"—for example, requirements of congressional fact-finding under statutes that enforce the Fourteenth Amendment—in order to promote a well-functioning legislative process.

Although such views point in the right direction, an institutionalist direction, they do not go far enough; in each case the arguments are only incompletely institutional. The cause of the problem, I shall suggest, is that each of these views commits the fundamental mistake of overlooking the collective character of judicial institutions—of overlooking that the judiciary, like Congress, is a "they," not an "it."[2] That mistake produces the critical and erroneous assumption that coordinated judicial adoption of some particular approach to legal interpretation is feasible and desirable. Once we drop that assumption, it becomes clear that the premises implicit in these views do not support their conclusions. To be sure, the conclusions might nonetheless be correct, even if the reasoning is invalid. We might fill in the missing premises of these views in ways that would make their conclusions hold. But we can only do so, I shall claim, if the new premises take account of second-best problems that stem from the costs of coordination within the judiciary. So these views would have to be justified, if at all, on entirely different grounds than the ones their proponents typically offer.

This is not a general impeachment of all interpretive approaches. The objection based on the collective character of judicial institutions applies only against approaches that, by their terms, require some threshold or critical mass of coordinated judicial action to provoke desirable legislative reactions. It does not apply against approaches that allow strictly marginal or divisible contributions by individual judges. So, for example, nothing I say here impeaches the claim that individual judges should interpret statutes purposively, not to provoke legislative responses but because purposivism is best quite apart from anticipated legislative reactions. Such a view can coherently be adopted by individual judges quite apart from what other judges do. By the same token, the formalist prescriptions I offer in Chapters 7 and 8 do not presuppose coordinated judicial action. On the institutional account of the benefits of formalism that I shall offer, adoption of formalism by individual judges will make the interpretive system marginally better, regardless of what other judges do. All I seek to establish here is that approaches that do require or presuppose large-scale judicial coordination fail. The choice between approaches that do not require such coordination must be made on different grounds.

Agreement, Disagreement, and Empiricism

Before proceeding, I shall forestall a puzzle, or an objection, about the relationship between the claims here and the claims in previous chapters. Here I emphasize the possibility of disagreement among judges. But I have criticized first-best interpretive theorists for ignoring the possibility of agreement—the possibility that judges might, bracketing high-level disagreements, converge to shared conclusions about the operating level of legal interpretation. Here I emphasize that democracy-forcing justifications for textualism (as well as other approaches) face serious second-best problems. But in Chapter 2 I criticized Eskridge for not engaging the claim that democracy-forcing textualism might itself constitute the best form of dynamic interpretation on Eskridge's own premises. Most generally, I have suggested that interpretive theory takes insufficient account of system effects, whereas here I am criticizing a suite of democracy-forcing arguments that themselves appear systemic. Are these claims consistent?

Yes, because they are offered to make the same point, just against different targets. As we have seen, first-best theorists of various stripes ignore the possibility of judicial agreement; second-best considerations may help judges with different commitments to converge on particular interpretive rules, as I argued they might with respect to legislative history. Here we shall see that democracy-forcing theorists ignore the possibility of judicial disagreement; second-best problems may cause democracy-forcing interpretation to have perverse effects. The common mistake in both these views is that the relevant arguments are fatally a priori or abstract, as opposed to empirical. The first camp assumes away the possibility of agreement; the second camp assumes away the possibility of disagreement.

The institutionalist position, by contrast, is that interpretive theory has no choice but to confront the empirical questions that underpin the competing approaches. In a certain state of affairs (with high levels of judicial coordination), democracy-forcing arguments might prove feasible, but given a different state of affairs they will fail. Likewise, abstract debates over first-best commitments are inescapable if convergence does not occur, as a factual matter, in many domains. But if convergence is widespread, again as a factual matter, then many principled disagreements can be ignored. So this chapter, like the last, has the modest aim of suggesting a possibility with second-best implications: on certain empirical premises about the feasibility of judicial coordination, democracy-forcing arguments will backfire. Part III then takes up, more systematically, the question what judicial interpreters should do, given pervasive empirical uncertainty about relevant institutional variables.

The Fallacy of Division

To generate the critique of democracy-forcing arguments, we need to introduce a piece of logical apparatus: the *fallacy of division*. Although the fallacy has been given several subtly different definitions, for present purposes we may usefully say that the fallacy rests on a mistaken treatment of factual or normative generalization. The fallacy arises when a claim that is true of, or justified for, a whole set is taken to apply to any particular member of the set. That an army is strong does not entail that any one of its soldiers is strong; that the world would be better if all nations disarmed does not entail that any particular nation should disarm unilaterally.[3]

My principal submission here is that democracy-forcing interpretation routinely trips over the division fallacy. Division problems occur when interpretive theorists ask, explicitly or implicitly, the following question:

"What is the best interpretive approach for judges (or courts) to adopt?" That question omits an essential feature of the problem. Imagine that a given judge, any judge, is deciding whether to be a textualist, an originalist, a purposivist, or something else and has turned to the academic literature on interpretive theory for guidance. (This is, of course, a strictly heuristic or expository device that simplifies the presentation.) The theorists' counsel speaks to the question which approach would be best if adopted by "the judges" or "the courts." But that is not the question that our particular judge needs to answer. Our judge wants to know what approach is best for her to adopt. The two questions will have very different answers if the other judges adopt different interpretive practices or rules than she adopts. That a given approach would be best for the whole court or judiciary does not entail that it would be best for any given judge taken alone if other judges do not coordinate on the same approach.

The logical mistake here is an invalid inference from a group-level claim to an individual-level claim. The inference fails if judicial coordination on a particular approach is infeasible or unlikely. The best approach for any given judge to adopt will vary depending on whether the other judges adopt the same approach or instead adopt any of several other approaches, either because they disagree with the first judge's normative conclusions, because they are incapable of full compliance with the relevant prescriptions, or for some other reason.

In this picture the interpretive theorist has gone wrong by casting the critical question at an excessively high level of abstraction. For reasons I shall explore later, the collective structure of judicial institutions means that it is simply inadequate to theorize about interpretation as if the judiciary were a unitary institution, perhaps conceived as a single individual (whether or not that single individual resembles Dworkin's superhuman judge Hercules). In the language of moral philosophy, the interpretive theorist has overlooked essential questions of nonideal theory, which asks what obligations people have when others will not or cannot comply with their (identical) obligations. In the language of economics and consequentialist political theory emphasized in Chapter 3, the interpretive theorist has overlooked essential questions of the second-best, which arise when a general or collective equilibrium cannot be attained. Under either description, the core problem is that the theorist has gone wrong by omitting essential institutional detail. It is an irony of interpretive theory that so much emphasis has been given to exploring the consequences of the legislature's collective character, while inadequate attention has been paid to the same problem in judicial institutions.

I shall begin by examining a range of democracy-forcing proposals, methods, and doctrines that commit the division fallacy. After examining circumstances in which any particular judge might do badly to adopt an interpretive approach that might be best if adopted by the whole judiciary, I shall suggest that a range of interpretive doctrines are fallacious in this way. This point knocks out arguments that would justify textualism by its disciplining effect on legislatures; that justify canons of construction, or interpretive default rules, by pointing to their democracy-forcing or information-eliciting effects; or that justify constitutional rules by reference to their beneficial effects on the lawmaking process. The common conceptual mistake in these arguments is the undefended assumption that sustained judicial coordination on a particular interpretive approach or canonical regime is feasible. Whether it is feasible is an empirical question; I shall give tentative reasons for believing that it is not feasible, in our system anyway. To the extent that coordination across judges is not feasible, I shall also claim, it will often be affirmatively harmful or perverse for any particular judge to adopt the approach that would be best if all judges coordinated on it.

Judicial Coordination and Interpretive Method

The division fallacy is to suppose that an interpretive strategy that would be beneficial if adopted by all judges should therefore be adopted by any particular judge. Whether the conclusion holds depends on what other judges are doing. Judges vote on cases within a collective judicial bureaucracy that, at appellate levels, always sits on merits cases in multijudge panels. The collective character of judicial institutions produces several reasons for believing that (or circumstances in which) a particular judge might do badly to adopt an approach that would be best if adopted by all judges. The essential idea is that interpretive accounts that explicitly or implicitly require a whole court or the whole judiciary to coordinate on a given course of action and to sustain that course of action over time demand too much of judicial institutions.

There are two separate and independent points here, one analytic, the other empirical. Analytically, the premise that it would be best for all judges to coordinate on a given approach does not, without more, yield the conclusion that any particular judge ought to adopt that approach. Whether that is so depends upon what other judges do. Empirically, it is often costly or simply infeasible for the judiciary to coordinate upon a particular course of action and to sustain that coordination to the degree necessary to affect the behavior of other institutions and actors. Much more work would have to be done to substantiate the empirical claim, but the opposite assumption—that judges can easily coordinate on an approach that would be best for the whole system (if it were agreed what approach that is)—is also unsubstantiated. Neither position has any natural or methodological priority. In Part III I give extended treatment to the question what judges should do in situations of irreducible empirical uncertainty of this kind.

Two qualifications are important. First, for simplicity I shall often speak of coordination across "the judiciary" or "all judges." "All" is of course shorthand for "whatever critical mass of judges is necessary to bring about the legislative reaction that the dynamic interpreter seeks to produce." I do not mean that literally all judges in the whole judicial system must comply. The division problem arises so long as any particular judge must coordinate with some critical mass or requisite proportion of other judges in order to produce the desired results, so that individual judicial action is useless.

Second, it is worth reemphasizing that the division fallacy only bites against interpretive accounts that explicitly or implicitly require coordinated judicial action. Some accounts lack this character. Nothing I say here underwrites an objection to interpretive theories that have a strictly marginal or divisible character—theories in which the choices of individual judges make separable and cumulative contributions to some good specified by the theory. But democracy-forcing accounts, I shall suggest, are not marginalist or divisible in this way. Rather, democracy-forcing accounts typically require or assume some threshold or critical mass of coordinated judicial action, and the division problem does bite on such accounts. Embedded structural features of judicial institutions, which I shall now survey, block the necessary coordination across judges.

Irreducible disagreement. The most important practical consequence of the collective character of the judiciary is to produce irreducible disagreement within the judiciary about competing interpretive approaches—

both disagreement within panels or courts and, over time, across panels or courts. The history of interpretive theory in American courts reveals persistent and deep disagreements among judges and courts about the proper methods and sources of legal interpretation. As to methods, judges who emphasize the ordinary meaning of constitutional and statutory text criticize those who emphasize the purposes of framers or legislators, who in turn criticize devotees of specific legislative intentions; each of these groups itself fractures into competing variants. As to sources, the history of American interpretation is full of cases that have become chestnuts precisely because text, history, interpretive canons, constitutional and statutory policies, and other sources pull in different directions in those cases, forcing judges to make consequential choices about their priorities. The competing camps of interpretive theory are not solely scholastic inventions; they reflect chronic, possibly intractable differences in judicial views about the proper treatment of recurring interpretive problems.

To be sure, the scope of judicial disagreement will be reduced, and its consequences ameliorated, to the extent that judges reach incompletely theorized agreements about interpretation. We have seen that judges who disagree on high-level principles may converge upon particular rules, canons, or statutory techniques. Consider the possibility, for example, that both textualists and intentionalists might converge on a rule excluding legislative history, the former because they think it irrelevant in principle, the latter because they come to believe, empirically, that legislative history misleads judges about legislative intent. A less useful version of the incompletely theorized agreement, however, occurs when judges who agree on high-level principles find that they disagree about a wide range of particular interpretive canons, rules, or problems. Self-described intentionalists might sharply disagree about, for example, the intentionalist value of rejected legislative proposals. The extent and scope of disagreement will also be heavily sensitive to the type of court at issue. The base rate for most lower appellate courts is a great deal of agreement in any type of case, so it is not surprising to find agreement on many statutory and constitutional cases as well. At the Supreme Court level, however, cases are harder, disagreements are sharper, and the effectiveness of precedent in dampening theoretical disagreement is reduced.

The most we can say, in the abstract, is that the possibility of muting disagreement in these ways needs much more empirical assessment than it has received so far. But any judge who thinks that it would be better for the court or for the judiciary as a whole to adopt method A rather than method B must consider the possibility that the next judge over is equally convinced that method B would be the best approach—not merely for that judge, but for all concerned.

Inevitable mistakes and noncompliance. Even where disagreement is absent, or at least not openly debated, different judges may do different things with similar statutory problems. Judges' behavior may differ even if their stated principles do not. An important possibility is sheer human error resulting from the cognitive load under which judges labor. Judges, like other people, face important shortages of time, information, and theoretical acumen. Decisions interpreting statutory and constitutional provisions will, with nontrivial frequency, announce rationales or reach results that contradict widely agreed-upon interpretive rules and thus count as mistakes from any normative perspective. In a large number of these cases the judges who issued the decisions might themselves condemn the decision if they reviewed it without constraints of time and information. But the feedback mechanisms that might promote this form of learning are feeble in the extreme. Judges rarely have the occasion to reevaluate old decisions unless a higher court reverses the decision and sends it back; even then, of course, the lower judge may attribute the reversal to principled disagreement or partisan biases rather than acknowledge that his initial decision was mistaken.

Less commonly, but more dramatically, we might imagine situations in which some judges engage in bad-faith noncompliance with agreed-upon interpretive rules. Very few deny that there is some domain, perhaps a large domain, of easy interpretive cases—cases in which the obvious meaning of a legal text captures a straightforward linguistic, legal, and social consensus, one that corresponds to a sensible account of constitutional or statutory policies, and in which other sources of meaning, if checked, would confirm the obvious meaning. Judges motivated by strongly held policy convictions that run counter to the text may write opinions that erroneously classify easy cases as hard ones, exaggerating minor statutory quirks into ambiguities that may be resolved with reference to grandiose claims about background interpretive principles. In some fraction of cases the Supreme Court may eventually correct the lower courts' mistake, but it is unclear how often this occurs; as we shall see later, Supreme Court review is probably inadequate to squeeze all disagreement and error out of the interpretive system.

Aggregation problems and cycling. Under certain circumstances the distribution of views across a multijudge court may produce Condorcetian voting cycles, in which judges who may choose from any one of three or more positions find that a majority coalition exists to defeat each position. Even if the judges' individual views are well ordered, the collective ordering is intransitive and therefore (in one sense of the term) incoherent, even irrational. Voting cycles of this sort may be suppressed by adopting a rule that arbitrarily stops the cycle at some point, such as a doctrine of precedent, but this produces a form of path-dependence: the content of law becomes highly sensitive to the order in which cases arise, which in turn empowers agenda-setters. Arrow's theorem[4] demonstrates that no decision-rule can avoid this dilemma, given certain reasonable-seeming stipulations about admissible views and permissible ways of ordering those views.[5]

The empirical significance of cyclical voting is unclear.[6] Under reasonable empirical assumptions, the arrangement of views across judges frequently displays no collective instability ("single-peaked preferences") or is sufficiently homogeneous that the most contestable stipulations of Arrow's theorem do not apply (Sen's "value-restricted preferences").[7] The sole point relevant here is that the work on judicial voting cycles generalizes fully from substantive views to methodological positions—to the choice of rules for constitutional and statutory interpretation. On a three-judge court, let us imagine, there are three possible views about the use of originalist evidence in constitutional interpretation. View 1 is that it should never be used; view 2 is that it should always be used; view 3 is a plain-meaning rule, under which the material is used only when the constitutional text is ambiguous or vague. The three judges rank these approaches differently. Judge A is a committed originalist: she believes that originalist evidence should always be used, but if that position is ruled out, she believes that it should at least be used in cases of textual ambiguity. (Judge A, that is, ranks the approaches in the order 2, 3, 1). Judge B is hostile to originalism and believes that the material should never be used; but if it is to be used, Judge B thinks that it is unrealistic to attempt to cabin it by a plain-meaning rule. (So Judge B ranks the approaches 1, 2, 3). Judge C thinks the plain-meaning approach best, but if that is rejected, thinks that total disavowal of originalist material is better than unrestricted use. (So Judge C ranks the approaches 3, 1, 2). Under this distribution of views, the court's method of constitutional interpretation will cycle endlessly or, if precedent applies to rules about interpretation, stop arbitrarily.

Exogenous and endogenous change. In some periods methodological disagreements, mistakes, and aggregation problems are temporarily muted or restrained by political consensus or aggressive Supreme Court oversight. An observer of American legal interpretation circa 1965, for example, might have thought that legislators, agencies, and judges had coordinated on a shared set of interpretive tools and methods praised by legal process theorists. Those methods prominently featured balancing tests in constitutional interpretation, purposive statutory interpretation, and easy recourse to legislative history.

But this sort of coordination of the interpretive system is rarely stable and rarely lasts for long. One possibility is that exogenous social shocks arising from political, economic, and technological developments will call into question the empirical premises on which the prevailing consensus rests and change the political valence of interpretive methods. Another possibility is endogenous oscillation between or among interpretive methods, which can operate either in place of or in addition to exogenously driven change. Consider the possibility that judicial use of legislative history will oscillate over time because increased use will cause legislators to pollute the history with obviously unreliable material, causing judges to downplay its importance, causing legislators to reduce their efforts at manipulation, and so on.

Even if judges craft a temporarily stable interpretive consensus, it may have no effect at all on legislative behavior in the short or medium term, just because of the lag built into the interpretive system. Old statutes (statutes enacted before the courts announced the new interpretive rule) will take some time to proceed through the lower courts and receive a definitive Supreme Court construction or a definitive adjudication of their constitutional validity. By the time new statutes (enacted after the newly announced rule) present themselves, the Court's composition may have changed, or new alliances and new doctrines may have formed. For an example of this dynamic, consider that the Rehnquist Court formulated several interpretive doctrines intended to increase congressional respect for federalism, such as the requirement of detailed congressional fact-finding under statutes that enforce the Fourteenth Amendment against states. In most cases those doctrines have been applied to statutes enacted before the new doctrine was announced. By the time new statutes dominate the pool of litigated cases, the relevant interpretive doctrines will have already passed into history.

Apart from the dynamic interplay between courts, legislatures, and agencies, endogenous change may arise from interpersonal dynamics within courts. One possibility is that various justices on the Supreme Court alter their interpretive positions over time in response to the positions colleagues take. Dynamics of this sort can occur if, for example, some justices wish to occupy the Court median while the Court as a whole is shifting to the right or left, if some justices move toward extremes to occupy roles left vacant by the departure of other members, or if like-minded justices polarize toward extreme views.

In light of these possibilities, it is unsurprising (though not predictable ex ante) that the legal process consensus had been shattered by the mid-1980s, after the resurgence of the Republican Party and the appointment of a cadre of conservative judges. All of the major elements of the legal-process consensus had either been discarded or were subject to serious critiques. Constitutional balancing tests were on the intellectual defensive; both constitutional and statutory interpretation were animated by newly formalistic approaches, including textualism and originalism; and legislative history had come under attack as legally irrelevant and excessively manipulable. For present purposes it does not matter whether the relevant changes were caused by exogenous political change or reflected endogenous oscillation or judicial dynamics of some kind. The important point is that interpretive method is highly unstable, at least in the medium and long term.

The Structure of Judicial Institutions

Taken singly or collectively, these institutional facts—irreducible disagreement, mistakes and noncompliance, aggregation problems, and change over time—undercut any argument that implicitly requires that a given interpretive approach be adopted by all judges (if it is to work for any judge) and sustained for long periods. Whatever interpretive account of this sort a given judge adopts, other judges will adopt different ones, both at the same time and over time. The heterogeneity of interpretive approaches will block the implicit generalization on which the relevant approaches depend.

A tempting mistake here is to think that heterogeneity and fluctuation cannot exist in a hierarchical court structure topped by a high court with power to lay down systemwide interpretive rules and to bind lower courts to substantive results. But the picture of a centralized, hierarchical judiciary is fantastic. It omits a number of institutional fault lines internal to the structure of judicial institutions that hamper judicial coordination on interpretive strategies:

Divisions within lower courts. Sometimes, or on some questions, lower courts follow a unified course of action within a common legal and intellectual framework. Often, however, they do not. Even if we put aside the district courts, whose judges are largely free to pursue their preferred interpretive and substantive policies in cases that the parties will not appeal (perhaps because they have been strongly encouraged to settle), the circuit courts are hardly a monolithic, unified actor. In some cases there are strong substantive disagreements across circuits; in some cases circuit mechanisms for internal coordination are unwieldy; most simply, messiness is pervasive just because there are hundreds of appellate judges spread across more than a dozen lower courts. Importantly, there is no a priori guarantee that certiorari review will bring uniformity to lower-court decisionmaking. Whether it does so is an empirical question that has received insufficient study,[8] and will undoubtedly have different answers in different legal contexts and in different eras.

Noncompliance by lower courts. Another possibility is that lower courts or a critical subset of them will defy the Supreme Court's instructions more or less covertly. Canonical examples are the district courts' foot-dragging after *Brown v. Board of Education*,[9] and, from a later period, the District of Columbia Circuit's sustained pattern of noncompliance with, even defiance of, the Supreme Court's instructions for interpreting the Administrative Procedure Act.[10] The possibility of defiance, at least on some issues and for some period, should be unsurprising. Although lower-court judges may experience a reputational cost if the Court reverses their decisions or admonishes them in a written opinion, it is hardly clear that the Court has the institutional capacity to catch an appreciable fraction of noncompliant decisions; and the Court lacks power to subject theoretically subordinate judges to any serious, direct sanctions, such as financial penalties.[11]

A notable recent example of lower-court recalcitrance involves the Commerce Clause. Despite two prominent Supreme Court decisions invalidating federal statutes for exceeding the Clause's boundaries, lower courts have consistently declined the Supreme Court's apparent invitation to expand the new analysis to statutes such as the Endangered Species Act, the Freedom of Access to Clinic Entrances Act, or various federal statutes that criminalize possession of machine guns and drugs. Remarkably, lower-court judges in recent years have voted to reject almost all Commerce Clause challenges to federal statutes, regardless of the judges' party or background views of federalism. This reluctance to press the Commerce Clause revolution is a nontrivial obstacle to the Court's new federalist majority, which typically waits for some lower court to invalidate a federal statute on federalism grounds before confirming the invalidation. Although no legal rule prevents the Court from invalidating a federal statute after the lower courts have uniformly sustained it, to do so would be a departure from the Court's ordinary certiorari practices. Overall, it is reasonable to speculate that the new federalist majority would prefer lower courts to do some of the work of the Commerce Clause revolution themselves, actively implementing the Court's decisions rather than bucking against the new Commerce Clause logic.

Instability within the Supreme Court. Even if, per impossibile, lower courts were perfect agents for the Supreme Court, the principal is itself multiple, composed of nine justices. Irreducible disagreement, aggregation problems, shifting alliances, and shifting membership over time combine to create systematic instability in interpretive doctrine, preventing the sustained judicial coordination that is necessary if interpretive doctrines are to be justified on dynamic grounds. The high court that is supposed to coordinate the hierarchical system is itself riven by disagreement, plagued by mistaken or disingenuous opinion writing, destabilized by aggregation problems, and buffeted by political change. Occasionally, to be sure, the jurisdiction's high court will come into the hands of a persistent and stable majority that can for a few years pursue a sustained course of coordinated action. Perhaps the Warren Court was like that, for a few years anyway, and later we shall see that the Rehnquist Court attempted to coordinate on new procedural rules for congressional law-making in constitutionally sensitive areas, such as federalism. But the Rehnquist Court was also a statistical anomaly in many respects, especially in the length of its justices' service. It is far more typical in American law that campaigns of coordinated action by high courts break down with surprising rapidity; we shall see a few examples in the next section.

The claim is not, of course, that judicial coordination on interpretive doctrine is somehow impossible. We might imagine circumstances in which a united majority of the Supreme Court sticks to an interpretive doctrine or strategy, brings lower courts into line through aggressive over-sight, and produces hoped-for reactions from other lawmaking institutions. My suggestion is simply that judicial coordination on interpretive doctrines and strategies is costly and unstable and thus tends to be both relatively rare and noticeably fragile. In this practical and institutional sense, rather than some logical sense, judicial coordination on ambitious interpretive doctrines and strategies is generally infeasible.

Democracy-Forcing Statutory Interpretation

Having indicated the conceptual and empirical problems, let us turn to some examples of democracy-forcing proposals. The conceptual mistake common to these proposals and arguments is that they all treat courts as a unitary actor. Although these proposals might be justified anew on empirical grounds, the relevant justifications would have to address the collective character of judicial institutions and the resulting fact that ju-dicial attempts to coordinate on the relevant interpretive approaches are threatened by instability.

Textualism. Textualists often argue for the primacy of statutory text over legislative history on democracy-forcing grounds. A central argument for textualism is that it improves legislative performance: judicial refusal to remake enacted text forces Congress to legislate more responsibly ex ante by anticipating and forestalling the sort of postenactment interpretive problems that H. L. A. Hart emphasized. The argument can also be put in the language of *preference-eliciting default rules,* a subcategory of democracy-forcing arguments that assumes fixed legislative preferences. On the preference-eliciting version, adherence to text will prod legislative coalitions into revealing their preferences explicitly.

The canon of avoidance. An important interpretive canon, or maxim, is the idea that statutes should be construed to avoid serious constitutional questions where it is fairly possible to do so. Although the canon's supporters propose a range of justifications, an important one is the idea that avoidance will elicit desirable deliberative behavior from legislators. Absent the canon, legislators might cross constitutional limits inadvertently or by indirection. The canon thus encourages legislators to focus their deliberations on the statute's limits and the extent to which the statute presses constitutional law in new directions; at the very least, legislators will be forced to speak clearly, perhaps in statutory text, if they wish to raise a serious constitutional question.

Clear statement rules and nondelegation canons. The canon of avoidance is a general precept that statutes should be interpreted to avoid serious constitutional questions. Courts have developed a potpourri of similar canons that (1) construe statutes to promote "underenforced" constitutional norms[12]—constitutional principles that courts are reluctant to enforce through full-fledged judicial review on the constitutional merits—or that (2) implement "nondelegation canons," interpretive canons that attempt to force Congress, rather than the executive, to focus on and speak clearly about especially sensitive decisions.[13] Examples include the ideas that statutes should be narrowly construed to avoid raising the question whether Congress has unconstitutionally delegated its legislative power to an administrative agency; that statutes must speak clearly if an agency is to be given the power to intrude upon traditional or essential state functions; and that statutes should be presumed prospective, as opposed to retroactive. In all of these cases the standard justifications for clear statement rules prominently feature the democracy-forcing idea that "constitutionally sensitive questions . . . will not be permitted to arise unless the constitutionally designated lawmaker has deliberately and expressly chosen to raise them."[14]

The rule of lenity. The rule of lenity is a venerable interpretive canon holding that penal statutes should, where fairly possible, be construed in favor of defendants. Here the democracy-forcing idea is that legislators should be encouraged to deliberate about criminal punishment and speak clearly when they decide to adopt it.

One criticism of these democracy-forcing proposals is that they rest upon mistaken empirical premises about legislative behavior and capacities. Perhaps Congress is in a strong sense institutionally incapable of fulfilling the procedural demands that these doctrines make; more weakly, perhaps the costs of congressional adaptation to those procedural demands are greater than any resulting benefits. The division problem suggests a different critique, one focused on judicial rather than legislative institutions: Information-forcing or deliberation-forcing arguments assume that judges can and will coordinate on the relevant canons, doctrines, and precepts. Such arguments thus ignore the possibility that interpretive approaches will fluctuate across courts and over time rather than achieving some stable, coordinated state.

If all (relevant) courts consistently eschewed legislative history or consistently adhered to clear statement rules or to the rule of lenity, Congress might encode policy choices in text, squarely face important constitutional questions, and speak clearly when imposing criminal punishments. But suppose that the federal judiciary persistently disagrees about the merits of these doctrines and about their applicability in particular settings, both within courts, such as the Supreme Court, and across courts, such as the courts of appeals. These persistent disagreements would then produce shifting coalitions and mutable doctrines; there would be no consistent, unified set of incentives to which Congress might respond, and no steady judicial policy of democracy-forcing or preference-eliciting interpretation.

At the empirical level, both variation and fluctuation are the norm for each of these interpretive tools. As for legislative history, the Supreme Court has alternately emphasized and downplayed it in an oscillating pattern. Its use rose from 1937 until about 1950, fell again until the late 1950s, then fluctuated uncertainly until a dramatic upward spike in the mid-1970s. Another slow decline began in the mid-1980s, but usage rose again in the mid-1990s before falling yet again toward the end of the decade. At any given time the Court's opinions vary in their willingness to resort to legislative history, even where that history is available. This persistent instability means that the textualist resurgence led by Justice Antonin Scalia is most unlikely to produce a sustained disciplining or democracy-forcing effect on statutory drafting. "Because Justice Scalia's critique never has commanded a majority on the Supreme Court, its principles cannot be attributed to the Court as a whole, let alone to lower courts."[15]

The same broad pattern of fluctuating, inconsistent usage holds true of the clear statement rules and the rule of lenity. As to the former, the Rehnquist Court's favored substantive canons differ markedly from the Burger Court's, which in turn differ from the Warren Court's; all in all, "these norms constitute a kind of ad hoc, judicial policymaking that Congress, ex ante, would find difficult to predict."[16] As to the rule of lenity, "judicial enforcement of lenity is notoriously sporadic and unpredictable. As often as not, the 'instinctive distaste' for extinguishing individual liberty without clear legislative warrant gives way to other tastes that can be satisfied only by broad readings of federal criminal statutes."[17]

The upshot is that at any given time some courts, panels, or opinions use the relevant interpretive tools, and some do not. Even where a given canon is nominally invoked, different judges or courts assign it markedly different weights. The rule of lenity, for example, is sometimes treated as a strong presumption, sometimes as a weak tiebreaker, while clear statement rules vary both in their strength and in the sources that may be used to rebut them—text alone, text or legislative history, or perhaps even legislative history alone. This variety and fluctuation make democracy-forcing or information-eliciting arguments premised on the sustained coordination of judicial behavior seem at best optimistic, at worst futile.

Democracy-Forcing and Perverse Results

Futility may not be the worst problem that democracy-forcing proposals face, however. In a regime marked by intractable variation across judges, courts, and decisions and by fluctuation over time, the standard assumption—that any particular judge ought to vote as she would if all other judges were to vote the same way—may be worse than futile. It may in fact be affirmatively harmful or perverse. If other courts, or other judges at different times, do not use democracy-forcing approaches or preference-eliciting canons, then local or episodic use by particular judges may produce bad case-specific consequences without the beneficial systemic effects said to justify the approach. Consider an *isolated* textualist decision that eschews legislative history on the theory that *universal* judicial textualism would have beneficial, democracy-forcing effects. If legislators' expectations are shaped by the bulk of decisions that do not adopt such a theory, then the isolated textualist decision might affirmatively misread legislators' instructions. The same point holds in reverse: an isolated decision consulting legislative history, on the ground that universal judicial intentionalism would produce beneficial consequences, is at best futile and at worst perverse if the enacting majority deliberately encoded its preferred policy in text while leaving legislative history to manipulation by dissenters.

This is a second-best problem that is structurally identical to the second-best problems with intentionalism and legislative history that we examined in Chapter 4. Here the cost of the division fallacy is that sporadic or isolated use of a rule or canon justified on systemic grounds produces decisions that are mistaken on those very grounds. Suppose that a given court, or panel, or judge justifies a dispositive invocation of the rule of lenity on the ground that it forces Congress to speak clearly to criminal punishments; suppose also that other courts, panels, or judges are not using the rule or are using it only inconsistently. Then an isolated instance of its use by one court will have no democracy-forcing effect. It merely gives the particular criminal defendant in the case at hand a windfall victory even though all other interpretive sources (text, legislative history, and so on), minus the rule of lenity, suggest that the statute covers the defendant's conduct. That might be a good or bad thing for independent reasons, but it cannot be justified as a democracy-forcing or information-eliciting approach.

As I have noted, one might save the arguments for democracy-forcing interpretation by assuming that the effect of judicial decisions is perfectly divisible or marginal. Suppose that judicial decisions become 1 percent more textualist, causing majority coalitions in the legislature to become 1 percent more likely to embody their preferences in statutory text rather than legislative history. From the textualist point of view, this should count as a good result; and it is a result attainable by individual judges. On this view, the democracy-forcing argument for textualism does not require coordinated judicial action; it thus steers clear of the fallacy of division. (I refer to textualism here for concreteness only; precisely the same point holds against any theory that justifies intentionalism or purposivism on democracy-forcing grounds.)

In my view, this sort of assumption is not at all plausible. For one thing, adding textualist votes to the judicial system will have no effect, not even a marginal one, if those votes are distributed across cases in the wrong way (from the textualist point of view). Imagine, in the limiting case, that textualist votes are only ever cast by dissenting judges; from the democracy-forcing standpoint those votes are wasted, except for the speculative possibility that they will change other judges' minds. For another thing, the legislative reaction to judicial decisions is probably lumpy rather than perfectly divisible or marginal. Starting from a baseline case in which all judges are intentionalist, the best initial assumption is that legislators will take no notice of textualism until the proportion of textualist judges or decisions reaches some threshold or critical mass. If so, then judges who are attracted to textualism on democracy-forcing grounds are again subject to coordination problems because textualism will be pointless, or even perverse, unless and until the requisite fraction of other judges goes along.

Whatever the merits of these competing empirical assumptions, however, the more important point is that merely to engage these arguments is already to have moved beyond the assumption of a unitary, internally undifferentiated "court" or "judiciary." The argument from the divisible or marginal effect of textualism only becomes necessary, or indeed intelligible, for textualists who have seen the division problem—for textualists, that is, who have gotten beyond or given up the idea that any individual judge should or will adopt the approach that would be best if adopted by all judges. So this argument exemplifies a qualifier I mentioned at the outset. Although we might save the conclusions of democracy-forcing arguments by supplying new empirical premises that take account of a collective judiciary—and that is all the divisibility argument does—we cannot save the invalid reasoning by which those arguments are typically defended in the current literature.

Democracy-Forcing Constitutional Interpretation

Parallel examples are to be found in the theory and practice of constitutional interpretation.

Due process of lawmaking. It is tempting to think that constitutional theorizing is intrinsically less susceptible to the division fallacy. Interpretive theorizing that assumes coordinated judicial action, the argument might run, is only relevant when the theorist hopes that judicial interpretation will influence the behavior of legislators in statutory drafting and of agencies in administrative rulemaking. Constitutional interpretation, on this view, is not forward-looking in the same way. After all, most of the Constitution's text is fixed, and amendments are rare events, so that adopting interpretive doctrines with a view to their deliberation-forcing effects on constitutional drafters would be pointless.

But this is wrong. Many constitutional rules and doctrines are justified on the ground that they will have valuable forward-looking effects on the behavior of current legislators. Under the general rubric of "due process of lawmaking,"[18] theorists have proposed a variety of precepts, approaches, and doctrines that structure the legislative process with a view to improving legislative deliberation and action. These doctrines universally assume that the requisite judicial action can easily be coordinated; they commit the division fallacy, in other words, by assuming that if it would be good for all courts to adopt a particular strain of due process of lawmaking, it would be good for a particular court or judge to do so.

Requirements of congressional factfinding. The Rehnquist Court's revival of constitutional federalism has been criticized and defended, in part, on due-process-of-lawmaking grounds. In the Commerce Clause area, *United States v. Lopez*[19] suggested, in part, that the validity of national legislation might turn, not on the Court's independent assessment of the statute's connection to commerce, but instead on the quality and quantity of the record evidence that Congress had provided to demonstrate a commercial connection. The later decision in *United States v. Morrison,*[20] however, seemed to reject the due-process-of-lawmaking strand in *Lopez*. In cases arising under Section 5 of the Fourteenth Amendment, the procedural strain has been quite marked. In *Kimel v. Florida Board of Regents*[21] and *Board of Trustees v. Garrett,*[22] the Court invalidated federal statutes subjecting states to suit under the Age Discrimination in Employment Act (ADEA) and the Americans with Disabilities Act (ADA), holding in both cases that the congressional findings accompanying the statute failed sufficiently to document the factual and legal predicates (a pattern of unconstitutional state behavior) necessary for congressional action. The Court usually leaves the point of these requirements unstated, but the only plausible account is that the Court is using constitutional invalidation as a sanction to encourage congressional factfinding and perhaps even deliberation of a certain kind and quality.

Standard criticisms of the Rehnquist Court's resort to due-process-of-lawmaking techniques focus on legislative capacities and prerogatives.

One idea is that Congress is structurally incapable of supplying the sort of judicialized factfinding and deliberation the Court is demanding; another idea is that these cases have bad expressive dimensions, suggesting a lack of interbranch comity and judicial respect for congressional autonomy. Given the fallacy of division, however, we may add another point: the Court's due-process-of-lawmaking enterprise, requiring as it does a steady course of coordinated judicial action, is extremely vulnerable to fluctuations in judicial behavior over time and to disagreements within the decentralized judiciary.

Those sources of instability have already begun to operate in the Commerce Clause cases. At the Supreme Court level, consider the contrast between *Lopez*'s interest in legislative procedure and *Morrison*'s exclusive focus on substance. Suppose that some justice, at the time of *Lopez*, joined the majority solely on the basis that a requirement of congressional factfinding, if consistently adopted by the whole Court, would eventually have beneficial effects on the quality and depth of congressional deliberation. The hidden premise of the argument is that judicial coordination of this sort is feasible not only in the case at hand but for the time necessary to alter congressional behavior. If, and to the extent that, the assumption fails because the requisite judicial coordination is infeasible, then a due-process-of-lawmaking approach resting on that assumption must fail as well.

To be sure, the new federalist majority did hang together in *Morrison*, even if it discarded the democracy-forcing rationale for *Lopez*. In the Section 5 cases, however, the majority changed course: the decision in *Nevada Department of Human Resources v. Hibbs*[23] upheld state-regulating provisions of the Family and Medical Leave Act, rejecting claims that the congressional record failed adequately to connect the legislation with a pattern of state violations of constitutional rights. Whether or not *Hibbs* can be reconciled with the previous Section 5 cases on technical grounds, it is quite clear that the Court has watered down its democracy-forcing conception of Section 5, at least for the time being.

A separate problem is that even a temporarily unified Court majority may be unable to force its agenda on the lower courts, which can hamper the Court's plan by simple failure to render active cooperation. As we have seen, that is just what has occurred in the Commerce Clause cases: the lower courts have overwhelmingly declined to extend the Court's precedents to new federal statutes, even where a fair reading of *Morrison* would suggest that invalidation is the obvious outcome. So even if the due-process-of-lawmaking rationale still animated the Court's Commerce Clause precedents, its effect might well have been diluted by lower-court recalcitrance.

Overbreadth and legislative deliberation. A similar example is the free speech overbreadth doctrine. Roughly speaking—the conceptual and doctrinal disputes here are exceedingly refined—overbreadth doctrine permits a litigant whose own conduct is constitutionally proscribable to challenge a statute on the ground that it has a nontrivial range of applications that violate the free speech rights of parties not before the court. So a statute that sweeps too broadly, combining constitutional applications with unconstitutional ones, will be invalidated in whole, not just in part, if it impinges on free speech (although not if it impinges on most other constitutional rights). Although overbreadth has been supplied with a variety of justifications, one idea is that "[o]verbreadth doctrine . . . provid[es] an incentive to legislatures to draft laws that may affect First Amendment activity with as much precision as practicable."[24]

That rationale holds only to the extent that the judiciary can coordinate, across judges and over time, on the relevant conception of overbreadth doctrine. But there is little reason to think that this sort of sustained judicial coordination is feasible. Consider *Massachusetts v. Oakes,* in which Justice O'Connor's plurality opinion said that an overbreadth claim becomes moot if the statute is amended, after the defendant's conviction, to eliminate the portion of the statute that the defendant challenges as overbroad.[25] This seemingly technical position is actually critical, for it would demolish the ex ante, democracy-forcing justification for overbreadth. As Justice Scalia noted in a partial concurrence that, on this point, attracted no less than five votes, under the plurality's rule the legislature might promulgate an overbroad law and then simply narrow the statute before the final appeal, thereby saving any convictions obtained under the initially overbroad statute.

Justice Scalia's incentive-based view is not the law, however, at least according to the judge-made rules governing the precedent effect of fractured decisions; three of the five votes supporting his view appeared in a dissenting opinion, and votes do not typically aggregate across judgments in this way.[26] Since *Oakes* various lower federal courts and state courts have reached opposing results on similar facts. A later decision from the

Supreme Court, *Osborne v. Ohio,*[27] further complicated the issue by holding that an overbreadth challenge could be mooted by a postenactment judicial narrowing, rather than legislative narrowing, of the challenged statute. Given this inconsistency across courts and arguable variation over time, it would be foolish for any judge to adopt Justice Scalia's forward-looking account of overbreadth in the hope that coordinated judicial action will discipline legislative behavior in speech-sensitive areas.

Precedent over time. What theory of precedent should judges adopt in deciding constitutional cases? (I offer further remarks on this issue in Chapters 7 and 8.) Accounts of precedent typically assume that all judges, including future judges, will coordinate on the same approach. The theoretical problems facing any particular judge who adopts any given approach will, however, change dramatically when other judges adopt different approaches.

Consider a sequence like the following. At time 1 a particular account of precedent prevails in the legal system. This account might hold, for example, that a precedent decided at time 1 may be overruled by a court sitting at time 2 only if there is some special justification for overruling it. At time 1 the jurisdiction's highest court issues a precedent decision. Under the prevailing account of precedent, it is not permissible for the time 2 court to overrule the earlier decision just because its members think that decision erroneous. When time 2 is reached, however, the judges then sitting happen to hold a different account of precedent. Under this account, judges may overrule any earlier decision that is mistaken in their current view. So the time 2 court overrules the earlier decision and substitutes a precedent decision that is the opposite of the earlier one.

Now imagine a judge sitting at time 3. This judge subscribes to the account of precedent that prevailed at time 1—that is, precedents may not be overruled unless there is special justification for so doing; it is not enough that the earlier precedent be erroneous. On this view, to which precedent does the time 3 judge owe allegiance—the decision issued at time 1 or the overruling decision issued at time 2? From the standpoint of the time 3 judge, the overruling decision was erroneous; it invoked a mistaken theory of precedent, and under the correct theory the time 1 decision would still be the law. The very theory of precedent that brands the time 2 overruling as mistaken, however, also bars the time 3 judge from voting to overrule the time 2 decision just because it was erroneous.

The theory held by the time 3 judge can be interpreted in procedural or substantive terms, and these interpretations now have sharply different implications.

This story is not fanciful; similar accounts are ubiquitous in constitutional law. Consider two narratives commonly encountered in originalist legal discourse:

- Before 1937 the Supreme Court issued restrictive decisions about the scope of national legislative power, the delegation of legislative power to agencies, and social and economic regulation. After 1937 these decisions were overruled, in some cases on the simple ground that then-sitting justices thought them mistaken. Should the current Court adhere to the overruling decisions, even though they were methodologically flawed, or reinstate the overruled decisions, even though to do so would require the current Court to adopt the same aggressive approach to overruling precedent that the post-1937 decisions adopted?
- The Warren and Burger Courts overruled a great many criminal-procedure precedents, expanding criminal defendants' constitutional rights in many settings. Moreover, the Court made some of its rulings prospective, in part to weaken the constraints of precedent (because prospectivity reduces the cost of overruling precedents). Should the current Court respect the Warren and Burger Court precedents, or should those decisions be treated in the same cavalier fashion as the older decisions they overruled?

The point here is not to assert that either of these accounts is historically accurate; it is merely to use them to illustrate the quandary that the time 3 judge faces. What should the time 3 judge do? There is no answer internal to the theory of precedent that the time 3 judge holds, because the theory is at odds with itself: its procedural instruction is to uphold the time 2 decision, while its substantive counsel is that the time 1 decision should be reinstated as the law that would obtain had the correct account of precedent been followed. The time 3 judge must choose between these two possibilities on other grounds entirely.

Some will counsel the time 3 judge to do as he would have others do, adhering to the procedural counsel of his theory. Others will counsel the time 3 judge to engage in a form of retaliatory activism: the judge should vote to overrule the Time 2 decision, even in violation of his theory's procedural counsel, in order to restore the law to the state that would obtain if the theory had been followed by all prior judges.[28] Proponents of the latter course will claim that failure to engage in retaliatory activism will, over time, produce a sort of ratchet effect: "conservative" courts, here defined as courts that afford great weight to precedent, will respect the decisions of "liberal" courts, here defined as courts that afford little weight to precedent. But liberal courts will not respect the decisions of conservative courts. Over time, legal change will systematically tend to come from liberal courts. If those courts also tend to be liberal in the political sense, the ratchet will also have a political valence over time.

These dilemmas arise because theories of precedent vary among judges and over time. Theories of precedent typically recommend that any particular judge adopt the theorist's approach because that approach would be best if adopted by all judges. But many other judges will adopt different approaches; when they do, accounts of precedential decisionmaking that implicitly require or assume generalization will go badly awry. Theories of precedent vary across judges and over time for the same reason that different judges prefer different canons of statutory interpretation and different approaches to constitutional interpretation: theories of precedent inevitably have controversial normative and distributive implications. To praise "conservative" judging as "restrained" because it respects past precedent is to build in a presumption in favor of existing distributions of legal rights, economic and property entitlements, and social conditions. To condemn conservative judging, so defined, is to build in systemic pressure for legal change. Over time, different judges with different preferences about the pace of legal change and about the substantive valence of change in different periods will adopt varying approaches to precedent. Any account of precedent that implicitly requires that account to generalize across courts and over time is, on this view, so unlikely as to be no account at all.

A Note on Positive Models

So far the examples, both statutory and constitutional, have involved normative arguments for particular interpretive canons. A second class of examples involves positive models of the dynamics of legislation. Consider the ingenious models advanced by sophisticated intentionalists ("conventionalists" might be more accurate) to rebut textualist claims about legislative history. In these models intentionalist statutory interpretation produces a self-fulfilling equilibrium: courts consider legislative history as accurate, and rational legislators anticipating the practice monitor legislative history to ensure that it does indeed accurately reflect the deal struck by the enacting coalition. Textualism might also produce a self-fulfilling equilibrium, albeit with the players coordinated on text rather than history. But if disagreement, mistakes, and noncompliance, voting cycles, or legal and political change cause different judges or courts to do different things with legislative history at different times, then no equilibrium model that implicitly depicts the judiciary as a unitary actor is very impressive; a more refined approach is necessary. The same point holds against the whole class of rational models that portray constitutional and statutory interpretation as the product of a unitary judiciary or simply an abstract "court."

To be sure, ever-more-sophisticated rational choice models might be constructed to account for the mutability and inconsistency of judicial interpretation. Perhaps, in a more complicated model, legislators might assess the probability that judges will use various interpretive strategies, resulting in an expected-value calculus that will tell legislators to decide how much to invest in creating text, legislative history, or other interpretive sources. In the limiting case we might adopt the assumption of complete divisibility, under which something like a 1 percent change in judicial behavior would produce a 1 percent change in legislative behavior; developing this sort of model in plausible ways would be an advance on the current suite of approaches. Yet this sort of approach puts even more strain than usual on our credulity about legislators' rationality, information, and computational abilities. Far more plausible, as we have seen, is to assume that legislative reactions are somehow lumpy, such that changing proportions of textualist or intentionalist decisions among the judiciary might produce no effect on enacting coalitions until some threshold is crossed. Whatever the merits of alternative modeling strategies, however, the key point is to advance beyond the typical approach that treats courts as unitary or internally homogeneous. Recognizing the division problems that result from the collective character of judicial institutions requires important modifications of the standard positive models of interpretive dynamics.

The Distributive Effects of Interpretive Method

With respect to both the normative and positive examples given earlier, the most general point is that the choice of interpretive method has controversial substantive and distributive consequences. Interpretation is not a pure exercise in coordination across judges and courts; interpretive method also determines or helps determine whose preferences the legal system satisfies, and to what degree. To be sure, many interpretive doctrines and canons do have a coordination component. The best outcome, from the systemic point of view, might be that all judges should adhere either to a rule of lenity or to a rule of severity, rather than mucking about inconsistently. But choosing canons or choosing between textualism or legislative history is not like choosing whether to drive on the left side of the road or the right. It is a mixed game of coordination and distribution in which judges desire to coordinate, but some judges would prefer that all coordinate on one particular rule, while other judges would prefer that all coordinate on a different rule.[29]

I take this to represent the chronic condition of judicial interpretation. Thus sophisticated intentionalists argue that a self-fulfilling equilibrium centered on legislative history is superior to an equilibrium centered on text, on the ground that the former better suits the organizational constraints under which legislatures act.[30] Likewise, an important criticism of the Rehnquist Court's frequent recourse to clear statement rules is that the Court's preferred rules, rather than being neutral coordinating regimes that merely allow legislators to signal their choices, inevitably have controversial normative and distributive implications. The Court's presumptive canons favor federalism, property rights, and other values, but the opposite presumptions would equally favor the opposite values, so normative argument and substantive conflict over the content of the interpretive regime are unavoidable. Finally, the rule of lenity will produce fewer convictions than would a rule that criminal statutes should be broadly construed ("the rule of severity"), and different judges will have different extrinsic reasons for preferring one outcome to the other. There need be nothing cynical about these observations; judges' preferences in these domains may flow from sincerely held jurisprudential commitments. The point, however, is that different judges have different commitments, in which case the distributive effects of interpretive rules will matter to them. In all of these areas the distributive consequences of alternative canons and interpretive tools are precisely what create the persistent disagreement, inevitable noncompliance, and political shifts that in turn prevent judges and courts from attaining the coordination benefits of uniform interpretive rules.

What Is to Be Done?

We may sum up the division problem as follows. In the examples given earlier, the division fallacy seduces theorists of judicial interpretation into errors of inadmissible generalization. The implicit premise of such theorizing—any approach that would be desirable if adopted by all judges should therefore be adopted by any particular judge—treats judicial institutions as unitary rather than riven by chronic disagreement, noncompliance with agreed-upon rules, and political conflict. Disagreement and conflict might be called the circumstances of judicial politics;[31] they arise from changing economic and social conditions and from the distributive effects of competing approaches to interpretation. Recognizing the division fallacy undermines a range of positions, doctrines, and arguments, including the claim that textualism may have a disciplining effect on legislatures, the idea that canonical regimes can serve as democracy-forcing default rules, and the Rehnquist Court's flirtation with due process of lawmaking.

If all this is right, what is a judge to do? I provide a positive answer in Part III. Here my point is strictly negative, an attempt to clear away some intellectual underbrush. Interpretive rules cannot be justified on democracy-forcing grounds that require ideal conditions for judicial coordination, conditions that cannot be attained by the decidedly nonideal structure of judicial institutions. To reiterate, that negative conclusion leaves other types of arguments untouched. So long as the relevant theory does not require or assume a critical mass or threshold of judicial coordination—so long as individual judges may make a strictly divisible or marginal contribution to the aims specified by the theory—then the infeasibility of sustained judicial coordination poses no problem. Strictly marginal or divisible grounds may be available for the conclusions whose democracy-forcing justifications have been erased. Thus textualists who must abandon the ex ante, democracy-forcing justification for textualism may fall back upon other justifications for the primacy of constitutional or statutory text; and intentionalists who must abandon the picture of legislative history as a self-fulfilling interpretive regime may turn to other arguments for legislative history.

Eliminating arguments nonetheless represents progress. The last chapter, focusing on judicial capacities, suggested that judicial use of legislative history to discover legislative intentions and purposes represents an excessively ambitious undertaking that may increase rather than reduce judicial error, even from an intentionalist standpoint. This chapter, focusing on system effects, has suggested that judges should eschew ambitious democracy-forcing arguments. The common theme is a sort of modesty, an argument for reducing judges' aspirations and ambitions in light of institutional concerns. This is vague; I mean here only to point down the road that Part III will travel.

First-Best, Second-Best, and Judicial Coordination

Most important, the discussion of system effects and judicial coordination in this chapter is intended to reemphasize the central themes of Chapter 3. There we distinguished two styles of interpretive theory, first-best and second-best. First-best theory is concerned with the ultimate normative aims of legal interpretation: the ideal interpreter should attempt to read constitutional and statutory provisions in ways that make the best sense of law's implicit principles, that accord with the best current theories in linguistics and semantics, that comport with the deep structural logic of the Constitution's separation of powers, or that promote social justice, suitably understood. Second-best interpretive theory is a different enterprise. It asks how nonideal interpreters of law should proceed in light of widespread disagreement about competing first-best theories and given the institutional constraints and political conditions that actually obtain in the legal system.

The point that second-best questions are inescapable is, I have suggested, especially damaging to a particular class of democracy-forcing arguments. Recognition of the collective structure of constitutional and statutory interpretation by judges and the resulting possibility of disagreement, incoherence, and instability in the theory and practice of judicial interpretation pushes strongly in the direction of second-best interpretive theory. The point is not, on this view, that first-best interpretive theory is worthless or conceptually mistaken. But first-best interpretive theory can never, all by itself, support normative recommendations addressed to actual interpreters in an actual legal system (judges or others). First-best theory must always be translated through supplemental empirical premises about institutional capacities and performance, the effects of disagreement across interpreters, and the changing political forces that buffet the lawmaking system.

— III —

Applications

So far we have rejected some old questions in Part I and asked some new ones in Part II. The new institutional and empirical questions about legal interpretation are inescapable, whatever answers we end up giving. In that sense, the argument of Parts I and II stands on its own foundation. Nonetheless, the crucial question is what, in the end, should actually be done about the empirical problems of institutional interpretation. Here I indicate a method for answering that question and offer conclusions about what the best answer or set of answers turns out to be.

From an academic perspective, the solution to empirical problems concerning legal and social institutions is to wait until the cumulative effort of social scientists provides answers in the long run. The central point of Chapter 6, however, is that some decisionmakers face institutional choices in the short run. The decisionmakers I have in mind are judges. The problem that judges face is that the choice of interpretive rules is inescapable now. When interpretive problems arise, any approach the judges select will rest on empirical and institutional assumptions, such that a different approach would be indicated with a different set of assumptions. Judges thus face what I shall call the *institutionalist dilemma*, which arises because judges labor under conditions of uncertainty and bounded judicial rationality. As for uncertainty, the crucial predicates for the choice of interpretive approaches are facts about institutional capacities and systemic effects, but judges lack the necessary information and have no way of acquiring it in the short run. As for bounded rationality, even the information judges do have may overwhelm their limited capacities for accurately processing information. The dilemma, then, is this: Where choice is inescapable, but empirical uncertainty is irresolvable and information-processing capacity is limited, what are judges to do?

Chapter 6 proposes a method for answering this question: judges should, indeed must, fall back upon a known repertoire of techniques for choice under conditions of profound uncertainty and bounded rationality. These techniques include allocating burdens of proof, cost-benefit analysis, the principle of insufficient reason, maximin, satisficing, picking or nondeliberative choice, fast and frugal heuristics, and others. These tools will at least enable judges to make reasonable decisions in the face of irreducible uncertainty, although their decisions may not be rational in any strong sense of the term. Given the conditions under which judges choose interpretive rules, however, reasonableness is the most that can be demanded.

Chapters 7 and 8 apply the techniques of interpretive choice to a range of crucial problems in statutory and constitutional interpretation, respectively. Here again, the substantive conclusions I generate can be either accepted or rejected while subscribing fully to the interpretive-choice argument of Chapter 6. Whatever conclusions the techniques of interpretive choice yield, those techniques are all that judges have. My conclusions are clear, however, and they run contrary to the current academic consensus in favor of flexible, dynamic, and policy-saturated legal interpretation that draws upon a rich array of legal and nonlegal materials. The most plausible responses to the uncertain conditions of interpretive choice suggest that courts' foremost concern should be to minimize their interpretive ambitions, especially by minimizing the costs of judicial decisionmaking and of legal uncertainty. That basic concern for interpretive modesty pushes interpretive doctrine in the direction of formalism in the institutional sense—that is, toward rules rather than standards, and toward a relatively small, tractable, and cheap set of interpretive tools rather than a relatively large, complex, and expensive set. Where no clear and specific text is at hand, interpretive modesty counsels judicial deference—both deference to agency interpretations of statutes and to legislative interpretations of the Constitution.

Concretely, Chapter 7 concludes that in the statutory arena courts should eschew legislative history altogether, should pick canons of construction rather than attempting to choose the best ones, and should defer to administrative agencies unless the statutory text directly at hand is clear and specific. Chapter 8 concludes that in the constitutional arena judges should adopt a Thayerian version of judicial review that defers to legislatures unless the constitutional text directly at hand is clear and specific. Again, however, these conclusions are simply byproducts of the central project of Part III, which is to describe the background conditions of interpretive choice and to think about how courts should reason under those conditions.

— 6 —

Judges, Uncertainty, and Bounded Rationality

Empiricism: Academic and Judicial

Part II outlined an empirical research program for institutionalists. The critical variables relevant to the choice of interpretive approaches, I suggested, fall into two large categories—institutional capacities and systemic effects—and include the choice between rules and standards (in various domains), the accuracy of decisions, the cost of decisions, the character of legislative and administrative responses, and the costs of judicial coordination. This is emphatically a research program for academics; and it is a program that will not be fulfilled or even well under way in the foreseeable future. Although social scientists and empirically inclined lawyers are beginning to study the empirical determinants of interpretive approaches, the institutional turn is still in its infancy.

From the academic perspective, this is the usual state of affairs across all disciplines. Waiting for empirical social science to provide one with relevant information is, for academics, a built-in occupational hazard; in academic discussion the discovery that disagreements are empirical is often taken to end the conversation. Thus academics must frequently rest content with what we may call *the stalemate of empirical intuitions.* We shall see in Chapter 8, for example, that some theorists support a strong form of judicial review, in part because they intuit that legislators have only weak incentives to comply with constitutional constraints on first-order legislative outcomes. We shall also see that other theorists oppose judicial review, intuiting that legislators' incentives for constitutional compliance are strong. Both camps can acknowledge that the dispositive questions are empirical, and that no empirical answers are currently available; so both can accept the mutual stalemate of intuitions. (However, both camps also tend to claim that their opponents should bear the burden of proof in the face of empirical uncertainty. The latter is a supplemental principle for resolving empirical uncertainty that we will examine later in this chapter.)

Academics and judges, however, operate on different time scales. In the sufficiently long run judges will absorb academic findings about the consequences of alternative interpretive doctrines if those consequences are studied, and they will do so without any formal training in social science methodology. People who are not doctors understand that vaccination immunizes the subject from a disease, something not even the most erudite of experts understood until the turn of the last century. But judicial decisions are not made in the long run. The stalemate of empirical intuitions is tolerable for academics interested in legal interpretation only because they do not make any decisions as academics (although the occasional academic-turned-judge, such as Judge Richard Posner, may wear both hats). Stalemate is not tolerable for judges who must actually choose interpretive rules on which decisions will be based today and tomorrow and the next day rather than a generation on.

From the standpoint of the institutionalist judge, then, the hard question is what to do in the short run, given the absence of necessary information and the limited capacity of boundedly rational judges to absorb whatever information is present. Suppose that given one set of empirical findings about the institutional determinants of interpretation, one set of operational doctrines would be best; given another set of findings, however, a different set of operational doctrines would be best. Suppose also that there are no such findings in either direction. If this is so, does institutionalism reach an impasse?

The Institutionalist Dilemma:
Uncertainty and Bounded Rationality

The real problem for institutionalists, then, is not that institutionalism is pointless without a high-level value theory of interpretation; as I argued in Chapter 3, that problem is much overblown. The real problem is that interpretive-choice questions are excessively demanding in two senses.

The first problem is *uncertainty:* the assessment of institutional capacities and systemic effects, the calculus of error costs, decision costs, and the costs of coordination requires information that judges do not have and will be unable to obtain in any useful time frame, at least in the short run. The reason for this pessimism is just that the range of relevant variables is too large, the society-wide scope of the variables too complex. Consider the daunting complexity of questions such as the comparative decision costs and error costs of the five or six possible legislative-history regimes or the effects of judicial behavior on the reciprocal expectations of legislatures, courts, agencies, and litigants. Not only are the relevant interactions staggeringly complex, they are in many cases intrinsically indeterminate, so much so that no decisionmaker can plausibly assign probabilities to the possible outcomes. This means that many of the relevant problems are objectively "uncertain" in the economists' technical sense, as I shall explain in detail later.

The second problem is that of *bounded rationality*. Construed in a broad sense, this includes limits on the information-processing capacity of otherwise rational agents. Real-world decisionmakers, including judges, have limited capacity to understand and use even the information they do have. The problem of bounded information is amplified by bounded decisionmaking capacity. Bounded rationality, however, is also relevant in a more pointed sense. Judges, like other decisionmakers, are never fully rational.[1] Like other decisionmakers, they are prey to cognitive failings, including the use of heuristics that misfire in particular cases, producing cognitive biases. Consider the phenomenon of salience, discussed in Chapter 1: salience causes decisionmakers to focus on vivid foreground particulars, such as the hardships suffered by parties in particular cases, while ignoring larger background abstractions, such as the systemic effects of interpretive rules. Cognitive misfires of this sort cause judges to overweight the information they obtain from observing the facts of particular litigated cases.

In what follows I shall for brevity often refer generally to "uncertainty" to include objective uncertainty, judges' lack of information (whether or not that information is actually available), and bounded rationality. From the standpoint of the institutionalist project, it matters little whether the institutionalist dilemma arises from the objective absence of information that is properly called uncertainty or from judges' limited knowledge and limited capacity to process information. In either case the problem is that judges are unable to put values to the variables that institutional analysis identifies as relevant. Uncertainty in this broad sense, then, threatens to strangle the institutionalist project in its crib. It puts institutionalists, or at least institutionalists who want to provide useful advice for judges, in a dilemma—maintaining simultaneously that institutional and interpretive choice are unavoidable, on the one hand, and that interpretive choice outstrips judges' informational resources, on the other.

One reaction to the dilemma is to say that judges should reject altogether the institutionalist framework outlined in Part II and instead simply adopt whatever interpretive rules appeal to their normative intuitions. Thus Jon Elster discusses the analogous problem that a consequentialist approach to designing constitutions is excessively demanding. Given that the "global net long-term equilibrium effects" of constitutional design are impossibly opaque, Elster says, we ought to eschew the consequentialist framework altogether, opting instead for whatever constitutional arrangements are "just."[2] But critics rightly see this as an attempt to escape the inescapable—as an attempt to dodge one horn of the dilemma that ends up impaling us on the other. If the core claim of Part II is correct—if institutional analysis is unavoidable—then the pursuit of "justice" without regard to institutional consequences may prove self-defeating. Because of second-best effects, the direct pursuit of justice may produce worse results relative to that very theory of justice than an indirect approach would have. "[T]he non-consequentialist has no way of showing, on his own premises, that he is not seeking a paradise that will eventually turn into an inferno."[3]

A better reaction to the institutionalist dilemma, in my view, is to fall back, not on justice (or, for that matter, Eskridgean public values), but on a repertoire of techniques for decisionmaking by boundedly rational agents acting under profound uncertainty. This view holds, in general, that if institutional analysis has to be done without full information, it just has to be done with whatever information is available or can be generated at acceptable costs. Judges will then use the relevant tools for decisionmaking with incomplete information. This is not the same as casual empiricism. Of course a type of casual empiricism is probably inevitable for any decisionmaker, emphatically including judges; but empiricism neither is nor should be completely formless. The techniques described later, techniques for boundedly rational agents making decisions under conditions of uncertainty or ignorance, improve upon casual empiricism by attempting to give reasons for acting on the basis of one picture of the world rather than another.

Interpretive Choice and Case-by-Case Decisionmaking

There is an objection to this formulation of the institutionalist dilemma. On this objection, judges do not "choose doctrines"; there is no such problem as interpretive choice. What judges do is decide cases. There may be a problem with the consistency of particular judicial decisions over time. But judges never sit down at any given point to choose the interpretive precepts or doctrines they will use.

If this means that interpretive choices may themselves prove inconsistent over time, then it is true and important. One of the claims of Chapter 5 was that the problem of inconsistency over time undercuts democracy-forcing interpretation. But if the objection means that there is something interpreting judges can do other than choosing interpretive precepts, then it is conceptually incoherent. The idea that judges should take each case as it comes, interpreting sensibly in light of the materials at hand, itself constitutes an implicit choice of interpretive method and an implicit allocation of interpretive authority. It is a choice to commit interpretation to the case-specific discretion of the judges on the spot, as opposed to the discretion of judges at other times and places who might formulate general interpretive doctrine to govern the adjudicative process. That choice is a contestable one and must be defended on the merits.

Of course it is true as a matter of judicial biography that we are not to imagine judges as sitting down at some point in time to decide which approach to interpretation to "adopt." Judicial styles are the product of complex social and legal processes that unfold over the course of a career. But it is true, nonetheless, that judges make choices about interpretive regimes whenever they decide what interpretive tools to bring to bear on a particular case. The judge who thinks of himself as "deciding cases" without an interpretive approach just has a particular interpretive approach without knowing it—like M. Jourdain, who was astonished to discover that he had been speaking prose all along.

Uncertainty, Bounded Rationality, and Interpretive Choice

So far I have merely described the institutionalist dilemma. I must now show that it actually exists. If courts had full information about the relevant empirical issues and unbounded ability to process that information accurately, the empirical character of institutional choice would pose few difficulties. But neither the condition of full information nor the condition of full comprehension plausibly describes the actual setting of interpretive choice. Rather, judges must make interpretive choices in the face of impoverished information, have only limited capacity to generate the needed information by postponing interpretive choices or by conducting experiments, and have limited capacity to accurately process the information they do obtain. These conditions make interpretive choice an exercise in choice under conditions of empirical uncertainty and bounded rationality.

Perhaps the most obvious problem is the sheer objective uncertainty inherent in the complex empirical questions made relevant by the institutionalist approach. Those questions may be called "trans-scientific," meaning that although they are empirical, they are also (in many instances) unresolvable at acceptable cost within any reasonable time frame.[4] It may be that the costs of acquiring the data needed to answer the empirical questions are prohibitive or at least greater than the benefits to be gained from choosing the best interpretive doctrine. It may also be, more simply, that the needed data cannot be obtained (or at least not obtained in full) at any cost, because uncertainty is objective and irreducible.

Trans-scientific questions abound not only in the natural sciences but also, or especially, in the social sciences, where the number of variables and the difficulty of collecting data often mean that empirical questions never achieve closure, despite seemingly endless study.[5] Consider, for example, a critical empirical question, debated in the interpretation literature,[6] about the weight to be afforded to statutory precedents. In jurisdictions where the courts adopt a strong rule of statutory precedent—and assuming heroically that different judges can coordinate on such a rule, which was the problem flagged in Chapter 5—will legislatures more frequently modify or override statutory precedents through new legislation than they will in jurisdictions with a weaker rule? The question is empirical but extremely difficult to resolve. The problem is not that the question is poorly formulated in the sense that it is only a pseudo-empirical question. There is a fact of the matter about relative rates of legislative response under different regimes of precedent. The problem is to fill in the actual values of the relevant variables, and it is a daunting problem.

The best way to get at the problem would be a direct experiment. I will say more about experimentation later. It suffices to note here that no experiment in a form acceptable to the standards of social science research could possibly be conducted. Such an experiment would require that several lawmaking systems, identical except for their rules of statutory precedent, be created—an absurd prospect. The alternative to direct experimentation is to fall back upon comparative and historical empiricism. A comparative project could attempt to estimate the relative rates of legislative override in states or nations that use different rules of statutory precedent. A historical project could compare legislative performance in a given jurisdiction as precedential rules have changed over time.

Yet in all likelihood neither inquiry will prove tractable. Some empiricists are ever aglow with the faith that anything can be tested, yet in social science settings like these it routinely proves too difficult to control for the myriad of potential variables and thus too difficult to trace effects to their proper causes or even to decide what is cause and what is effect. Suppose that two otherwise similar states with different rules of statutory precedent—one strong, one weak—display different rates of override. It is possible that the causation runs from legislative activity to the precedent rule, rather than the other way around. The courts of the state with a strong rule of statutory precedent might have adopted that rule precisely because the greater activity of the state legislature, produced by completely unrelated factors, gave the courts confidence that obsolete statutory precedents would not linger forever without legislative correction. Or suppose that in a certain state the change from an absolute rule to a softer rule coincided with a diminished rate of legislative activity. No conclusion whatsoever follows, certainly not the conclusion that weakening the precedent rule enervates legislatures, for both changes might well have been independent products of some external event, such as the rise of a new political party that independently influenced the behavior both of the legislature and of the elected judiciary.

The precedent example is hypothetical, principally because so little work has been done to assess the empirical consequences of interpretive choice. But similar problems afflict even the small body of work that has been done. One of the best studies by a lawyer of the empirical effects of interpretive method is Eskridge's examination of congressional "overrides" of the Supreme Court's statutory decisions in the period from 1967 to 1990.[7] The study is wide-ranging, but for present purposes its most interesting component is Eskridge's attempt to specify whether Congress is relatively more likely to override decisions that rely primarily on statutory text, or rather decisions that rely primarily on legislative history or judicial beliefs about legislative purposes. The study examines the "primary reasoning" of Supreme Court statutory decisions overridden by Congress and finds that decisions primarily based upon the "plain meaning" of statutory text were more likely to be overridden than decisions primarily based upon legislative history, purpose and policy, and precedent.

The study poses the right questions. As we have seen, a central argument for textualism is that it has a democracy-forcing effect: judicial refusal to remake enacted text forces Congress to legislate more responsibly ex ante. Critics of textualism respond, in part, that Congress simply cannot assume the degree of responsibility that democracy-forcing arguments assign to it. Legislation will inevitably have effects unforeseeable even by the most conscientious legislators, and the need to secure political compromise ensures that legislation will often contain vague generalities or artful ambiguities. The promise of Eskridge's study is to give scholarship some purchase on the actual effects of interpretive method on legislative response—still bracketing the separate systemic objection to democracy-forcing, based on the costs of judicial coordination, that I advanced earlier.

The study's methods, however, suffer from ill-defined categories and omitted variables. First, the criteria used to determine the primary reasoning of the case are remarkably ill-defined: consider such predicates as "the placement and length of the Court's analysis," "the persuasiveness of the Court's analysis," and "the Court's own apparent confidence in its decision." There are equally slushy supplemental principles. For example, "if the Court's legislative history argument was subordinate to, but more convincing than, what appeared to be a makeweight textual argument, the study identified the primary reasoning as legislative history."[8]

Second, even if one supposes those criteria to have been consistently applied in every instance, the study fails to account for important variables and thus fails to establish its conclusions. Eskridge suggests, for example, that decisions by textualist or formalist interpreters (who focus on "the statutory language as understood by both Congress and the President at the time of enactment") are more likely to be overridden,[9] and that formalist interpretation captures the enduring or aggregate preferences of Congress over time less accurately than nonformalist approaches.[10] The dramatic charge is that formalism is "countermajoritarian."

But all this is just an extended example of the fallacy of composition: the assumption that a feature true of a subset of cases will hold true when generalized to all cases.[11] Eskridge is using data about rates of congressional override of formalist decisions in a world in which there are both formalist and nonformalist decisions and implicitly extrapolating to evaluate formalist proposals that judges ought to move to a world in which all decisions are formalist. That extrapolation need not hold, and it is exceedingly difficult to know whether it would. The nub of the democracy-forcing argument for textualism is that in a nontextualist interpretive regime congressional coalitions sometimes signal their preferences through legislative history and other sources. Those same coalitions, the argument supposes, when faced with a consistently textualist judiciary, will consistently express their preferences in statutory text rather than in legislative history or in other sources that are disfavored on a textualist approach. A consistently textualist regime might capture majoritarian preferences far more accurately than do either textualist or nontextualist techniques in the period Eskridge has studied. The textualist argument is speculative, of course, but it is just the sort of predictive argument for interpretive choice that, although empirical rather than jurisprudential, is nigh impossible to resolve through standard empirical techniques.

Eskridge's study is among the best available work about some fundamentally important empirical determinants of interpretive choice. But even that study's foundations seem infirm in critical respects, and the infirmities illustrate the structural problems that afflict empirical work on interpretation. The first problem is that questions about the empirical determinants of interpretive choice, such as rates of legislative response under different rules of precedent or the democracy-forcing effects of textualism, lie at one extreme of the spectrum of complexity. They are questions that implicate many actors and institutions (legislators, agencies, lawyers, judges), many jurisdictions, and many different types of legal sources. Another problem is that interpretation scholarship must begin its empirical work from a starting point that is very far from the goal. Only recently has interpretation scholarship taken an empirical turn, and the recent work laments the startling lack of serious empirical studies. This means that the returns from investment in empirical work on interpretation lie well into the future.

It is tempting to sidestep the problems of interpretive empiricism with the observations that some data are always better than no data, and that empiricism can supply helpful or suggestive data even if it cannot supply dispositive answers. This is correct in the long run, at least net of the costs of gathering data, but it is excessively optimistic as to the short run. The assumption here is that the gains from empiricism are continuous, so that incremental additions of empirical work produce incremental gains in the time period in which the work occurs. But there is no particular reason to think that empirical problems usually display that sort of continuity.[12] The benefit of gathering data may just as easily prove to be nil—not even helpful—until the amount of data reaches some discontinuous threshold, perhaps a very high threshold. Just as knowing only the first digit of a phone number is essentially useless, so too, if we currently know 5 percent of what we would have to know to choose between the alternative rules of statutory precedent, then we might increase our knowledge tenfold and still only know half of what we need to. Investments in empiricism are investments in long-term basic research that will pay few short-term dividends for interpretive practice.

All told, the trans-science problem considerably dilutes the promise of empiricism for the normative theory of statutory interpretation. Courts would like to choose the doctrines that best implement their interpretive aims or (in the absence of consensus about interpretive aims) choose doctrines on which judges would reach an incompletely theorized agreement. But empirical uncertainty makes interpretive instrumentalism difficult to execute; not only is critical information lacking, but, as discussed more fully later, courts can do little to generate new information. Accordingly, many of the relevant empirical questions cannot be solved in the short or medium term, and courts must choose between plausible candidate doctrines under conditions of severe empirical uncertainty.

Uncertainty, Trans-Science, and Skepticism

I have claimed that the empirical problems relevant to interpretive choice are often trans-scientific: they are empirical in principle but intractable in practice, given current information. A necessary caution is that this claim has nothing to do with any form of skepticism about knowledge. Of course it is true that decisionmakers can often proceed quite confidently on the basis of empirical hunches, based on general knowledge of the world and its causal properties. We can reject without further ado a proposal that jurors be authorized to hear the cases of close relatives, even if we do not know in any scientific or demonstrable sense that biased outcomes will result.

My claim, however, is that the empirical questions relevant to large-scale interpretive choice are not of this character; no simple problems of this sort are in the picture. The jury example I have just given is reminiscent of a crude claim we shall examine in Chapter 8: that judicial review of legislation for constitutionality is necessary because legislators cannot be allowed to judge the limits of their own power. The claim fails because strong forms of judicial review allow judges to determine the limits of their own power, and because the institutional insulation necessary to liberate judges from current politics liberates them to pursue goals other than constitutionalism, as well as depriving them of much relevant information. The institutional costs and benefits of judicial review are highly complex, as are the associated empirical questions. Overall, what makes the trans-science problem daunting for interpretive choice is that the large-scale character of the institutional variables bars decisionmakers from proceeding on the sort of confident intuitive hunches that often prove useful for quotidian decisions on a smaller scale.

Judges, Scientists, Engineers, and Experimentation

On the picture just sketched, judges are often faced with empirical and predictive questions that would (if answered) determine the choice of interpretive doctrines. But the needed information will often be absent. In such a situation one reaction is to delay the moment of choice until the needed information comes to hand or can be generated. The analogy would be to the process by which scientific controversies are resolved. The norms that govern the process of scientific research suggest that judgment should be suspended until the needed experiments have been performed and data collected.[13]

Yet this seems infeasible for judges; it is another version of academic, as opposed to judicial, empiricism. In trial litigation scientific criteria of accuracy are often subordinated to practical concerns of the legal system, such as the swift resolution of controversies or skepticism about juries' judgment. So too, social and institutional considerations will often make it impossible for courts either to suspend judgment until the facts are in or to generate needed information themselves. It follows that judges engaged in interpretive choice should be wary of scientific analogies and of calls for experimentation. A more plausible analogy would compare judges constructing a system of interpretive doctrine to engineers. The engineer often cannot experiment, unless experimentation is so broadly defined as to become equivalent simply to learning from observation and experience. The engineer would in principle like to build a full-scale prototype of the project and observe its performance under the conditions that will affect the project. Yet the size and costliness of the project will usually forbid such an effort and condemn the engineer to uncertain estimates and extrapolations.

Similar problems afflict the idea that judicial experiments with candidate doctrines of interpretation can generate the information needed for the informed exercise of interpretive choice. Two principal forms of experimentation should be distinguished. First, judges might engage in *provisional interpretive choice*. Here the idea is that the judges should choose an interpretive doctrine in a tentative fashion, with an explicit proviso that the doctrine may be revised in the future. The hope is that deciding a stream of future cases under that doctrine would provide information that will later enable the original choice to be updated, either by confirming that choice or by switching to a new doctrine. Second, judges might adopt a *decentralization* strategy. The Supreme Court, for example, might explicitly permit the circuit courts of appeals to adopt divergent interpretive doctrines in the hope that a comparison of cases arising from different circuits will illuminate the effects of candidate doctrines.[14] Nether of these approaches seems feasible, however. The collateral costs of judicial experimentation, especially the costs of legal uncertainty, will often prove prohibitive.

Provisional interpretive choice. Under provisional interpretive choice, judges might choose a doctrine and then hope that deciding a stream of future cases under that doctrine will provide them with information that will enable them to update their original choice. But updating will by no means prove a cure-all. The stream of future cases will provide information only about the doctrine chosen. The question of interpretive choice is comparative, however, and there will be no new information about the doctrine not chosen. Switching to the originally rejected doctrine in order to generate information about that alternative is possible, but highly destabilizing. Whether the information gained justifies the attendant costs in legal uncertainty will itself prove to be a contestable question with empirical components, a question on which the experiment will provide no guidance.

A related problem is that the institution that provisionally chooses the interpretive doctrine may not itself receive the updated information. The Supreme Court, for example, may choose between possible doctrines based on the justices' empirical hunches, but the lower courts will handle the bulk of the subsequent cases. If the doctrine chosen is applied by the lower courts in a (nominally) uniform fashion, the Supreme Court will probably not revisit it no matter how bad it is on other grounds, for the Court's certiorari policy rarely provides grounds for review in the absence of an express conflict between the lower courts. The uncertain transmission of information within the multitiered structure of the judicial hierarchy makes talk of updating, derived from a rational statistical model of individual decisionmaking, largely inapposite.

Decentralization. Another possible form of experimentation would be for the Supreme Court to decentralize statutory interpretation doctrine. The Court could allow the various federal courts of appeals, say, to experiment with different doctrines of interpretation; the Court would refrain from granting certiorari in order to allow the beneficial "percolation" of ideas to proceed (but only for a time, so this idea overlaps with provisional interpretive choice).

It is hardly clear that much useful information could be gained in this way. The implicit analogy between percolation and federalism is quite remote, for the judicial circuits are not independent jurisdictions; they are subject to a common legislative body and a common executive, and that will complicate the interpretation of the experiment. If two states adopt two different interpretive doctrines, empiricists can in principle isolate the policies' comparative effects (although controlling for all important variables routinely proves impossible in practice). But if the Fifth Circuit adopts a presumption in favor of extraterritoriality and the Eleventh Circuit adopts a presumption against it, Congress must react to both regimes simultaneously—or, rather, to one regime of disuniform interpretive doctrine. The experiment will not yield comparative information about congressional reaction to one (uniform) default rule or the other. If the aim of the decentralizing experiment is to supply the Supreme Court with the data necessary to choose a default rule, then that missing information is precisely what is needed.

It is not obvious that the Court could decentralize statutory interpretation doctrine even if it wanted to. The example just given is implausible. Lawmakers would be most unlikely to accept a situation in which, say, the extraterritorial application of federal statutes, and thus American relations with the affected nations, turned upon the fortuity of which internal judicial district happened to have jurisdiction. The problem might be less severe for other doctrines of solely domestic significance, but it also might not be. The costs of disuniformity and the perceived injustice and arbitrariness that accompany disuniformity would probably not be tolerated if the relevant interpretive doctrines happened to find application in civil rights cases, in cases affecting other interests of constitutional stature, in cases affecting interstate commerce, and in environmental cases—which is to say most of the statutory interpretation cases that matter in the federal system.

Neither provisional adjudication nor decentralization, then, will prove of much help. In general, the idea behind provisional adjudication and decentralization is salutary. It is to lower the stakes of interpretive choice by gathering information before choices are made and by confining the effects of the necessary experiments, either temporally or jurisdictionally. But it is itself an empirical question of interpretive choice whether the costs of instability, disuniformity, and repeated decision and reevaluation imposed by such policies are worth the information obtained. Moreover, the experimental results will not, in fact, provide the information needed to (eventually) choose uniform interpretive rules. In general, judges, like engineers, are subject to cost constraints that sharply limit their ability to generate full information before making crucial decisions under uncertainty. For judges, "experimentalism" is a misleading metaphor.

Informational Advantage and Judicial Capacities

This picture of the empirical posture of interpretive choice is bleak, but it would be misleading to make the picture uniformly bleak. Courts have relatively better information or capacity to generate and assimilate information about certain types of questions pertinent to interpretive choice than they have about other types.

The elements of interpretive choice for which the judges' informational advantage seems most pronounced are the costs of adjudication and the effects of various interpretive rules on the judges' caseloads—two critical components of decision costs. "Decision costs" is a broad rubric that might encompass the direct (out-of-pocket) costs of litigation to litigants and the judicial bureaucracy, including the costs of supplying judges with information needed to decide the case at hand and formulate doctrines to govern future cases; the opportunity costs of litigation to litigants and judges (that is, the time spent on a case that could more profitably be spent on other cases); and the costs to lower courts of implementing and applying doctrines developed at higher levels.

The hypothesis of informational advantage seems strongest with respect to direct judicial decision costs under various interpretive and substantive rules; presumably judges know how they spend their own time. But judges probably also understand the direct costs of litigation to parties, or at least the judges understand those costs better than they understand the wholly external effects of judicial decisionmaking. Most judges have practiced law, and all judges observe litigation frequently. Judges also observe the relative costs and benefits of rules and standards, but only insofar as the choice of legal form bears on their own decisionmaking. The time spent to develop a rule in the present case reduces decision costs in future cases, whereas adopting a standard now increases decision costs later. Judges at any particular level of the judicial hierarchy will probably know less about the decision costs incurred by judges at other levels than they do about their own, but will probably have a decent sense of decision costs at lower levels in the hierarchy, at least if decision costs do differ significantly between the appealed and unappealed cases. And the Supreme Court should have a decent sense of the overall caseload in the system and perhaps even some sense of the direction in which changes in judicial doctrine push the caseload.

None of these factors are perfectly known to judges by any means. The right comparison, though, is not to perfect knowledge, but to judges' understanding of other empirical components of interpretive choice that predictably lie far beyond the judges' realm of competence. The reaction of legislative coalitions and agencies to changes in interpretive doctrine, for example, is in principle a critical question for interpretive choice. But as Chapter 4 emphasized, generalist judges in many cases have neither background expertise concerning internal congressional and administrative mechanics nor the time to acquire it, engrossed as they are in the details of particular cases. So the judges will have a weak grasp of the institutional understanding and positive political analysis needed to predict or observe the reactions of other institutions to interpretive change.

Even if judges focus solely on observable legislative outputs, only a fraction of statutory changes ever come to the judges' attention. So claims about the effects of interpretive doctrine on legislative behavior and output will prove extremely difficult for individual judges to assess. Separate problems of coordination also afflict the judges at the collective level, as Chapter 5 emphasized.

A further complication is that even if the judges do possess informational advantage with respect to certain components of interpretive choice, the usefulness of the advantage is unclear. Many interpretive choices rest on a mixture of components, about some of which judges plausibly have better information than others. Whether the judges should consult legislative history, I suggested in Chapter 4, encompasses the following factors, among others: the judicial decision costs of the possible legislative-history rules; the number and gravity of errors under the candidate rules (measured against some specified end, say, the median legislator's intent); and the costs to legislators of transferring instructions from legislative history to text (or vice versa) under the candidate rules. The first factor is probably more susceptible to judicial estimation than the second, and both of those determinations are probably far easier for judges than is the third.

Most problems of interpretive choice, then, will display a mixture of two kinds of empirical variables, some subject to judicial experience and informational advantage and some largely mysterious to generalist judges. The resulting question is obvious: How exactly should judges proceed under conditions of radical uncertainty in general, and especially where the empirical components of interpretive choice on which the judges lack informational advantage are as important to the overall decision as the more tractable components? How can judges get beyond the stalemate of empirical intuitions that chronically afflicts academic work?

Interpretive Choice under Uncertainty

Here I survey a range of strategies or techniques for the choice of interpretive rules under conditions of empirical uncertainty and bounded judicial rationality. My aims are both descriptive, to catalogue some techniques invoked, almost always implicitly, in debates over interpretation, and also evaluative, to indicate which of those techniques appear particularly cogent, manageable, or fruitful in the interpretive setting. My aim is emphatically not to analyze choice under uncertainty generally or acontextually, nor to prescribe a method or methods for choice in all settings of uncertainty. As will become clear, no method for choice under uncertainty is globally best. So the following discussion should be read as qualified, throughout, by the enterprise we are pursuing, which is to identify techniques that judges and other interpreters might use to overcome the stalemate of empirical intuitions.

Allocating the burden of uncertainty. A typical lawyer's response to empirical uncertainty is to allocate the burden of overcoming uncertainty to one party or the other. Burden allocation takes many forms. A common variant is to allocate the burden of proof[15] to those advocating a change in the legal status quo: unless the existing rule is demonstrably inferior to the proposed substitute, the existing rule will prevail. In this version the allocation of the burden in essence puts into the scales the costs of transition from one legal regime to another and weighs those costs against the party proposing the transition. Consider two examples from statutory interpretation:

> *Legislative history.* One response to textualist critiques of legislative history illustrates the use of burden allocation. After noting that the choice between formalist and antiformalist approaches to legislative history turns upon a range of uncertain empirical and predictive judgments, the response argues that "in light of our long-standing traditions [that license the use of legislative history], a dramatic shift of the sort proposed by Justice Scalia [who would have the courts ignore legislative history most of the time] bears a heavy burden of justification, and he has not met that burden here."[16]
>
> *Statutory precedent.* Critics of proposals for a strong rule of statutory precedent suggest that the proposal faces a "heavy burden of demonstrating that [the] rule would stimulate the legislature to greater involvement in its constitutional responsibility for updating statutes."[17] This is in part a status quo version of the burden-allocation technique; the suggestion is that "[t]he evidence is insufficient to reject the Court's longstanding willingness to overrule its statutory precedents in compelling circumstances."[18]

Often the range, and therefore the usefulness, of the burden-allocation strategy will be limited. The idea that the proponent of legal change should bear the burden of empirical uncertainty is particularly vulnerable to this charge. The character of the status quo will often be highly contestable, and the more energy courts and commentators must invest in deciding what it is, the sillier the enterprise becomes; why not just spend that time figuring out the best rule? The limiting case of this problem occurs when none of the alternative rules is currently in place because an entirely novel issue of interpretive doctrine has come to the Court's attention. In recent memory, for example, the weight to be afforded presidential signing statements, which explain the executive's interpretation of a statute, became a significant issue only during the Reagan administration. These situations are not infrequent, and the burden-allocation strategy supplies little help in their solution.

It is sometimes possible to extend the scope of the burden-allocation strategy by analogical reasoning. The role of presidential signing statements in statutory interpretation, for example, might be determined by analogy to their prominent role in treaty interpretation.[19] But the relevance of the analogy will often be subject to theoretical and factual debate—the president's role in treaty formation, for example, differs importantly from his role in the legislative process. In that case the proper allocation of the burden will once again become as contestable as the underlying question.

A different use of burdens of proof in situations of empirical uncertainty is to allocate the risk of decisionmaker error to one side or another. The presumption of innocence in criminal law supposes that decisionmakers will sometimes err, and that the harms from an erroneous conviction are much greater than the harms of an erroneous acquittal. That example is fairly uncontroversial, but often the consequences of the alternative errors will be sufficiently unclear that the assignment of a burden will prove as controversial and time-consuming as a full examination of the underlying cases would have been.

Burdens of proof are perhaps most successful when used to generate information, as when, for example, an adjudicator can allocate burdens so as to elicit information from the party or parties who possess it.[20] In situations of interpretive choice, however, the central problem is not that the information necessary for the choice needs to be elicited from some other actor, but that the information is objectively unavailable, unobtainable at reasonable cost, or excessively complex for judges' limited capacities. In that context, burden shifting will often have the rhetorical function of saddling one view or another with the weight of irresolvable uncertainty. Since the proponent of change cannot demonstrate with certainty that the proposal will prove beneficial (it is, after all, a change), there will always be a residual uncertainty that can be used to defeat the proposal if the burden is set sufficiently high.

Expected utility maximization and cost-benefit analysis. The lawyer's burden-shifting approach is undertheorized, but other disciplines have more articulate answers to the problems of decisionmaking under uncertainty. In economics, philosophy, and elsewhere, "decision theory" is the branch of rational choice that studies decisionmaking by rational actors subject to various constraints. A brief overview of the methods of decision theory will frame the specific strategies to be discussed in subsequent sections and help illuminate the conditions under which those strategies aid the project of interpretive choice.

In its normative dimension, decision theory suggests that rational decisionmakers should maximize expected utility. How can this be done under conditions of incomplete information? A few distinctions help. On the standard account, "risk," "uncertainty," and "ignorance" have precise meanings.[21] Decisions under risk refer to decisions in which the decisionmaker knows both the payoffs of various outcomes and the probabilities attached to those outcomes. In such cases the decisionmaker can straightforwardly maximize expected utility by weighting outcomes according to their probabilities. For simplicity, though with some inaccuracy, I shall use the term "cost-benefit analysis" for this enterprise of maximizing expected utility. Uncertainty, by contrast, denotes the class of situations in which the decisionmaker knows the payoffs associated with various outcomes but not the probabilities that the possible outcomes will come to pass.[22] Under ignorance, not even payoffs are known.

Decisions under uncertainty can be reduced to decisions under risk and thus made tractable by assigning probabilities to outcomes. Probabilities may be assigned in two ways: frequentism and Bayesian subjectivism.[23] Under the first method, probabilities are derived from the frequency with which the various possible outcomes have occurred in similar choice situations in the past. Where the relevant decision is one in a repetitive series of similar decisions, the decisionmaker may have, or be able to acquire, information about the objective frequency of the occurrence of possible outcomes across the whole series.

The second method for assigning probabilities to outcomes is subjectivist. Under this approach, decisionmakers assign subjective probabilities to possible outcomes through a poorly understood process of judgment and intuitive hunch. In the fog of war, a general attempting to decide whether to commit his reserves has no choice but to assign subjective probabilities to the possible consequences, or so the most dogmatic Bayesians claim. Indeed, the most extreme version of the Bayesian view is that uncertainty does not exist.[24] Probabilities can always be assigned somehow or other, so all decisions can be described either as decisions under certainty or under risk.

In many cases, however, neither frequentist nor subjective methods of reducing uncertainty to risk are wholly rational. Many decisions are not plausibly described as one of a long series of similar decisions from which frequencies can be derived, because unusual or even unique features of the decision will dominate the features it has in common with past situations of choice. The decisions facing Napoleon at Waterloo could not have been aided by frequentism, for they were not the same decisions he faced at Austerlitz or Jena. Moreover, even where the decision situation is repetitive, the particular decisionmaker may participate in only one or a few such decisions. Jurors, for example, may sit on only one of many similar cases.

Subjectivism often fares no better.[25] Two problems are particularly serious. First, there is some experimental evidence that subjective probability assignments turn on the procedure by which the assignments are elicited.[26] If so, those assignments are an artifact of the framing and presentation of the choice situation, rather than anything that relates to the world external to the decisionmaker. Second, and more generally, decisionmakers will sometimes simply lack the background information or sources of judgment necessary to form a probability estimate that has any epistemic credentials. In many difficult situations there is little reason for confidence that subjective probability assignments have any grounding in fact. Often the only reasonable answer to a question of probabilities is "Who knows?"

Bayesians deny that uncertainty exists because choosers can always attach subjective probabilities to outcomes. This is a non sequitur, however. From the fact that subjective probabilities can always be attached to outcomes, it just does not follow that objective uncertainty does not exist; nor does it follow that the subjective probabilities have any significance.[27]

From the normative standpoint, in an important range of cases subjective probabilities have no epistemic credentials; they are simply meaningless. "One could certainly elicit from a political scientist the subjective probability that he attaches to the prediction that Norway in the year 3000 will be a democracy rather than a dictatorship, but would anyone even contemplate *acting* on the basis of this numerical magnitude?"[28]

In the analyses of statutory and constitutional interpretation in Chapters 7 and 8, I shall take a catholic approach to the tools of decision theory. Where probabilities can plausibly be assigned, I shall view the relevant problems through a cost-benefit lens, asking how judges might choose interpretive rules so as to maximize the expected net benefits to the interpretive system. I have emphasized, however, that in many cases the usual techniques for reducing risk to uncertainty get no traction. In such cases decision theory must turn to other tools.

The principle of insufficient reason. There is a more radical technique for reducing uncertainty to risk: the "principle of insufficient reason" (also called the principle of indifference or the equal assignment rule). Where uncertainty is real, so that decisionmakers' subjective probability assignments are not meaningful, the principle of insufficient reason instructs decisionmakers to assume that the unknown probabilities are equal and thereby transforms situations of uncertainty into situations of risk.[29] This procedure, however, assumes that the full range of possible outcomes is already given. Of course, this is sometimes not true; different descriptions of the situation will yield different partitions of possible outcomes, and in such cases the application of the principle of insufficient reason will be highly sensitive to how the decisionmaker does the partitioning.[30] Yet this is a slightly technical objection, in the pejorative sense. Sometimes outcomes do come prepartitioned by the nature of the problem or by established conventions. In any event some version of insufficient reason seems an inevitable tool of decisionmaking under severe uncertainty.[31] The decisionmaker simply assumes that variables of unknowable importance, cutting in opposed directions, have equal values and thus systematically cancel out.

Consider the following example: When judges reject a proposal to depart from the doctrinal status quo on the ground that the proposal is "speculative," we may view the argument through the lens of insufficient reason. On this construal, opponents of the proposal reason that the costs of transition from the status quo to the proposed alternative are clearly positive. Since the comparison of other costs and benefits between the two alternatives is speculative, they are assumed to wash out to a tie, and the transition cost breaks the tie in favor of the status quo. This calculus implicitly assigns equal values to the other components of the total expected costs of the status quo and the proposed alternative. The same reasoning can be applied to other sorts of costs. Consider the following argument against a strong rule of statutory precedent: While the other consequences of the rule are speculative, perhaps indeterminate, one certain and substantial consequence will be that bad precedents remain on the books. All else equal, then, the proposal should be rejected.

Perhaps deciding this way is nonrational or even irrational. The values of the other variables are unknown in the alternative regimes, but that does not mean that they are equal. Rather, the unknown costs of one regime may well dwarf the unknown costs of the other. The principle of insufficient reason might be akin to trying to pick the larger of two numbers by choosing the one with the larger digit in the second decimal place, even if one knows nothing about the digit in the first decimal place.[32]

But the principle of insufficient reason retains a nagging force and cannot be too easily dismissed. If the decisionmaker knows that one component of cost is higher in one regime than in the other, but has little other information, on what other basis could the decision be made? The possible effects of various courses of action and the probabilities that particular effects (rather than other possible ones) will indeed come to pass often lie well beyond the limits of human calculation, either because the decisionmakers' cognitive capacities are limited, because it is too expensive and time-consuming to obtain the needed information, or simply because the needed information cannot currently be obtained with any amount of effort. Yet in such situations decisionmakers do not retreat into paralysis. Rather, they eliminate imponderables from both sides of the scales and focus instead on the variables that can be grasped. Jon Elster puts the point this way:

In many, indeed most, decision problems there are associated with each of the options a number of unknown and essentially unknowable possibilities whose materialization depends on the future development of the universe. When trying to make up one's mind, one has to assume that those and other unknowable factors on each side cancel out, so that one can concentrate on the knowable ones. Even among the latter, one has to focus mainly on the known ones, because of the direct costs and opportunity costs of collecting and processing information. The ensuing decision, although not ideally rational from the point of view of an omniscient observer, will at least be as rational as can be expected.[33]

The principle of insufficient reason seems most plausible under two conditions. First, the decisionmaker ought to have a pronounced informational advantage with respect to the consideration that is given dispositive weight, as compared with the considerations pronounced imponderable and therefore dropped from the decision. Otherwise there is no reason to think that a decision made on the basis of that consideration will prove more successful than one made on some other, equally speculative basis. Second, the decisionmaker should be able to discern that the consideration given dispositive weight is, in some rough sense, of the same order of importance as the discarded imponderables. If the dispositive consideration can be seen to be of trivial weight when compared with other possible consequences of the choice, the decision will display the irrationality of picking the larger of two numbers by focusing on the second decimal. It would, for example, be strange to propose the exclusion of legislative history on the ground that exclusion will at least (all else equal) save the federal judiciary the costs of buying copies of the United States Code Congressional and Administrative News. The greatest possible benefit attainable from that consideration seems predictably trivial in relation to the overall costs and benefits of legislative history.

The maximin criterion. The principle of insufficient reason is a last-ditch attempt to reduce uncertainty to risk by assigning equal probabilities to possible outcomes. But even if this attempt fails, and uncertainty genuinely cannot be reduced to risk, decision theory is not yet exhausted. Sometimes a choice may be dismissed because it will produce worse outcomes than the other possible choice(s) under any state of affairs. Conversely, the "dominance" or "sure-thing" principle holds that some choices dominate others even in the absence of probability information because the dominant choice produces better outcomes than the outcomes of the alternative(s) under some or all states of affairs and never produces a worse outcome.

Often enough, however, these happy contingencies fail to hold, and there is no sure-fire or dominant choice among the set of possible choices. In hard cases of this sort, decisionmakers can adopt several possible criteria for choice under uncertainty. The most prominent, though by no means the only, criterion is "maximin": choose the option whose worst possible outcome is better than the worst possible outcomes of the alternatives (that is, maximize the minimum payoff).[34] In Chapters 7 and 8 I shall draw upon maximin where cost-benefit analysis, even as supplemented by the principle of insufficient reason, runs out of useful insights because the decision problems seem genuinely to be problems of uncertainty rather than risk.[35]

We must also touch upon a more pessimistic possibility. For many decision problems implicated by the choice of interpretive rules, it is not even clear that decisionmakers know the payoffs of the various outcomes, let alone the probabilities that the outcomes will occur. In such cases the uncertainty that afflicts interpretive choice is even more daunting than uncertainty in decision theory's technical sense; it is in fact a deep form of ignorance.

The theory of decisionmaking may still provide indirect guidance, but decisionmakers facing cases of this sort can aspire to nothing more than a rough sort of reasonableness. Decision theory describes strategies or approaches that decisionmakers can draw upon even if the formal conditions that describe those strategies are not satisfied, for decision-theoretic criteria will often have informal, pragmatic analogues. The maximin strategy, for example, is well defined only if the payoffs of various outcomes are specified. Even if this is not true—perhaps especially then—the more general idea that decisionmakers should minimize the downside, attempting to stave off disaster, is coherent.[36] Other strategies also have analogues in practical reason, as I shall suggest later. In short, where this sort of profound ignorance is at issue, decisionmakers may not be able to make decisions that are fully rational in any strong sense, but they may at least aspire to make decisions that are reasonable.

Satisficing. So far we have been examining strategies by which rational or boundedly rational decisionmakers attempt to maximize some value in the face of either risk or uncertainty. A nonmaximizing response to uncertainty or bounded rationality is *satisficing*, in which a decisionmaker searches among options or choices until, but only until, one is found that meets some preset aspiration level—until, but only until, the choice is "good enough."

The conceptual issues here are complex. In the simplest versions of the standard model of rational choice, the feasible set of actions or options is just given. Here the idea of satisficing is incoherent. How could it be rational, in a static context, to choose anything other than the best available action—to do anything other than maximizing? Some philosophers suggest that it can be rational to choose less than the best so long as the action chosen is satisfactory.[37] But if the action chosen is less than the best and also satisfactory, than the best action is also satisfactory, and satisficing gives no reason to choose the former over the latter.[38] In static contexts the superiority of maximizing to satisficing is conceptually entailed by the scale of value the decisionmaker uses.

Satisficing comes into its own, however, when decisionmaking is viewed more dynamically.[39] In many real-world decisions the set of options is itself (at least partially) the product of earlier decisions. One of the most important questions decisionmakers face is the extent of rational search: how many options and how much information should be sought out and considered before an ultimate choice is made? Here satisficing is coherent; as Herbert Simon emphasized, satisficing is a constraint on further search for new information and new options.[40] The satisficer searches only until a choice is found whose outcomes, or expected outcomes, are good enough.

Here is an example of the utility of satisficing for highly uncertain questions of interpretive choice. Should judges review statutes for constitutionality? (I examine this critical issue at length in Chapter 8.) An important defense of judicial review turns on the following implicit appeal to satisficing: "Judicial review might be the best system for our society, but our acceptance of it outruns our belief that it is theoretically best . . . One reason is that it works well enough, and it would be too costly and risky to reopen the question whether, abstractly considered, it is the best possible arrangement."[41] Here "well enough" means that the institution of judicial review meets some implicit aspiration level, defined in absolute rather than relative terms.[42]

The idea of satisficing, however, is open to serious conceptual and methodological objections. One standard claim is that it is necessarily irrational deliberately to settle for less than the best choice within the set of available choices.[43] Where satisficing seems to occur, it is just that the decisionmaker has implicitly calculated that the costs of acquiring further information outweigh the benefits—and that is itself a fully optimizing or maximizing decision, one that itself takes the costs of decisionmaking into account.[44] Most important, the source of the satisficer's aspiration level is mysterious, and its location arbitrary; why is it set in one place rather than another?

Neither objection is fatal, however. As to the conceptual problems, satisficing is clearly not a maximizing strategy with respect to particular local decisions. To be sure, satisficing may itself be a globally maximizing strategy in a higher-order sense: the satisficer will, over a series of decisions, end up better off than a decisionmaker who is insensitive to the direct costs and opportunity costs of search and decisionmaking. Yet satisficing is not just a weird term for maximizing-under-constraints. The satisficer and the constrained maximizer, who does account for decision costs, still employ different *stopping rules,* or rules for constraining further search among possible options. The constrained maximizer stops searching when the marginal benefit of finding a better option, discounted by the probability of finding such an option, is equal to or less than the cost of further search. The satisficer stops searching when she finds an option that is good enough. Although the two strategies sometimes yield similar choices, sometimes they do not,[45] and even if they were extensionally equivalent, the two strategies would still embody different rules for choosing.[46] Note here also that the constrained maximizer's stopping rule requires subjective probability assignments and thus gets no purchase in situations of genuine uncertainty.

As to the problem of aspiration levels, the satisficer's aspirations need not be exogenously fixed once and for all; they can be endogenously formed as decisionmakers acquire experience with the relevant settings. In many domains experience will suggest that the band within which an aspiration level might plausibly be set will be quite narrow. Although such practical considerations are not conceptually satisfying, it is not clear that satisficing rules themselves have or need have any aspiration to be conceptually satisfying. So long as they fulfill their primary mission of truncating the costs of search and decisionmaking at a point that is beneficial when repeated over a series of decisions, they are good enough.

Beyond these theoretical points, satisficing has strong practical warrant. It captures an important practical truth about how boundedly rational people make decisions under conditions of uncertainty or ignorance. I shall suggest in Chapters 7 and 8 that interpreting judges might well satisfice at rather low levels of aspiration. Judges, that is, should adopt restrictive limits on permissible search through the sources of interpretive information and should adopt interpretive precepts that are good enough, in some modest sense, rather than attempting to produce the very best interpretive regime.

Picking. Part of the impetus toward satisficing is that maximizing can acquire a self-defeating or pathological character, particularly in the presence of extremely high decision costs. Imagine a maximizer, irrationally insensitive to the opportunity costs of decisionmaking, who spends a whole day choosing the very best cereal in the supermarket. Closely related to satisficing is the idea that in such situations the decisionmaker should simply pick a course of action rather than choosing one.[47] Shoppers faced with a selection between different brands of similar goods will often simply pick one rather than investing a great deal of time and energy examining the goods' particular features. The investment necessary to fully informed choice would dwarf any possible gains from picking the slightly superior brand.

This is a low-stakes situation, but decisionmakers also pick when high stakes are involved, especially if there is no reason to think that even a great deal of further information-gathering and deliberation will make the problem significantly more tractable. A traveler lost at a crossroads might pick one path or the other, even if the decision is very important, simply because no amount of deliberation will reveal which path is the right one. Picking might take the form of random selection (flipping a coin) or perhaps the deliberate use of an irrelevant characteristic (perhaps the shopper always chooses the toothpaste in the blue tube).

Overt picking is rare in law generally and in the formulation of interpretive doctrine in particular. Judges do not often say that they are simply picking between candidate doctrines, perhaps because the ordinary rhetoric of opinion writing often tries to suggest that every judicial decision is fully reasoned in a way that picking cannot be. Justice Scalia, however, has said about the canons of construction that "what is of paramount importance is that Congress be able to legislate against a background of clear interpretive rules,"[48] which suggests that any clearly established canonical default rule is better than judicial vacillation between the possible rules. And picking is closely related to the justifications for precedent,

such as Holmes's claim that "one of the first things for a court to re-
member is that people care more to know that the rules of the game will
be stuck to, than to have the best possible rules."[49] The connection is that
both picking and precedent attempt to conserve on the costs of deciding
(for picking) and redeciding (for precedent) when there is little reason
to think that the uncertain gains of making the very best decision will be
worth the actual costs of the process itself. So picking is not alien to
interpretive choice, although the political constraints on judicial resort to
picking, especially resort to random selection, are likely to be formidable
in many cases.

Fast and frugal heuristics. Finally, recent experimental work has identified
a set of tools for boundedly rational decisionmakers that draw upon satisficing, picking and other strategies: so-called fast and frugal heuristics.[50]
An important example for our purposes is the "take the best" heuristic,
under which decisionmakers employ a deliberately simplistic stopping
rule to constrain their own search for, and consideration of, information
present in the environment. Under the "take the best" rule, the decisionmaker uses a single reason—the single most valid cue or predictor of
some trait the decisionmaker values—and ignores other, less valid cues,
predictors, or reasons. A female guppy attempting to identify the more
fit of two male suitors will choose the more orange of the two; only if
the two are about equally orange will she look to other considerations.[51]

"Take the best" is obviously frugal and fast. It is also surprisingly accurate. Cognitively constrained decisionmakers who employ "take the
best" will reach more accurate decisions, where the single best cue often
points in the right direction, than they would using more complex and
information-intensive decision rules.[52] Part of the reason is that more
complex decision rules demand too much of decisionmakers whose ability
to process information is limited. Fast and frugal heuristics, by contrast,
can be "ecologically rational"—well adapted to aiding boundedly rational
decisionmakers as they navigate particular informational environments.
This is not always so, of course; where the price for using simple decision
rules is very high, fast and frugal heuristics fare poorly. Yet it is clearly
wrong to assume that boundedly rational decisionmakers always do better
by considering more information than frugal heuristics provide. Instead,
they often do worse.

In sum, it is not the case that more information is always better than less, and it is not the case that searching for more information is always better than stopping short. In Chapters 7 and 8 I apply these claims to the question of how far afield boundedly rational judges should search for interpretive information. I suggest that judges, starting from a wide range of interpretive value theories, should converge on a simple interpretive strategy akin to "take the best." Judges, that is, should stop the interpretive search with the meaning apparent on the surface of clear and specific statutory and constitutional texts, where there is such a meaning. This view excludes any interpretive search-procedure that instructs judges to search beyond clear and specific texts with a view to impeaching the texts' apparent meaning by reference to sources such as legislative history and background principles of law.

Two Objections

We must consider two obvious objections, even at this preliminary stage. The first is that boundedly informed or boundedly rational judges will be no more competent in choosing second-order methods for reasoning under profound uncertainty than they are at the first-order reasoning itself. There is an air of paradox about the idea that judges should evaluate and use a repertoire of tools for reasoning under uncertainty. If the judges can assess the consequences to which this reasoning appeals, why can they not assess the consequences of interpretive decisions as well? But there is no real paradox here. The view I am suggesting simply holds that even boundedly rational judges can understand what it is they do not understand, can know the limits of their own knowledge, and can reason in light of those limits. Such second-order decisionmaking is common, perhaps inevitable, in law and elsewhere.[53]

A second objection is that the techniques of interpretive choice are only weakly determinate. As the examples have illustrated, and as Chapters 7 and 8 will further suggest, standard techniques of interpretive choice can appear on both sides of operational-level questions, and there is no general, higher-order procedure for choosing which approach should prevail. This objection is indisputable, but not very significant. It restates what is just the chronic condition of reasoning under severe uncertainty or ignorance. Where formal rationality runs out, a range of choice-procedures and choices are typically reasonable.

The dilemma of interpretive choice is precisely that it is both uncertain and inescapable. So the indeterminacy point is fatally noncomparative, because there just is no other type or mode of reasoning on offer in such situations. Concretely, the choices are that judges use some repertoire of weakly reasonable techniques, on the one hand, or nothing at all, on the other. It is quite possible, of course, that the techniques of interpretive choice discussed here are the wrong ones or at least not a complete list, and that considering a different set would yield more determinate and perhaps less formalist prescriptions. The issue cannot be settled abstractly; we must examine the consequences of various reasonable choice-procedures. The next chapter does so.

— 7 —

Statutory Interpretation

We turn now to more extended examples and concrete suggestions. In this chapter I attempt to move beyond the stalemate of empirical intuitions that so often arises in academic discussion of interpretive theory. I do so by applying the tools of interpretive choice developed in Chapter 6 to some crucial problems of statutory interpretation. My conclusions, in brief, are these. When the statutory text directly at hand is clear and specific, judges should stick close to its surface or apparent meaning, eschewing the use of other tools to enrich their sense of meaning, intentions, or purposes. When the statutory text at hand is ambiguous or vague, judges should defer to the interpretations of administrative agencies or executive agents rather than attempting to fill in gaps or ambiguities by reference to other sources. In either type of case the tools that should be excluded from the judicial kit-bag include legislative history, many of the canons of construction, and holistic textual comparison, which supplements or overrides the provisions at hand by reference to other provisions of the same or other statutes. Finally, judges should apply a strong doctrine of statutory precedent, subject, however, to defeasance by later administrative interpretations. I shall arrange the relevant questions and claims as follows:

- Recall the *Holy Trinity* problem from Chapter 4. When there is clear and specific statutory text in the picture, should judges consult legislative history to confirm or disconfirm the apparent meaning or to ascertain legislative intentions or purposes? On cost-benefit, maximin, and satisficing grounds, I shall suggest that the answer is no. Legislative history imposes certain costs for conjectural benefits, and clear statutory text will do well enough, enough of the time, at capturing legislative intentions or purposes. Judges should stick to the surface meaning of such texts, not attempting to tailor them to underlying policies or purposes.

- For similar reasons, moreover, judges should not supplement or impeach the clear and specific meaning of provisions immediately at hand by invoking other traditional tools of construction, such as canonical default rules or holistic comparison with other provisions and statutes.

- Even where there is no clear and specific text at hand, the tools of interpretive choice suggest that judges should not draw upon legislative history, related statutes, or canons of construction to fill gaps or resolve ambiguities. Instead, judges should apply a strong version of the so-called *Chevron* rule of deference to administrative agencies and executive agents. Understood in institutional terms, *Chevron* should apply whenever there is a statutory gap or ambiguity, regardless of what process the agency uses to develop its interpretation of the statute. *Chevron* should apply to criminal statutes as well as civil ones. Most generally, my suggestion is that judges announce a *second-order default rule* that agencies rather than judges will be allowed to choose the interpretive default rules, such as the canons of construction, unless statutes clearly say otherwise.

- Judges should accord very strong weight to statutory precedent, subject only to the proviso that new administrative interpretations of statutes should trump previous judicial interpretations, unless clear and specific text says otherwise.

A Note on Statutory Rules of Statutory Interpretation

In what follows I bracket the possibility that the rules and decision-procedures governing judicial interpretation of statutes might be legislated, rather than developed by judges themselves.[1] Past history shows that it is most unlikely that Congress will enact rules of interpretation that will generally resolve the disputed issues of interpretive choice.[2] For good reason, the literature on statutory interpretation, both past and present, focuses on the question of what interpretive rules judges should use absent legislative intervention; that is my focus here as well. The project is just to ask what interpretive decision-procedures judges should adopt, treating the institutions of the legal system as otherwise fixed. For similar reasons, in Chapter 8 I shall bracket the possibility that the approach to constitutional interpretation that I advocate should be implemented through statutory or constitutional changes to the voting rules that govern the judiciary.

Two Types of Statutory Cases: An Overview

As a first cut at the problem, we may divide statutory cases into two types. In type 1 cases there is a clear and specific text directly at hand and on point. I argued in Chapter 4 that the statutory text in *Holy Trinity* squarely dictated the government's position. The Court itself acknowledged that claim, and Dworkin and Scalia agree, with Eskridge the lone dissenter. In all cases of this sort, the key question is whether judges may or should turn to the grab-bag of other sources that the Court calls the "traditional tools of statutory construction"[3]—chiefly legislative history, other provisions or statutes in the code, and the so-called canons of construction. The traditional tools are used in this category of cases to impeach the surface meaning of the text, perhaps by tailoring the surface meaning to a more refined account of legislative intentions and purposes. On the conventional understanding, *Holy Trinity* presented just this sort of conflict between clear text and evidence of intentions or purposes suggested by the legislative history. (I claimed in Chapter 4 that the conventional understanding of the case is wrong, and that the legislative history reinforced rather than contradicted, the plain meaning; but I put that point aside for the present discussion.)

In type 1 cases the surface meaning of clear and specific text provides a kind of *baseline level of interpretive information*. There is a converging agreement among all the standard value theories that clear and specific statutory text provides the best information about the interpretive aims judges should, on any particular theory, be attempting to promote. This is obvious for textualist interpreters who believe that capturing ordinary textual meaning is the criterion of good interpretation, but it is just as true for intentionalist or purposive interpreters. All versions of intentionalism or purposivism acknowledge that clear (or "plain") statutory text provides the best source of information about legislative intentions or purposes.[4] Sometimes intentionalists even say, as did the Court in *Caminetti v. United States*,[5] that "the language being plain, it is the sole evidence of the ultimate legislative intent." In what follows I shall offer an institutional justification for the *Caminetti* principle.

Given the informational baseline of clear and specific text, the further question is an empirical inquiry into the marginal benefits of additional sources, such as legislative history. This, however, is the daunting sort of empirical inquiry that judges must conduct under conditions of uncertainty, even ignorance. Judges laboring under bounded information and rationality face the following set of questions: Is there anything to be gained by looking to marginal sources that go beyond the baseline level of information? What are the costs of further search? How might we decide what to do, given limited information about costs and benefits?

My general suggestion in this type of case will be that judges should stop with the clear and specific text, refusing to go beyond the baseline level. The *Caminetti* rule, which treats clear and specific text as conclusive, is an interpretive version of the fast and frugal heuristic "take the best" discussed in Chapter 6. "Take the best" looks to the single most useful informational cue or source in the environment and follows it where it has a definite value.[6] Boundedly rational judges should do likewise. The leading interpretive approaches all treat clear and specific text as the single best source of interpretive information (about meaning, intentions, or purposes). When that single best source points clearly in a particular direction, judges should stop the interpretive search instead of proceeding to see whether the text can be impeached by reference to legislative history and other nontextual sources.

In what follows I shall also put this point in cost-benefit terms (supplemented by the principle of insufficient reason), in terms of the maximin criterion, and in terms of satisficing. Here the various tools for decisionmaking under risk or uncertainty all point in the same direction. To preview the arguments: In cost-benefit terms, the marginal benefits of going beyond the baseline level of information are diminishing and highly conjectural, while the costs are certain and large, relative to any plausible value theory.[7] In maximin terms, sticking to the surface meaning of clear and specific text yields the best worst-case outcome for judicial decisionmakers. The worst worst-case outcome would be to incur all the marginal costs of departing from the interpretive baseline, searching further and further afield through the interpretive sources, yet without improving the accuracy of outcomes at all. In satisficing terms, the baseline level of information is good enough, relative to any plausible value theory.

Satisficing interpreters think that searching for information beyond the baseline level is a type of perfectionism that makes the best the enemy of the good. On any of these approaches, the core point is that to depart from the baseline of clear and specific text is to incur certain loss for speculative benefit.

Here is an analogy. In discussing Holmes's strong conception of statutory precedent, Judge Posner offers the following intuition: "If like Holmes you lacked confidence that you or anyone else had any very clear idea of what the best decision on some particular idea would be, the pragmatic posture would be one of reluctance to overrule past decisions, since the effect of overruling would be to sacrifice certainty and stability for a merely conjectural gain."[8] If we ignore the reference to Posner's brand of pragmatism, for the reasons discussed in Chapter 3, I suggest that the insight here generalizes very widely. Going beyond the baseline level will clearly incur losses in terms of decision costs and the costs of legal uncertainty, while the benefits side is unclear; so judges should rest content with the baseline level.

A parallel analysis applies in type 2 cases, where the statutory text at hand contains a linguistic gap or ambiguity. Here judges often turn to the traditional tools of construction to generate further information, but this is bad practice. Although the text at hand is of lower informational value in such cases, there is a better solution than ambitious judicial gap-filling. Judges should instead turn to administrative agency interpretations, deferring to agencies when the statutory provisions at hand contain a gap or ambiguity and the agency interpretation falls within the scope of the gap or ambiguity. I shall suggest that on a wide range of interpretive value theories, judges will plausibly do better by deferring to agency interpretations than by themselves using the traditional tools to search widely and deeply for the best interpretation. Finally, in both types of cases the considerations developed here point to a strong doctrine of statutory precedent, defeasible, however, by a contrary agency view.

Two Stock Objections

Before proceeding, we must pause to clear away some stock objections. One objection will be to question the idea that the statutory text at hand can be clear and specific apart from resort to other interpretive tools. On this sort of view, whether a text is clear or ambiguous is itself a function of the tools judges use. If, for example, legislative history suggests intentions or purposes at odds with the surface meaning of a statutory provision, there is a sort of ambiguity (albeit one that we might classify as extrinsic rather than intrinsic).

It is not clear that this objection poses any problems. If it is correct, the result would simply be that many, perhaps most, cases would be sorted into our second category, largely to be resolved by agencies rather than judges. But I think that the objection can also be met on its own terms, for two reasons. First, what I am proposing is that judges should simply stick to the surface meaning of texts that lack any intrinsic or linguistic ambiguity, eschewing further, ambitious inquiries into sources that might create extrinsic ambiguity. There is no conceptual or linguistic problem with that proposal. The question is just whether it produces better results, relative to a consensus of value theories, than do alternative approaches.

We might read the objection to say something more ambitious: that even the intrinsic meaning of texts is, conceptually or as a matter of the nature of language, a function of the interpretive tools and sources judges use. But this is a sophistry. We saw in Chapter 2 that texts may be perfectly clear, relative to the surface-level norms of some linguistic community. Here the complementary suggestion is that statutory texts may be linguistically plain, even if further sources might bring a sort of ambiguity to light. Unless we suffer from an implausible version of language-skepticism or from an attachment to some version of the long-discredited thesis that legal language is pervasively indeterminate, the relevant questions about this proposal sound in institutional terms, not conceptual ones.

There is a second objection, related to the first. What happens if and when judges disagree about whether the statutory text immediately at hand is clear and specific? Perhaps some judges will think the language clear while others think it ambiguous. Perhaps different judges will all think the language clear, but will also think that it clearly says different things, and thus will disagree about what it does (clearly) say. In all such cases, the objection might run, it might be difficult to sort cases into one type or another and difficult to decide whether there is a gap or ambiguity sufficient to trigger *Chevron* deference.

The general answer, one I shall take as understood throughout the following discussion, is that there is nothing special about such cases.

Judges can disagree for many reasons, including that they hold different views about whether statutory language is clear. None of this is an argument for consulting legislative history, for holistic textual comparisons, or for other tools whose exclusion I shall counsel. Those sources, I shall suggest, might provoke as much judicial disagreement as they resolve. Judges disagree after reading legislative history as well as before doing so. In general, it is unclear whether judicial disagreement increases or diminishes as sources are added beyond the statutory provisions at hand. The only definite effect of adding further sources is to increase the costs of decisionmaking, especially when the large costs of compiling and consulting legislative history are incurred. Whatever set of interpretive sources judges are allowed to consult, disagreements are resolved through voting, and that is also the mechanism for resolving judicial disagreement in the regime I suggest. My overall claim is that the informational benefits of legislative history and other collateral interpretive tools are conjectural or dubious, while the institutional costs of their use are definite and substantial, so the interpretive system is better off without them. Nothing in that claim is impeached by the observation that judges will sometimes disagree about whether language is clear.

Type 1 Cases: Text and Legislative History

Where there is a clear and specific text at hand, should judges consult legislative history in search of further information about legislative intentions or purposes or about textual meaning? (Recall from Chapter 4 that even judges who subscribe to an ordinary-meaning account of the aim of statutory interpretation may consult legislative history as relevant information about meaning; something like this was Holmes's view). I suggest that burden allocation gets little traction here, but that tools such as cost-benefit analysis, insufficient reason, maximin, and satisficing all suggest that judges should eschew legislative history in this category of cases. Clear text sets a baseline level of information that is useful on any interpretive value theory. Searching beyond the baseline level promises large and certain costs for, at best, conjectural benefits.

Relevant variables. The empirical dimensions of the legislative-history problem are daunting. That problem requires interpreters to assign values to, and compare, a large and complex set of variables. Is the legislative history a reliable indicator of the median legislator's intent (for the intentionalist), of legislative aims (for the purposivist), or of the ordinary use of statutory terms (for the textualist who admits "persuasive" or "informative" legislative history)? Will judges of limited competence err more, and more seriously, under some approaches to legislative history than under others? Will adoption of one doctrine produce beneficial changes in legislative output, self-defeating changes in legislative output, or perhaps no appreciable change? What are the decision and litigation costs of the various regimes, both for judges and parties?

Many of these questions have intricate empirical interconnections. For example, to the extent that legislative history frequently supplies unreliable evidence relevant to some interpretive aim, or no evidence at all, the litigation costs of legislative history become less justifiable; the judicial system gets less for its money. Reliability and costs interact with judicial error as well. The felt imperative to reduce spiraling costs of research and litigation may cause lawyers (and consequently judges who rely upon lawyers) to truncate their inquiries into expensive sources, thus increasing the rate of error if that is determined by reference to a hypothetical, fully informed judge.

Given the number and complexity of these variables, what should judges do? Chapter 4 showed that even from an intentionalist standpoint, judges might well minimize error by excluding legislative history. But that discussion demonstrated only one empirical possibility. The question here is how judges should proceed, starting from a range of high-level value commitments, in the face of severe uncertainty and the limits of the judges' own information-processing capacity. I shall review a range of approaches to the problem.

Burden allocation. One critique of textualist attacks on legislative history emphasizes a burden-allocation strategy in the frequently seen form that places a burden on opponents of the (claimed) status quo.[9] In light of the long-standing tradition of judicial resort to legislative history, the argument runs, the textualist has the burden of overcoming a presumption in favor of that tradition; but the textualist attack rests on dubious empirical premises, and the burden of opposing legislative history has not been overcome.

Here the burden-allocation strategy misfires for the usual reason: the character of the status quo is uncertain, even perhaps in flux. The Court's use of legislative history rose slowly between 1892 (the date of *Holy Trinity*) and World War II, reached an apogee during the Burger Court,[10] and declined sharply after Justice Scalia joined the Court. In the 1992 term, for example, only 18 percent of the Court's cases cited legislative history.[11] The proportion is now rising slowly again, but the balance still weighs against legislative history. In the Court's 1996 term, 51 percent of the Court's majority opinions in statutory cases did not use legislative history, and the figure was 54 percent for all opinions.[12] The most that can be said about legislative history is that it was not used (or hardly ever used) before 1892—about half of our national history—that its use has periodically waxed and waned since then, and that nowadays it is eschewed a bit more often than it is used. So there is no settled tradition with respect to legislative history, and no settled status quo. One might say that the status quo is that the Court will use legislative history sometimes, and that this has been the status quo at least since 1892. But this seems too clever, because it entails that the status quo would be set in favor of legislative history even if the Court used it in, say, 1 percent of the cases.

This point disposes of another idea of Eskridge's, one that goes beyond the legislative-history issue in the strict sense, that flexible judicial interpretation of statutes is the status quo, that it has not produced "disastrous consequences," and that "the burden of proof is on scholars . . . who want to change these practices."[13] In the past century waves of judicial flexibility have alternated with formalist retrenchments in rough and uneven ways so that the judicial record contains a hodgepodge of formalist and antiformalist elements. Decisions reveling in legislative history contrast with decisions rejecting it; decisions praising flexible, purposive interpretation contrast with mechanical surface-level textualism. Because the status quo is itself uncertain, internally conflicted, and in flux, there is no fixed point against which a burden-of-proof argument can gain traction.

The passing reference to avoiding disaster is overblown. The interpretive regime that disfavored legislative history before 1892 and generally favored a relatively wooden or formalist interpretive style produced no disasters either. Although the stakes involved in legal interpretation are substantial, the stability of society or the legal order is probably not seriously affected by whatever interpretive regime the judges use. We might, however, interpret the reference charitably as an invitation to judges to adopt a satisficing rather than a maximizing worldview, restricting their ambitions in important ways. If that is Eskridge's point, it is well taken, but I shall suggest that it cuts against, rather than in favor of, interpretive flexibility and judicial use of legislative history.

Cost-benefit, insufficient reason, maximin, and satisficing. I now turn to a complex of arguments for judicial formalism about legislative history— that is, a rulelike prohibition on its use. These arguments are grounded in ordinary cost-benefit analysis; in the principle of insufficient reason, under which the speculative benefits of legislative history should be assumed away in favor of attention to its known costs; in the maximin idea of acting so as to produce the best worst-case outcome; and in the satisficing idea of stopping when an aspiration level of successful interpretive search has been reached.

We begin with the cost-benefit approach, supplemented by the principle of insufficient reason. Because judges possess informational advantages with respect to the question of decision costs, even boundedly rational judges can ascertain that the costs of legislative-history research and litigation to courts and parties—and thus the total judicial decision costs of legislative history—are high. But the external and collateral costs and benefits of legislative history—its relevance and reliability, and the effects of its use on the quantity and quality of congressional lawmaking—are at best difficult to specify and at worst wholly indeterminate. Those costs and benefits should be assumed to wash out, per the principle of insufficient reason. All else equal, then, legislative history would be excluded.

Let us examine these points in more depth. Judges possess far better information about the relative litigation and decision costs of differing legislative-history rules than about legislative history's external effects. The rapid fluctuation over time of judicial resort to legislative history, even within very short time frames, has meant that many judges have had some opportunity to observe litigation under changing judicial practices. The other effects of judicial resort to legislative history—questions of reliability, judicial error, and legislative response—are certainly important, but busy generalist judges have almost no reliable information or background knowledge about those questions and no way to acquire the information at acceptable cost. Such questions of legislative behavior and reaction and of error costs are precisely the sort of question least susceptible to judicial prediction. So it is plausible that judges would do best by choosing the rule respecting legislative history that promises to min-imize decision costs, subject to a reasonable threshold of satisfaction on the dimension of accuracy. Judges should focus on the costs of decision because their information about that concern is far superior.

If decision costs are to be minimized, subject to some threshold aspi-ration level of accuracy—a crucial qualifier I emphasize later—legislative history should be excluded. A prominent theme in judicial critiques of legislative history has been the practical point that legislative-history re-search is, simply put, too costly and time-consuming. That legislative history is massively voluminous and expensive to research is also widely, although not universally, believed by academic commentators, even by those otherwise critical of textualism.[14] Legislators' incentives make it pre-dictable that legislative history will be, over the run of statutes, far more voluminous and costly to research than text or other sources. Legislators must, on average, spend far more political capital to insert material into statutory text than to insert the same material into legislative history, so text will be produced in far less volume than legislative history.

Legislative history's contemporary defenders do not typically deny that legislative history is costly. Some say rather that the costs of legislative-history research will diminish with changes in technology. But as I em-phasized in Chapter 4, cheaper technology makes it easier not only to research legislative history but also to generate it, so the increase in volume might outstrip the increasing capacity for research. Other de-fenders of legislative history say, more simply, that the high decision costs are worth incurring for the informational value of legislative history. But that response is empirically far too ambitious. Whether the costs are worth it is deeply controversial and will remain so for a long time, pre-cisely because most of the costs and benefits on either side are trans-scientific. There is far less uncertainty surrounding the question of deci-sion costs; a regime that excludes legislative history will predictably be cheaper, if one considers only the direct costs of litigation and decision, than any regime that admits legislative history. Canceling out other con-siderations, per the principle of insufficient reason, suggests that legislative history should be excluded. If one starts from the baseline level of inter-pretive information, provided by clear statutory texts on the issue at hand, the marginal costs of adding legislative history seem very large, while the marginal benefits seem speculative in the extreme.

The point can also be put in terms of a maximin approach to decisionmaking. Suppose the following situation: Consulting legislative history is very expensive, but might provide much further valuable information about statutory meaning or legislative intent. It also might not; legislative history might actually increase the rate and gravity of judicial error, as Chapter 4 emphasized. The probabilities of these outcomes are very hard to gauge, so it is hard to speak meaningfully of an expected-value approach to legislative history. Moreover, the judges will be hard pressed to gauge the overall error costs of resort to legislative history, even after they have decided many statutory cases. In this situation maximin supports the exclusion of legislative history. If legislative history is excluded, the worst possible outcome is that the judges will get statutory cases wrong with indeterminate frequency. If legislative history is consulted, the worst possible outcome is that the judges will get statutory cases wrong with indeterminate frequency, *and* the enormous expense of legislative-history research will be incurred. Choosing the rule that excludes legislative history improves the worst possible outcome.

Finally, the argument can be put in terms of satisficing as well. In the type of cases we are discussing, clear statutory text provides a baseline level of interpretive information and thus a baseline level of accuracy that is good enough. Judges should stop there, satisficing at the baseline level. Cost-benefit analysis worries that further search into sources such as legislative history brings definite and very high decision costs while producing only speculative benefits on dimensions such as accuracy. The satisficer worries, more roughly, that to go beyond the baseline level is to let the best become the enemy of the good. Judges should restrict their aspirations by sticking to clearly useful sources instead of wandering into terrain in which there is much to be lost and little to be gained.

An interesting implication of the satisficing account is that the interpretation the court produces might be sensitive to the order in which materials are considered. In a case like *Holy Trinity*, a satisficing court that considered legislative history before statutory text might conclude that the legislative history offered a fully satisfactory account of legislators' intentions. The bare idea of satisficing, by itself, cannot justify a rule that intentionalist interpreters should stop with the plain (and satisfactory) meaning of the text, as opposed to the plain (and satisfactory) meaning of the legislative history. But this is no serious objection to the satisficer. In any decisionmaking setting in which less than all possible alternatives are to be searched out and considered, one must begin somewhere. Decisionmakers who employ the "take the best" heuristic discussed in Chapter 6 use the best single cue available in the environment to which they have adapted, while ignoring other cues. So too the satisficing interpreter will form a second-order estimate, based on experience, about which source provides the best clues to the goal made relevant by the interpreter's value theory (say, legislative intentions), but will then ignore other information. Forming such an estimate requires far less information than does consulting all potentially relevant interpretive sources in each case. And, as discussed earlier, a variety of interpretive approaches have converged on a common view about what the best cue actually is. They have converged on the view that clear statutory text is the single best indicator of statutory meaning and of legislative intentions or purposes— the single best cue that boundedly rational interpreters can use.

Intermediate solutions? A rule of exclusion is not the only logically possible response to the high decision costs and speculative collateral benefits of legislative history. Intermediate solutions include a rule that admits only reports from congressional committees, or that consults legislative history only if the statute lacks a plain meaning. We might even imagine judges dipping at random into the legislative history, selecting a few pages to read, on the theory that random spot-checking might, as a probabilistic matter, produce informational gains at low cost.

The promise of these solutions is to control decision costs while providing large benefits in interpretive accuracy. But that promise is never fulfilled, because in practice such intermediate solutions prove highly unstable over any extended period and inevitably dissolve back into plenary consideration of legislative history. One cause of the instability is Eskridge's insight that "once you open the door to consideration of legislative history, it is hard to exclude any type of evidence without viewing it in the context of the whole story."[15] Courts that prefer committee reports accordingly end up interpreting or contradicting the committee report with evidence from floor debate.[16] Another cause of the instability is that the triggering conditions for these intermediate doctrines are vague. Courts that profess to consult legislative history only when statutory text is ambiguous, for example, end up evaluating the legislative history even when the text is plain because they must rebut arguments from dissenting judges or parties.[17] The great virtue of the wholesale exclusion of legislative history, from the standpoint of judicial decision costs, is that it provides a comparatively (although not perfectly) stable and enforceable rule. Just as abstinence is easier than moderation, so too judges will find it easier not to look at legislative history at all than to look only at certain parts of the legislative history in an ill-defined sequence, or to look at the whole legislative history only under certain poorly specified conditions.

Decision costs and accuracy revisited. The point of all this is not that decision costs should be minimized *tout court.* If it were, judges might flip coins to decide cases or simply close the courthouse doors. The suggestion, rather, is that institutionalist judges would do well to adopt a modest aspiration level. Rather than trying to minimize both decision costs and the costs of error, as might a system designer with complete information, judges who are cognitively bounded should minimize on the dimension on which their information is best (decision costs), subject to the satisficing constraint that the interpretive rules appear to produce some threshold level of accuracy about legislative intentions or purposes or about textual meaning. That threshold level of accuracy is provided, I have claimed, by the baseline of clear and specific statutory text on the issue at hand. In cost-benefit terms, the key point is that the question of legislative history is marginal, not absolute. The question is just whether sources like legislative history that are added to the baseline level of clear and specific text produce net benefits. They might do so—only a full empirical inquiry could support a conclusion one way or another—but my claim is that judges should act on the assumption that they do not.

To be sure, a cost-benefit analysis with complete information might or might not show, in the end, that legislative history is cost-justified, all things considered. Excluding legislative history might unduly impoverish the courts' sources of information (about legislative intent, textual meaning, or any other end specified by the underlying theory), thereby increasing the risks of judicial error. Perhaps legislative history generally tends to make statutory cases more determinate because legislative history frequently clarifies ambiguous statutes or qualifies overly broad ones. In any case its exclusion might also impoverish the parties' sources of information about how courts will rule, and that in turn might increase legal uncertainty and the rate of litigation as opposed to settlement. Exclusion might even raise the costs of litigation and adjudication in statutory cases if it causes parties to spend exorbitant amounts of time and money parsing statutory text, searching dictionaries and databases to find helpful usage, or paying linguists to opine in support of the parties' preferred readings.

But all these points identify merely conjectural benefits of legislative history, benefits that should be discounted because they are conjectural. The costs of legislative history, on the other hand, are large, quite certain to be incurred, and well known to judges. Given these conditions, a reasonable judge should choose not to move beyond the baseline posture, even if doing so might, in the end, prove net beneficial. If the baseline level of information were routinely very low, even judges alert to the direct costs and opportunity costs of decisionmaking could rationally decide to demand more or search further. But as we have seen, the baseline level is said to be quite high by all standard value theories. Statutory text is widely thought to provide the best evidence of legislative intent or purpose; the reliability and relevance of legislative history is often questioned; and the era before *Holy Trinity* licensed recourse to legislative history did not witness extravagant varieties of textualism. From this perspective, the central vice that afflicts judicial use of legislative history is neglect of the direct costs and opportunity costs of decisionmaking that is information-intensive. Overlooking collateral institutional costs, legislative-history enthusiasts on the bench search beyond the point at which reasonable decisionmakers would decide to truncate the inquiry.

It is important to clearly distinguish two theses here. The first is that boundedly informed and boundedly rational judges are likely to do worse if they consult legislative history than if they do not. The second is that boundedly informed and boundedly rational judges are unlikely to be able to determine whether or not they should consult legislative history. I mean to advance the first thesis and deny the second. As discussed at the end of Chapter 6, that combination of views is not paradoxical or self-contradictory. It supposes only that judges can know what they do not know and can act with awareness of the limitations of their own information and abilities. This posture is in a sense theoretically unsatisfying. But I claim only that it is reasonable, not that it is theoretically rational in any strong sense. When making choices under uncertainty, decisionmakers can and must make second-order decisions about how best to proceed in light of their first-order limitations. Judges can do no better than the modest posture I recommend. Under any more ambitious decisional approach, they may well do far worse.

Type 1 Cases: Other Sources

Let us extend this analysis to some of the other traditional tools of statutory construction. The most important of these are the canons of construction and the text of related provisions and statutes (what lawyers sometimes call statutes "in pari materia"). Much of what we said about legislative history applies, on a smaller scale, to these other tools. Although the costs of these tools are lower, their benefits are lower as well. Where judicial use of the traditional tools is inevitable, as may sometimes be the case for canonical default rules, judges should pick a clear and limited set of defaults and use them inflexibly over time, rather than attempting to maximize the benefits of the traditional tools by indulging in case-specific, fine-grained adjustments of the interpretive regime.

The canons of construction. The canons of construction are maxims of interpretation, judicially developed rules of thumb. They may be sorted into the linguistic (such as the idea that "the expression of one term excludes another" by negative implication) and the substantive (such as the idea that statutes should be presumed, absent a clear contrary statement, not to apply outside the territory of the United States). We have seen some substantive canons, particularly of the clear statement variety, in Chapter 5 as a component of democracy-forcing accounts of interpretation—accounts I criticized for ignoring the systemic costs of coordination necessary to create a critical mass of democracy-forcing judicial decisions.

Karl Llewellyn tried to debunk the canons by exposing their indeterminacy, arguing that for each canon there is an equal and opposite countercanon.[18] Later scholars have in turn debunked Llewellyn by arguing that the opposed pairs of canons just list a presumption and its exceptions, so that there is no conflict after all, and more generally that the canons supply useful interpretive default rules. As default rules, the canons are conventionally justified either (1) as rules that track legislators' preferences and thus function as off-the-rack terms that reduce legislative drafting costs or else (2) as democracy-forcing rules that courts might use to provoke desirable legislative responses. As suggested in Chapter 5, and as I shall suggest later, the democracy-forcing justification is untenable in light of the costs of judicial coordination on a particular democracy-forcing regime.

What of the canons' purported informational role as what Einer El-hauge calls "preference-estimating" rules that attempt to capture what most legislators intend most of the time?[19] The linguistic canons are typically free from the distributive effects that (according to Chapter 5) cause persistent disagreement over the content of the default rules, with resulting coordination failures and inconsistency over time. At the very least those distributive effects are not predictable ex ante where linguistic canons are concerned. Compare the canon favoring Native American tribes,[20] whose distributive effects are palpable and always run in one direction, with the rule that statutory singular terms will always be read to include plural terms unless the legislature clearly says otherwise.[21] Because distributive effects and therefore political controversy are muted for many linguistic canons, judicial coordination on a particular set of linguistic canons seems a far more realistic aspiration than coordination on a set of substantive canons, especially to the extent that the political valence of the substantive canons is predictable ex ante.

The crucial question for preference-estimating canons is not coordination. It is whether such canons will supply useful information, net of costs, that courts may use to fill statutory gaps. At first blush preference-estimating canons seem a more promising additional source than legislative history from the marginal point of view. The extreme volume and heterogeneity that make legislative history uniquely costly and uniquely susceptible to judicial mishandling (I argued in Chapter 4) do not fairly characterize the canons, at least not in as great degree.

Even if the canons do better than legislative history on the cost side, however, they also promise much less in the way of informational benefits. This is trivially true, of course, if Llewellyn was right. If each canon has an equal and opposite countercanon, the informational value of the total set is nil. But even if the indeterminacy point is bracketed, the canons provide low-value information about statutory meaning or about legislative intentions or purposes. One point is that legislatures are unlikely actually to draft legislation in light of judge-made default rules. As Judge Posner puts it, "with a few exceptions, [the canons] have no value even as flexible guideposts or rebuttable presumptions, even when taken one by one, because they rest on wholly unrealistic conceptions of the legislative process."[22] Another point is that the canons are entirely generic and thus often unhelpful. The off-the-rack quality that gives the linguistic canons an aura of neutrality is in fact an unappealing trait from the informational standpoint. The canons' generic quality means that canons never speak directly to the particulars of the interpretive problem at hand and thus provide, at best, secondary or collateral information about statutory meanings, intentions, or purposes.

I intend to foreshadow here a contrast with agency interpretations, which are typically the product of deep familiarity with the particular statute at hand and its particular underlying policies. For now, the point is just that the same decisional approach we pursued in the setting of legislative history applies to the canons, albeit with reduced weights on both the cost side and the benefit side. Although the costs of using the canons are plausibly small, especially for the less controversial linguistic canons, the informational benefits in preference-estimating terms are also small; and the benefits are far more conjectural than the costs. On cost-benefit and maximin grounds, judges would do best to dispense with the canons altogether where that is possible.

In some domains, however, canonical interpretation may not be optional. It has been suggested that some classes of canons, especially the linguistic canons, are inevitable, at least in some category of cases.[23] On this view, where statutes do not speak explicitly one way or another, it is not clear what it could possibly mean to interpret without default rules, set in one way or another; and linguistic canons are merely default rules about how ordinary drafters and interpreters use and understand language. For a linguistic example, suppose that a statute contains a list that can either be read as exhaustive or illustrative. How can the court possibly escape choosing one or the other reading? In that sense, the argument runs, the court cannot avoid adopting, at least for the occasion, either the maxim that lists are exhaustive ("the expression of one is the exclusion of another") or the opposite maxim that lists are illustrative.

The same point may hold for some of the substantive canons as well. Suppose that a statute bars employment discrimination on racial grounds without specifying whether the statute applies to American firms outside the United States or only domestically.[24] It seems that some default rule or other on the question whether statutes apply extraterritorially must be set. But other substantive canons are thoroughly dispensable. Consider the canon that statutory veterans' preferences are to be broadly construed.[25] Abolishing that canon would not institute a sort of antiveteran interpretive default rule. It would just mean that veterans-benefit statutes are to be construed "reasonably," as Justice Antonin Scalia puts it, without any thumb on the scale in one direction or another.[26]

Even where canonical default rules are inevitable, it does not at all follow that *judges* must be the ones charged with selecting the default rule one way or another. When there is an agency in the picture—and in the regulatory state there almost always is, especially if we count prosecutors as agencies charged with interpreting criminal statutes, as I shall discuss shortly—then the conclusion of the argument from inevitability no longer holds. Where an agency has first-line interpretive authority, courts may simply code the sort of puzzles described here as statutory ambiguity and then defer the issue to agency resolution. In the linguistic example, the agency might be given authority to decide whether the list is illustrative or exhaustive, or to decide whether statutes apply extraterritorially. In our schema these are not type 1 cases at all. They are to count as type 2 cases, and agencies should be given authority to choose the relevant interpretive default rules.

In other words, it may be inevitable that some interpreter must develop default rules to govern cases of this kind, but it is not at all inevitable that courts must do so. Whether courts or agencies should hold that authority is always a separate institutional question. My suggestion later will be that courts should conceive the *Chevron* rule of agency deference as a kind of *second-order default rule:* a default rule that authorizes agencies to select the first-order canonical default rules unless Congress clearly says otherwise. Judges, in other words, should code the problem of selection between different possible default rules as itself an instance of statutory silence or ambiguity. Then the *Chevron* default rule will itself commit the choice of the canonical default rules to relevant agencies under particular statutes.

In a residual and ever-diminishing class of cases there may even today be no relevant agency in the picture. In such cases judges will do best by simply picking default rules, in the special sense of "picking" introduced in Chapter 6. At the level of individual judges, when canons are picked, the judges themselves will conserve the nontrivial costs of argument over the content of the canons. From the systemic standpoint of minimizing legal uncertainty and the decision costs incurred by legislators, agencies, and litigants, it matters far more that there be a single canonical regime, consistently adhered to over time, than that judges constantly engage in fine-tuning and case-specific adjustments in the hope of producing the maximally correct regime.

The problems of coordination-with-distribution discussed in Chapter 5 are relevant here, but can be overcome at least with respect to canons that have little in the way of distributive effects that are predictable before the fact. Not only do the linguistic canons fall into this category, but some substantive canons do as well. It is very hard for any judge to predict, over a range of future cases, whether a default rule for or against extraterritorial application of statutes will benefit or harm the judge's interests. In such cases the canon will have an uncertain valence over many future cases, and this puts the judges who must pick canons behind a veil of uncertainty or ignorance that reduces the distributive stakes. The substantive canons discussed in Chapter 5, by contrast, were precisely those lacking any such unpredictable valence. The rule of lenity never cuts in the government's favor, but the canon against extraterritorial application sometimes will, sometimes will not.

The idea that where there is no agency in the picture, canons should be picked, not chosen, need not rest on the view that the content of canonical default rules does not matter at all. There is a fact of the matter, albeit a fact that is extremely difficult to discover, about whether and in what settings legislators tend to use language in such a way as to create exhaustive lists or illustrative ones. The better argument for picking is that the gains from identifying the very best default rule in any particular setting will be overwhelmed by the costs of making the identification. The judges might vacillate for many more years about the issue, but when the argument was done, the benefits of having arrived at the right rule would be far smaller than the costs in legal uncertainty for legislators and litigants and in decision costs for judges produced by the vacillation itself. All this suggests that fixing the system of canons with a minimum of fuss—by dispensing with judicial canons where possible, by allowing agencies to choose second-order default rules, and by judicial picking where necessary—will provide tangible savings in decision and uncertainty costs, savings that dominate the speculative benefits of getting the maximally best canonical regime. Consistency in adhering to canons will not cure the endemic problems of competing canons (Llewellyn's point), or canons with vague triggering conditions, or democracy-forcing canons with predictable distributive effects like the rule of lenity. But those problems are reduced as much as possible by the regime of second-order default rules and agency deference that I propose.

Related statutes. Similar points apply to the collateral text of related statutes. Textualists are prone to use such statutes as a substitute for legislative history, while intentionalists and purposivists are prone to use such statutes as collateral evidence of legislative intentions and purposes. This enterprise—call it *holistic statutory interpretation*—often fails cost-benefit analysis, however, for the marginal benefit of consulting the collateral sources is lower than is the marginal cost of consulting them.

For concreteness, I shall begin by considering the value of related statutes from a textualist standpoint and then generalize the argument to include other first-best approaches. Suppose that an interpreter believes that the aim of interpretation is to capture the ordinary meaning of statutory or constitutional text, quite apart from anyone's intentions. (I bracket here, as irrelevant for present purposes, the possible high-level justifications for this view.) The textualist interpreter faces a range of implementation issues that must be confronted to make her high-level commitment operational. How exactly should the textualist view be embodied in decision-procedures that interpreters will use? Of these implementation questions, I consider only the following: *How much* text should the interpreter consider? Suppose that there is both a primary text, a statutory section or constitutional clause whose interpretation will settle the rule of law that applies between the parties, and collateral texts, such as other provisions of the Constitution or of the relevant statute, or other statutes. How widely should the textualist interpreter cast the net, and how much weight should be given to collateral texts?

This issue underlies important debates in both statutory and constitutional interpretation. In the statutory arena the Court has at times adopted a strong presumption of textual coherence across whole statutes, on the view that textual similarities and differences across provisions are at least presumptively significant. Justice Scalia's opinion for the Court in *West Virginia University Hospitals v. Casey*[27] goes even further, suggesting that interpreters should treat the whole *United States Code* as though terms are used consistently across statutes. As I discuss in Chapter 8, there is a similar approach in constitutional interpretation. Thus Akhil Amar defends an "intratextualist" view that makes extensive use of comparisons across constitutional clauses, even to the point of insisting that words appearing in widely separated contexts be given similar meanings.[28] Elsewhere in the constitutional arena there are occasional hints of an even more expansive "intertextualist" view, analogous to the *Casey* opinion. On this view, the Constitution would be read in light of collateral legal texts, such as the Declaration of Independence and the Northwest Ordinance.[29] What these views have in common is a more or less expansive commitment to holistic or coherentist textualism,[30] as opposed to the sort of clause-bound textualism that focuses principally or solely on the statutory or constitutional provisions directly applicable in the case at hand.

There is a simple intuition behind such approaches, although I shall suggest in a moment that the intuition is mistaken. The textualist interpreter seeks the ordinary meaning of a legal term in the provision at hand. Other provisions of the same text or other legal texts use the same term or use different terms in ways that illuminate by contrast. The holistic textualist reasons that interpreters should consult collateral texts as widely as possible and give them whatever weight they intrinsically deserve, all things considered, to whatever extent they happen to provide relevant evidence of ordinary meaning. Indeed, on this construal there is nothing at all special about legal texts. Any sources of ordinary meaning will do, such as dictionaries, literature, or the testimony of linguists.

On cost-benefit grounds, however, the holistic enterprise is dubious. The key points are familiar. First, if one holds constant the quality of decisions (from a textualist perspective), the direct decision costs and opportunity costs of holistic textualism are real and perhaps quite high. The refined and comprehensive comparisons required by holistic textualism take time that needs to be allocated across an array of cases. The time spent searching out and comparing usage across the whole Code or within a database means less time to be spent on considering directly relevant texts in other cases. Most important, the marginal value of the additional texts is low because the meaning of other statutes bears indirectly, at best, on the meaning of the statute under interpretation.

Second, if one holds the costs of decisionmaking constant, holistic textualism may do worse even according to the very value theory presupposed by holistic textualism itself. As compared with *clause-bound textualism*—textualism focused on the directly dispositive clauses or provisions at hand—holistic textualism requires a more complicated and information-intensive inquiry that will reduce decisional accuracy whenever fallible interpreters read the comparison texts mistakenly. The comparison to collateral texts may cause boundedly rational interpreters to arrive at a better interpretation of the text at hand, but the effect may also be the opposite. The collateral comparison may drive the interpreter away from the best interpretation of the text at hand, provoking an error that would not have occurred under clause-bound textualism. In general, there is no particular reason to think that the illuminating effect of holistic texualism will predominate over its error-producing effect.

Third, and related to the second, holistic textualism is a dangerous tool in the hands of fallible interpreters. It risks producing a holistic, highly coherent, but fundamentally mistaken analysis that enforces a simultaneous misreading of a whole set of related provisions. Risk-averse interpreters might prefer the limited incoherence of clause-bound interpretation to a sweeping, integrated, but erroneous universal account.

In Chapter 8 I translate these points to the constitutional arena, where they undermine holistic textualism in constitutional interpretation. Here I want to suggest that these points generalize across a range of first-best accounts of statutory interpretation. On cost-benefit grounds, the holistic enterprise is a poor bet whether the interpreter's value theory is textualist, intentionalist, or purposivist. On the intentionalist and purposivist approaches, collateral statutes are evidence—information about what legislators intended or hoped to accomplish. Yet from the informational standpoint, searching further and further afield in the code for statutes that use similar terms is an exercise in diminishing marginal returns. The most important common feature of other statutes is that they are not the statute before the Court, and any information they supply will be at best collateral or low-value.

For exactly these reasons, intentionalist interpreters sometimes urge the Court to minimize reliance on collateral statutes in favor of sources directly tied to the particular statute at hand, like legislative history. But that proposed substitute fares no better, or so I have argued earlier. The better alternative to wide-ranging holistic textualism, I suggest later, is a strong regime of agency deference. Agencies, not courts, should be authorized to determine how far afield to go in search of collateral evidence of legislators' intentions or purposes. The intentionalists' instinct that interpretation should focus on the statute at issue, as opposed to collateral statutes of marginal relevance, is correct. But that focus should be implemented by deference to agencies who have a deep understanding of particular statutes and expertise in the relevant statutory policies.

Type 2 Cases: The Institutional Premises of the *Chevron* Rule

Let us turn now to type 2 cases—those in which the statutory text immediately at issue contains, as a linguistic matter, a gap or ambiguity.

Here I shall emphasize two alternatives. Courts may proceed in these cases by emphasizing the traditional tools of construction, drawing upon a rich brew of judge-made canons and collateral sources, or else by deferring to agency interpretations that fill the gap or resolve the ambiguity. Of course, these options are, as I have presented them, extremes on a continuum; traditional tools and agency deference may be combined in various ways. In a string of prominent recent decisions, for example, the justices pay lip service to principles of agency deference, but draw upon the traditional tools to decide whether there is a gap for the agency to fill.[31] That procedure in effect reads agency deference out of the picture by narrowing agencies' gap-filling power to the residual area in which judicial tools run out. Here I shall criticize such decisions, arguing that courts should defer to agencies, without bringing traditional tools to bear, whenever the statutory text immediately at hand contains an intrinsic gap or ambiguity. In essence, I shall suggest that judges should defer to agencies' choices about whether, when, and how to employ the traditional tools where a linguistic gap or ambiguity exists in the provision immediately at hand.

I have said that the traditional interpretive tools are costly and of dubious value on a wide range of interpretive approaches or value theories. But where the statutory provisions at hand are ambiguous, what exactly is the alternative? If statutes contain gaps or ambiguities, yet the turn to legislative history, canons, collateral statutes, and other traditional interpretive tools produces definite costs but only uncertain benefits, where then should courts turn? It is occasionally suggested, for example, that judges who eschew the use of legislative history must turn to the canons or related statutes to find the interpretive materials they need to decide cases. But this idea assumes that judges must do all the interpreting. I shall suggest, to the contrary, that where statutes contain gaps, judges will do best, relative to a wide range of interpretive values, by ceding interpretive control to agencies.

There are two extant views I mean to criticize here. One view simply confines itself to judicial interpretation, remaining largely blind to the role of agencies. We have seen in Part I the startling fact that leading modern theorists of interpretation, among them Eskridge and Posner, spend relatively little time discussing interpretation by agencies, despite the preeminent interpretive role of agencies in the modern state. Even where agency interpretation is discussed, the most prominent strand of theory spends a great deal of energy attempting to "reconcile" deference to agencies with the interpretive authority of judges. Here the typical claim is that in a wide range of settings, Congress itself should be taken to have instructed the judges to defer.[32]

I shall try to provide an alternative account that rejects the formalist (in the sense of conceptual or essentialist) premises of that view, emphasizing instead the strictly institutional justifications for agency deference. The Constitution neither requires nor bars judicial deference to agencies, nor do extant statutes plausibly instruct judges to defer to agencies, as a general matter. The argument for agency deference is not to be drawn from formal sources of law. Rather, the argument is simply that the interpretive system will be better off, on a wide range of interpretive value theories, if judges defer to agencies when statutory texts are not clear and specific.

The Chevron *rule and some institutional questions.* How should courts approach agency interpretations of law? Should courts decide legal questions on their own, or should they give some weight to the views of the relevant agency? For many years the answer to this question was sharply disputed. It received an authoritative answer in *Chevron v. NRDC*,[33] which sets out a two-step inquiry. Under step one, the question is whether Congress has "directly decided the precise question at issue," or whether Congress has unambiguously banned what the agency proposes to do. Under step two, courts ask whether the agency's interpretation of the statute is reasonable. The result is that under *Chevron*, agency interpretations of law should be upheld if they are reasonable and if they do not contradict the clear instructions of Congress. The court is not authorized to reject the agency's interpretation merely because the court disagrees, all things considered, about how the statute should be interpreted.

How is *Chevron* to be evaluated? It is generally agreed that courts must follow congressional instructions on the question of deference. If Congress has unambiguously instructed courts to defer to agency interpretations of law, or not to do so, courts must do as Congress says. With this premise, many people have defended or challenged *Chevron* by reference to enacted law. Some urge, for example, that the Administrative Procedure Act, which asks courts to "decide relevant questions of law," argues in favor of an independent judicial judgment on the legal question. But on reflection, statutory law is generally indeterminate on the crucial question. To be sure, courts are told to decide relevant questions of law; but *Chevron* might be one of the legal rules courts are to apply. Under statutes in which agencies are exercising delegated authority, perhaps the meaning of the relevant law just is what agencies say that it is. At the very least, this is a plausible reading of statutes that delegate rulemaking and adjudicative authority to agencies. Plausible, but not necessary; candid observers, on all sides, acknowledge that Congress has not authoritatively required or forbidden the *Chevron* principle.

The best defenses of *Chevron* do not rest on formal claims of this sort. Rather, they attempt to read ambiguous congressional instructions in a way that is well attuned to institutional considerations. As the simplest illustration, consider Peter Strauss's view.[34] Strauss emphasizes that the Supreme Court is able to resolve a small percentage of cases involving ambiguities in regulatory law. He suggests that because of the sheer number of courts of appeals, independent judicial interpretations of regulatory law would make it extremely difficult to ensure national uniformity. If *Chevron* is followed faithfully, agency interpretations will be authoritative unless there has been clear error; and this means that if the Environmental Protection Agency, the Federal Communications Commission, or the National Labor Relations Board interprets its governing statute in a particular way, national law is likely to be genuinely national. If *Chevron* were not the law and were not followed faithfully, regulatory law—involving, for example, the environment, communications, and labor-management relations—would inevitably be highly variable across the country. *Chevron* therefore works against balkanization of federal law. This idea, which justifies agency deference by emphasizing the Supreme Court's low capacity for coordinating the actions of the federal judiciary, fits snugly with the account of judicial coordination problems laid out in Chapter 5.

Variables and choices. Strauss's point, of course, is only meant to address one of the relevant institutional variables. The other variables flow directly from what we have said earlier. Will agencies do better or worse than courts at judging legislative intentions or purposes? At reading legislative history? What of the costs of decisionmaking for parties, for agencies in the first instance, and then additionally (in a nondeferential regime) for courts deciding whether the agency's interpretation is correct by the judges' lights? Courts might resolve such questions by turning to the traditional tools of construction, drawing upon legislative history, canons, and related statutes to generate further information about meanings, intentions, or purposes. Even after *Chevron* this style of judicial gap-filling persists; indeed, it has attained new prominence in recent years.

On the institutional perspective, however, the simple question is whether courts pursuing a range of interpretive approaches will do better or worse with this rich palette of interpretive colors than with a more limited set. A natural view is that more tools are better than fewer, and that more sophisticated tools are better than simpler ones. I suggested earlier that the natural view has it backwards. The basic point is that there is little reason to think that judges will improve their performance, relative to any standard interpretive approach, by using any more ambitious decision-procedure than the one I have suggested for this category of cases. Conversely, by virtue of their specialized competence and relative accountability, agencies are in a better position than are courts to assess the relevant considerations. Agencies will often possess far better information about the legislative process that produced the statute, about the specialized policy context surrounding the statute's enactment, and about the resulting legislative deal. Certainly there is no general reason to think that courts will systematically outperform agencies with regard to the institutional variables we have discussed. Only a kind of blind confidence in judicial capacities could suggest that judges are systematically superior to agency administrators in determining what legislators intended, or what purposes an enacting majority meant to pursue, or what policy tradeoffs the statute made.

It is sometimes suggested that agencies cannot function well as interpreters of original legislative intentions or purposes. On this view, agencies' political responsiveness makes them sensitive to current politics, particularly the desires of current legislators and legislative committees, rather than to original intentions. Current political responsiveness is indeed a strength of agencies, as I shall emphasize later. But it hardly follows that agencies are therefore inferior to courts as intentionalist or purposivist interpreters; agencies may be superior on both the originalist dimension and the dimension of current political accountability or responsiveness. In baseball, speed may trade off against power at the frontiers of performance, but one player may nonetheless be both speedier and more powerful than another.

As far as information is concerned, specialized agencies are closer to the statute, its legislative history, and its original purposes and compromises than are generalist judges.[35] Agencies are also typically far more familiar with the congressional process and its heterogeneous outputs. As for political responsiveness, one point is that agencies may refer to legislative history to resist current political pressures from new congresses or from the executive.[36] A second point is one of motivation and institutional incentives: courts' political insulation does little to ensure that courts will implement original intentions or purposes revealed by legislative history. The basic mechanisms of judicial insulation (principally life tenure and an irreducible salary) liberate judges from current politics, but they do nothing at all to guarantee that judges will faithfully implement past political deals or search for original legislative intentions. Political insulation frees current judges to implement whatever values they happen to hold. Some judges will be faithful intentionalists, but there is little reason to suppose that that is systematically true, or more true than it is for agencies. Overall, political insulation and the generalist character of the federal judiciary together reduce the judges' informational capacities, rendering them unfamiliar both with the specialized policy contexts of particular statutes and with the legislative processes that produce particular statutory schemes and accompanying legislative history.[37] Although agencies are systematically more responsive and accountable than courts, it is hardly clear that judicial resort to the traditional interpretive tools produces better accounts of original legislative intentions or purposes than does judicial deference to agencies.

What judicial resort to the rich palette of traditional tools does clearly do, however, is to layer an enormous additional set of process and decision costs on top of the administrative system. Not only are the direct decision costs of the traditional tools high, but those tools also create significant uncertainty for agencies, legislators, and regulated parties. Where canons of various sorts, legislative history with its high volume and internal heterogeneity, and indeed the whole enacted code are all in the judicial kit-bag waiting to be used, agencies and other actors will find it difficult to predict what the eventual fate of an agency interpretation will be.

Relative to any of the standard interpretive approaches, then, there is no reason at all to think that the tools of judicial gap-filling are superior to agency interpretation, but judicial gap-filling does bring with it large costs of decisionmaking and uncertainty. Both of the latter costs would be eliminated by a regime in which judges defer whenever statutes contain surface-level gaps or ambiguities. On cost-benefit and maximin grounds, then, that modest regime dominates the more ambitious regime that uses the whole set of traditional tools. Again, the point here is not to suggest that minimizing the costs of decisionmaking and uncertainty is the sole aim. If it were, courts could simply close up shop altogether. The point is that the concern with accuracy functions only as a kind of satisficing target or aspiration level, such that judges should minimize the costs of decision and uncertainty once that level has been met. Where gaps or ambiguities exist, agencies will frequently do well as interpreters of law; there is no particular reason to think courts will do better; and the traditional tools of judicial interpretation produce definite costs. The appropriate judicial posture, then, is one of modesty and deference to administrative conclusions rather than interpretive ambition.

In making this suggestion, I mean to draw attention to two ways of analyzing the issue of deference to agencies in type 2 cases. The first, and perhaps the most common, is to speak in terms of constitutional considerations, separation of powers, and congressional instructions. If any of these were clear, the question would be at an end. But here, as, in the many other contexts discussed in Parts I and II, the relevant sources of law do not resolve the choice of interpretive approaches. The other way of analyzing *Chevron* is frankly institutional. The questions about judicial deference to agencies are questions about alternative institutional regimes for accomplishing aims that are valuable on a wide range of high-level interpretive theories. As throughout the project, moreover, the submission here is twofold, and the first part is independent of the second. First, institutional arguments, however they might be resolved, are the best way to think about the problem. Second, I have suggested a particular resolution of the institutional analysis: courts should defer to agencies whenever the statutory text at issue, viewed on its face and without recourse to the traditional tools, contains a surface-level gap or ambiguity.

Agencies, criminal law, and the rule of lenity. We must take a closer look here at one of the most significant traditional tools of interpretation, briefly discussed in Chapter 5: the rule of lenity, under which courts are to resolve ambiguities in criminal (or "penal") statutes in favor of criminal defendants. Lenity is sometimes thought to implement or symbolize a larger background point about the differences between criminal cases and civil cases. Whatever the role of agencies in civil cases, courts must use the rule of lenity to force Congress itself to legislate with specificity on the subject of criminally enforceable obligations; such legislation cannot be delegated to agencies or courts. Lenity is also thought to respect a constitutional obligation, rooted in due process, that potential criminal defendants have specific notice of their obligations, rather than being convicted under ambiguously worded laws.

From our perspective, however, the standard arguments for lenity are fatally abstract, failing to account for the institutional capacities involved. Yale legal scholar Dan Kahan has argued that Congress is structurally incapable of legislating with greater specificity in criminal arenas. The alternative of greater criminal common lawmaking by federal courts, Kahan argues, is infeasible, partly because "the sheer number of district court and court of appeals judges who [would participate in criminal common law] . . . would pose immense obstacles to its consistent and rational exercise."[38] The last point, bearing on the costs of judicial coordination, undermines the democracy-forcing argument for lenity, as I suggested in Chapter 5.

Kahan's institutional solution is to extend *Chevron* to federal criminal law by urging courts to defer to reasonable interpretations of criminal statutes advanced by the Department of Justice prior to prosecution. The last proviso ensures that the notice function of lenity is satisfied, although notice is provided by administrative regulations rather than statutory text. The important point is Kahan's resolutely institutional, rather than conceptual, focus: his central proposal is that the interpretation of federal criminal statutes would work better, in light of a wide range of values, under a *Chevron* regime than under the current nondeferential one. At the very least, Kahan has shown that there is no reason for the additional complexity that arises from having different interpretive regimes across the criminal-civil divide. Courts may well produce better criminal policy by extending *Chevron* universally, and the extension will certainly increase the simplicity of the interpretive regime, with resulting benefits in terms of reduced decision costs and reduced legal uncertainty.

Agencies and formalism. To clarify something implicit in the previous discussion, the suggestion here is for a dual interpretive regime in type 2 cases. In such cases, I have suggested, courts should defer so long as the statutory text directly at issue contains a surface-level gap or ambiguity.

Agencies might themselves, however, draw upon a wider range of sources, tools, and considerations. Although I have urged that courts adopt a restricted repertoire of formalist interpretive techniques, I have also suggested that agencies themselves need not do so. Attention to institutional considerations can show why agencies might be given the authority to use this richer interpretive palette, even if courts should be denied that authority.

Two points are relevant here. First, agencies are likely to be in a better position to decide which procedures for gap-filling and which sources of interpretive information provide the greatest marginal benefits in light of statutory and administrative policies. This is so mostly because agencies have a superior degree of specialized technical competence, a superior understanding of legislative processes (both in general and in the setting of particular statutes), a superior knowledge of the legislative history and the original intentions, purposes, and compromises it reflects, and a degree of political responsiveness that gives them superior information about both public values and policy-relevant facts. Second, agencies are likely to be in a better position to know whether departures from the text will seriously diminish predictability or otherwise unsettle the statutory scheme. If agencies are not concerned about the risk of unsettlement, there is some reason to think that the risk is low. Because of these points, the case for formalistic interpretation by judges is stronger than the case for formalistic interpretation by agencies. That is a substantive claim; methodologically, the key points are just that agencies need not be required to interpret statutes in the same way as courts.

Of course any judgment on this point itself depends on contextual factors, the same variables we have examined throughout. One such question is whether a regime of purposive, flexible interpretation by agencies and formalist interpretation by courts would be stable. We might imagine, pessimistically, that the anticipation of judicial review by formalist courts would cause agencies to adopt similar methods simply to maximize the chances of having their decisions sustained; agencies' authority to depart from formalism would then become strictly nominal. If so, it would provide a reason, all else equal, for courts and agencies to adopt the same interpretive approach, although we would still face the important choice between formalism and flexibility across the board.

But there is nothing inevitable about this scenario. Reviewing courts could simply defer to agencies' adoption of a purposive or nonformalist interpretive approach even if the same courts would themselves adopt a formalist approach when deciding cases with no agency in the picture. Just as a regime of second-order default rules would allow agencies themselves to choose the relevant interpretive default rules within their areas of expertise, so too on a larger scale *Chevron* can easily be understood to allow the agency latitude to choose between interpretive approaches and to vary from the approach the court itself would adopt. Under this proposal, the agency would have no need to mimic the judges' own interpretive approach, so a regime of agency purposivism and judicial formalism would not be unstable.

Agencies, courts, and the allocation of complexity. I have suggested that in cases where there is no clear and specific text on point, agencies might properly engage in a more complex form of interpretation than courts do. On institutional grounds, that is, courts might eschew the use of many of the traditional tools of interpretation in such cases, remitting their resolution to agencies through relatively simple rules of deference. Is this suggestion excessively judge-centered, falling into exactly the sort of mistakes emphasized in Chapter 2? Perhaps the arguments from maximin, satisficing, cost-benefit, and the principle of insufficient reason, if considered from the standpoint of agencies rather than judges, would also suggest that agencies ought to eschew complex interpretation. Conversely, perhaps reducing the ambition, burdens, and costs of judicial decision-making by judicial deference to agencies where texts are vague or ambiguous would merely shift decision costs onto agencies less able to bear them. Under certain empirical assumptions, this sort of shift could even make the overall interpretive system worse off.

Here two points are critical. First, these concerns, even if correct, would show at most that agencies themselves should eschew complex interpretation as well. The interpretive system would then become globally much simpler than it is, but this is no objection to my central claim that judicial interpretation should become much simpler than it is. To make these concerns bite, one would have to defend the facially implausible thesis that there is a law of the conservation of interpretive complexity across the whole interpretive system, so that the costs of ambitious interpretation can only ever be redistributed from judges to agencies, not reduced overall. No reason for holding such a view suggests itself. The danger here is an unreasoned prejudice that the status quo level of systemwide interpretive complexity is optimal or at least inevitable. Perhaps some minimum of interpretive complexity is inevitable in a modern legal system, but the current level may also be far above that minimum.

Second, I have given reasons to believe that the costs to agencies of engaging in complex interpretation, using the traditional interpretive tools, are lower than the costs to courts. Specialist agencies, for example, are far better positioned to comprehend the complex legislative histories of their particular statutes than are generalist judges. If this is so, then reducing judicial decision costs by deference to agencies would produce a net reduction in systemwide decision costs as well, for an overall gain. The interpretive complexity shunted out of the judiciary would be managed at a lower cost by agencies. General assessments of this sort are themselves empirical, of course. Here we bump up against the limits of the trans-science thesis discussed in Chapter 6. Where complex interpretive information must be processed, to deny the benefits of agency specialization is to cross the indistinct but real boundary between laudable agnosticism and debilitating skepticism.

The Scope of *Chevron:* The *Mead* Muddle

I have suggested that the scope of judicial deference to agencies should be wide indeed: courts should defer so long as the text immediately at hand contains a surface-level gap or ambiguity. There are actually two issues here. One question is whether other interpretive sources, the traditional tools of interpretation, should be taken to override the agency's views where there is a conflict. I have urged that the answer be no. A distinct issue, however, involves the question which types of agencies, using which types of decisionmaking processes, are entitled to *Chevron* deference where a gap or ambiguity is conceded to exist. That latter question is addressed in the most important administrative law decision in many years: *United States v. Mead,*[39] which curtailed *Chevron* deference and adopted a resolutely noninstitutional account of *Chevron's* rationale.

I shall suggest that *Mead* is close to disastrous on institutional grounds. *Mead* attempts to develop a fine-grained jurisprudence of deference, sensitive to the differences among the multiple policymaking instruments that agencies use; the Court's basic impulse was to "tailor deference to variety."[40] But this impulse overlooks the increasing cognitive and institutional load that the increasing complexity of *Mead*'s legal regime imposes on lower courts, litigants, and other actors. On the account I offer, the Court should return to the much broader version of *Chevron* deference urged in dissent by Justice Scalia.

The Mead *opinion.* Two questions were at issue in *Mead:* should the two-step test for deference articulated by *Chevron* apply to a letter ruling of the Customs Service, and if not, should the less formal deference standard of *Skidmore v. Swift & Co.*[41] apply instead? The Court's nominal answers were also clear enough: no to the first question and yes to the second. My focus is on the first question and the large reframing of the law of deference that the Court implemented.

The *Chevron* opinion itself is best read as an attempt to simplify and clarify the preexisting and notoriously muddled law of deference to agency interpretations. Doctrinally, *Chevron* announced a straightforward set of ideas: Congress sometimes intends to delegate lawmaking authority to agencies; such delegations may be express or implied; statutory ambiguities and gaps will be taken as implied delegations of agency authority to make law by interpreting the ambiguity in one direction or the other or by filling in the gap. From this follows the famous *Chevron* two-step, under which courts first ask whether Congress has spoken clearly to the question at hand, and, if not, whether the agency interpretation is reasonable. The first question asks whether there is an ambiguity or a gap to be filled; the second asks whether the agency's chosen interpretation falls permissibly within the domain of the ambiguity or impermissibly outside it. On this view, the key innovation of *Chevron* is to create a global interpretive presumption: gaps and ambiguities are, without more, taken to signify implicit delegations of interpretive authority to the administering agency.

Mead reverses this global presumption. Rather than taking a gap or ambiguity to signify delegation, *Mead* establishes that the default rule runs against delegation. Unless the reviewing court affirmatively finds that Congress intended to delegate interpretive authority to the particular agency at hand in the particular statutory scheme at hand, *Chevron* deference is not due and the *Chevron* two-step is not to be invoked. This need not mean that absent a delegation, the reviewing court decides the interpretive question without regard to the agency's views. The agency's views are, under the alternative *Skidmore* standard, still deserving of a certain inchoate "respect," due to the agency's policy expertise and to the intrinsic persuasiveness of its position. Note, however, that (both before and after *Mead*) there is a set of interpretive questions as to which the agency's views are irrelevant, except to the extent that any litigant's views are considered; an example is the interpretation of the Administrative Procedure Act itself. So *Mead* establishes a finely graded structure of deference with three categories or tiers: *Chevron* deference, *Skidmore* deference and no deference. Justice Scalia's dissenting view, by contrast, would have recognized only two tiers: *Chevron* deference, and no deference at all, with the former triggered by any authoritative agency interpretation. Scalia's alternative, then, is *Chevron* as a global default rule.

Two blows against institutionalism. Note two aspects of the *Mead* opinion that run contrary to the institutionalist view of agency deference I have articulated here. First, the justification for *Chevron* deference is, in the view of the *Mead* Court, simply that Congress intends courts to accord agencies deference under certain circumstances. This is a formalist idea (in the old and inadequate sense of formalism); it is emphatically not the institutional idea I have defended, under which the justification for *Chevron* is simply that judicial deference to agencies produces better consequences than nondeference. Second, the *Mead* Court moves away from *Chevron*'s relative simplicity toward a far more complex regime of deference standards.

We must unpack the second point a bit. If congressional intentions determine deference, in what circumstances should the reviewing court find affirmative evidence of congressional intent to delegate (thereby assigning the issue to *Chevron* deference rather than *Skidmore* deference)? One idea, pressed by some academics and members of the administrative bar, would have been to say the following: *Chevron* deference is owed if, but only if, the agency possesses a statutory delegation of rulemaking or formal adjudicative authority and has used that authority to produce the interpretation at issue. *Mead*, however, does not adopt this relatively simple approach. The opinion is quite clear that although the agency's authority to use, and actual use of, the relevant procedural formats—formal rulemaking or adjudication and informal rulemaking—should usually be taken as sufficient to evidence a congressional intent to delegate, formal agency procedure is not necessary.[42] The requisite delegatory intent may be found even as to agency action outside these categories—

including informal adjudication, interpretive or procedural rules excepted from notice-and-comment obligations, and other varieties of action—so long as "circumstances" evidence a delegatory intent. *Mead* is thoroughly vague about what circumstances count as evidence of such an intent, and what the evidentiary weights of various circumstances are. I shall indicate some of the relevant considerations later. It is clear, however, that the Court was greatly concerned that making procedural formality a necessary condition for *Chevron* deference, as well as a sufficient condition, would be too crude an approach; it would fail adequately to (in the Court's words) "tailor deference to variety," here the variety of procedural formats by which agencies generate interpretations.

Mead: *An indictment.* It is not too early to offer some tentative generalizations about the heavy burdens of implementing *Mead,* burdens that fall principally upon lower courts and litigants rather than the Supreme Court itself. From the Supreme Court's relatively detached and abstract perspective, the global *Chevron* alternative urged by Justice Scalia might have seemed unacceptably crude. Adding a layer of refinement to the deference analysis may well have seemed an obviously sensible move, an easy way to "tailor deference to variety." In this section I shall suggest, however, that the seductive theory of *Mead* has worked out badly in the trenches of lower-court decisionmaking. Important cases purporting to apply *Mead* have devolved into extensive, and likely inefficient, litigation over threshold questions; have taken *Mead* to license an all-things-considered de novo judicial determination whether the agency's interpretation is correct or incorrect; and have taken *Mead*'s threshold inquiry into delegation to support a sort of generalized hostility to delegated agency authority. On the ground, I shall suggest, *Mead* has produced a great deal of confusion and error; and I shall offer some reasons why this might be so.

Uncertainty, error, and decision costs. The most obvious point or set of points emerges from the distinction between rules and standards. When and why might it be best for high courts in a jurisdiction to use rules rather than standards? One type of answer draws on principal-agent models, in which lower courts are taken as agents and the high court as principal. Standards raise the costs to the principal of monitoring the behavior of its agents, so a higher court may use rules in part to confine the discretion of lower-court judges, who would otherwise exploit standards to implement their own preferences.

But rules might have other benefits, even where all lower-court judges attempt to faithfully implement the high court's instructions. The principal benefits are that rules might, all else equal, reduce uncertainty in the legal system, reduce the cost to lower courts of reaching decisions, and even reduce the rate and gravity of the errors that lower courts make. Rules might reduce uncertainty for litigants if they make planning easier; they might reduce decision costs for lower courts because they reduce the range of facts and questions that are legally relevant. Most surprisingly, rules might sometimes reduce error on the part of lower-court judges even though rules are overinclusive and underinclusive relative to the rules' background justifications. If the cognitive load imposed by open-ended standards is large, so that decisionmakers using such standards will frequently (even in good faith) stray widely from the background justification, then even the distortion that rules create might produce greater net accuracy than would a comparable standard. As to all of these points, there are many variables to be considered.

Along these lines it is a valid, if rather obvious, objection to *Mead* that it overvalues the decisional benefits of standards and undervalues the decisional benefits of rules. In some passages the *Mead* Court seems to talk as though the mere existence of a background goal or justification—here, the idea that deference is a function of congressional intent—entails as a conceptual or logical matter that only an all-things-considered inquiry into that justification is legally permissible. This is nonsense, of course; rules and standards are simply different, equally permissible devices for structuring the decisionmaking environment. (Nor did the *Mead* Court itself follow through on its claim; recall that the *Mead* Court, despite its sneer at Justice Scalia's relatively rulelike alternative, filters the congressional intent inquiry through rulelike procedural categories designed to make the inquiry more tractable.) Even short of that nonsensical claim, however, it is equally a mistake for higher courts to adopt doctrinal structures that require finely tailored inquiries while ignoring or underestimating the resultant decisional burdens. In what follows I shall explore less obvious variations on this theme. But it remains a forceful objection to *Mead* that it implements an ambitious, even perfectionist search for precision in the legal norms governing agency deference, precision whose benefits are, on the evidence to date, outweighed by the collateral costs.

Predecision costs. In a variety of areas, law incurs not only first-order decision costs, but what might be called predecision costs—costs of allocating decisions between or among different jurisdictions, different decisionmakers, or different standards of review by a given decisionmaker. Sometimes the legal system's willingness to incur predecision costs reaches grotesque extremes, as when parties litigate which forum's choice-of-law rule will determine which forum's conflict-of-law rule will determine which forum's substantive law will determine the merits,[43] or when judges or justices extensively debate constitutional standards of review that even academic experts find it nigh impossible to differentiate. Predecision costs inflict deadweight losses whenever, after the fact, the difference between alternative decisionmaking forums or standards of review makes no difference.

Mead requires lower courts to incur extensive predecision costs. Consider a post-*Mead* decision of the federal Court of Appeals for the District of Columbia Circuit, *Federal Election Commission v. National Rifle Association*,[44] in which the circuit court conducted an extensive analysis to decide the preliminary question whether to afford *Chevron* deference to a formal advisory opinion of the FEC. This sort of preliminary litigation over which standard of review applies to the ultimate statutory questions may consume far more lawyer time and judge time and present many more complexities than the statutory merits. Given that there is at least a substantial domain of cases that come out the same way under either *Chevron* or *Skidmore*—the FEC case is one—the benefits of *Mead*'s fine-tuning of the applicable standards of review may be swamped by the extra predecision costs it creates.

Are tiers of deference possible? The principal effect of *Mead* is to add an extra tier to the potentially applicable standards of judicial review. Rejecting Justice Scalia's proposal for a regime containing *Chevron* deference or no deference, *Mead* creates a regime with *Chevron* deference, *Skidmore* deference, and no deference. The analysis of predecision costs just given suggests that *Mead*'s attempt to refine the deference analysis is not cost-justified. A different and more radical critique suggests that adding an extra tier of deference is, in a pragmatic sense, simply infeasible, given the cognitive constraints under which real-world adjudication occurs. Judges can operate in a mode of deference and in a mode of independent decisionmaking, but more refined, intermediate modes are either psychologically unattainable or nonexistent. As Judge Posner puts it:

[Judicial] endorsement of multiple standards of review . . . greatly ex-aggerates the utility of verbal differentiation. It reflects the lawyer's ex-aggerated faith in the Word. I think I understand the difference between plenary review and deferential review. In the former setting the appellate judge must say to himself, "The issue has been given to me to decide, and while I shall pay due attention to what the district judge (or other trier of fact) had to say on the question the ultimate decisional respon-sibility is mine and must be exercised independently." In the latter set-ting the appellate judge must say to himself, "The issue is not mine to decide; because the district judge (or magistrate or administrative agency or whatever) has a better feel for it, or for other institutional reasons (such as to discourage appeals), the responsibility for deciding has been given to him and I must go along unless persuaded that he acted un-reasonably, or in other words unless I am clear in my mind that he erred." What is the intermediate position? There is none.[45]

If anything like this view is correct, of course, *Mead*'s attempted re-finement of *Chevron* is so much wasted paper. Its only effect will be to increase the frequency with which judges operate in a nondeferential mode as opposed to a deferential one; and when judges are in the former mode, they will ignore the agency's views entirely. Another case from the District of Columbia Circuit, *Motion Picture Association of America v. Federal Communications Commission,*[46] provides an example of this effect. The panel overlooked that it was supposed to be deciding on the level of deference, collapsed the *Mead* inquiry into the merits, and decided the statutory question without affording the Federal Communications Com-mission even the polite nod that *Skidmore* deference affords.

Standards as externalities. Finally, we may again invoke rules and stan-dards to analyze the relationship between the Supreme Court and the lower courts, although with a different emphasis. We have seen that a principal might choose rules over standards in order to minimize the costs of front-line decisionmaking by subordinate agents. But the con-verse point is that the articulation of standards by the highest court in a jurisdiction shifts decisionmaking costs onto lower courts. Those costs will not be truly externalized if the jurisdiction's high court will subse-quently incur the costs of the standard-based regime, perhaps in the form of later appeals from fact-specific rulings in the courts below. But if the high court can avoid all or some of those subsequent costs, for example, by strategic use of discretionary certiorari jurisdiction, then a genuine externalization is possible, in which case high courts may produce too many standard-based decisions, from the social point of view.

It is not hard to see *Mead* in this light. If the Court desires to cast its own jurisprudence in a more fine-grained fashion than the global *Chevron* regime that Justice Scalia urged, the costs of that jurisprudence will be felt most immediately and keenly by the District of Columbia Circuit rather than the Court itself. To the extent that the Court can use its discretionary certiorari jurisdiction to avoid entanglement in the fact-bound metalitigation that *Mead* requires—and there is every reason to believe that it not only can do this, but will—then the Court will have failed to account for the full social costs of its preferred legal regime.

Back to the future? In light of these points, I think that it is not too early to declare *Mead* a failure. What matters here, however, is the methodological point: *Mead* fails for want of attention to the institutional consequences of the deference regime the Court sought to create. Consider the Court's sneering dismissal of Justice Scalia's argument for an exclusive reliance on *Chevron*'s global, relatively rulelike approach. The Court dismissed the global *Chevron* alternative by invoking the stock argument that rules are overinclusive relative to their purposes; Justice Scalia's approach, which would afford *Chevron* deference even where the majority's approach would find no delegatory intent, failed sufficiently to "tailor deference to variety." But of course the *Mead* majority could have gone even further than it did to "tailor deference to variety"; instead, it chose to develop procedural proxies that serve as subrules. The question is why the Court chose to stop where it did on the continuum defined at one end by Justice Scalia's approach and at the other by a genuine totality-of-the-circumstances test. The unfortunate, and almost surely unintended, implication of the Court's sneer is that any attempt to limit the range of considerations to less than all the relevant circumstances amounts to an impermissible failure to capture congressional intent, even if the costs of the all-things-considered search are much higher than the costs of a more structured inquiry would be.

Taken together, these considerations suggest that *Mead*'s compromise position, suspended uneasily between *Chevron*'s relatively clear global presumption and a genuine totality-of-the-circumstances test, is intrinsically unstable. At the Supreme Court level, it may well slip in one direction or another, either back toward *Chevron*'s former scope or in the other direction, toward an even soupier approach than the *Mead* Court was willing to permit. My central suggestion here has been that the former outcome—a reinstatement of global *Chevron* deference—would be highly desirable in light of the high costs of decisionmaking and uncertainty under the *Mead* regime, and *Mead*'s very uncertain benefits.

Precedent, Judges, and Agencies

The foregoing discussion anticipates important issues concerning the weight to be afforded statutory precedents. Let us begin with the strictly judicial case, in which later judges decide what weight to accord precedents issued by earlier judges; we shall then bring agencies into the picture. In general, from an institutional perspective, the precedent debate has occupied the wrong terrain. Proponents of a strong or even absolute rule of statutory precedent have generally grounded their arguments on a democracy-forcing claim that an absolute rule will force desirable legislative responses.[47] But in light of the discussion of precedent in Chapter 5, there is no reason to believe that judges can systematically coordinate on a democracy-forcing approach. Different judges will have different theories of precedent, different views of democracy-forcing, and different views of what the resulting rules should be. This coordination failure matters if, as I have suggested, democracy-forcing rules need some critical or threshold mass of judicial participation to accomplish their ends. What is needed is an account of precedent that allows strictly marginal contributions from individual judges, such that individual votes may contribute marginally to systemic goods even if many other judges do not vote similarly.

If individual judges cannot generate the critical mass of participation needed for democracy-forcing to work, they may nonetheless contribute, at the margin, to a reduction in the overall decision costs of precedent. If the effect of strong statutory precedent on legislative response is highly conjectural, the effect on judicial decision costs is not. All else held constant, the stronger the rule of statutory precedent, the less frequently litigants will seek overruling, and the less time must be spent on redeciding previously decided questions. This is a strictly marginal phenomenon, such that each judge who subscribes to strong precedent contributes to reducing decision costs for the whole system.

To be sure, parties, especially institutional litigants, will also invest more in cases of first impression, because the stakes are higher with a strong rule of precedent. But that increased investment occurs in cases that would usually be brought anyway, because cases of first impression are typically hard cases in which the law favors neither side strongly. The increased investment will be dwarfed by the subsequent reduction in decision costs resulting from many potential future cases that are never brought at all because litigants who object to the precedent anticipate a lower chance of success. This gain in legal certainty and stability is tangible, while the collateral costs and benefits of precedent are speculative. Holmes said of himself that "I am slow to assent to overruling a decision. Precisely my skepticism . . . makes me very unwilling to increase the doubt as to what a court will do."[48] In our terms, judges should adhere to a strong doctrine of precedent on cost-benefit, maximin, and satisficing grounds, minimizing the clear costs of legal uncertainty because the benefits of overruling are typically conjectural.

It follows from our earlier discussion, however, that the picture changes when agencies participate in setting the first or subsequent interpretation. On one view, a judicial interpretation of a statute freezes the law in place; the judicial precedent should trump any later agency interpretation even if the agency interpretation would, in a case of first impression, have been a reasonable interpretation of a statutory gap or ambiguity.[49] From the institutional standpoint, however, this is misguided. Judicial precedent should give way to an agency interpretation if that interpretation is otherwise permissible. Allocating override authority to the agency in this way increases, rather than reduces, legal certainty, for the reasons Peter Strauss gives: centralizing interpretive authority in agencies reduces the disuniformity of law across judicial circuits and thus reduces the net uncertainty and decision costs of the interpretive regime.[50] Strauss's point holds for subsequent interpretations just as for earlier ones. To be sure, if the Supreme Court itself (as opposed to the lower courts) could decide all statutory cases, then uniformity would also be secured by judicial supremacy (bracketing the question of disuniformity within the Supreme Court itself, as discussed in Chapter 5). But the premise of Strauss's argument, a premise that no one seriously disputes, is that the Court lacks the institutional capacity to take all interpretation upon itself in that way.

The judicial-supremacy approach is typically justified on the essentialist basis that agency override of judicial precedent is inconsistent with the grant of "judicial power" to the courts, or with courts' power to "say what the law is," but these are typically unhelpful abstractions. Similar points have been urged against *Chevron* itself. Here, as there, the right essentialist counter is simply that the law itself might include a rule of agency override, in which case the rule does not contravene courts' law-declaring power. Such reasoning is empty, no matter whether offered in favor of *Chevron* or against it. Abstract argument does not come to grips with the institutional considerations on which arguments for or against agency override must be based.

Agencies and Common-Law Interpretation

There is a larger point here, about the role of agencies as interpreters who develop statutes over time in common-law fashion. The question whether new agency interpretations may override judicial precedent is a special case of the larger phenomenon of statutory drift. The great strength of Eskridge's dynamism is the descriptive premise that the import of both statutes and judicial precedent changes over time with changes in ordinary usage of language, changing technology and policy questions, and new contexts of application. As I suggested in Chapter 2, however, Eskridge goes wrong when, in his earlier work, he supposes that courts must be the institutions charged with adjusting statutes to changing circumstances.

A premise of *Chevron* deference is that agencies may adjust their interpretations to new facts, policies, and even political values, switching to new rules that fill statutory gaps or resolve ambiguities. On this view, agencies are best suited to function as common-law courts because of their superior information, superior capacities for policy analysis, and more direct pipeline to the changing political and public values that Eskridge wants courts to incorporate into statutory interpretation. Where agencies rather than courts are charged with updating statutes to reflect public values, it follows that courts should defer to agencies whenever the current meaning of a statute discloses a gap or ambiguity.

In previous discussion I suggested grounds for a converging agreement between textualists, on the one hand, and intentionalists or purposivists, on the other, as to rules excluding legislative history, mandating deference to agencies, and other matters. We have here the basis for another converging agreement, this time between originalist interpreters, who think that the original meaning of statutory language as of the time of enactment governs, and dynamists like Eskridge, who think that current meaning is paramount. Both camps might agree to defer to agencies when either the original meaning or the current meaning discloses a gap or ambiguity. Originalists would do so because, as I suggested earlier, there is little reason to think that courts will do much better at recovering legislative intentions or purposes than agencies will, in part because of agencies' much greater familiarity with legislative processes, while judicial interpretation produces discernibly large systemic costs. Dynamic interpreters, on the other hand, will accept judicial deference because agencies will be better suited to play the role of common-law courts.

There is nothing inconsistent about saying both that originalist interpreters might opt for a regime of strong agency deference and that agencies might be best situated to function as statutory updaters on dynamic premises. The suggestion is that relative to judges, agencies' institutional capacities make them superior interpreters on both originalist and dynamic views of statutory interpretation. At least, agencies are not so clearly inferior as interpreters that judges should incur the collateral systemic costs of ambitious judicial interpretation to fill gaps or ambiguities. This suggestion provides the basis for the converging agreement I have outlined. So far as agency deference goes, no high-level choice of interpretive values over time, no high-level theory of the legitimacy of statutory drift, seems necessary.

Coordination and Marginal Contribution

Importantly, nothing in the interpretive decision-procedure I have sketched here aims to produce desirable reactions from Congress or other institutions; no democracy-forcing is in the picture. No threshold or critical mass of judicial coordination is necessary to implement these proposals. Rather, the contribution that individual judges can make is strictly marginal or divisible. By declining to consult legislative history, eschewing a wide set of holistic sources, and deferring to agency interpretations where the text at hand is not clear and specific, individual judges can reduce systemic decision costs and legal uncertainty at the margin.

Coda: *Chevron,* Textualism, and a Model Opinion

I conclude by showing, rather than describing, what I take to be the appropriately modest judicial posture in statutory interpretation. The model opinion I wish to exhibit is Justice Kennedy's plurality opinion in *K Mart v. Cartier,*[51] which upheld certain Customs Service regulations that permitted the importation of "gray-market" goods—trademarked goods manufactured abroad and imported without the consent of the American trademark holder.

The statutory provision immediately at hand in *K Mart* made it illegal to import, without the American trademark holder's consent, "into the United States any merchandise of foreign manufacture if such merchandise . . . bears a trademark owned by [an American citizen or corporation]." Although the Court addressed several issues and fractured badly, a majority found that the agency had validly interpreted the language to permit importation in situations where the foreign and American trademark holders were subject to common control—for example, where a foreign firm incorporated an American subsidiary that then held the domestic trademark. Justice Kennedy's plurality opinion upheld the regulation principally because the phrase "merchandise of foreign manufacture" could, as a linguistic matter, refer either to goods manufactured in a foreign country or goods manufactured by a foreign company; there was thus an ambiguity for the agency to resolve.

At the level of method, the Kennedy opinion provided a highly deferential version of the two-step *Chevron* test. In this version, the agency prevails whenever "the plain meaning of the statute" is "silent or ambiguous with respect to the specific issue addressed by the regulation." Of course, a major issue, as we have seen, is what the scope of "the statute" is—whether "the plain meaning of the statute" can be generated by incorporating collateral statutory provisions drawn from other titles or sections or even from other statutes entirely. Justice Scalia's dissent in *K Mart* followed this strategy, rejecting the claim of ambiguity on the ground that collateral statutes and regulations used the key term "merchandise of foreign manufacture" in ways inconsistent with the agency's view. But the plurality suggested a narrower, less ambitious approach, indeed the very approach I have urged here: the agency prevails unless the particular provision at hand clearly bars the regulation, without consideration of legislative history, holistic textual comparison to collateral provisions, or other tools. Although the Kennedy opinion paid lip service to the principle that the court must look to "the language and design of the statute as a whole," not merely the "particular statutory language at issue," the opinion took back the lip service in an important passage:

> I disagree with Justice Scalia's reasons for declining to recognize this ambiguity. . . . First, the threshold question in ascertaining the correct interpretation of a statute is whether the language of the statute is clear or arguably ambiguous. The purported gloss any party gives to the statute, or any reference to legislative history, is in the first instance irrelevant. . . . I believe that agency regulations may give a varying interpretation of the same phrase when that phrase appears in different statutes and different statutory contexts. There may well be variances in purposes or circumstances that have led the agency to adopt and apply dissimilar interpretations of the phrase "of foreign manufacture" in other regulations implementing different statutes.[52]

It has frequently been suggested that a textualist approach to *Chevron* might systematically result in less deference to agencies than a nontextualist approach. On this view, as Justice Scalia himself puts it, "one who finds *more* often (as I do) that the meaning of a statute is apparent from its text and from its relationship with other laws, thereby finds *less* often that the triggering requirement for *Chevron* deference exists."[53] *K Mart* suggests that this account embodies at most a partial truth, and a rather misleading one. As the *K Mart* dissent demonstrates, most of the work in anti-deferential textualism is done by recourse to collateral statutes and provisions. Where courts both eschew legislative history and restrict themselves to the statutory provision at hand, there will be little material with which to override an agency resolution of a linguistic ambiguity.

It is true, however, as Justice Scalia also says, that the approach I urge here will bar deference where ambiguities are extrinsic rather than intrinsic—where, as in the conventional understanding of *Holy Trinity*, the clear and specific text of the provision at hand is inconsistent with legislative history. But my suggestion has not been that agencies should always win, or that courts should defer whenever the agency can cite some legal material in support of its view. My basic claims are these: First, courts should adopt an interpretive decision-procedure or set of rules that satisfice on the dimension of accuracy (about meanings, or intentions, or purposes) while minimizing the collateral costs of decision and uncertainty. Second, the decision-procedure that meets these criteria is for courts to defer to the agency's views unless clear and specific language, in the provision immediately at issue, bars the agency interpretation. This is certainly a humble posture for judges, one that restricts courts to a small set of small tasks. But our aim, from the systemic perspective, is not to find a decision-procedure that makes cases interesting for judges. It is to find arrangements that take best overall account of the institutional capacities of courts, agencies, and other actors in the interpretive system.

— 8 —

Judicial Review and
Constitutional Interpretation

Part I diagnosed various types of institutional blindness on the part of prominent theorists of legislation and statutory interpretation. The principal recommendation of Part II was that the theory of statutory interpretation should take an institutional turn. Chapter 7 recommended that judges choosing interpretive rules under conditions of uncertainty and bounded rationality should opt for a rule-bound combination of plain meaning and agency deference. What of constitutional interpretation? In this chapter I shall claim that all of these recommendations generalize, with appropriate modifications, to the constitutional setting. The institutional turn is fully appropriate, indeed necessary, for constitutional as well as statutory interpretation. Judicial review of statutes for constitutionality and judicial decision-procedures for constitutional interpretation must be assessed in light of institutional capacities and systemic effects. The problem of interpretive choice under uncertainty thus arises in the constitutional setting and must be resolved with the tools developed in Chapter 6.

My conclusions parallel those of Chapter 7. On cost-benefit, maximin, and satisficing grounds, judges should choose a rule-bound decision-procedure for constitutional cases. The baseline judicial function in constitutional cases is to enforce clear and specific constitutional texts. But judges should eschew ambitious forays beyond this baseline. Judges should thus defer to legislatures on the interpretation of constitutional texts that are ambiguous, can be read at multiple levels of generality, or embody aspirational norms whose content changes over time with shifting public values. The category of provisions to be remitted to legislative enforcement includes the principal provisions of the Bill of Rights and the Fourteenth Amendment, especially the guarantees of free speech, due process, and equal protection.

This is a surprising conclusion, of course, and one that will strike many supporters of robust judicial review as beyond the pale. Must the Court really sit back and permit legislatures to choke off political speech, or to curtail rights of privacy and reproductive autonomy? As against this sort of reasoning from a set of vivid particulars, I emphasize the rule-consequentialist case against judicial review. For every rights-protective Supreme Court decision, there is a decision that undermines rights. The question is not whether, say, the Court's decision in *Brown v. Board of Education* is "good" or "bad" in isolation. Ambitious judicial review is an institutional rule that necessarily produces a package of outcomes, both good and bad. If the package includes *Brown,* it also includes horrors such as Chief Justice Taney's proclamation in *Dred Scott v. Sandford* that there is a constitutional right to own slaves. To favor ambitious judicial review is to favor an interpretive regime that sweeps well beyond the particular results beloved by judicial review's defenders. Nor is there any mechanism by which the judges can be constrained to produce only the good outcomes and not the bad ones. The key question then, is whether any more ambitious form of judicial review than the one I propose is beneficial in net effect. I think that the answer is no. Given the high risks and strictly conjectural benefits of ambitious judicial review and its definite systemic costs, our legal order is better off without it.

Two general qualifications are in order. First, the Constitution is, of course, not the same as a garden-variety statute. The difference in the material being interpreted and in the broader settings may affect the answers that a thoroughly institutional analysis will produce, even if it does not affect the variables that must be considered. Because the constitutional setting differs from the statutory settings in important ways, the same inquiry into institutional capacities and system effects may produce different answers. In general, however, my conclusions are familiar: courts should adopt an unassuming and unambitious posture, deferring to other institutions whenever the legal materials at hand do not clearly and specifically resolve the legal questions.

Second, academic theory about constitutional law does better, on the score of institutional sensitivity, than academic theory about statutory interpretation. As I shall suggest later, constitutional theorists have in part already taken the institutional turn, with important work beginning in the 1970s. And the conclusions I reach are firmly within a burgeoning strand of constitutional theory that I dub *neo-Thayerian*. At the same time, the institutional turn is as yet incomplete in constitutional theory. The treatment of basic questions in constitutional law, such as judicial review, has always suffered from institutional blindness; there remain important pockets of contemporary theory that are resolutely oblivious to second-best questions; and my institutional justifications for the Thayerian position are very different than the historical, populist, or jurisprudential grounds that other theorists tend to emphasize.

Overview

I begin by emphasizing the extent to which the foundations of interpretive theory in constitutional law are deficient on the score of institutional sensitivity. Here the critical case is, of course, *Marbury v. Madison*[1] and its inadequate (because excessively abstract and conceptual) justification for judicial review. After sketching the partial and salutary turn to institutional analysis in modern constitutional theory, and especially in the most recent work, I then turn to the basic question whether judicial review is desirable on institutional grounds. Here I survey a range of leading accounts, defenses, or versions of constitutional judicial review, accounts that go well beyond *Marbury*'s conceptualisms. Among them are Alexander Hamilton's principal-agent conception of judicial review, John Hart Ely's representation-reinforcing view, Ronald Dworkin's account of constitutional interpretation, Antonin Scalia's version of originalism, Akhil Amar's "intratextualism," Lawrence Lessig's translation theory, Larry Alexander and Frederick Schauer's attempt to ground judicial supremacy in the settlement function of law, and David Strauss's common-law constitutionalism.

Despite their sophistication, I claim that all of these accounts suffer from institutional deficits. The premises of these accounts do not reach all the way down to the operational level; they cannot explain why, and to what extent, courts should be entrusted with the power to review legislation for constitutionality. The basic claims here are familiar. At a minimum, accounts of constitutional interpretation are incomplete without reference to institutional capacities. Second, and more ambitiously, institutional considerations may enable constitutional lawyers to converge upon interpretive approaches in operation, bracketing first-best accounts of constitutionalism or simply remaining agnostic about them.

After clearing the ground in this way, I analyze judicial review and constitutional interpretation from the standpoint of institutional choice and interpretive choice. Whether, and to what extent, judicial review is desirable turns upon a range of empirical and institutional variables, including the agency costs, error costs, and decision costs of the alternative regimes, moral-hazard effects, the optimal rate of legal change, the costs of transition from one regime to another, and the relative capacities of legislatures and courts at updating obsolete constitutional provisions. As in the parallel case of statutory interpretation, the empirical variables are highly uncertain, judges' information is limited, and their capacity to process information is poor.

I then turn to applying the suite of tools for choosing interpretive regimes under conditions of uncertainty and bounded judicial rationality. I conclude that the basic decision-procedures for constitutional interpretation should track the basic decision-procedures for statutory interpretation suggested in Chapter 7. Courts should enforce, through substantive judicial review, only the sort of clear and specific constitutional texts that tend to promote structural and coordinating goals. In cases where constitutional texts are ambiguous, can be read at multiple levels of generality, or embody vaguely stated political aspirations, courts should defer to legislatures as an institution better placed to update the Constitution over time. These conclusions parallel those of Chapter 7. Just as I suggested that courts should defer to agencies when statutes contain gaps or ambiguities, so too I shall suggest that courts should defer to legislatures when constitutional provisions contain gaps or ambiguities. Because the Constitution contains less clear and specific text than do most modern regulatory statutes, however, in operation these recommendations will mean that courts have a smaller role in constitutional interpretation than in statutory interpretation.

To attach a useful label to all this: I shall urge, on institutional grounds, a Thayerian version of judicial review. Courts should enforce the Constitution only where, as the nineteenth-century legal scholar James Bradley Thayer suggested, no reasonable basis for interpretive dispute exists, because the constitutional text is clear and specific. This proposal in effect makes most of the vague, ambiguous, and aspirational pronouncements of the Bill of Rights nonjusticiable; it restricts courts to enforcing, for the most part, the more specific structural and coordinating provisions of Articles I–VII of the Constitution. This was in essence the view not only of Thayer, but of Judge Learned Hand and of Justice Felix

Frankfurter. Although their defense of this view was not institutional in the present sense, I mean to proceed in the spirit of their views, and I reach similar conclusions.

Marbury v. Madison

Is judicial review desirable? Does the Constitution call for it? These are old and much-debated questions. The modest goal here is to draw attention to a serious problem: Many of the best-known arguments on behalf of judicial review, including those in *Marbury* itself, are blind to institutional considerations. They ignore the risk of judicial error and the possibility of dynamic consequences. In American law, Chief Justice John Marshall might even be deemed the father, or the founder, of the kind of institutional blindness that we are criticizing.

Indeed, what is most striking about Marshall's arguments for judicial review is that they depend on a series of fragile textual and structural inferences, ignoring the institutional issues at stake. Much of Marshall's emphasis is on the unobjectionable claim that the Constitution is "superior paramount law"; but it is possible to accept that claim without also thinking that courts are authorized to strike down statutes that violate that law. A constitution is "superior paramount law" in many legal systems that offer little or no judicial review of legislation. When Marshall famously asserts that "[it] is emphatically the province and duty of the judicial department to say what the law is," he is offering a conclusion, not an argument on its behalf. Marshall invokes the Supremacy Clause,[2] which certainly means that a law repugnant to the Constitution must yield. But that clause offers nothing in support of the institutional claim that courts have the power to strike down laws that, in their judgment, are unconstitutional. When Marshall gives examples of unconstitutional laws, he confines himself to the easiest of cases under the most determinate of texts, such as a hypothetical statute requiring only one witness to convict of treason. But this tells us little about the role of judicial review in hard cases, where text is ambiguous or silent. Overall, Marshall's textual and structural inferences are very weak, and no source of constitutional meaning clearly settles the question. Any evaluation of Marshall's conclusion must depend, in large part, on institutional considerations.

If it appears odd to suggest that judicial review need not be a part of the American constitutional fabric, a reading of the historical materials should dispel the appearance.[3] The constitutional theorist Larry Kramer urges that for the framers, the "Constitution was *not* ordinary law, *not* peculiarly the stuff of courts and judges."[4] Instead, it was "a special form of popular law, law made by the people to bind their governors."[5] For many members of the revolutionary generation, constitutional principles were subject to "popular enforcement,"[6] that is, public insistence on compliance with the Constitution, rather than judicial activity. "It was the legislature's delegated responsibility to decide whether a proposed law was constitutionally authorized, subject to oversight by the people. Courts simply had nothing to do with it, and they were acting as interlopers if they tried to second-guess the legislature's decision."[7] Kramer traces the controversial early growth of the practice of judicial review, with many seeing it as an "act of resistance." At the founding, a "handful of participants saw a role for judicial review, though few of these imagined it as a powerful or important device, and none seemed anxious to emphasize it. Others were opposed. . . . The vast majority of participants were still thinking in terms of popular constitutionalism and so focused on traditional political means of enforcing the new charter; the notion of judicial review simply never crossed their minds."[8]

In Kramer's account constitutional limits would be enforced not through courts, but as a result of republican institutions and the citizenry's own commitment to its founding document. Kramer raises serious doubts about the understanding in *Marbury v. Madison* and in particular about judicial supremacy in the interpretation of the Constitution. Critically, he suggests that for some of the framers, judicial review was "a substitute for popular resistance" and—here a Thayerian strand emerges from the historical record—to be used "only when the unconstitutionality of a law was clear beyond dispute."[9] What is important for our purposes is the idea that at the American founding, the supremacy of the Constitution was clear, but judicial enforcement was not, in part because of ambivalence about which institutions would be well suited to ensuring compliance.

That ambivalence was and is perfectly sensible. As I discuss at length later, many liberal democracies have refused, to a greater or lesser extent, to give judges the power to strike down legislation.[10] If judges are corrupt, biased, poorly informed, or otherwise unreliable, it hardly makes sense to entrust judges with that power. And if legislative officials can be trusted to be faithful to constitutional commands, the need for judicial review is greatly diminished. Or suppose that a constitutional system feared, with reason, that the power of judicial review would weaken the attention paid by other institutions to constitutional requirements—so that judicial review, it was thought, would weaken the grip of constitutional limitations on other branches. This conjecture is empirical in character. A system without judicial review might be accepted on second-best grounds; we might believe emphatically in constitutionalism, but also think that judicial review will tend to undermine rather than to promote its goals. Hence the analysis of the *Marbury* question itself must depend, in part, on the same institutional considerations stressed throughout Parts I and II.

It is possible to draw a general conclusion. In many domains the question is posed whether one institution should review the acts of another, and if so, the intensity with which that review should occur. This question arises, for example, in the context of constitutional challenges; attacks on criminal convictions; review of punitive damage awards by juries; appellate review of trial court findings; and judicial review of agency decisions of law, fact, and policy. In all these areas it is important to pay close attention to institutional variables. The costs of error and the costs of decision are crucial. It is necessary to examine systemic effects. There is no sensible acontextual position on the question whether review, of one institution or another, should be intense or deferential, or indeed available at all.

A Note on Constitutional Existence Conditions

Legal scholars Matthew Adler and Michael Dorf have argued that in some domain, judicial review is conceptually necessary—something akin to a precondition for any constitutional order to be intelligible.[11] In their motivating example, Adler and Dorf suppose that a party presents a document to a court, claims that it is a duly enacted federal statute, and asks that it be enforced. The court, Adler and Dorf say, must decide whether the document really "is" a federal statute—whether a statute "exists," or whether "constitutional existence conditions" have been met. That inquiry in turn requires the court, as a conceptual matter, to identify the institution that counts as "Congress" and to decide whether that institution has followed the constitutionally specified procedures for enacting legislation. Traditionally, courts facing such problems applied the "enrolled bill rule," under which the statement of legislative officers that a bill had been duly enacted was conclusive on the court.[12] But the enrolled bill rule has weakened in recent years,[13] and even that rule still requires the court to identify which individuals validly hold the relevant legislative offices.

Let us grant some such point for the sake of argument. Adler and Dorf explicitly acknowledge, however, that outside the extremely narrow domain of identifying valid statutes, no conceptual or logical necessity requires judicial review. Many liberal democracies have denied or currently deny to their constitutional courts the authority to conduct this further form of judicial review, at least of national legislation. It would be odd to suggest that these polities are somehow riven by a logical contradiction. Adler and Dorf also acknowledge that courts might have good reasons, among them "democracy," for denying judicial review of a whole range of other issues, including free speech claims, equality rights, and rights to fair process. So the analysis from constitutional existence conditions is narrow. My aim here is to supplement their analysis by adding that democracy is too abstract a commitment to cut between various positions on the desirability of judicial review. The choice between those positions turns on questions of institutional capacities and systemic effects.

Modern Constitutional Theory: Institutional Blindness Redux

Judicial review, I mean to suggest, poses questions of interpretive choice. Even given some high-level conception of the aims of constitutionalism, it is a further question whether judges should be given interpretive authority over the Constitution, and in what domains. There are further questions as well: Should judges' interpretive authority be initial or final, supplemental to legislatures or exclusive of legislatures? What decision-procedures for interpreting the Constitution should judges use, given some allocation of interpretive authority across institutions?

Remarkably, a great deal of prominent constitutional theory is oblivious to these questions. Theorists proceed without regard to the institutional capacities of legislatures and judges, or at best on the basis of stylized abstraction about institutional capacities; often systemic effects and the interactions among institutions are neglected. Here I shall survey some of the most prominent theorists with a view to diagnosing institutional blindnesses of the same types we encountered in Chapter 1. Not all of these theorists are institutionally insensitive; we shall see, in particular, accounts of judicial review by Larry Alexander, Frederick Schauer, David Strauss, and Mark Tushnet that usefully incorporate institutional considerations. Even there, however, the institutional analysis is incomplete in important respects.

Hamilton and agency. Let us begin with an account that both predates *Marbury* and is more sophisticated than Marshall's effort: Alexander Hamilton's defense of judicial review in *Federalist* 78.[14] Hamilton suggests that judicial review is justified by a principal-agent model of constitutionalism. The "People" are the principals, government officials are their agents, and the Constitution is a contract or charter that specifies the terms of the agency relationship. Judicial review, then, is like judicial enforcement of a standard principal-agent contract in private law. On this view judicial review is not at all countermajoritarian in inspiration; judicial enforcement of limits on governmental authority, particularly on legislatures, occurs by virtue of delegation from the People themselves.

Hamilton's account has been criticized on many grounds; here I confine myself to two crucial institutional points. The first is a problem about judicial motivations. Why would current judges want to enforce the original terms of the agency charter? The constitutional privileges of life tenure and irreducible salaries block the crudest threats that current politicians might make against the judges. But this is no guarantee that judges will enforce the past political arrangements, including agency agreements, embodied in constitutional texts. Life tenure and salary protection liberate the judges to pursue whatever version of constitutionalism they find attractive. Some judges will be Hamiltonians, but others will be Rawlsian liberal democrats, free-market libertarians, socialists, or Christian fundamentalists. There can be no general answer to the questions how judges will behave or what they will value once they are freed from the blunt pressures toward reappointment, reelection, or financial security that affect many other types of officials.

We shall even see later some examples of constitutional cases in which judges may have acted to protect the institutional, professional, or material interests of the judges. This too cannot be ruled out by the Hamiltonian story. Perhaps legislators and other agents tend to act so as to enlarge their powers, in violation of the original agency agreement. But judges too are agents and cannot simply be assumed a priori to stick to the original agreement while other agents are busy violating it. Perhaps judges are self-interested agents, intent upon expanding their institutional power or prone to shirk their duties so as to increase their leisure. Perhaps they are not, or not always; the question is empirical.[15] Hamilton gives no answer to the question why one set of agents (the legislature) cannot be trusted to monitor its own behavior, while another set of agents (the judges) is trusted to set the limits of its own power.

Second is a point about judicial capacities. Suppose that all judges are Hamiltonians and desire to enforce the original terms of the agency agreement. Still, judges are boundedly rational and cognitively fallible and will make mistakes about what the agency agreement requires, forbids, or permits. To err by adopting an excessively narrow construction of governmental authority is, on an agency view, no better than to err by adopting an excessively broad view. Viewed in more dynamic terms, the former error may actually be worse than the latter one. Thayer suggested that the costs of a judicial decision mistakenly declaring legislation unconstitutional are systematically higher than the costs of a judicial decision mistakenly declaring legislation constitutional because the former decision, unlike the latter, cannot be corrected by ordinary legislative processes.[16]

Finally, Hamilton's account assumes away the existence of cases as to which the terms of the original agency agreement are ambiguous or silent. (Recall that Marshall likewise jiggered the case in favor of judicial review by providing examples of highly determinate or rulelike texts.) Where the agreement is ambiguous or silent—including the special and important case of ambiguity that arises from meanings that may be construed at multiple levels of generality—it is not clear what it means to say that judges are merely enforcing "the agreement." Consider especially the problem that changed circumstances over time may render portions of the original agreement obsolete. Later theorists, such as Lawrence Lessig, have emphasized this objection to originalist constitutional interpretation, just as Eskridge emphasizes it against originalist statutory interpretation. We shall see later, moreover, that the same institutional blindnesses that afflict Eskridge afflict the dynamic theorists of constitutional interpretation as well.

Ely and representation-reinforcing review. John Hart Ely's great book *Democracy and Distrust*[17] articulates a representation-reinforcing view of constitutional adjudication that has proven widely influential among political theorists as well as lawyers. The basic idea, drawn from a famous footnote in an otherwise obscure Supreme Court decision known as *Carolene Products*,[18] is to "clear the channels of political change" by using judicial review to police the political process against self-entrenchment by legislative majorities, and against prejudiced or discriminatory legislation that arises because "discrete and insular minorities" are systematically excluded from politics. Ely's main project is to justify the Warren Court's interventionist decisions in free speech and equal protection of the laws while simultaneously condemning the pre–New Deal Court's interventionist decisions protecting economic liberties. Process theory underwrites this "preferred position" for civil liberties as against economic ones, remitting the latter to ordinary politics.

Despite the panache and style of his book, Ely's basic process-based recommendation shares the stylized and asymmetrical institutionalism that afflicted the legal process school generally, particularly Hart and Sacks's legal process account of statutory interpretation (critiqued in Chapter 1). Ely's treatment appears particularly jejune in light of new contributions to process theory, from the 1990s and after, that feature an increasingly sophisticated and multifaceted treatment of institutional attributes and capacities. As I emphasized in Chapters 1 and 2, lawyer-economists like Neil Komesar and Einer Elhauge have drawn upon transaction-cost economics and interest-group theory to undermine Ely's suggestion that judges take an aggressive representation-reinforcing posture in constitutional cases. In Komesar's case Ely is one of his principal targets, while in Elhauge's case the target is the claim in public choice theory and constitutional economics that judges should intervene to correct failures in political markets that result from interest-group pressures.

Ely's argument exemplifies what Komesar calls "single-institutional" analysis: it fails to compare all relevant costs and benefits of the available institutional alternatives. Ely assumes away the problem of judicial capacities by assuming that the only relevant variation is in legislative performance: where legislatures function successfully in pluralist fashion (as in the economic arena), courts should stay their hand, whereas courts should intervene where legislatures are subject to process failures. Komesar, and Elhauge, however, make clear that process failures in the form of rent-seeking activity and differential interest-group access afflict the courts as well (Elhauge), and that whatever relative insulation judges enjoy comes at the price of severe informational deficits (Komesar), so that the judges are prone to stumble into empirical pitfalls. Ely's one-sided process theory does not engage the sophisticated institutional questions that Komesar, Elhauge, and others have explored.

In some quarters Ely's process theory has degenerated into the crude idea that courts *must* engage in judicial review to protect "minorities" from "the tyranny of the majority." But as observed by a string of political scientists and legal scholars, from Robert Dahl to Michael Klarman, protecting minorities is hardly a plausible description of what judicial review actually does.[19] Courts are majoritarian institutions, albeit ones that may adjust more slowly than legislatures to changes in majoritarian beliefs, values, and preferences. What is clear is that few judicial declarations have been able to withstand sustained majoritarian pressure for more than a generation or so because of threats of retaliation from other institutions, because judges are appointed by majoritarian institutions, and because, in the long run, judges come to think the way most other people think. Systemic effects are critical here: especially if courts are unwilling to conduct second-order interventions into the cost of funding rights,[20] legislatures may undo even the few countermajoritarian decisions that are issued by simply restricting public largesse on another margin. Consider the claim that the Warren Court's interventionist decisions on criminal procedure have been undermined by low legislative funding of defense counsel.[21]

Most important for our purposes, the appeal to the tyranny of the majority overlooks judicial fallibility and the resulting possibilities for error. Suppose that judges, acting in the name of minority rights, often restrict legislative power well beyond what any textual, historical, or structural account of constitutional interpretation would support; suppose that such decisions even go beyond any plausible account of the rights minorities should have as a matter of political morality. It would then be clear that countermajoritarianism was doing more harm than good, and that retrenching the scope of judicial review would not harm anyone's legitimate rights. It is even possible that courts will act to create affirmative constitutional injustices and impose them upon other political actors; consider *Dred Scott v. Sandford*,[22] the infamous Supreme Court decision that declared a constitutional right to own slaves and thus helped destabilize the fragile sectional equilibrium that collapsed in the Civil War. In light of such examples, perhaps legislatures acting without judicial oversight would even do better than courts, in net effect, at minimizing harms to both minorities and majorities. This possibility demonstrates that the scope of judicial review cannot be read directly from some high-level concern, such as majoritarian tyranny; it turns, rather, on institutional capacities and performance.

Dworkin's constitutional jurisprudence. Dworkin's approach to constitutional law is nicely illuminated by an unusual brief submitted to the Supreme Court as it was deciding whether there is a constitutional right to assisted suicide.[23] Widely known as "The Philosophers' Brief," the submission is in Dworkin's distinctive style, and indeed Dworkin is listed as lead counsel. "The Philosophers' Brief" offers an ambitious argument with considerable appeal. It says that some "deeply personal decisions pose controversial questions about how and why human life has value. In a free society, individuals must be allowed to make those decisions for themselves, out of their own faith, conscience, and convictions." The brief urges that distinctions between "omissions" (failing to provide continued treatment) and "acts" (providing drugs that will produce death) are "based on a misunderstanding of the pertinent moral principles." Drawing on the abortion cases, the brief says that every person "has a right to make the 'most intimate and personal decisions central to personal dignity and autonomy,'" a right that encompasses "some control over the time and manner of one's death." The brief thus urges the Court to declare a constitutional right to physician-assisted suicide. Dworkin's personal gloss on the brief says that it "defines a very general moral and constitutional principle—that every competent person has the right to make momentous personal decisions, which invoke fundamental religious or philosophical convictions about life's value for himself."

Simply as a matter of political morality, the argument in "The Philosopher's Brief" is certainly reasonable, and it cannot easily be shown to be wrong. But suppose that the Court was convinced by the argument in principle; should the Court have held that there is a right to physician-assisted suicide? Not necessarily. Before accepting the argument, it is necessary to ask about judicial competence to evaluate moral arguments of this sort, and also to ask about facts and incentives. Perhaps the Court is not especially well equipped to evaluate those arguments; and if consequences matter, the moral arguments might not be decisive in light of the second-best risk that any right to physician-assisted suicide would, in practice, undermine rather than promote the autonomy of patients.[24]

Many people, including Dworkin himself, appear to think that the Supreme Court should not much hesitate to find a constitutional right of some kind if it is presented with convincing (to the judges) philosophical arguments for that right, at least if the right "fits" with the rest of the legal fabric. For those who take an institutional perspective, this view is wrong. Courts may not understand what justice requires or may not be good at producing justice even when they understand it. In these circumstances courts' understanding of the Constitution is partly a product of their judgments about their own distinctive role as a social institution. Note that this claim does not depend on skepticism about moral or political arguments. It is reasonable to believe that judges are not well equipped to engage in theoretically ambitious tasks without also believing that political theory is itself problematic or useless.

Amar's intratextualism. Akhil Amar describes his preferred approach to constitutional interpretation as "intratextualism."[25] The term denotes a textualism that makes extensive use of comparisons across clauses, even to the point of insisting that words appearing in widely separated contexts be given similar meanings—a technique capable of generating dramatic readings, such as the claim that the key to understanding the meaning of "speech" in the First Amendment is the meaning of "speech" in the Speech and Debate Clause. Amar's target is what he calls "clause-bound" interpretation, the judicial practice of reading constitutional provisions and their accompanying history and precedent in (partial) isolation from textually related provisions.

In its emphasis on the authority of constitutional text and in its populist underpinnings, Amar's account appears to lie at some polar opposite from Dworkin's, in which the constitutional text does relatively little work and populism is hardly a defining ideal. From the institutional perspective, however, the two accounts are on a par. What Dworkin and Amar share is a deep commitment to a sort of constitutional holism: a commitment to reading the Constitution (whether that is taken to denote the document's text or the moral principles underlying constitutional law) as a coherent, integrated whole. It is this shared feature of holism or coherentism that unites the institutional critique of Dworkin with the institutional critique of Amar. Amar, like Dworkin, pays too little attention to the possibility that real-world judges charged with holistic interpretation will simply blunder, producing a pattern of incoherent outcomes or, worse yet, an internally coherent but misguided vision of public law.

Amar recommends intratextualism as a tool suitable in the courtroom as well as the classroom; indeed, most of Amar's intratextualist heroes are famous judges, especially John Marshall. Yet Amar pays little attention to the institutional capacities of the real-world judges who would be charged with practicing intratextualism; he largely ignores the judges' interpretive capacities or their likely performance under the alternative regimes of intratextualism, on one hand, and clause-bound interpretation, on the other. Compared with the clause-bound alternative, intratextualism requires a more complicated and information-intensive inquiry, one that will reduce decisional accuracy whenever judges read the comparison texts mistakenly. So, for example, a judge who looks to the Speech and Debate Clause to illuminate the Free Speech Clause might well go badly wrong, given that the former provision predated the First Amendment and addresses very different problems. Amar gives us no reason to think that the illuminating effect of intratexualism will predominate over its error-producing effect.

What is worse, intratextualism in the hands of fallible judges risks producing a holistic, highly coherent, but fundamentally mistaken analysis, one that constitutionalizes a simultaneous misreading of a whole set of related provisions. Justice Douglas's opinion in *Griswold v. Connecticut*,[26] for example, offered a holistic, coherent account of the Bill of Rights as based upon a general principle of privacy; and it is an account that Amar himself thinks is deeply mistaken.[27] If Amar had a more realistic view of judges' abilities as constitutional interpreters, he might prefer the limited incoherence of clause-bound interpretation to a sweeping, integrated, but erroneous universal account. What Amar has done, in short, is to overlook the principle of second-best. Rather than asking "What interpretive methods should judges use?" Amar has asked, "What interpretive methods would I use, were I a judge?"—the question that is a common cause of institutional blindness in interpretive theory, as I suggested in Chapter 1.

Scalia's second-best originalism. Justice Antonin Scalia articulates an originalist account of constitutional interpretation in which the original public understanding of constitutional texts is authoritative, and in which history is to be used to capture original public understandings. In comparison with Hamilton, Scalia's originalism is far more institutionally sophisticated. Some have suggested that Scalia's principal justification for originalism is that it restrains judicial "discretion," and there is some justice in this; Scalia does say that "the main danger in judicial interpretation of the Constitution . . . is that the judges will mistake their own predilections for the law."[28] But in fact Scalia's argument goes a level deeper than that standard claim. The argument, rather, is best understood to rest on a complex view of judicial capacities.

The first-best ideal, Scalia suggests, is a kind of compromise or balancing between the claims of original understanding, on the one hand, and the need to update the Constitution in light of changed circumstances, on the other. Judges, however, will usually err on the side of updating, just because their values tend to be current values. Originalism, Scalia suggests, compensates for predictable judicial bias, offsetting it so as to produce a closer approximation of the ideal compromise:

> [T]he principal defect of [originalism]—that historical research is always difficult and sometimes inconclusive—will, unlike nonoriginalism, lead to a more moderate rather than a more extreme result. The inevitable tendency of judges to think that the law is what they would like it to be will, I have no doubt, cause most errors in judicial historiography to be made in the direction of projecting upon the age of 1789 current, modern values—so that as applied, even as applied in the best of faith, originalism will (as the historical record shows) end up being something of a compromise. Perhaps not a bad characteristic for a constitutional theory. Thus, nonoriginalists can say, concerning the principal defect of originalism, "oh happy fault." Originalism is, it seems to me, the librarian who talks too softly.[29]

This is a kind of second-best account, in which an interpretive approach should be chosen so as to offset some predictable error or skew in judicial decisionmaking. As such, it is a remarkable echo of Blackstone's second-best defense of rule-bound formalism in statutory interpretation. Recall from Chapter 1 Blackstone's argument that "law, without equity, tho' hard and disagreeable, is much more desirable for the public good, than equity without law; which would make every judge a legislator, and introduce most infinite confusion [by producing] as many different rules of action laid down in our courts, as there are differences of capacity and sentiment in the human mind."[30] Scalia is addressing a different question—the optimal rate at which the Constitution should be updated (by judges), rather than Blackstone's question whether judges should read facially clear texts so as to tailor them to their background purposes or to background conceptions of equity—but in both cases the argument takes a second-best form.

Despite Scalia's institutional sophistication, however, he fails to consider the alternative possibility that legislatures, rather than judges, should be solely entrusted with the authority to update the Constitution. Scalia says that "[a] democratic society does not, by and large, need constitutional guarantees to ensure that its laws will reflect 'current values.' Elections take care of that quite well."[31] But Scalia's second-best originalism is premised on the assumption that judges will be charged with interpreting vague or ambiguous texts—the "equal protection of the laws" leaps to mind—and will inevitably read those texts in light of current values. These two premises are in some tension with each other if judges are simply stipulated to have interpretive authority across the whole Constitution, including ambiguous or aspirational provisions that need updating over time in light of the polity's changing circumstances.

The tension can be dissolved, as I shall suggest later, by the Thayerian option: remitting judges solely to the enforcement of a narrow set of clear and highly specific texts, while committing open-ended or aspirational norms that change over time, such as the Constitution's guarantees of equal protection and due process, to legislative enforcement. Second-best originalism is an ingenious device intended to compensate for shortcomings in judicial capacities. But the alternative solution, which would make second-best originalism unnecessary, is just to transfer the relevant category of questions out of the judges' hands altogether. What Scalia has failed to consider, then, is a systemic question about the allocation of interpretive tasks across different institutions in light of their distinctive capacities.

Lessig, translation, and compensating adjustments. Similar problems beset Lawrence Lessig's account of constitutional interpretation, which sees that practice as an exercise in "translation."[32] Translation is a particular version of originalism, of "fidelity" to the Constitution of the founding era. Lessig's important insight is that judges might, in principle, act more faithfully to the original constitution by updating constitutional rules to meet changed circumstances than by adhering woodenly to the specific text chosen by the founding generation or to their specific expectations. Just as a translator might do better to choose a colloquial analogue that captures the flavor of the original, rather than simply using a literal equivalent, so too the original meaning of the constitutional structure might, in changed circumstances, best be preserved by departures from the original understanding. In the area of federalism, for example, Lessig urges the Court to "make-up" constitutional rules that restore the original balance between federal and state authority. "[T]o be faithful to the constitutional structure, the Court must be willing to be unfaithful to the constitutional text."[33]

Translation is best viewed as a first-best account that refines legal process purposivism: like Hart and Sacks's approach, translation boosts the level of interpretive generality from the specific intentions or expectations of a law's framers to their ultimate aims or ends. But Lessig's account also shares purposivism's insensitivity to institutional considerations. Lessig fails to consider the possibility that judges might be poor translators, garbling meanings so badly that a simpleminded transliteration would preserve more of the original than would an ambitious and mistaken attempt to capture the original's real sense. Judicial mistakes might make ambitious attempts at translation self-defeating, driving results further away from the original meaning rather than pushing results closer to it. In the federalism setting, for example, it is by no means obvious that making up rules to approximate the original balance is, even on Lessig's theoretical premises, the right prescription for the Court. The Court might overshoot the mark by announcing stringent restrictions on federal authority that push constitutional law further away from the founding balance than would deference to national political processes.

Here is another example, taken not from Lessig's own work but from the secondary literature applying Lessig's insights. Suppose that the original Constitution, rightly understood, bars delegations of legislative authority to the executive and also bars the legislative veto. (Of course, I do not mean to endorse or oppose either claim here.) The circumstances of modern government are such, however, that delegations of legislative authority are pervasive, and there is no prospect of returning to the original understanding in this regard. The translation theorist might argue that judges should vote to uphold the legislative veto, even though it is clearly unconstitutional in isolation, on the ground that it is a "compensating adjustment"[34] needed to restore the original structural balance among the branches of government. On this view, the legislative veto will allow the legislature to limit and police the sweeping delegations of authority that it cannot avoid making. In fact, Justice White's dissent in the decision that invalidated the legislative veto urged upholding the veto on just this ground.[35]

Of course, there is a competing account. Perhaps the legislative veto falls afoul of the translated Constitution because it aggravates the power of self-interested private groups over processes of lawmaking, thus defeating the goal of bicameralism and presentment, which is (on this view) to reduce the role of factions in government. On this view, for the Court to uphold the legislative veto might move public law further away from, rather than closer to, the structure and purposes of the original Constitution. Now this view may be wrong. The problem is that it is no simple task for judges laboring under constraints of time, information, and expertise to identify the deep commitments of the Constitution that are to be translated to fit modern circumstances.

From the institutional perspective, the idea that judges should translate original structures by searching for offsetting constitutional adjustments is defective if it is unaccompanied by an account of judicial capacities. It takes great confidence in those capacities to think that judges can identify the net effects of such large-scale reforms with enough precision to warrant jettisoning clear constitutional provisions. The overall effect of the legislative veto or of its invalidation is a major research question for experts in political science.[36] There is little reason to believe that generalist judges, devoting a brief time to the subject and possessed of limited information, can form even a plausible view of the relevant complexities. Translation assumes an optimistic account of the judges' abilities as translators, an account that becomes increasingly questionable as judicial departures from text and original expectations become increasingly ambitious, and as the systemic effects of the adjustment become increasingly difficult for generalist judges to predict.

Breyer and active liberty. Another version of purposivist judicial review is Justice Stephen Breyer's proposal that judges should interpret the Constitution to promote "active liberty," or democratic self-government.[37] As in statutory interpretation, Breyer does not take account of the institutional questions that intervene between high-level principles and ground-level practices. Active liberty could underwrite an originalist approach, because active liberty is exercised in the constitution-writing process. That was Hamilton's argument: enforcing higher law does not detract from self-government because the people are just binding "themselves." On the other hand, active liberty could fit with a Thayerian view, involving great deference to legislatures, because active liberty is also exercised through representative legislatures. Praise for active liberty says little about what, concretely, judges should do.

Alexander, Schauer, and the settlement function of law. We turn now to a sophisticated and important defense of a strong form of judicial review. Larry Alexander and Frederick Schauer highlight the settlement function of law, including constitutional law: although it is important to settle issues correctly, it is also important that they be settled one way or another. The stability of constitutional rules over time is a good in itself, apart from the content of the rules. From this premise, Alexander and Schauer conclude that the constitutional order needs a single, authoritative interpreter who is jurisdictionally empowered to settle conflicts, and to whom all other institutions must defer (on questions of constitutional meaning). Alexander and Schauer suggest that this interpreter should be the Supreme Court; they thus defend, not merely judicial review but a form of "judicial supremacy," in which Congress and the president would be required to defer to the Court's constitutional interpretations—not merely the Court's judgments in particular cases.

By examining judicial review and judicial supremacy through an institutional lens, Alexander and Schauer are asking exactly the right questions. But their answers are unsatisfactory, because Alexander and Schauer fail to follow through on their institutional commitments. Even if the other premises are granted, Alexander and Schauer do little to justify the assumption that the single authoritative interpreter must be the Supreme Court. A regime of legislative supremacy, in which courts lacked any power to review legislation for constitutionality, would also satisfy Alexander and Schauer's criteria for stability.

The crucial questions here are emphatically empirical:[38] would legislative supremacy produce more or less stability than judicial supremacy? Inertia or structural status quo bias is built into legislative institutions by voting rules, bicameralism, and other features. Is this stronger or weaker than the status quo bias built into judicial institutions? If the answer is "stronger," then the Court might display more short-term oscillations and reversals than does Congress, in which case legislative supremacy would be preferable so far as stability goes (although other institutional considerations would also be relevant).

David Strauss's common-law constitutionalism. Chicago law professor David Strauss offers an important account of constitutional interpretation and adjudication that shares some of the strengths and weaknesses of Alexander and Schauer's account.[39] Strauss's central point is a descriptive claim that is both inarguable and important: modern constitutional law is often doctrinal rather than text-based. Courts deciding constitutional questions frequently proceed in the mode of what Strauss dubs common-law constitutionalism, basing their decisions on precedent rather than on inferences from text, structure, and history.

Strauss leverages this descriptive claim into a normative defense of common-law constitutionalism, which Strauss praises as a form of "rational traditionalism." Both halves of this formulation are important. Strauss's traditionalism is not reverence for the past for its own sake or praise for the craft mysteries of the common-law guild. Rather, it is a form of Burkean epistemic humility that takes traditions to represent the aggregated judgments of many generations. This is itself a type of sophisticated second-order rationality that takes account of the bounded information and cognitive capacities of the judges sitting at any particular time. As for rationalism, here the updating function of precedent comes to the fore. Common-law constitutional interpretation allows judges to update obsolete constitutional norms and structures over time, incorporating changes in felt public needs and values. Strauss is suggesting a form of dynamic constitutional interpretation parallel to Eskridge's account of statutory interpretation, albeit with a greater emphasis on common-law incrementalism.

On this picture, what role does the constitutional text play, if any? The text, Strauss argues, is not irrelevant; it is just that its functions are far more limited than textualist or originalist accounts of constitutional interpretation acknowledge. The text principally serves a coordinating or conventional role: it settles structural questions as to which it is more important to have the issue settled than to have it settled right. An example is the age minimum for the presidency. In such domains Strauss suggests that interpreters with different commitments can reach an overlapping consensus (or an incompletely theorized agreement) to follow text, simply because existing text serves as a focal point for resolution of the issue. In other areas, however—areas where it is more important that the law be settled right and adjusted over time than that it be settled once and for all—common-law constitutionalism proceeds without much in the way of textual support and without needing such support.

There is a missing step in Strauss's view, however, just as in Alexander and Schauer's proposal. Why exactly should courts, rather than legislatures alone, be the institutions charged with the enterprise of common-law constitutionalism? Recall that despite the court-centered overtones of the "common law," Strauss has stripped the concept of its standard connotations. For Strauss, common-law constitutionalism denotes incremental constitutional decisionmaking, informed by a presumptive respect for past settlements and decisions and grounded in epistemic humility. But legislatures as well as courts proceed incrementally, generating norms and institutional structures that produce a presumptive deference to the past. Strauss acknowledges that legislatures engage in common-law constitutionalism in some form. Although legislative precedent is not as theorized or self-conscious as judicial precedent, the norms of legislative discourse permit or even encourage legislators to oppose new ideas as inconsistent with past legislative settlements. And the institutional rules that govern legislatures quite possibly build in a greater status quo bias than the rules that govern courts, as we mentioned earlier. It would plausibly be more costly to secure a congressional repeal of a major statute than to secure a Supreme Court overruling of a major precedent. The questions again are mostly empirical, and Strauss has done no more to justify his court-centered assumptions than have Alexander and Schauer.

What of the creative and rationalistic side of Strauss's vision, in which common-law constitutionalism updates constitutional law over time to accord with changing circumstances and public values? Here many of the points urged in Chapters 2 and 7 against Eskridge's version of dynamism are also relevant. Granted that it would be good to have the Constitution updated over time in incremental fashion. The institutional-choice question is then whether legislatures or courts are the better updaters. Plausibly, legislatures have far better access to changing public norms than do courts and are no worse along the other institutional dimensions that Strauss values. Just as Eskridge overlooks that agencies may be the best common-law statutory interpreters, Strauss overlooks that legislatures may be the best common-law constitutional interpreters.

These points suggest that Strauss has conflated two different questions. One question involves the different modalities of constitutionalism. Here we may applaud Strauss's distinction between the role of text, which provides the basis for incompletely theorized agreements that settle structural questions, and common-law incrementalism, which updates the Constitution over time in other areas. An entirely different question, however, is how responsibility for these functions should be allocated across different institutions. Imagine a system in which courts are responsible solely for enforcing coordinating or conventional settlements created by specific constitutional texts, such as the presidential age minimum. Other questions, such as the changing interpretation of aspirational norms over time—norms such as equality or fair process—are committed to legislatures on the basis of an institutional judgment that legislatures are superior to courts in executing common-law constitutionalism. This is essentially the Thayerian system that I shall defend later, in which courts defer to legislatures on all questions except those clearly settled by specific texts. Nothing in Strauss's account rules out, in principle, a Thayerian implementation of his commitments.

Of course, these observations do not actually demonstrate that the Thayerian alternative is superior, nor are they intended to. I merely emphasize that the key questions are empirical, involving legislative and judicial capacities, the systemic effects of different approaches, and the allocation of functions across different institutions. Strauss's account, though elegant, finally fails to come to grips with these questions in an adequate fashion.

Some generalizations. The points I have made so far generalize in two ways that are familiar from Chapter 3. The first point is that a master principle of constitutional authority or value—the original understanding (Hamilton), law as integrity (Dworkin), the primacy of constitutional text (Amar), fidelity through translation (Lessig), the settlement function of law (Alexander and Schauer), or rational traditionalism (Strauss)—taken by itself, can yield no conclusions at all about judicial review or about proper interpretive method. With a certain assessment of judicial capacities, judges might do better, by Amar's own lights, with clause-bound interpretation than with intratextualism. On Lessig's own premises, fallible judges might be better translators if they stick to the unambitious transliteration that Lessig disparages. As for Dworkin, consider the possibility that a highly fallible judge charged with implementing law-as-integrity might do best, from the moral point of view, by opting for a relatively "wooden" or "mechanical" adherence to the apparent meaning of enacted texts, described at a low level of generality, than by ambitiously attempting to bring principled coherence to large areas of law. Thus, as

Strauss emphasizes, an epistemically humble Dworkinian judge might even behave like Amar's clause-bound textualist in some domains, especially where the settlement function of law comes to the fore.

The same holds true for judicial review and the allocation of authority across institutions. Scalia's emphasis on judicial restraint, Strauss's emphasis on common-law incrementalism, and Alexander and Schauer's emphasis on settlement might all be best implemented through a regime of legislative supremacy or Thayerian deference to legislatures than through a regime of judicial supremacy or any weaker form of judicial review. Likewise, nothing in Hamilton's originalism entails, by itself, that judicial review is necessary for, or even conducive to, the enforcement of the original agency agreement. The further questions, about judicial and legislative capacities, are inescapable, even on these thinkers' own premises.

The second point is the possibility of incompletely theorized agreements about interpretive method in constitutional cases. Interpreters who hold various first-order accounts of constitutional authority might converge, for example, on a practice of clause-bound textualism where the relevant texts are highly specific. The Amarian would do so to avoid large-scale, coherent mistakes by fallible intratextualist judges; the Dworkinian would do so because any more ambitious attempt at integrity-based coherence or large-scale purposivism might predictably do worse, on Dworkin's own moral criteria, in the hands of judges who do not resemble Hercules, Dworkin's idealized judge. Moreover, where agreements of this sort are possible, the underlying disagreements between competing accounts of the Constitution's authority could be bracketed or ignored. As Strauss rightly emphasizes, with respect at least to the role of clause-bound textualism and the interpretation of specific textual settlements, it would be possible to choose an approach to interpretation without committing to any such first-best position.

Any of these second-best accounts might or might not be plausible. The important point here is just that constitutional interpretation is not the same in a second-best world as in a first-best world. As with statutes, so with the Constitution: any account of constitutional interpretation that overlooks the decisive role of institutional considerations is for that reason defective.

The Thayerian Strain and Its Revival

So far I have been critiquing constitutional theory for institutional blindness. But I do not mean to claim that *Marbury*'s crude form of blindness, resolutely oblivious to institutional questions, fairly represents all subsequent constitutional theory in America. Many important strands of post-*Marbury* theory have been grounded in accounts of institutional capacities. We saw, for example, that Scalia's originalism is principally justified on such grounds, although Scalia fails to consider alternatives that might be superior on his own premises. Likewise Strauss, Alexander, and Schauer offer accounts of judicial review and interpretation that have important institutional dimensions, although these accounts also fail to follow through on their institutionalist premises by considering whether some version of legislative supremacy or Thayerian deference would prove superior, given the values these accounts posit. In general, it is unsurprising that modern constitutional theory—a body of theory pervasively structured around the question why unelected judges should have the power to nullify legislation—should display some sensitivity to institutional role, if only in the stylized, abstract manner of Ely and the legal process tradition.

Crucial for our purposes is an institutionalist strand of constitutional theory, to which I have referred several times, stemming from James Bradley Thayer. The core of Thayerism is an argument for judicial deference to legislatures in constitutional matters. In Thayer's original version this was a "rule of clear mistake": courts should defer unless no plausible interpretation would sustain the challenged statute. Later versions adumbrated the general idea that the Constitution might properly be treated or interpreted in one way by a legislature and another way by a court, in light of the distinctive characteristics of the interpreting institution. Among the modern versions of this idea are Alexander Bickel's legal process account of the distinctive attributes of courts as constitutional interpreters, although that account glorified courts' insulation ("the ways of the scholar") while overlooking the informational deficits that insulation produces;[40] and Lawrence Sager's idea that legislatures might properly be charged with responsibility for underenforced constitutional norms.[41]

A currently influential strand in recent constitutional theory might be called neo-Thayerian; it is represented by Jeremy Waldron,[42] Mark

Tushnet,[43] and Larry Kramer,[44] among others. These thinkers' views diverge in important respects, and not all of them subscribe to the specifically Thayerian idea that statutes should be upheld unless they are unconstitutional on any reasonable interpretation. I lump them together as Thayerian on the basis of a common spirit and general orientation. Waldron, whose interests are primarily jurisprudential, has examined how legislative institutions help resolve otherwise intractable political disagreements. Tushnet has revived and enriched the Thayerian concern with the debilitating effects of judicial guardianship on legislative performance and has examined legislators' incentives to enforce the Constitution. Kramer, as we have seen, has worked to dispel overheated claims on behalf of ambitious, interventionist judicial review, especially by impeaching its historical pedigree.

In what follows I shall attempt to refine and improve the neo-Thayerian view by putting it squarely on institutional grounds rather than historical and populist grounds (as does Kramer for the most part) or philosophical ones (as does Waldron for the most part). My approach is closest to that of Tushnet, who is greatly concerned with the systemic effects of judicial review on legislative responsibility, and to that of the lawyer-economists Komesar and Elhauge, whose concern is comparative institutional competence. I attempt to go beyond these theorists, however, by refusing to rest content with the stalemate of empirical intuitions. The analysis can be pushed forward by asking what decision-procedures boundedly rational judges should adopt in the face of uncertainty about the empirical questions that the neo-Thayerians have put into play.

Institutional Variables

We have seen that two questions are central. One is the question whether authority to interpret the Constitution should be lodged exclusively in the judiciary (Alexander and Schauer's judicial supremacy), lodged exclusively in the lawmaking process (legislative supremacy), or shared between them in some fashion. Another is the question of interpretive choice: given some allocation of review authority across courts and legislatures, what methods of constitutional interpretation should courts use? As I have emphasized before, these questions are mutually interdependent. A fully specified interpretive theory would answer both sets of questions simultaneously, in a form of reflective equilibrium. I have also emphasized that normative analysis of these questions is necessarily an institutional exercise. High-level commitments, for example, to integrity, the settlement function of law, or to an originalist principal-agent model of constitutionalism, prove too abstract to cut between institutional options of this sort or to underwrite conclusions at the operating level of the legal system.

What, then, are the institutional considerations that bear upon the allocation of constitutional authority and upon the methods of interpretation judges should use? The next section attempts to isolate some relevant variables; in the following section I shall take up the sort of questions examined in Chapters 6 and 7 about what regime to choose under conditions of irreducible empirical uncertainty. I shall exclude proposals such as Robert Bork's idea that Congress should be empowered to override constitutional decisions by a two-thirds vote.[45] As in earlier chapters, I mean to hold constant our current institutional structures, including voting rules. Instead, I ask what interpretive methods judges should adopt, given the current structures. For simplicity, I shall assume that the only options under consideration are judicial supremacy in the mode of Alexander and Schauer, legislative supremacy, or the intermediate Thayerian decision-rule, under which courts defer unless legislation violates the clear and specific coordinating and conventional texts to which Strauss rightly draws attention. This is, of course, unrealistic, and deliberately so. Although one might imagine many more complex combinations or allocations of legislative, executive, and judicial authority to interpret the Constitution, I simplify here in order to isolate the relevant considerations.

The principal variables are the agency costs and error costs of judicial review, decision costs and the costs of uncertainty, systemic effects (especially a form of moral hazard), the optimal rate of constitutional updating, and the transition costs of switching from one regime to another. Each of these considerations, however, implicates a tangle of subsidiary questions. As in the case of statutory interpretation, it will become clear that the information needed for fully specified institutional and interpretive choice far exceeds the judges' epistemic resources.

Agency costs, error costs, and institutional capacities. We have seen that Hamilton's defense of judicial review in *Federalist* 78[46] supposes a simple principal-agent model with multiple agents: the people as principal appoint legislative representatives subject to the terms of the agency agreement (the Constitution) and also appoint the judiciary as another agent to enforce the agreement. If the judges were both infallible and perfectly faithful, the Hamilton model would be persuasive on its own terms, although vulnerable to external criticisms. We have also seen, however, that judges are neither infallible nor predictably faithful to the original constitutional agreement. The critique of Hamilton thus raises the question of the relative agency costs and error costs of judicial review and of legislative supremacy.

We may roughly classify such costs into two forms, agent incompetence and agent self-dealing. Both produce interpretive error relative to a first-best account of constitutionalism; the first does so by virtue of agents' bounded capacities, the second by virtue of slippage between agents' incentives and the principal's goals. The competence issue is whether even faithful or well-motivated agents suffer informational and cognitive constraints that cause them to make errors or mistakes, where "mistake" is defined according to some particular constitutional value theory or according to an incompletely theorized agreement across different value theories. On any value theory, not merely Hamiltonian originalism, faithful but fallible legislators will misinterpret the Constitution.[47] Faithful but fallible judges will also misinterpret it, issuing erroneous rulings of constitutionality and of unconstitutionality. Excessively lax review suggests that judicial review is unnecessary, excessively stringent review that it is affirmatively harmful. Note that we cannot assume optimistically that random errors in either direction will wash out, because we also care about the constitutional variance produced by our institutional choices. A legislature or a judiciary that made a precisely equal number of constitutional errors in either direction would be far worse than one that made no errors at all.

The self-dealing issue is whether epistemically perfect agents will use their authority to divert gains to themselves. Here too the consequence will be erroneous constitutional decisions by legislators or judges, although caused by self-interest rather than incompetence. Constitutional theory in the public choice vein has detailed many forms of legislative self-dealing and agency slack in legislatures. But judges too may engage in self-interested interpretation, both as individuals and as a collective bureaucracy. Consider whether or not it is plausible that self-interest distorts judicial review of statutes that alter judicial compensation, as in

United States v. Will,[48] or review of statutes that the justices lobbied against in the legislative process, as in *United States v. Morrison,*[49] or review of electoral outcomes that will determine the identity of the Justices' colleagues, as in *Bush v. Gore.*[50] The latter two cases might also be described as examples of vanity rather than self-interest, and all the cases emphasize that the distinction between incompetence and self-interest is fuzzy. Cognitive mechanisms such as motivated reasoning and self-serving bias may transmute self-interest into "sincere" error.

Of course, I do not mean to restrict attention to the agency costs inflicted by imperfect judiciaries; that would be just another example of the single-institutional analysis, or asymmetrical institutionalism, rightly condemned by Komesar and Elhauge. The ideal procedure would be to compare the net agency costs of fallible legislatures and fallible courts under the alternative institutional schemes of judicial supremacy, legislative supremacy, and a Thayerian regime. With or without *Marbury*-style review, legislatures may erroneously reject bills on constitutional grounds or erroneously fail to do so. *Marbury*-style review adds the possibility that insufficiently vigorous constitutional review by legislatures will be corrected, but also adds the possibility of erroneous judicial invalidations of statutes correctly judged constitutional by legislatures. Indeed, erroneous judicial invalidations might combine with erroneous legislative rejections of bills to produce dramatic overenforcement of constitutional rules.

We must dispel a crude, but common, answer to the comparative inquiry into agency costs and error. On this view, courts will prove systematically superior to legislatures at enforcing constitutional rules. Legislators seek reelection above all and so will implement current popular preferences rather than enforcing countermajoritarian constitutional norms; while courts' political insulation, created by life tenure and salary protection, gives them superior capacities to resist populist politics.

Both halves of this claim are far too simple. We have already seen that life tenure and salary protection may liberate judges from political threats, allowing them to pursue whatever aims they happen to hold. But it does not follow that their aims will coincide with any particular conception of good constitutional judging, including the protection of minorities from current popular majorities. Moreover, political insulation produces an informational deficit on the part of judges, including a dearth of information about the consequences of constitutional decisions, and this blinkering can produce blunders of constitutional law and policy. In any event, whatever the incentive structures surrounding judicial office, scholars such as Michael Klarman have emphasized that judges are people too and tend to share the norms of current society, at least its elite professional sector (from which many legislators are also drawn). It is not obvious a priori, then, that judicial review will produce significant enforcement of constitutional protections against current majorities; and Klarman reads the historical record to suggest that in fact it does not.[51]

As for the legislative side of the issue, even on the crudest model of legislators as reelection maximizers, legislators will enforce constitutional rules if that is what constituents demand. There is ample evidence that constituents do so demand, at least some of the time.[52] Moreover, many legislators enjoy a great deal of slack from their constituents, especially because gerrymandering has increased the number of safe legislative seats in the Congress. Such legislators tend to switch their aims at the margin, from maximizing their chances of reelection to other goals, including the making of good public policy, which in turn includes good constitutional policy.[53] Legislators may also arrange internal legislative institutions and processes in ways that build in a kind of precommitment to serious constitutional deliberation. Among these checks are expert staff charged with flagging constitutional problems in legislation, procedural default rules that require deliberation about constitutionality, and special rules that grant legislative minorities preferred rights to object to bills on constitutional grounds. In these ways, legislators may design a kind of Thayerian Congress.

Decision costs and uncertainty. Given some allocation of interpretive tasks to the judiciary, an important consideration involves the decision costs of interpretive methods. This is obvious in the case of originalism. Even Antonin Scalia, one of originalism's chief defenders, says that "[p]roperly done, the task requires the consideration of an enormous mass of material" and "an evaluation of the reliability of that material"; in general, originalism is "a task sometimes better suited to the historian than the lawyer."[54] The costs of originalism spike sharply upwards as constitutional texts become increasingly ambiguous or can be understood at multiple levels of generality. Consider the vast corpus of writings by academic historians and lawyers about the original understanding of the Fourteenth Amendment's Equal Protection Clause, a debate that has as yet reached no conclusive results.

We ought not to underestimate the decision costs of other approaches, however. Common-law constitutionalism, for example, often requires elaborate inquiries into a welter of conflicting precedents. Such inquiries are no less historical than originalist examination of documents from constitutional conventions of various types. The only difference is that the subject matter of the historical research needed under common-law constitutionalism is the history of courts.

The decision costs of interpretive methods are chiefly out-of-pocket costs and opportunity costs for litigants and judges deciding constitutional cases in domains where interpretive authority has already been allocated to the judiciary. Yet decision costs are also important to the initial choice of allocation of authority between courts and legislatures. *Systemic decision costs* are the costs of reaching constitutional settlements of contested issues, holding constant the content of those settlements.

Consider, as one important systemic decision cost, the resources spent on judicial selection in a regime of vigorous judicial review. Recent events surrounding the Senate confirmation process suggest that the greater the constitutional authority of the judges, the higher the stakes of selection to judicial office (notably the Supreme Court, but also the lower federal courts), and the more interest groups and others invest in the struggle over judicial selection and confirmation. Holding constant the quality of judicial candidates, this large expenditure of resources is a deadweight loss to society, at least if we ignore the very dubious possibility that the confirmation wars create some sort of spillover educational benefit for the public at large. Perhaps the confirmation wars have on average raised the quality of judicial candidates, but that would be a very optimistic assessment. Another possibility is that the increasing contentiousness of confirmation tends to reward mediocrity, at least at the margin.

The most critical component of systemic decision costs is the cost of uncertainty created by multiple constitutional decisionmakers. The existence of multiple decisionmakers increases the costs of predicting constitutional settlements. Those costs fall upon citizens, legislators, litigants, and other actors affected by constitutional law. Consider the possibility, again holding eventual outcomes constant, that adding judicial review to a system of legislative decision of constitutional questions dramatically increases the costs of uncertainty about how and when constitutional questions will eventually be resolved. From this standpoint, an advantage of a regime of legislative supremacy would be a reduction in the costs of legal uncertainty that result from layering judicial review on top of legislative decisionmaking. The additional or marginal legal uncertainty will be very low, however, if courts are limited to invalidating legislation that clearly violates highly specific coordinating or conventional texts of the sort Strauss mentions.

This point is distinct from Alexander and Schauer's claim that the settlement function of law is best promoted by having a single, authoritative constitutional decisionmaker. There is an ambiguity in that claim that may be elicited in the following way. Imagine two constitutional decisionmakers, Legislature and Court. Imagine also that the universe of potential constitutional claims is divided into two categories, type 1 cases and type 2 cases. (The labels for the decisionmakers and the categories are entirely arbitrary.) If type 1 cases are assigned exclusively to Court and type 2 cases are assigned exclusively to Legislature, it is not clear whether there is a single constitutional decisionmaker in Alexander and Schauer's sense. Two institutions are deciding constitutional questions, but any given question falls within the jurisdiction of only one institution.

From the standpoint of systemic decision costs, however, the latter point is the critical one. The marginal or additional costs of uncertainty arise when, and because, a given question can be decided and redecided in successive fashion by several institutions, each authorized to reverse the decision of the previous decisionmaker. In the regime we have described, no such marginal costs occur. So long as the jurisdictional allocation is known to all in advance, and so long as the costs of sorting cases into the relevant categories are not prohibitive, constitutional actors need take account of the constitutional rulings of only one institution for any given question, although more than one constitutional decisionmaker exists.

System effects. A further layer of complication is the possibility of systemic interaction effects between legislative and judicial determinations of constitutionality. One possibility is a form of moral hazard. If judicial review is a constitutional insurance policy against erroneous legislative determinations, judicial review may dilute rather than strengthen legislators' incentives to take precautions against erroneous enactment of unconstitutional statutes. This was Thayer's concern, in his famous reflections on John Marshall, that review would dilute the statesman's sense of constitutional responsibility.[55] The concern is parasitic on the assumption that judges are fallible. If judicial review catches all and only those unconstitutional statutes that responsible legislators would catch anyway in a regime without judicial review, then the moral-hazard effect changes no outcomes. But if judges are fallible, then moral hazard may act as a multiplier, causing a net increase in the number of constitutionally objectionable statutes that survive both legislative and judicial scrutiny.[56]

The converse possibility, however, is that judicial practices may have few systemic effects on legislative behavior. We emphasized in Chapter 5 that democracy-forcing is not a plausible aspiration for constitutional judging. This is also a systemic point, although a negative one. It suggests that judicial interpretation may have little systemic effect on legislatures absent some threshold level of internal coordination that the judiciary is unlikely to reach. The strain of constitutional theory known as "due process of lawmaking" hopes that judges can develop doctrines that will force or encourage legislatures to deliberate well about constitutional and policy questions. A range of constitutional-law doctrines and quasi-constitutional doctrines are often justified in this way, including the canon that statutes should be construed to avoid constitutional questions and the recent practice in which judges review the legislative record for sensitivity to federalism values. To the extent that these doctrines require sustained judicial coordination to force legislative deliberation, however, they assume, without empirical evidence, that sustained judicial coordination is feasible. If it is not, these doctrines will be futile or even perverse on second-best grounds.

Optimal rate of constitutional updating. So far I have assumed that judicial review "invalidates" statutes. This ignores that the practical effect of review is merely to delay changes in legal and constitutional policy until the process of presidential appointment aligns the Court's holdings with the nation's wishes.[57] To be sure, this point is perhaps too Olympian. If the delay is a generation or so, then the difference between invalidation and delay has no cash value to anyone alive at the time of the initial decision. Consider the federal statutes barring child labor that the Court invalidated in the 1920s; by the time the Court reversed itself in the 1940s, a generation of child laborers had come and gone.[58] In any event the Court's erroneous ruling may itself generate new interest groups and social movements that will subsequently immunize the ruling from reversal—one account of the aftermath of *Roe v. Wade*.[59] But in the main the point is correct and important.

There is an important question, then, about the optimal rate of legal change and constitutional updating in light of changing circumstances. Suppose that legislatures update the Constitution at some rate, either by formal amendments or by enacting quasi-constitutional "super-statutes"[60]—the 1964 Civil Rights Act is paradigmatic—that become entrenched in the constitutional culture. Suppose also that courts will delay legislatures' constitutional updating for some time, but never permanently. Then the question is simply whether legislatures, by themselves, are updating at a desirable or optimal rate, and whether adding a layer of judicially imposed delay moves the system closer to or further from the optimal point.

It is quite possible, of course, that the answer is "further from." Madison was intensely concerned with slowing the rate of legal change, which he saw as excessive because of the "inconstancy and mutability" of legislative lawmaking,[61] but at the constitutional convention he said very little about judicial review; he sought to build in the necessary delay through bicameralism, long legislative terms, and other institutional structures. Adding judge-created delay to those structures is very possibly excessive, perhaps amounting to a form of double-counting. To answer these questions requires an account of what the optimal rate of updating is, but also requires empirical information about the rates of updating that do or would prevail in regimes with or without judicial review. And, as usual, it might be possible, in light of that information, to bracket high-level disputes about what the optimal rate of updating is. It might well turn out, for example, that judicially imposed delay results in an excessively slow rate of constitutional updating on any plausible high-level account of where the optimum lies.

Transition costs. A final consideration involves the costs of transition from one regime to another. Suppose, for example, that current law embodies Alexander and Schauer's proposal for judicial supremacy, under which legislators defer all constitutional questions to courts. The question whether to abolish "judicial review," in that sense, would not be the same as the question whether to institute it in the first place, because the status quo position matters. The neo-Thayerian opponents of judicial review I mentioned earlier tend to elide this distinction, in Waldron's case because his basic concern is to prevent the introduction of full-scale judicial review into the British legal system.[62]

The concern about the costs of transition between regimes interacts with the other considerations we have examined, often in subtle ways. Thayer's moral-hazard concern that judicial review debases legislative responsibility, for example, might suggest that a sudden switch from a regime of vigorous judicial review to one of legislative supremacy could prove disastrous. Legislators accustomed to a judicial backstop for catching constitutional errors, and thus rendered constitutionally irresponsible by the previous regime, could hardly adjust instantly to their new obligations. If the moral-hazard effect dissipated very slowly, the interim period might pose a real risk that legislatures would treat constitutional restrictions cavalierly. Even if the new long-term equilibrium were better than the old judicial-review equilibrium, the transitional disruption might prove so severe as to block any path from the latter to the former. In that case the current regime of judicial review would constitute a local-maximum trap, akin to the problem facing subsistence farmers who are unable to switch to more productive technologies because they will starve to death in the meantime.

Empiricism, Uncertainty, and Choices

As in Chapters 6 and 7, the ultimate question is what judges should do about all this. As I argued earlier, the Constitution neither requires nor forbids judicial review; there is no valid deductive inference from the Constitution's status as binding law to the particular enforcement mechanism of judicial review. Nor does the Constitution require or forbid judges to use any particular method of constitutional interpretation. It is not even clear, conceptually, that it could do so, for the constitutional command to use a particular method of constitutional interpretation would itself have to be interpreted. The questions, then, are at bottom ones of institutional allocation and interpretive choice in light of the aims specified by a high-level conception of constitutionalism or by a converging agreement among such conceptions at the operational level.

Quite clearly, however, a staggering amount of information would be required for a full institutional analysis of the questions surrounding judicial review and constitutional interpretation. It is not feasible for judges to acquire the necessary information, at least at any reasonable cost within the short or medium term. Even if the information could be obtained, it would rapidly outstrip the information-processing capacity of boundedly rational judges. To be sure, comparative work on judicial review in political science and economics has outlined some of the relevant variables,[63] but it has yet to make much progress on specifying their magnitudes or even their signs. The complexity of social and political systems means that it is difficult in the extreme to include controls for all plausibly relevant variables.

Consider a recent and sophisticated large-number study that attempts in part to ascertain whether "constitutional review," defined as a function of both judicial review and the difficulty of amending the party's constitution, increases political freedom.[64] As the authors note, although freedom and constitutional review are certainly correlated, an obvious hypothesis is that some other factor produces both conditions. As it turns out, when the continent of the relevant polity is controlled for, there is no statistically significant correlation between freedom and constitutional review.[65] Whether judicial review (what the authors call "constitutional review") increases freedom seems to depend upon where one lives, which means that other, unknown factors are doing the work.[66]

Overall, what comparative work provides are large-scale points that are useful mostly to debunk lawyers' shibboleths. One such shibboleth, especially popular among law students, is that the absence of judicial review will immediately result in majoritarian tyranny. It is a useful tonic for such views that the absence or sharply limited scope of judicial review (at least of national legislation) in the Netherlands, Switzerland, Belgium, the United Kingdom, and other nations has not produced a swathe of fascist dictatorships. Beyond demarking the outer boundaries of the problem, however, comparative work offers little assistance.

If the desirability of judicial review is an institutional question, but a trans-scientific one (at least in the current state of political science and legal theory and probably for the foreseeable future as well), what conclusion should we reach? One reaction is to abandon consequentialist analysis altogether. We have already encountered Jon Elster's view: because the complexity of "global long-term net equilibrium effects" makes institutional choice indeterminate, we ought to choose institutions that comport with whatever nonconsequentialist theory of justice or of politics we hold.[67] But those theories will in most settings prove too abstract to cut between the choices available to us at the level of constitutional design. A commitment to democracy, for example, is compatible with a very strong form of judicial supremacy if we jigger the institutional variables the right way. Thus Hamilton, in *Federalist* 78, squares representative government with judicial enforcement of the Constitution by resolutely ignoring the error costs, agency costs, and decision costs of judicial review.

As I emphasized in Chapters 6 and 7, the only other recourse is to invoke an eclectic group of tools for institutional and interpretive choice under conditions of profound uncertainty, tools found in decision theory, rhetoric, and other disciplines. I shall proceed to apply some of these tools to the interlocked questions whether judges should engage in (some form of) judicial review, and what methods of constitutional interpretation judges should use.

Transition costs and the status quo. Judicial review is sometimes defended by reference to the idea that opponents bear the burden of empirical uncertainty, if only because there are costs of transition away from the status quo (which is said to license or require judicial review). Sometimes this seems largely spurious, for example, the claim that opponents of judicial review bear the "burden of proof"—a device that courts properly use to reduce decision costs and allocate the risk of error in the face of uncertainty, but when used by academics is usually a rhetorical device to close down argument. So when Judge Posner says that Waldron and the other neo-Thayerian skeptics have not proved that judicial review is a bad idea,[68] we are entitled to ask whether Judge Posner has proved that it is a good one.

There is a legitimate version of this argument, however, based on the principle of insufficient reason. That principle instructs the decisionmaker to count only known costs, eliminating other, unknown and unknowable costs from both sides of the ledger by assuming that they will wash out. This sort of reasoning may end up incorporating the status quo into the analysis just as a burden-of-proof rule does, but on more respectable grounds. If the costs of transition from one institutional arrangement to another, for example, are clearly positive, and the other variables on both sides are imponderable, this approach counsels against disrupting the status quo in the search for speculative gains.

The point supports a criticism of my proposals here. I shall shortly suggest that judges should decline to enforce all but clear and specific constitutional texts. This is a seemingly radical proposal that would overturn the current status quo, since today's justices and judges routinely exercise robust judicial review under vague, ambiguous, or aspirational provisions. The radicalism of my recommendation, the criticism might run, is impermissible on the very same institutional grounds I have given. Suppose all other variables bearing on judicial review are uncertain. Should not modest, unambitious judges continue to do what judges have recently been doing—which is to exercise robust judicial review under the Bill of Rights and other vague or ambiguous provisions?

The same point can be put in satisficing terms. Consider David Strauss's defense of judicial review, mentioned in Chapter 6: "[O]ur acceptance of [judicial review] outruns our belief that it is theoretically best. . . . One reason is that it works well enough, and it would be too costly and risky to reopen the question whether, abstractly considered, it is the best possible arrangement."[69] I take this to rest on an implicit appeal to satisficing. Strauss would say that the appeal is Burkean. The two formulations are compatible, because a Burkean reluctance to upset the status quo must rest at bottom on the claim that the status quo is sufficiently tolerable to meet some ill-defined aspiration level.

Despite the general merits of the principle of insufficient reason and of satisficing, I do not think that such arguments succeed in this setting. One major problem is that "judicial review" has no clear referent; it simply does not denote a well-defined institutional arrangement. The rules and practices conventionally lumped under the label of "judicial review" in American courts include a bewildering variety of strands, themes, norms, doctrines, and constitutional and statutory provisions. There is a strand of judicial supremacy, sometimes with originalist coloratura, represented by some Rehnquist Court opinions;[70] there is a Thayerian strand, represented by other Rehnquist Court opinions,[71] and by an older tradition stemming from Holmes, Hand, and Frankfurter; there is a process tradition stemming from the Warren Court and its academic rationalizer John Hart Ely; overlapping all of these, although distinct from them, is an important strain of common-law constitutionalism. As far as judicial review goes, it is not clear what the status quo is, or even that there is a well-settled status quo in the first place. We cannot appeal to insufficient reason or satisficing to defend "judicial review," for it is not at all clear what we would be defending.

If there is a status quo, moreover, it is in fact more Thayerian than otherwise, despite appearances. In a wider perspective, abolishing judicial review in the high-profile, politically charged cases arising under the ambiguous provisions of the Bill of Rights would only amount to a marginal tweak of the status quo. By force of economic, social, and institutional developments, the constitutional order has settled on extensive legislative authority to decide constitutional questions, especially at the federal level. Although the judiciary can and does review federal statutes for constitutionality, in many domains the realities of modern government ensure that Congress's authority to decide constitutional questions is effectively paramount. Neil Komesar has insisted upon this point,[72] although constitutional-law scholars have largely ignored it, perhaps because it is empirical rather than conceptual.

In the twentieth century nonjudicial institutions of government grew much faster than the judiciary; consider that in 1999 the total federal judicial budget was $3.9 billion, while the administrative budget of the national political branches alone ran to some $80 billion—twenty-one times larger.[73] Congress, the White House, and the federal administrative agencies, both executive and independent, together form an institutional system whose current scale and scope—measured by resources, revenue, personnel, outputs, or any other dimension—dwarf the scale on which courts operate. This disparity ensures that the judiciary lacks the logistical capacity to review more than a small fraction of political-branch decisions, including congressional decisions embodied in statutes that raise constitutional questions. The Court's peak capacity runs to about 200 cases per year, most of which concern statutory interpretation rather than constitutional adjudication, whereas in the past few decades Congress has produced many hundreds of new public laws every year, and administrative agencies annually produce thousands of new regulations.[74] Many of these laws pose no constitutional questions, and to some extent the Court can compensate for its capacity constraints by deciding fewer cases (as it has in recent years) but issuing broader rules in the cases it does decide.[75] In general, however, the gargantuan congressional-administrative process produces more lawmaking than the comparatively minuscule judiciary has the capacity to review for constitutionality.

So it is unsurprising that the Supreme Court has itself retreated from judicial review of most congressional decisions. Consider the following selection of congressional activities and determinations with important constitutional dimensions that the federal courts decline to review, either de jure under the rubric of justiciability and political-question doctrines or de facto under the rubric of "rational basis" review:

- The procedural validity of constitutional amendments[76]
- The procedural validity of enacted statutes[77]
- The creation and validity of internal congressional rules[78]
- "Economic and social" regulation,[79] a huge category that includes the following:

    (1) Regulation of the channels and instrumentalities of interstate commerce and of intrastate activity that substantially affects interstate commerce[80]

    (2) Regulation of property rights, short of a physical appropriation or total deprivation of value[81]

    (3) Regulation of contractual obligations[82]

- Spending for the general welfare, both conditional[83] and unconditional
- Use and disposition of the property of the united States[84]
- Delegation of rulemaking authority to the executive or to independent agencies[85]
- The division of war powers between Congress and the executive[86]
- Establishing rules and regulations for the military[87]
- Simultaneous service in the legislature and in the executive[88]
- The admission and naturalization of aliens[89]
- Confirmations and impeachments[90]
- Enforcement of the "Republican Form of Government" Clause[91]

The Court still reviews statutes on constitutional grounds, of course. The important point is that the substantive scope of the unreviewable or largely unreviewed exercises of political-branch power together amounts to a large slice of the activities of government. Komesar is right about the big picture: by and large, the Supreme Court has retreated to policing a restricted domain of highly salient individual-rights issues, such as free speech and abortion rights; to occasionally invalidating novel interbranch encroachments in the name of the separation of powers; and to occasionally striking down novel exercises of congressional power in the name of federalism. In other domains, which is to say in a great deal of what government does, the political branches are the ultimate arbiter of constitutionality.

The upshot is that the status quo objection mistakes a small corner of the picture for the whole canvas. There is a residual category of non-

Thayerian judicial review in the system, but it occupies a small domain, in which emotionally charged issues receive disproportionate attention. To abolish that residual would not be a radical overturning of the status quo, but rather a mopping-up operation. I argue next that the costs of non-Thayerian review are definite and substantial, while the benefits are entirely conjectural. If that is so, the small transition cost of moving to a Thayerian regime does not suffice to tip the decision-calculus the other way.

Cost-benefit, insufficient reason, maximin, and satisficing: The case for Thayerism. Let us turn to the affirmative considerations supporting Thayerism. In my view, the tools for choice under uncertainty developed in Chapter 6 support a Thayerian regime of judicial review and constitutional interpretation. Thayer's idea was the rule of clear mistake, but I mean to suggest a more specific interpretation or conception of that position. Under this conception, courts would be limited to enforcing, through judicial review, only clear and specific constitutional texts—the sort of texts that Marshall used as examples of judicial review in *Marbury* itself.

Examples of clear and specific constitutional texts might include such things as the qualifications for federal office (including the composition of the legislature, legislative tenure, the rules governing presidential elections, and presidential term limits), the rules governing appointment of federal administrative officials (but not their removal, as to which the Constitution is largely silent), and the rules governing congressional procedure, statutory enactment and constitutional amendment, and life tenure and salary protection for judges. Not included would be the clauses vesting "legislative," "executive," and "judicial" power in the branches of the national government; the vaguer grants of power to the national government, such as the power to regulate "commerce" among the several states; and the "majestic generalities" of the Bill of Rights, especially including the First Amendment's guarantee of "the freedom of speech" and the Fourteenth Amendment's guarantees of "life, liberty and property" (not to be deprived without "due process of law") and the "equal protection of the laws." The general contrast here is well drawn by Justice Frankfurter, who sorts the Constitution's provisions into two types: "explicit and specific" provisions, on the one hand, and "[g]reat concepts," such as commerce, due process, and liberty, on the other. Frankfurter says that the latter "relate to the whole domain of social and economic fact" and "were purposely left to gather meaning from experience."[92] The last idea hints at the view I shall expound later: adjusting the interpretation of the great constitutional concepts as circumstances change over time is a task best remitted to legislatures rather than entrusted to courts.

Of course, there will be boundary problems about these two categories, and marginal cases. Perhaps I have misclassified some provisions in either direction. But there is no question about what examples lie at the polar extremes: "liberty" and "equal protection of the laws" at one end and Marshall's example of the Treason Clause at the other. In many cases it is important that constitutional text will clearly and specifically rule some things out of bounds, even if the text does not pick out a unique answer within those bounds. Consider the clause, prominent in *Bush v. Gore* and the 2000 election controversy, providing that state "legislatures" may direct the manner in which presidential electors are appointed.[93] Whatever this includes—does it include rules developed by judges through flexible construction of statutes?—it is quite clear that it does not include, say, a freestanding gubernatorial command. In general, if we agree with Frederick Schauer that there is a large category of easy cases in constitutional law,[94] it will not do to be excessively skeptical about how to sort cases into and out of these categories.

These two categories map onto David Strauss's fundamental distinction between coordinating rules, where it is more important that the question be settled than settled right, and rules whose content matters. In the latter category, vague or ambiguous constitutional texts must be adjusted over time to reflect the polity's changing circumstances and values. To be sure, one might point out that there is no necessary identity between (1) clear and specific texts and (2) coordinating texts. Clear provisions might happen to address subjects as to which content matters more than coordination. While this point is correct at the conceptual level, under our Constitution the extension of the two categories overlaps a great deal (as I read Strauss to assume). The bulk of the Constitution's very clear and specific texts address structural questions where coordination is paramount—how many senators shall each state have?—while most of its vague or ambiguous texts address subjects as to which substantive preferences, judgments of value, and aspirations have changed and have been contested over time.

An institutional mechanism explains this correlation. Clear constitutional texts in noncoordination domains are at much greater risk of falling out of step with deep shifts in social and political values, and when they do, they risk being repealed or altered. Consider the very clear Prohibition Amendment of 1919, which was repealed fourteen years later because the moral tide that produced it had receded and the difficulties of enforcement had mounted, or the clear provision that slaves would count as three-fifths of a person for apportionment purposes, overridden by a clear proviso in the Fourteenth Amendment. By contrast, vague or ambiguous provisions in noncoordination domains can simply be reinterpreted by the judges and will then live on to be reinterpreted again in later periods.

The Thayerian position differs from Strauss's position in the following way: Strauss would entrust both categories of constitutional provisions to judicial oversight, whereas Thayerians would remit to legislative supervision the whole enterprise of common-law constitutionalism under vague or ambiguous constitutional provisions. On the Thayerian view, courts are limited to enforcing clear and specific constitutional texts. Overall, this proposal runs parallel to the one in Chapter 7 that courts deciding statutory cases should enforce only clear and specific statutory texts, otherwise deferring to agencies under an expansive version of the *Chevron* doctrine. As *Chevron* is in the statutory arena, so Thayerism is in the constitutional arena: absent some clear and specific text, courts should defer to legislatures, abandoning judicial review to that extent.

So far I have merely described the Thayerian position, not justified it. Let us begin, as we did in Chapter 7, with the *interpretive baseline* provided by clear and specific constitutional texts. Strauss argues, quite correctly in my view, that judicial review is and should be most formalistic, in the sense of literal and rule-bound, under specific structural provisions as to which coordination and settlement are more important than is the content of constitutional law. Examples involve the legislative veto, which the Court invalidated on textual grounds in *INS v. Chadha*,[95] and the attempt by Congress to appoint executive officials, which the Court rejected on textual grounds in *Buckley v. Valeo*.[96]

Strauss further suggests that as to such coordination-type questions, competing conceptions of constitutionalism and judicial review can reach an overlapping consensus that constitutional doctrine should track clear and specific text.[97] This seems correct and important. Competing high-level accounts of statutory interpretation converge, for institutional reasons, on the view that judges should enforce clear and specific statutory texts (or so I argued in Chapter 7). So too it is hard to imagine a plausible specification of institutional variables under which judges should not enforce clear and specific constitutional texts. In such cases the risks of error are very low, as are the costs of judicial decisionmaking and legal uncertainty, and the benefits of authoritative settlement are high. True, in such situations legislatures are also unlikely to err by enacting clearly unconstitutional statutes. But cases like *Buckley* show that legislatures sometimes will do so. The point is that judicial review in this category can make a valuable, albeit modest, marginal contribution because the risks of erroneous judicial invalidation are low, as are the collateral costs of judicial review. In this setting, the additional screening mechanism that judicial review provides can act as a kind of low-cost backstop, blocking the occasional wild pitch that legislatures throw. And because there is clear and specific text in the picture, there is far less reason to fear the offsetting error of erroneous invalidation of statutes that should be sustained.

Suppose, then, that judges are to enforce clear and specific coordinating texts in the formalist or rule-bound style the Court displayed in *Chadha* and *Buckley*. The next question is also marginal: is it beneficial on net for judges to expand review beyond the interpretive baseline of clear and specific texts? Beyond that baseline constitutional texts are ambiguous on the issue at hand or are open-ended and aspirational, susceptible of readings at multiple levels of generality. Here the content of constitutional law matters more than does the settlement function of law; here the content of constitutional law must continually be updated over time to reflect changing political, social, and economic circumstances.

In my view, judges should refuse to extend judicial review beyond the interpretive baseline. The marginal gains of more expansive review seem entirely speculative, while the decision costs and the costs of legal uncertainty that are created by layering judicial review on top of legislative action are substantial and quite definite. This is put in cost-benefit terms, but, as in Chapter 7, we can put the point in satisficing terms as well. Judicial review works well enough as a backstop against violations of clear constitutional texts. To move beyond that aspiration level is to embrace a kind of perfectionism, a vaulting judicial ambition that threatens to do far more harm than good from the larger standpoint of the constitutional system.

Let us begin with the gains side of the ledger. There is no particular reason to believe that judges are better positioned than legislators to update constitutional principles and rules through incremental decision-making over time. Much the more straightforward assumption is that legislators have systematically better access to changing public values than do courts, a point made by theorists as diverse as Scalia and Ely. At most, we might say with Klarman that judges share the values of the broader society, at least its elite sector. But then it would not be at all obvious what would be gained, at the margin, by adding judicial review in the updating mode.

This point escapes many commentators who seek to defend judicial review under the Constitution's open-ended and aspirational provisions by saying that judicial review is also majoritarian in character. This defense undermines itself, because majoritarian judicial review is at grave risk of being superfluous. Suppose that judicial review merely adds another, cumulative layer of majoritarian decisionmaking, one that does not systematically improve outcomes but instead shifts them unpredictably, with accompanying process and decision costs. Then what good is it?

Of course, constitutional updating must proceed with reasonable caution. Constitutional law's response to changing circumstances should be to optimize the rate of legal change, not to maximize it, and there is a reasonable concern that legislators will respond too quickly to shifts in current politics. Perhaps a layer of judicial review will act as a constitutional balance wheel, adjusting the pace of constitutional change toward the optimum. Note, however, that this is the opposite of saying that judicial review is majoritarian. Under the latter account, judicial review is a procyclical force that accelerates trends rather than a countercyclical force that slows them.

In any event, we cannot begin with the bare fact that legislators, unlike judges, are elected and then somehow deduce that judicial review will push the pace of constitutional change toward the optimum. As far as epistemic humility and presumptive respect for the past are concerned, it is not at all clear that legislatures do worse than courts. Nor is it clear that the more highly theorized doctrine of precedent that judges employ is superior, on any margin, to the loose precedential norms that arise in Congress. Those norms are backed up by institutional rules, such as bicameralism and supermajority requirements, that build a definite status quo bias into legislatures, and for which there is no clear structural analogue in the judiciary. These institutional forces could mean that legislatures in a Thayerian world would change the Constitution at the optimal rate, or even too slowly—in which case adding a judicial balance wheel would make things worse, not better. The claim that judicial review acts as a valuable balance wheel is utterly conjectural. In general, the gains side of the ledger is all rank speculation.

On the cost side of the ledger, however, things are much more definite. Judicial review beyond the interpretive baseline clearly and sharply increases systemic decision costs and the costs of legal uncertainty. Where constitutional texts are ambiguous on the question at hand, or vague, or aspirational, judges must resort to a far wider and costlier set of interpretive and jurisprudential materials, including elaborate inquiries into originalist history, the precedential history of the courts, the looser precedents established by political decisionmaking, and the multiple sources of vaguely specified constitutional traditions. Citizens, legislators, and litigants have far less to go on in predicting constitutional decisions; the sheer overall complexity of constitutional interpretation rises sharply. I shall return to this last point later.

To be sure, legislators engaged in constitutional interpretation beyond the baseline will also incur many of the out-of-pocket costs of complex constitutional interpretation. But systemic decision costs and uncertainty costs are cumulative where judicial review is layered on top of legislative interpretation. Citizens, legislators, and litigants must look to the successive decisions of two institutions to determine constitutional law, not merely the unreviewable decision of one. And in addition to the baseline level of social resources spent on selecting legislators (holding quality constant), a large additional increment must be spent on fighting over the high-stakes selection of powerful constitutional judges (holding quality constant).

All else equal, it is clear that this layering increases the systemic decision costs and uncertainty costs of the interpretive regime. As I emphasized in Chapter 7, systemic decision costs and costs of uncertainty are variables about which judges can be relatively confident of their empirical estimates even when they properly lack confidence in their estimates of the relative risks of majoritarian oppression, or process failure, or constitutional injustice. And if, as I have suggested, there is no particular reason to believe that an additional layer of constitutional review improves outcomes when pushed beyond the interpretive baseline, then there is little to offset these extra costs of decision and legal uncertainty. Certain and substantial costs would be incurred for speculative or conjectural gain. On cost-benefit grounds, supplemented by the principle of insufficient reason, judges should ignore the speculative benefits and avoid the certain costs.

This point can also be put in maximin terms, from the judges' point of view. The worst possible outcome of the Thayerian regime, let us suppose, is that the best conception of aspirational constitutional rules is frequently violated, or that constitutional updating takes place at the wrong pace (either too quickly or too slowly), or that majoritarian excesses occur, or some mix of these. The worst possible outcome of any more expansive regime of judicial review, I am suggesting, is that all of these harms also occur, and that judicial review imposes large systemic costs. If the judges cannot estimate the probabilities of these alternative scenarios, they can at least say that the latter outcome is worse than the former and should be avoided on maximin grounds.

Here too, as in Chapter 7, the point is not simply to minimize the decision costs of judicial review. If it were, the answer would be full legislative supremacy, not the intermediate Thayerian regime. Rather, the problem judges face is to estimate, under conditions of radical uncertainty and bounded rationality, where the judicial aspiration level should be set—where the clear systemic decision costs of further judicial review exceed any definite hope for additional benefits. The Thayerian interpretive baseline of clear constitutional texts, I am suggesting, represents both a floor and a ceiling. Under uncertainty, it is or should be judges' best bet about how far judicial review should extend without going too far.

Can Cumulative Review Be Avoided?

The costly layering of cumulative review is not peculiar to any particular regime of judicial review. It is inevitable, no matter how restricted the domain of judicial review and no matter how exclusive the judges' authority within that domain. To begin with, cumulative review exists even in the regime of judicial supremacy Alexander and Schauer propose. In that regime nonjudicial officials have a reason, of indeterminate weight, to defer to the decisions of the Supreme Court merely by virtue of their existence (apart from their content). But that reason can be overridden or outweighed by other considerations that Alexander and Schauer leave unspecified,[98] and presumably those considerations can or must include nonjudicial officials' independent assessment of just how wrong the Court's interpretation is. All this reduces, to an uncertain degree, the cost side of the equation, relative to a regime of fully cumulative interpretation. But it reduces the benefit side of Alexander and Schauer's regime as well, because this defeasible judicial supremacy also produces less settlement. The paired reductions in costs and benefits wash out, leaving the same conclusion in place: there is little reason to incur (even reduced) certain costs for speculative (and reduced) benefits.

It might seem that Alexander and Schauer pull their punches by making judicial decisions a mere reason for deference that can be outweighed by other reasons. What if judicial review were both exclusive and utterly conclusive, at least as to some questions? Perhaps this more thoroughgoing form of judicial supremacy could avoid the systemic costs of cumulative review altogether by placing some set of constitutional questions in the hands of judges alone. What about a rule or norm instructing legislators to entirely disregard the Constitution, or some subset of its provisions, leaving the relevant constitutional questions to the judges to sort out?

The short answer is that such a regime is ruled out by the structure of the lawmaking process. If legislators are rational, even if not self-interested, they will attempt to predict whether the courts will validate or invalidate bills they pass. Even the most public-spirited legislator must decide how to allocate her time and will be reluctant to invest in promoting a bill sure to be invalidated. (The legislator who is not public spirited, of course, may invest in promoting a bill precisely because it is sure to be invalidated.) The norms of the legal regime can instruct legislators to ignore the courts' future decisions altogether, but legislators cannot and will not comply. What rules out a regime of true judicial exclusivity—even one limited to a few provisions, say, free speech, due process, and equal protection—is the fixed institutional fact that legislators move first and can thus anticipate judicial rulings. In this sense, at least, cumulative review and its systemic costs are inevitable once any form of judicial review is in the picture.

Thayerism, Coordination, and Marginal Contribution

A separate point of note is that nothing in the Thayerian picture requires or assumes the sort of democracy-forcing interpretation I questioned in Chapter 5. The point of the interpretive decision-procedure I have sketched here is not to produce desirable reactions from Congress or other institutions. No threshold or critical mass of judicial coordination through agreed-upon behavior is necessary to implement it. Rather, the contribution that individual judges can make to the Thayerian regime is strictly marginal or divisible: each judge's Thayerian decisionmaking, at the margin, reduces systemic decision costs and legal uncertainty by shifting control over the incremental updating of the Constitution from courts to legislatures, at the margin.

In any event, the proposal here takes out of the judges' hands the very set of cases that are most likely to produce inconsistency over time. I suggested in Chapter 5 that coordination failures are most likely where interpretive rules have distributive effects as well as coordination effects— where, that is, judges not only care about coordination on some set of stable rules, but also care about what the content of the rules actually is. That is why, I have urged, judges deciding constitutional cases should confine themselves to enforcement of the sort of clear coordinating rules as to which settlement is more important than content. In that domain the substantive disagreements that produce coordination failures and judicial inconsistency over time are at a minimum.

Legislatures as Common-Law Constitutionalists

A corollary of the Thayerian position is that where vague, ambiguous, or aspirational constitutional texts are concerned, common-law updating over time is best left to legislatures. In Chapters 2 and 7 I emphasized the role of agencies as common-law courts, updating vague or ambiguous, statutory texts over time to reflect changes in social circumstances, policy expertise, and public values. Here I emphasize the parallel ability of legislatures to fill the role typically assigned to courts by common-law constitutionalists: that of adapting certain types of constitutional provisions to political and social change over time.

Constitutional texts change over time because of linguistic drift and changing social conditions. Change occurs at very different rates for different types of provisions. In Marshall's example, the Treason Clause's requirement of two witnesses does not have a significantly different meaning today than it did when it was drafted, because the text is pointedly clear and specific, and because our language still has much in common with the language of the late eighteenth century, when specific terms are at issue. Highly general, vague, or aspirational provisions such as the Due Process and Equal Protection Clauses, by contrast, are vessels into which new generations pour new conceptions of liberty, equality, and fair procedure.

With respect to such provisions, the task of updating the Constitution over time is not work for which the distinctive and rather narrow expertise of judges and lawyers is relevant. When constitutional rules fall hopelessly out of step with large-scale changes in public values, common-law constitutionalists want the Constitution to adapt to those changes. But it is not at all obvious that lawyers, as a professional class, enjoy any superior capacity to identify the relevant values, as compared with legislators drawn from a relatively broader range of professions, regions, and backgrounds. This is just the downside of the lawyer's technical expertise. Specialized training produces a narrowness of beliefs and commitments that reduces lawyers' information about values current in the larger polity.

Judges' political insulation gives them some distance from current electoral politics, which might help them sort passing political frenzies from deep shifts in public values. But insulation frees judges to do anything they want, within broad limits, and there is no guarantee that what they do will correspond to any account of what makes for good constitutional updating. Even more important, we have seen that judges pay a very large price for insulation in the form of reduced information about what actual people desire and believe. The need to secure reelection forces federal and state legislators into closer contact with a broader range of views, professions, and social classes than most judges encounter. There is no general reason at all to be confident that common-law interpretation by judges can update constitutional rules in ways that more closely track enduring changes in public values.

I suggested earlier that the systemic costs of committing politically charged aspirational provisions to judicial oversight are quite definite and plausibly large, not least because it raises the stakes of judicial appointments and thus raises the amount that interested groups will invest in the confirmation wars. Here the converse point is that the benefits, even from the standpoint of common-law constitutionalists, are entirely conjectural at best and nonexistent at worst. The tools of interpretive choice, then, suggest that the task of updating such provisions should be committed to legislatures.

What about *Brown v. Board of Education?*

I have suggested a particular specification of, and justification for, Thayerism: under conditions of severe uncertainty and bounded rationality, judges' best bet is to limit themselves to enforcing clear and specific coordinating texts and leave more aspirational or open-ended provisions to legislatures. This is not, in historical perspective, a particularly radical suggestion. To be sure, a surprisingly common belief at present is that of course the Supreme Court must engage in the type of vigorous, even aggressive judicial review that it currently does. Does not the rule of law require it? So it is worthwhile to remind ourselves that the Thayerian position is a venerable one in American law, and that some of our greatest judges have embraced it, including Learned Hand, Felix Frankfurter, and (intermittently) Oliver Wendell Holmes.[99]

Thayerian judges have often been tasked, however, with taking a position that would suggest that *Brown v. Board of Education* was wrongly decided.[100] Surely we cannot, as Hand and Frankfurter would have, treat due process and equal protection as aspirational provisions committed to legislative enforcement. Would not public-school segregation have been upheld? Some have claimed that any respectable account of constitutional adjudication must be able to justify *Brown*. In view of such claims, theorists have gone to implausible lengths to square their accounts with *Brown*. Faced with embarrassing evidence that the framers of the Fourteenth Amendment found segregated schooling acceptable, some originalists strain to find offsetting evidence,[101] while others depart from the general originalist practice of reading aspirational clauses at low levels of generality, claiming instead that the Equal Protection Clause embodies a higher-order principle that condemns segregation.[102] Some textualists claim, implausibly, that the clause's cryptic language must be read to condemn segregated schools, perhaps if we stare hard enough at the word "equal."[103]

It is pusillanimous to duck a challenge, so I acknowledge that on the view I have suggested here, *Brown* was indeed wrong, in the sense that the judges had no business deciding that sort of question in the first place. That said, the view that accounts of constitutional interpretation and judicial review should be tested against any particular decision is seriously misguided. That view overlooks the rule-consequentialist critique of judicial review. As emphasized in Chapter 3, the choice of an interpretive regime is always and inevitably a choice over packages of outcomes. To approve *Brown* is to approve an interpretive regime that licenses the Court to reach rights-denying decisions as well as rights-protecting ones. What matters is whether the overall regime is net beneficial.

Under a Thayerian regime, it is true, the Court would not have declared segregated public schooling unconstitutional. Nor would it have declared a constitutional right to own slaves *(Dred Scott v. Sandford)*, invalidated a generation's worth of legislation against child labor *(Hammer v. Dagenhart*[104] and *Bailey v. Drexel Furniture Co.*[105]), or invalidated congressional attempts to provide legal redress for gender-motivated violence *(United States v. Morrison)*.[106] The right question is not whether *Brown* was right or wrong, taken in isolation. The question is whether a jurisprudential record containing neither *Brown* nor these and other abominable decisions would have been better than a jurisprudential record containing all of them. A persistent illusion among academics as well as judges is the faith that "I can have all the invalidations I like and none of the ones I don't"—a perfectionist faith that overlooks the fallibility of judicial institutions. To license good decisions is to license bad ones as well. There is no general mechanism that can produce only happy endings.

The rhetorical punch of the *Brown* question plays on a set of half-conscious assumptions: *Brown* helped eliminate racial segregation; absent *Brown*, there might still be segregation today. Both the implicit causal claim and the implicit counterfactual claim are dubious in the extreme. On the causal side, political scientist Gerald Rosenberg has demonstrated that *Brown* had little or no effect on segregation. Rather, the 1964 Civil Rights Act and the 1965 Voting Rights Act, products of causal forces largely independent of *Brown*, were the prime movers of change.[107] On the counterfactual side, legal scholar Michael Klarman has shown as well as such things can be that the processes of national politics would have eliminated segregation even absent *Brown*.[108] The point in both cases is that segregation was a political regime, not just a legal regime. Large-scale political change was a precondition for eliminating segregation, and the Court follows large-scale change rather than producing it.

Sometimes the appeal is not to *Brown*, but to other actual or hypothetical horrors that legislatures in a Thayerian regime might produce. Absent vigorous judicial review, the idea goes, tyranny is certain to ensue. What if Congress enacted a law suppressing the political speech of Democrats or requiring racial minorities to surrender a kidney to benefit members of the majority?

There is a remarkably persistent strain in constitutional law of this sort of crude slippery-slope reasoning. By "crude" I mean slippery-slope reasoning that (1) lacks any mechanism that will push outcomes down the slope[109] and (2) overlooks the possibility that alternative institutional protections might be superior to judicial review. As to the second point, structural design changes within Congress might well be a more effective way to protect constitutional rights and interests than judicial review, as I suggested previously. Certainly Madison's principal idea, at the time of the constitutional convention anyway, was that legislative tyranny would be checked by bicameralism and the structure of representation rather than by judges. As to the first point, it is poor engineering to prevent a remotely possible disaster by adopting a structure that produces large costs in run-of-the-mill operation. That is why real engineers do not build houses capable of withstanding an asteroid strike. As I emphasized earlier, there is no systematic evidence from comparative law that the institutional mechanism of judicial review is necessary to prevent liberal democracy from sliding into illiberalism or nondemocracy or both; nor is there evidence that judicial review is sufficient to check the slide if other political institutions fail. There is, however, abundant evidence of the systemic costs of vigorous judicial review. To the extent that those costs represent insurance premiums against phantom risks of legislative tyranny, they are a pure social loss.

Levels of Lawmaking and a Note on Voting Rules

There are two more points that need attention. In one respect, it is misleading to call the view I suggest here Thayerian. Thayer principally addressed judicial review of federal statutes by the Supreme Court, and some of his arguments do not generalize well to the state setting, such as the claim that nondeferential review of federal statutes expresses a kind of disrespect for a coordinate branch of the federal government.[110] Thus some Thayerians, or Thayerian fellow-travelers, have drawn an important distinction between review of federal and state statutes. Holmes famously said that the Republic could maintain itself without review of federal statutes, but that review of state statutes was a necessity.[111]

I bracket this issue here; my principal concern is with national legislation alone. Tentatively, however, there seems little reason to draw such a distinction because there is little reason to think that the basic analysis differs significantly across this divide. A Thayerian regime for review of state statutes might increase the disuniformity of law nationwide because state legislatures have a wider scope to experiment with policies that would otherwise be invalidated by courts under provisions like due process and equal protection. No extant theory of federalism, however, tells judges with any specificity what the optimal level of legal uniformity is; it would be sheer assertion to say that the current level of uniformity, which is higher than the level that would obtain under the Thayerian regime, must be the right one. Here too judges should attend to the certain reduction in systemic decision costs and uncertainty that would follow from abjuring aggressive review of state statutes, while ignoring the strictly conjectural benefits of moving beyond the Thayerian baseline. The gains of moving beyond the baseline are obscure, while the losses are not. All this said, however, the preceding analysis of judicial review of national laws stands by itself, whatever conclusions we reach as to judicial review of state laws.

We must also glance at the possibility that Thayerism might itself best be instituted by a hard-edged voting rule rather than by the sort of interpretive decision-procedure I have proposed. Legal scholar Evan Caminker has examined the possibility that supermajority rules might be used to institutionalize deference, in response to a long history of similar proposals.[112] Under proposals of this sort, for example, a two-thirds majority of the Supreme Court—six justices rather than a bare five—might be required to invalidate federal statutes. Obviously many variants are possible here.

Caminker's valuable work addresses voting rules while holding all other institutional rules constant. Once we put institutional changes on the table, however, we might tinker along many other design margins as well. Perhaps an even better regime would require judicial bicameralism, with a majority vote of two panels of the high court needed to invalidate statutes, or repeat voting, with majority votes in two successive terms of court required; and there are a myriad of other possibilities. Of course, there is nothing wrong with Caminker's limited inquiry; not everything can be discussed all at once. My inquiry, in like vein, holds all relevant institutional rules constant, asking only what account of interpretation judges should adopt, given the current rules, without requiring structural reforms. Just as, in Chapter 7, we bracketed the proposal that Congress should enact binding rules of statutory interpretation, so too I proceed here while bracketing the important questions that Caminker raises.

Institutions, Interpretation, and Contingency

There is a final caveat related to the preceding point. The prescriptions I offer here, and in Chapter 7 as well, are emphatically prescriptions for our legal system, with the institutions it currently has. As I emphasized in Chapter 3, a corollary of the institutional approach to interpretation is the recognition that prescriptions are empirically contingent. If our institutions were importantly different than they actually are, the relevant prescriptions would differ as well. At other times our institutions have been different than they are today, and other polities today have institutions different from our own. It follows that interpreters in other times or places might do best to adopt interpretive decision-procedures other than the ones I have urged here.

Consider, for example, the possibility that judicial review in new or transitional democracies might properly take an aggressive role in protecting property rights, promoting market institutions, and protecting civil liberties and political rights. Suppose that legislatures and regulatory agencies are especially ill motivated and inexpert, that legislative outcomes are frequently and crudely oppressive of disfavored groups, and that electoral institutions are shaky. In such circumstances the values of the variables we have discussed would be different, and different prescriptions might make sense. I have suggested that aggressive judicial review is not plausibly best for our polity today, but that is strictly because our institutional circumstances do not warrant it. Although the institutional questions do not differ across time or across polities, the answers may well differ.

Coda: Interpretation and the Commitment to Complexity

There is something of a paradox in the suggestions offered in both Chapters 7 and 8. It seems odd that a prescription in favor of rule-bound, inflexible interpretation—"formalist" interpretation in one sense of the term—would follow from my emphasis on the empirical difficulties of interpretive choice, indeed, on the judges' (and the academy's) current ignorance about the empirical determinants of interpretive doctrine. Rules are often thought to demand more information from the formulators—in this case the judges who choose interpretive doctrine—than do standards, for the latter allow information generated at the point of application to be taken into account. If information is what the courts lack, then a flexible approach to interpretation that allows judges to take received information (like legislative history) into account might be better than a rigid approach.

But the paradox is only apparent, not real. Inflexible, rule-bound behavior is often the best response to a decisionmaking problem in which the decisionmaker has very poor information or a very low capacity to process the information that is received.[113] The absence or unreliability of information, or the decisionmaker's poor processing capacity, makes a wide and flexible repertoire of behavior a bad bet in marginal terms, because the chances that any additional action will better the situation are slight. So the decisionmaker should opt for a small set of relatively wooden behaviors and decision-rules.

It is true that I have proposed, for both statutes and the Constitution, an interpretive decision-procedure that leaves little room for judicial creativity, for the aesthetic rigors and rewards of lawyerly guild-craft in its more baroque forms, and for the elaborate study of Supreme Court decisionmaking. Cutting hard against this proposal is a cultural phenomenon that holds sway across large sectors of the legal academy and legal profession. It is something like *a commitment to complexity* in matters of legal interpretation. Lawyers, judges, and academic theorists often seem instinctively to resist suggestions for the radical simplification of judicial decisionmaking; they seem to believe that the sort of rich, ambitious, complex, and highly coherentist judicial decisionmaking envisioned by Hart and Sacks is somehow natural for law, even necessary or inevitable in any legal system.

This is an illusion for the most part. Some minimum of interpretive complexity might be inevitable in a modern liberal democracy. But the level of interpretive ambition and complexity varies, over time and across legal systems. To a large extent it is a product of people's choices, over and above the structural constraints. Perhaps the commitment to complexity is simply generational, a byproduct of Hart and Sacks's grip on elite lawyers educated in the post–World War II period. But there may be something else, and deeper, here as well. In Chapter 1 we examined mechanisms that produce a kind of institutional blindness in judges, lawyers, and academic theorists of legal interpretation. As a bookend for the whole discussion, we shall conclude this chapter by examining some mechanisms that produce something like a commitment to interpretive complexity, a commitment to promote the most ambitious and challenging forms of judicial decisionmaking, on the part of lawyers and judges.

Self-interested motivation and cost-externalization. For Bentham, the mechanism that generates legal complexity was obvious: self-interested collusive behavior on the part of lawyers and judges. Judge and Company benefits jointly and severally from a highly complex, even mysterious legal system in which laypeople must pay rents to lawyers to steer through the thickets that the lawyers themselves have created.[114] Although the claim is little discussed today, it had better institutional foundations when Bentham wrote. Consider that judges were commonly paid from the fees of litigants, and that one of Bentham's principal reforms was to urge that judges be put on regular government salaries.

Legal scholar Peter Schuck puts Bentham's argument in more modern terms and less conspiratorial ones by observing that the costs and benefits of complex legal interpretation are unequally distributed over different actors and groups. Producers of law, including legislators as well as judges and lawyers, may capture the benefits of complex law while externalizing its costs onto poorly organized groups.[115] Consider the claim advanced in Chapter 7 that the *Mead* decision allows the Supreme Court to capture the benefits of formulating deference in complex, highly reticulated terms while externalizing onto agencies, lower courts and litigants the costs of that complexity. Of course, there is a base rate of complexity in the legal system, no matter what judges and lawyers do. Legislators may also externalize complexity, enacting intricate and obscure statutory schemes that agencies and courts must struggle to implement. But my project here is to hold constant the level of complexity in the statutory and constitutional sources and focus on the question why standard attitudes toward judicial interpretation of those sources would add complexity even beyond that baseline.

Neglect of opportunity costs. Bentham's account, as updated by Schuck, points to self-interested motivations on the part of lawyers, judges, and other legal actors. But there is a cognitive mechanism operating as well that plausibly affects even public-spirited legal actors and specialized academics. I refer to the neglect of opportunity costs relative to direct costs, a neglect that occurs because opportunity costs are less salient or available for cognitive recall than are direct costs. This cognitive tendency tends to make decisionmaking excessively intensive and complex, rather than brisk and mechanical, because decisionmakers focus to excess on the costs of getting a particular decision wrong while overlooking the costs that a protracted process of decisionmaking itself creates. "The neglect of the opportunity costs that are created by the fact that *decision making takes time* is . . . an important and pervasive source of irrationality."[116]

The approximation assumption. I have argued throughout that ambitious, perfectionist interpretation falls prey to second-best problems. Interpretive complexity and refinement, when undertaken by judges with limited capacities, often produce mistakes that push the legal regime away from the desired aim rather than toward it. Suppose that a judge who subscribes to some high-level theory of interpretive authority, or a theorist urging judges to subscribe to that account, argues along these lines: "To be sure, it is clear that mistakes will be made, so the ideal I advocate is unattainable. But it is nonetheless a worthy ideal, and we usually think it praiseworthy, perhaps even morally obligatory, to pursue our ideals as far as possible, even if we will never fully attain them." Is the argument sound?

Not at all. It rests on the *approximation assumption:* the fallacious view that the best course of action is the one that approximates an unobtainable ideal as closely as possible.[117] To the contrary, if an ideal state of affairs cannot be fully realized, partial implementation of the ideal is often worse, as judged by the very criteria that support the ideal in the first place, than abandoning it entirely. We have already seen examples of this in various interpretive settings. Consider the possibility from Chapter 4 that the search for legislative intentions will often backfire when judges move beyond statutory text to seemingly more informative legislative history.

I believe, although I cannot demonstrate, that much of the preference for interpretive complexity stems from a kind of misguided idealism on the part of judges, lawyers, and perhaps especially academics, who tend to specialize in particular fields. The case at hand really is difficult, the considerations really are multifactored and subtle, and the interpretive problems are engrossing. Why should interpreters voluntarily blind themselves to any part of the relevant problems? Surely they should just do the best they can. But then we recall that Icarus, too, did the best he could, strove as high as he could. Like Icarus, I have suggested, judges and the legal system might be better off closer to the ground.

Conclusion

Interim Interpretive Theory

I conclude by emphasizing that the view I have urged in Part III is, by its terms, an interim theory of legal interpretation. It is a theory good only for an awkward transitional period in which academics and judges have begun to appreciate that the dispositive questions about the interpretive system are empirical and institutional rather than conceptual, but in which the relevant empirical information is largely absent. In this period, judging under uncertainty is the only type of judging on offer.

This picture follows from the two theses, methodological and substantive, that I have pursued throughout. Parts I and II argued that the determinants of interpretive theory are empirical findings about institutional performance, principally legislative, administrative, and judicial capacities and the systemic effects of interpretive decision-procedures. Part III moved beyond the methodological position to confront the inadequacy of our current information and the resulting stalemate of empirical intuitions. Judges designing interpretive decision-procedures cannot help but choose operative rules for interpretation, one way or another. It is impossible for judges just to "decide cases," for this is itself an interpretive decision-procedure. The institutionalist dilemma is that their choices must rest upon institutional variables, but the information needed to fill in the values of these variables does not yet exist. I suggested that judges acting in these circumstances must fall back upon a repertoire of techniques for decisionmaking under uncertainty. Those techniques counsel judges to adopt an unassuming posture of rule-bound, relatively inflexible decisionmaking, using a small set of interpretive tools and deferring to agencies and legislatures where texts are anything less than clear and specific.

My substantive suggestions are emphatically revisable. The cumulative progress of empirical findings might, in principle, eventually point toward a much different set of interpretive decision-procedures, although I happen to believe that any such prospect lies in the relatively remote future. I emphasized in the Introduction and at the beginning of Part II that the methodological thesis and the substantive thesis are partially independent. One can subscribe to the former while holding that the institutionalist dilemma should be resolved in some way other than the one I have suggested. Here the point is different. If the methodological thesis is correct, then interpretive theory, in the sense of suggestions to judges about what to do with statutes and the Constitution, can only be provisional. It is a recommendation to judges that is good only for a particular moment—namely, the transitional moment at which interpretive theory becomes resolutely empirical and institutionalist, but in which the vast bulk of the necessary empirical work has yet to be done.

I believe that the theory of legal interpretation has recently entered a transitional period of this sort. In this period judges and theorists have shrugged off the conceptualism of yesterday, but they see only dimly into tomorrow; that is what makes the institutionalist dilemma particularly acute. In this period the only useful service that can be rendered to judges by theorists of interpretation, as opposed to social scientists studying the empirical determinants of interpretive approaches, is to offer counsel about how legal actors might best proceed under conditions of uncertainty. This is a less elevated role than academic theorists have been used to playing. Supplying the first-best conceptualism that dominates interpretive theory is headier stuff than devising fumbling, cautious recommendations for judging under uncertainty. But the question whether interpretive theory is intellectually satisfying to its practitioners strikes me as entirely irrelevant from a social point of view.

As for judges, the interim character of interpretive theory suggests a new interpretation of the blindness of justice. In the traditional figure, the goddess of justice is blindfolded to represent her impartiality. In the revised interpretation, justice is blind because it cannot see the facts on which the proper design of the operating rules of justice depends. Justice, then, must step tentatively forward, minimizing the harms of various courses of action and abandoning any aspirations to perfection. I believe that we show the blind goddess more reverence by offering counsel that is realistic about her capacities than by urging her to heights she cannot attain.

Notes

Index

Notes

Introduction

1. See Hilary Putnam, *The Collapse of the Fact/Value Dichotomy and Other Essays* (2002).
2. The possibility of formalism in the operational, rule-based sense, justified on the basis of claims about judicial competence and ex ante effects, has recently commanded a great deal of interest in the literature on contract interpretation. See, e.g., Eric A. Posner, "A Theory of Contract Law under Conditions of Radical Judicial Error," 94 *Nw. U. L. Rev.* 749 (2000); Robert E. Scott, "The Case for Formalism in Relational Contract," 94 *Nw. U. L. Rev.* 847 (2000).

1. Interpretation without Institutions

1. Harold Demsetz, "Information and Efficiency: Another Viewpoint," 12 *J.L. & Econ.* 1, 1–4 (1969).
2. See Jeremy Waldron, *Law and Disagreement* 9 (1999).
3. See Henry Hart and Albert Sacks, *The Legal Process: Basic Problems in the Making and Application of Law* 1111–1380 (William N. Eskridge and Philip P. Frickey eds., 1994) (1958).
4. See 1 William Blackstone, *Commentaries on the Laws of England* *58–62.
5. Hart and Sacks, supra note 3, at 1170–71.
6. Blackstone, supra note 4, at *59.
7. Id. at *61.
8. Id.
9. Id. at *60.
10. Id. at *62.
11. John Dinwiddy, *Bentham* 59–69 (1989).
12. See Jeremy Bentham, *A Comment on the Commentaries and A Fragment on*

Government I.9, II.2 (J. H. Burns and H. L. A. Hart eds., 1977) [hereinafter Bentham, *Comment on the Commentaries*].

13. See id. at 111, 160. Bentham sometimes intimates that he endorses purposivism and the absurd-results canon only in cases of ambiguous statutory language. See, e.g., id. at 160. But it requires some work to square that qualification with Blackstone's example, so it is not clear how seriously we are to take it. See also Jeremy Bentham, *The Theory of Legislation* 155 (C. K. Ogden ed., Fred B. Rothman and Co. 1987) (1864) (urging that "laws should be literally followed").

14. Jeremy Bentham, *Of Laws in General* 239 (H. L. A. Hart ed., 1970) [hereinafter Bentham, *Of Laws*].

15. Id. at 240.

16. Id.

17. Bentham, *Of Laws,* supra note 14, at 241; Dinwiddy, supra note 11, at 68–69.

18. I do not discuss the realists themselves, though it is noteworthy that they tended to argue for candid and open-ended judicial policymaking in the face of ambiguous statutes, without grappling with the risks posed by judicial discretion. See, e.g., Karl N. Llewellyn, "Remarks on the Theory of Appellate Decision and the Rules or Canons about How Statutes Are to Be Construed," 3 *Vand. L. Rev* 395, 399 (1950), which, after challenging the canons of construction, suggests that courts should "strive to make sense *as a whole* out of our law *as a whole*" (emphases in original), without engaging the obvious institutional problems raised by any such effort. Max Radin, "Statutory Interpretation," 43 *Harv. L. Rev.* 863, 884 (1930), criticizes the conventional sources of interpretation and suggests that the real question is "Will the inclusion of this particular determinate in the statutory determinable lead to a desirable result?" Radin does not address the difficulties that courts might face in answering that question. Of course, I do not deny the possibility that the sources of law favored by the formalist—above all, the text—will leave ambiguities; in such cases institutional considerations are highly relevant to the decision how to proceed. *Chevron v. NRDC,* 467 U.S. 837 (1984), represents an institutionally grounded choice to leave the resolution to the relevant administrative agency. I take up *Chevron* and related issues in Chapter 7.

19. Hart and Sacks, supra note 3, at 158–172 (surveying the major lawmaking institutions and their relationships).

20. Id. at 1271–1312 (examining administrative interpretation of statutes).

21. H. L. A. Hart, *The Concept of Law* 124–136 (2d ed. 1995).

22. See id. at 128.

23. Id.

24. Id.

25. Id.
26. Id.
27. Id. at 129.
28. Id.
29. Id. at 130.
30. Id.
31. See Hart and Sacks, supra note 3, at 1374–80.
32. Id. at 1374.
33. Id. at 1377.
34. Andrei Marmor, "Should We Value Legislative Integrity?" in *Legislatures and Constitutionalism: The Role of Legislatures in the Constitutional State* (T. Kahana and R. Bauman eds.) (forthcoming Cambridge University Press).
35. See Ronald Dworkin, *Law's Empire* (1986).
36. Id. at 243.
37. Id.
38. *TVA v. Hill*, 437 U.S. 153 (1978).
39. Dworkin, supra note 35, at 347.
40. Congress promptly established an administrative mechanism for granting exemptions from the Endangered Species Act, see Pub. L. No. 95-632, 92 Stat. 3751, 3752–60 (1978), and Congress itself specifically exempted the dam at issue in *TVA v. Hill*, see Pub. L. No. 96-69, 93 Stat. 437, 449 (1979).
41. John F. Manning, "Textualism as a Nondelegation Doctrine," 97 *Colum. L. Rev.* 673, 695 (1997).
42. Id. at 728.
43. See *In re Sinclair*, 870 F. 2d 1340, 1342 (1989) (Easterbrook, J.) ("Legislative history may be invaluable in revealing . . . the assumptions its authors entertained about how their words would be understood. . . . [J]udges may learn from the legislative history even when the text is 'clear'. Clarity depends on context, which legislative history may illuminate.").
44. But see John F. Manning, "Constitutional Structure and Statutory Formalism," 66 *U. Chi. L. Rev.* 685, 686 (1999) (rejecting the "contention that the Constitution has little to say about the choice between formalist and antiformalist methodologies"). Manning's view here is appropriately nuanced; he disavows any suggestion that "inferences from constitutional structure will always provide clear answers to questions of interpretive design" and notes that "[w]hen they do not, the judiciary may have room to make choices among particular interpretive strategies." Id. at 692–693.
45. Compare John F. Manning, "Textualism and the Equity of the Statute," 101 *Colum. L. Rev.* 1, 10–15 (2001), and John F. Manning, "Deriving Rules of Statutory Interpretation from the Constitution," 101 *Colum. L. Rev.* 1648 (2001), with William N. Eskridge, Jr., "All about Words: Early Understand-

ings of the 'Judicial Power' in Statutory Interpretation, 1776–1806," 101 *Colum. L. Rev.* 990 (2001).

46. See Stephen Breyer, *Active Liberty: Interpreting Our Democratic Constitution* 85–101 (2005).

47. Steven Knapp and Walter Benn Michaels, "Against Theory," 8 *Critical Inquiry* 723 (1982).

48. Stanley Fish, *There's No Such Thing as Free Speech* 180–199 (1994).

49. Steven Knapp and Walter Benn Michaels, "Intention, Identity and the Constitution: A Response to David Hoy," in *Legal Hermeneutics: History, Theory, and Practice* 187, 196 (Gregory Leyh ed., 1992).

50. Fish, supra note 48, at 184.

51. For a current metaethical treatment of this distinction, see Brad Hooker, *Ideal Code, Real World: A Rule-Consequentialist Theory of Morality* (2000).

52. As to judges, see Adrian Vermeule, "Constitutional Amendments and the Constitutional Common Law," in *Legislatures and Constitutionalism,* supra note 34; Frederick Schauer, "Do Cases Make Bad Law?" (forthcoming *U. Chi. L. Rev.*). For a comparison of courts and legislatures in these terms, see Jeffery J. Rachlinski, "Bottom-Up versus Top-Down Lawmaking" (forthcoming *U. Chi. L. Rev.*).

53. See Scott Plous, *The Psychology of Judgment and Decision Making* 125–126, 178–180 (1993) (discussing the salience heuristic and the closely related heuristics of vividness and availability). Cf. Robert M. Reyes, William C. Thompson, and Gordon H. Bower, "Judgmental Biases Resulting from Differing Availabilities of Arguments," 39 *J. Personality and Soc. Psychol.* 2, 5–12 (1980) (demonstrating that vivid, concrete information exerts greater influence on mock jury deliberations than abstract, pallid information). For the impact of cognitive illusions and affective forces on judges, see Chris Guthrie, Jeffrey J. Rachlinski, and Andrew J. Wistrich, "Inside the Judicial Mind," 86 *Cornell L. Rev.* 777 (2001).

2. Dynamism and Pragmatism

1. See William N. Eskridge, Jr., "The New Textualism," 37 *UCLA L. Rev.* 621 (1990).

2. See William N. Eskridge, Jr., "Dynamic Statutory Interpretation," 135 *U. Pa. L. Rev.* 1479 (1987) [hereinafter Eskridge, "DSI"].

3. Id. at 1509.

4. See, e.g., Max Radin, "Statutory Interpretation," 43 *Harv. L. Rev.* 863, 870–871 (1930) (rejecting legislative intent and legislative history on realist grounds).

5. See John Copeland Nagle, "Newt Gingrich, Dynamic Statutory Interpreter," 143 *U. Pa. L. Rev.* 2209, 2222–35 (1995) (book review).

6. See Richard A. Posner, "Legal Formalism, Legal Realism, and the Interpretation of Statutes and the Constitution," 37 *Case W. Res. L. Rev.* 179, 190 (1987) ("No text is clear except in terms of a linguistic and cultural environment, but it doesn't follow that no text is clear.") [hereinafter Posner, "Legal Formalism"].

7. See Dan Kahan, "Democracy Shmemocracy," 20 *Cardozo L. Rev.* 795 (1999).

8. Eskridge, "DSI," supra note 2, at 1482, 1496.

9. Id. at 1494.

10. See Cass R. Sunstein, "Is Tobacco a Drug? Administrative Agencies as Common Law Courts," 47 *Duke L.J.* 1013, 1020, 1055–63 (1998). For elaboration of this claim, see Edward Rubin, "Dynamic Statutory Interpretation in the Administrative State," in *Issues in Legal Scholarship: Dynamic Statutory Interpretation* (2002), available at www.bepress.com/ils/iss3/art2.

11. Sunstein, supra note 10, at 1060.

12. William N. Eskridge, Jr., "The Dynamic Theorization of Statutory Interpretation," in *Issues in Legal Scholarship: Dynamic Statutory Interpretation* (2002): Article 16, available at www.bepress.com/ils/iss3/art16 at 22–23.

13. Id. at 21.

14. Eskridge, "DSI," supra note 2, at 1530.

15. Id.

16. See William N. Eskridge, Jr., "Textualism, The Unknown Ideal?" 96 *Mich. L. Rev.* 1509, 1541 (1998) [hereinafter Eskridge, "Textualism"].

17. See William N. Eskridge, Jr., "Norms, Empiricism, and Canons in Statutory Interpretation," 66 *U. Chi. L. Rev.* 671 (1999).

18. William Eskridge and John Ferejohn, "The Article I, Section 7 Game," 80 *Geo. L.J.* 523 (1992).

19. McNollgast, "Positive Canons: The Role of Legislative Bargains in Statutory Interpretation," 80 *Geo. L.J.* 705 (1992).

20. See generally William N. Eskridge, Jr., and Phillip P. Frickey, "Law as Equilibrium," 108 *Harv. L. Rev.* 26 (1994).

21. See McNollgast, "Legislative Intent: The Use of Positive Political Theory in Statutory Interpretation," 57 *Law & Contemp. Probs.* 3 (1994); McNollgast, supra note 19.

22. See Jerry L. Mashaw, *Greed, Chaos, and Governance: Using Public Choice to Improve Public Law* 99 (1997).

23. Posner, "Legal Formalism," supra note 6.

24. 1 William Blackstone, *Commentaries on the Laws of England* *61.

25. See, e.g., Richard A. Posner, *Law, Pragmatism, and Democracy* chs. 8–9 (2003); Richard A. Posner, "Pragmatic Adjudication," in *The Revival of*

Pragmatism: New Essays on Social Thought, Law, and Culture 235–53 (Morris Dickstein ed., 1998).

26. Richard A. Posner, "Judges' Writing Styles (and Do They Matter?)," 62 *U. Chi. L. Rev.* 1421, 1432–33 (1995).

27. Posner, "Pragmatic Adjudication," supra note 25, at 244.

28. Id. at 250–251.

29. Richard A. Posner and William Landes, "The Independent Judiciary in an Interest-Group Perspective," 18 *J.L. & Econ.* 875 (1976).

30. See Richard Posner, "What Do Judges Maximize? (The Same Thing Everybody Else Does)," 3 *Sup. Ct. Econ. Rev.* 1 (1993). See also Frederick Schauer, "Incentives, Reputation, and the Inglorious Determinants of Judicial Behavior," 68 *U. Cin. L. Rev.* 615 (2000).

31. Posner, "Pragmatic Adjudication," supra note 25, at 243–244.

32. See Michel Troper et al., "Statutory Interpretation in France," in *Interpreting Statutes: A Comparative Study* 171, 192 (D. Neil MacCormick and Robert S. Summers eds., 1991).

33. Frederick Schauer, "The Practice and Problems of Plain Meaning: A Response to Aleinikoff and Shaw," 45 *Vand. L. Rev.* 715 (1992).

34. See John F. Manning, "The Absurdity Doctrine," 116 *Harv. L. Rev.* 2387, 2437–38 (2003).

35. Richard Epstein, "The Perils of Posnerian Pragmatism," 71 *U. Chi. L. Rev.* 639, 650–651 (2004).

3. The Institutional Turn

1. Neil K. Komesar, *Imperfect Alternatives: Choosing Institutions in Law, Economics, and Public Policy* (1994).

2. Einer R. Elhauge, "Does Interest Group Theory Justify More Intrusive Judicial Review?" 101 *Yale L.J.* 31 (1991).

3. Although some have tried. See Thomas W. Merrill, "Does Public Choice Theory Justify Judicial Activism after All?" 21 *Harv. J.L. & Pub. Pol'y* 219, 221–222 (1997) (responding to Elhauge and Komesar).

4. See William N. Eskridge, Jr., "Dynamic Statutory Interpretation," 135 *U. Pa. L. Rev.* 1479, 1530 (1987).

5. Cass R. Sunstein, "Must Formalism Be Defended Empirically?" 66 *U. Chi. L. Rev.* 636 (1999).

6. Eskridge, supra note 4, at 1494.

7. Here I draw freely on the massive literature on rules and standards. Some of the most important contributions include the following: Colin S. Diver, "The Optimal Precision of Administrative Rules," 93 *Yale L.J.* 65 (1983); Louis Kaplow, "Rules versus Standards: An Economic Analysis," 42 *Duke*

L.J. 557 (1992); Frederick Schauer, *Playing by the Rules: A Philosophical Examination of Rule-Based Decisionmaking in Law and in Life* (1991); and Cass R. Sunstein, "Problems with Rules," 83 *Calif. L. Rev.* 953 (1995).

8. See generally Steven Shavell, "Optimal Discretion in the Application of Rules," Harvard John M. Olin Center Discussion Paper No. 509 (03/2005) (available at www.law.harvard.edu/programs/olin_center).

9. See Lee Epstein and Jack Knight, *The Choices Justices Make* 138–181 (1998).

10. See Francis Leiber, *Legal and Political Hermeneutics* 19 (1880) ("The British spirit of civil liberty induced the English judges to adhere strictly to the law, to its exact expressions. This again induced the law-makers to be, in their phraseology, as explicit and minute as possible.").

11. See *Millar v. Taylor*, 98 Eng. Rep. 201 (1769); but see *Pepper v. Hart*, 1 All E.R. 42 (1993) (announcing new rule that parliamentary debates may be consulted to resolve ambiguities). See generally T. St. J. N. Bates, "The Contemporary Use of Legislative History in the United Kingdom," 54 *Cambridge L.J.* 127 (1995).

12. *United States v. E. C. Knight Co.*, 156 U.S. 1 (1895). On the similarities and differences between Langdellian formalism and the formalism of the pre–New Deal Supreme Court, see Thomas C. Grey, "The New Formalism," 6–9 (2002) (unpublished draft).

13. *INS v. Chadha*, 462 U.S. 919 (1983).

14. See Schauer, supra note 7. See also Grey, supra note 12 (identifying a strand of formalism that emphasizes rule-following and legal determinacy).

15. See Cass R. Sunstein and Edna Ullmann-Margalit, "Second-Order Decisions," 110 *Ethics* 46 (1999).

16. See John Copeland Nagle, "Corrections Day," 43 *UCLA L. Rev.* 1267 (1996).

17. For a nuanced treatment of the effects of formalism on planning costs in tax law, suggesting that formalism might increase planning costs by encouraging strategic behavior, see David A. Weisbach, "Formalism in the Tax Law," 66 *U. Chi. L. Rev.* 860 (1999).

18. See R. G. Lipsey and Kelvin Lancaster, "The General Theory of Second Best," 24 *Rev. Econ. Stud.* 11 (1956).

19. See Cass R. Sunstein, "Incompletely Theorized Agreements," 108 *Harv. L. Rev.* 1733 (1995).

20. Richard A. Posner, *Law, Pragmatism, and Democracy* 65 (2003).

21. Ronald Dworkin, "Order of the Coif Lecture: In Praise of Theory," 29 *Ariz. St. L.J.* 353, 364 (1997).

22. Robert K. Merton, *Social Theory and Social Structure* Part I, ch. 2 ("On the Sociological Theories of the Middle Range") (1968).

4. Judicial Capacities

1. *Holy Trinity Church v. United States,* 143 U.S. 457 (1892).

2. 23 Stat. 332 (codified as amended at 29 U.S.C. § 2164 (1901)), superseded by Act of Mar. 3, 1903, Pub. L. No. 162, 32 Stat. 1213.

3. *Aldridge v. Williams,* 44 U.S. (3 How.) 1, 24 (1845).

4. See *United States v. Des Moines Navigation and Ry. Co.,* 142 U.S. 510, 530 (1892) (citing congressional debates as supporting authority); *Am. Net & Twine Co. v. Worthington,* 141 U.S. 468, 474 (1891) ("[R]eference to the [legislative history] may properly be made to inform the court of the exigencies [surrounding a bill's passage]."); *Jennison v. Kirk,* 98 U.S. 453, 459–460 (1879) (consulting internal legislative history to ascertain the statute's legal and social background, but not its construction); *Blake v. Nat'l Banks,* 90 U.S. (23 Wall.) 307, 317–320 (1874) (tracing passage of a bill through the congressional record, but conceding that legislative history was indeterminate); *Collector v. Richards,* 90 U.S. (23 Wall.) 246, 258 (1874) (referring to a Senate report, but only as an additional authority). See generally Hans W. Baade, " 'Original Intent' in Historical Perspective: Some Critical Glosses," 69 *Tex. L. Rev.* 1001 (1991).

5. See Record, Case No. 13,166, at Record Item No. 6, *Holy Trinity Church v. United States,* 143 U.S. 457 (1892) (No. 143) (on file at the Supreme Court Library).

6. Alien Contract Labor Act of 1885, ch. 164, § 1, 23 Stat. 332, 332 (codified as amended at 29 U.S.C. § 2164 (1901)), superceded by Act of Mar. 3, 1903, ch. 1012, § 4, Pub. L. No. 162, 32 Stat. 1213.

7. Id. § 5, 23 Stat. at 333 ("[N]or shall the provisions of this act apply to professional actors, artists, lecturers or singers, nor to persons employed strictly as personal or domestic servants.").

8. See Michael J. Brodhead, *David J. Brewer: The Life of a Supreme Court Justice, 1837–1910* 128–129 (1994).

9. *Holy Trinity Church,* 143 U.S. at 459.

10. Id. at 465 (quoting 15 Cong. Rec. 5359 (1884)).

11. Id. at 464–465 (quoting 15 Cong. Rec. 6059 (1884)).

12. Id. at 465–471.

13. See, e.g., *Lynch v. Donnelly,* 465 U.S. 668, 718 (1984) (Brennan, J., dissenting) (referring to "the days when Justice Brewer could arrogantly declare for the Court that 'this is a Christian nation' " (quoting *Holy Trinity,* 143 U.S. at 471)).

14. See, e.g., Carol Chomsky, "Unlocking the Mysteries of *Holy Trinity*: Spirit, Letter, and History in Statutory Interpretation," 100 *Colum. L. Rev.* 901, 939 (2000).

15. See 15 Cong. Rec. 5349 (1884) (statement of Rep. Hopkins) ("The bill just read was prepared by my colleague on the committee, the gentleman from Ohio. . . . He has made a very careful, elaborate, and able report on the subject."); see also id. (statement of Rep. Bland).

16. See, e.g., 15 Cong. Rec. 5368 (statement of Rep. Jones) ("While I approve the objects of the bill, I could not vote for it in its present form. The friends of the bill have . . . drawn a bill altogether too rigorous in its provisions."); id. at 5368–69 (statement of Rep. Cutcheon) ("I am in hearty sympathy with the purpose of this bill, as I understand it. I think there are very serious imperfections in the draught of the bill, which I hope may be remedied by amendment.").

17. Id. at 5354 (statement of Rep. Kelley).

18. Id. at 5358 (statements of Rep. Adams and Rep. O'Neill).

19. See A Universal and Critical Dictionary of the English Language 130 (Joseph E. Worcester ed., 1881) (defining "clerk" as "[a] writer employed in a public or private office, under a superior; one employed under another; a writer or assistant in an office, store, &c").

20. See 15 Cong. Rec. 5371 (passing bill on voice vote without roll call).

21. Id. at 6059 (quoting the Senate committee report).

22. Id.

23. See id. at 5729 (statements of Sen. Blair and Sen. Morrill).

24. Id. at 6057 (statement of Sen. Blair).

25. Id.

26. See id. at 6058 (yeas 26, nays 14).

27. Id. at 6059 (statement of Sen. Ingalls).

28. Id. at 6059 (statement of Sen. Blair). Blair stated: "I design to move the modifications alluded to in the Senate report, which are to change the expression, wherever it occurs, 'service or labor,' which is very general, to 'manual service or manual labor,' so that the provisions of the bill would then be restricted to the evil that exists."

29. See id. at 6067 (statement of President pro tempore); see also William D. Popkin, Materials on Legislation: Political Language and the Political Process 233 (2d ed. 1997) (suggesting that the Senate adjourned discussion of the bill because, having amended the bill, the Senate would have to resubmit it to the House for concurrence).

30. 16 Cong. Rec. 1621–22 (1885) (statement of Sen. Blair).

31. Id. at 1632 (statement of Sen. Morgan).

32. See id.

33. Id. at 1633.

34. Id. Morgan went on to say, "People who can instruct us in morals and religion and in every species of elevation by lectures . . . are not prohibited."

Id. This might be read to support a claim that a minister counts as a "lecturer" under the express exemption of section 5 of the act. That claim is wholly consistent with the view of *Holy Trinity* advanced here. It is, however, worth noting that the more natural reading of Morgan's remark is merely that any alien who immigrated to give lectures on religious topics would fall within the exemption for lecturers. It does not follow that anyone who "instruct[s] . . . in morals and religion" would count as a "lecturer."

35. See 16 *Cong. Rec.* 1837.

36. Id. at 2032 (statement of Rep. Hopkins).

37. Chomsky, supra note 14, emphasizes the background context and the broad purposes of the bill's original drafters. But Chomsky never comes to grips with the facts that (1) the bill's language was never tailored to those purposes and (2) the specific understandings of the bill's sponsors and supporters about what the language meant perfectly tracked the text rather than their more general purposes. This is a standard mistake of purposive interpreters: background intentions and purposes are always subject to being narrowed or broadened by the compromises, concessions, and deals brokered in the legislative process. See John F. Manning, "The Absurdity Doctrine," 116 *Harv. L. Rev.* 2387, 2424–25 (2003).

38. *Holy Trinity,* 143 U.S. at 458.

39. See Ronald Dworkin, "Comment," in *A Matter of Interpretation: Federal Courts and the Law* 115, 118 and n.8 (Amy Gutman ed., 1997)[hereinafter *Interpretation*]; Antonin Scalia, "Common-Law Courts in a Civil-Law System: The Role of United States Federal Courts in Interpreting the Constitution and Laws," in *Interpretation,* id., at 3, 18–23.

40. See Brief for Plaintiff in Error, *Holy Trinity Church v. United States,* 143 U.S. 457 (1892)(No. 143) 8–12 (on file at the Supreme Court Library) [hereinafter Brief for Plaintiff]. The brief merely refers to "Webster" without citation, but the definitions appear to be taken verbatim from the 1891 edition. See *Webster's International Dictionary of the English Language* 821 (Noah Porter ed., 1891) (defining "labor"); id. at 1316 (defining "service").

41. Dictionaries of the period consistently define "service" in both a narrower sense (as menial work) and a broader sense (as any employment or position). See, e.g., *A Dictionary of the English Language* 920–921 (Rev. James Stormonth ed., 1885) (defining "service," inter alia, as "labour, physical or mental, performed in course of duty"; "employment"; and "official duties of a clergyman"); *A Law Dictionary* 513 (John Bouvier ed., 1892) ("Service. In contracts. The being employed to serve another."); *A Universal and Critical Dictionary of the English Language,* supra note 19 (defining "service" as both "menial office" and "employment; business; any duty, public or private"); *Universal Dictionary of the English Language* (Robert Hunter and

Charles Morris eds., 1897) (defining "service" as "(1) [t]he act of serving; the performance of labour or offices at the command of or for another; menial duties. . . . (6) [d]uty performed in or appropriate to any office, charge, position or employment"). For judicial decisions that show the broad application of the word, see, for example, *United States v. Langston,* 118 U.S. 389, 394 (1886) (referring to the "services" rendered by public officials); *Hall v. Wisconsin,* 103 U.S. 5, 8–9 (1880) (same); *Boyd v. Gorman,* 157 N.Y. 365, 367 (1898) (interpreting "services" to include both "[t]he services of a day laborer and those of a professional man," because "the lawyer serves his employer, the same as a hodcarrier").

42. See, e.g., 16 *Cong. Rec.* 1625 (1885) (statement of Sen. Hayard) (stating that the bill applies to aliens "brought here . . . to perform labor or service" or whose "services are contracted for in advance, no matter how favorable to him or to the people of this country whom he is to serve"); 15 *Cong. Rec.* 6059 (1884) (statement of Sen. Blair) (referring to the phrase "service or labor" as "very general"); id. at 5354 (1884) (statement of Rep. William Kelley) (describing the bill as unduly broad because it "contain[s] a provision prohibiting citizens from employing an unnaturalized resident of the country in the performance of any service").

43. *Holy Trinity Church,* 36 F. 303, 305.

44. Brief for Plaintiff, supra note 40, at 15–16.

45. See Chinese Exclusion Act of 1882, ch. 126, 22 Stat. 58 (as amended and extended in 1884, 1888, 1892, 1902, and 1904); repealed by Act of Dec. 17, 1943, Pub. L. No. 78–199, 57 Stat. 600.

46. See, e.g., *In re Tung Yeong,* 19 F. 184 (D.C.D. Cal. 1884). Later decisions slightly broadened the interpretation to make clear that manual labor included both skilled and unskilled labor and also encompassed persons dependent on their own manual labor to earn a living, whether or not they were actually employed as laborers at the time of adjudication. See, e.g., *United States v. Chung Ki Foon,* 83 F. 143 (D.C.N.D. Cal. 1897).

47. See, e.g., *In re Ho King,* 14 F. 724, 725 (D.C.D. Or. 1883) (holding that actors are not "laborers" because the statute did not "have in view the protection of what are called the professional or mercantile classes").

48. See 16 *Cong. Rec.* 1630 (1885) (statement of Sen. Blair).

49. See Laurence Tribe, "Comment," in *Interpretation,* supra note 39, at 65, 92–93.

50. Brief for Plaintiff, supra note 40, at 18–21.

51. See McNollgast, "Legislative Intent: The Use of Positive Political Theory in Statutory Interpretation," 57 *Law & Contemp. Probs.* 3 (1994).

52. Jerry L. Mashaw, *Greed, Chaos, and Governance: Using Public Choice to Improve Public Law* 99 (1997).

53. This point, although little discussed, has not gone unrecognized. In particular, Cass R. Sunstein and Frederick Schauer have each contributed important, if brief, discussions of the issue. See Frederick Schauer, "The Practice and Problems of Plain Meaning: A Response to Aleinikoff and Shaw," 45 *Vand. L. Rev.* 715, 728–733 (1992); Frederick Schauer, "Statutory Construction and the Coordinating Function of Plain Meaning," 1990 *Sup. Ct. Rev.* 231; and Cass R. Sunstein, "Justice Scalia's Democratic Formalism," 107 *Yale L.J.* 529 (1997).

54. These considerations do not necessarily speak to the use of legislative history by nonjudicial interpreters such as agencies. I touch on the relationships among judicial interpretation, agency interpretation, and legislative history in Chapter 7.

55. Richard J. Pierce, Jr., "The Role of the Judiciary in Implementing an Agency Theory of Government," 64 *N.Y.U. L. Rev.* 1239, 1258 (1989); see also E. Finley, "Crystal Gazing: The Problem of Legislative History," 45 *A.B.A. J.* 1281, 1284 (1959) ("The printed hearings of the 85th Congress alone (1957–58) occupy almost seventy feet of shelf space. If complete compiled histories of all laws were to be undertaken, there would probably have to be a whole new agency to do the job.").

56. See W. David Slawson, "Legislative History and the Need to Bring Statutory Interpretation under the Rule of Law," 44 *Stan. L. Rev.* 383, 408 (1992).

57. Note that the 10,000-plus pages of legislative history for the Clean Air Act Amendments of 1990 by themselves amount to more than a third of the total pages in the United States Code, which in 1988 consisted of 27,308 pages. See Slawson, supra note 56, at 402.

58. Patricia M. Wald, "Some Observations on the Use of Legislative History in the 1981 Supreme Court Term," 68 *Iowa L. Rev.* 195, 200 (1983).

5. Systemic Effects and Judicial Coordination

1. Einer Elhauge, "Preference-Estimating Statutory Default Rules," 102 *Colum. L. Rev.* 2027 (2002).

2. With apologies to Kenneth A. Shepsle, "Congress Is a 'They,' Not an 'It': Legislative Intent as Oxymoron," 12 *Int'l Rev. L. & Econ.* 239 (1992).

3. In the first example the division problem arises because of a semantic equivocation: "strong" has two relevant senses. In the second example the problem seemingly stems from a causal confusion—a form of magical thinking in which nation 1's disarmament will somehow cause nations 2 through *N* to reciprocate. We might or might not want to define the division and composition fallacies to cover both semantic equivocation and causal

mistakes; analytic philosophers and social theorists have debated such matters inconclusively. See, e.g., William L. Rowe, "The Fallacy of Composition," 71 *Mind* 87 (1962); Jon Elster, *Logic and Society* 97–106 (1978). For my less refined purposes, the precise source of generalization mistakes and the precise definition of the fallacy are immaterial. All I mean to do is to use division as a shorthand label for a complex of conceptual errors that arise from mistakes about generalization and show important family resemblances.

4. See Kenneth Arrow, *Social Choice and Individual Values* (1951).

5. See Frank H. Easterbrook, "Ways of Criticizing the Court," 95 *Harv. L. Rev.* 802 (1982).

6. For an impressive claim that voting cycles almost never arise in Congress, see Gerry Mackie, Democracy Defended (2003). On cycling in courts, see Maxwell Stearns, "The Misguided Renaissance of Social Choice," 103 *Yale L.J.* 1219, 1283 and n. 253 (1994).

7. See A. K. Sen, "A Possibility Theorem on Majority Decisions," 34 *Econometrica* 491–499 (1966).

8. The empirical political science literature suggests that a surprising amount of lower-court conflict goes unresolved. See S. Sidney Ulmer, "The Supreme Court's Certiorari Decisions: Conflict as a Predictive Variable," 78 *Am. Pol. Sci. Rev.* 901, 901–911 (1984) (finding that between 1947 and 1976 the Court denied certiorari in more than half the cases involving conflict with Supreme Court precedent or intercircuit conflict). The importance of the conflicts that go unresolved is, of course, a separate question.

9. See J. W. Peltason, *Fifty-eight Lonely Men: Southern Federal Judges and School Desegregation* (1971).

10. See Antonin Scalia, "Vermont Yankee: The APA, the D.C. Circuit and the Supreme Court," 1978 *Sup. Ct. Rev.* 345.

11. Cf. Jonathan R. Macey, "Transaction Costs and the Normative Elements of the Public Choice Model: An Application to Constitutional Theory," 74 *Va. L. Rev.* 471, 496–499 (1988) (judges face collective action problems because judicial salaries cannot be adjusted to penalize defectors).

12. Lawrence Gene Sager, "Fair Measure: The Legal Status of Underenforced Constitutional Norms," 91 *Harv. L. Rev.* 1212 (1978).

13. Cass R. Sunstein, "Nondelegation Canons," 67 *U. Chi. L. Rev.* 315 (2000).

14. Id. at 331.

15. Victoria F. Nourse and Jane S. Schacter, "The Politics of Legislative Drafting: A Congressional Case Study," 77 *N.Y.U. L. Rev.* 575 (2002).

16. Jane S. Schacter, "The Confounding Common Law Originalism in Recent Supreme Court Statutory Interpretation: Implications for the Legislative History Debate and Beyond," 51 *Stan. L. Rev.* 1 (1998).

17. Dan M. Kahan, "Lenity and Federal Common Law Crimes," 1994 *Sup. Ct. Rev.* 345.

18. Hans A. Linde, "Due Process of Lawmaking," 55 *Neb. L. Rev.* 197 (1976).

19. *United States v. Lopez,* 514 U.S. 549 (1995).

20. *United States v. Morrison,* 529 U.S. 598 (2000).

21. *Kimel v. Florida Board of Regents,* 528 U.S. 62 (2000).

22. *Board of Trustees v. Garrett,* 531 U.S. 356 (2001).

23. *Nev. Dep't of Human Res. v. Hibbs,* 538 U.S. 721 (2003).

24. Alan K. Chen, "Statutory Speech Bubbles, First Amendment Overbreadth, and Improper Legislative Purpose," 38 *Harv. C. R.–C. L. L. Rev.* 31 (2003); *Broadrick v. Oklahoma,* 413 U.S. 601, 611–12 (1973) (overbreadth ensures that speech restrictions "represent a considered legislative judgment that a particular mode of expression has to give way to other compelling needs of society.").

25. *Massachusetts v. Oakes,* 491 U.S. 576 (1989).

26. See *Martin v. Commonwealth,* 96 S.W.3d 38, 53 (Ky. 2003) (noting that "the five votes fragmented between concurring and dissenting opinions in *Oakes* cannot be characterized as a 'holding' for purposes of precedent") (citing *Gregg v. Georgia,* 428 U.S. 153, 169 n.15 (1976)).

27. *Osborne v. Ohio,* 495 U.S. 103 (1990).

28. I take this to be Stephen Smith's basic argument. Stephen F. Smith, "Activism as Restraint: Lessons from Criminal Procedure," 80 *Tex. L. Rev.* 1057 (2002).

29. This mixed game is usually modeled as "the Battle of the Sexes," in which Male wants to attend a quilting bee, Female wants to watch roller hockey, but each would prefer to attend the other's event rather than spend the evening alone. See, e.g., Eric Rasmussen, *Games and Information: An Introduction to Game Theory* 31 (1989). Given the distributive effects of interpretive choices, the Battle provides a better lens for understanding interpretation than do pure coordination games. See David A. Strauss, "Common Law, Common Ground, and Jefferson's Principle," 112 *Yale L.J.* 1717, 1734 (2003). Although focal points can produce stable equilibria in the Battle, as well as in pure coordination games, see id.; James D. Morrow, *Game Theory for Political Scientists* 94–97 (1994), it is also possible that no stable cooperative regime will emerge, because players "hold out for a distribution of benefits of a regime more favorable to their immediate interests." James D. Morrow, "Modeling the Forms of International Cooperation: Distribution versus Information," 48 *Int'l Org.* 387, 413 (1994).

30. William N. Eskridge, Jr., and John Ferejohn, "Politics, Interpretation, and the Rule of Law," in *Nomos XXXVI: The Rule of Law* 277 (Ian Shapiro ed., 1994).

31. With a debt to Waldron's idea of the "circumstances of politics," itself indebted to Rawls's "circumstances of justice," which in turn is adapted from Hume. See Jeremy Waldron, *Law and Disagreement* 102 (1999); John Rawls, *A Theory of Justice* 109 (rev. ed. 1999).

6. Judges, Uncertainty, and Bounded Rationality

1. See Chris Guthrie, Jeffrey J. Rachlinski, and Andrew J. Wistrich, "Inside the Judicial Mind," 86 *Cornell L. Rev.* 777 (2001).

2. See Jon Elster, "Arguments for Constitutional Choice," in *Constitutionalism and Democracy* 303, 307–316 (Jon Elster and Rune Slagstad eds., 1988).

3. Giovanni Sartori, *Comparative Constitutional Engineering: An Inquiry into Structures, Incentives, and Outcomes* 198 (2d ed. 1997).

4. See Alvin M. Weinberg, *Nuclear Reactions: Science and Trans-Science* 4 (1992) (Trans-scientific questions are those that "can be asked of science and yet *cannot be answered by science.* . . . [T]hough they are, epistemologically speaking, questions of fact and can be stated in the language of science, they are unanswerable by science.").

5. See, e.g., Edward E. Leamer, "Let's Take the Con out of Econometrics," 73 *Am. Econ. Rev.* 31, 34–40 (1983) (discussing the pervasive difficulty in controlling for hidden variables in econometrics); David Hendry, "Econometrics—Alchemy or Science?" 47 *Economica* 387 (1980).

6. See Lawrence C. Marshall, "Let Congress Do It: The Case for an Absolute Rule of Statutory Precedent," 88 *Mich. L. Rev.* 177, 183 (1989) (statutory precedent should be absolute because "it is critical to reinvolve Congress as an active participant in [the] ongoing process of statutory lawmaking. One way to do this is to let Congress know that it, and only it, is responsible for reviewing the Court's statutory decisions, and that it, and only it, has the power to overrule the Court's interpretations of federal statutes"); William N. Eskridge, Jr., "The Case of the Amorous Defendant: Criticizing Absolute Precedent for Statutory Cases," 88 *Mich. L. Rev.* 2450, 2453 (1990) [hereinafter Eskridge, "Amorous Defendant"].

7. See William N. Eskridge, Jr., "Overriding Supreme Court Statutory Interpretation Decisions," 101 *Yale L.J.* 331 (1991) [hereinafter Eskridge, "Overriding"]. Other works of similar character include James J. Brudney, "Recalibrating Federal Judicial Independence," 64 *Ohio St. L. J.* 149 (2003), and Michael E. Solimine and James L. Walker "The Next Word: Congressional Response to Supreme Court Statutory Decisions," 65 *Temple L. Rev.* 425 (1992). In political science, an important recent study is Jeb Barnes, *Overruled? Legislative Overrides, Pluralism, and Contemporary Court-Congress Relations* (2004). Barnes, however, does not focus on the question Eskridge is

interested in: the relationship between overrides and the interpretive methods used by judges.

8. Eskridge, "Overriding," supra note 7, at 347 n.38.

9. See id. at 347–351, 406 ("Congress is more likely to override Supreme Court statutory decisions following such a formalist approach.").

10. See id. at 408–409.

11. See Jon Elster, *Political Psychology* 105–106 (1993) (defining the fallacy of composition as "the belief that whatever is true at the margin will remain true when generalized to all cases").

12. Cf. Bruce Talbot Coram, "Second Best Theories and the Implications for Institutional Design," in *The Theory of Institutional Design* 90, 94 (Robert E. Goodin ed., 1996) (detailing the "fallacy of continuity" in problems of institutional design).

13. See H. Tristram Engelhardt, Jr., and Arthur L. Caplan, *Scientific Controversies: Case Studies in the Resolution and Closure of Disputes in Science and Technology* 8–16 (1987) (noting that "sound argument closure" of controversies, based on rational evaluation of experiments, is the prescriptive ideal of science, in place of closure on grounds such as force and bargaining). A different analogy would be to the economic theory of investment under uncertainty. One important account says that rational investors enjoy "option value" from the ability to delay irreversible investments until new information has come to light. See Avinash K. Dixit and Robert S. Pindyck, *Investment under Uncertainty* 6–9 (1994). In those terms, I shall proceed to suggest that the option value to judges of the ability to choose interpretive doctrines later, rather than now, is probably low because waiting is itself costly and because little information will emerge in the interim.

14. The terms "provisional interpretive choice" and "decentralization" are adapted from Michael Dorf, who uses the terms "provisional adjudication" and "decentralization." See Michael Dorf, "Legal Indeterminacy and Institutional Design," 78 *N.Y.U. L. Rev.* 875 (2003).

15. I shall use the phrase "burden of proof" as shorthand that elides technical distinctions among burdens of proof, burdens of production, and burdens of persuasion.

16. Cass R. Sunstein, "Justice Scalia's Democratic Formalism," 107 *Yale L. J.* 529, 548 (1997).

17. Eskridge, "Amorous Defendant," supra note 6, at 2453 (1990).

18. Id.

19. See Michael P. Van Alstine, "Dynamic Treaty Interpretation," 146 *U. Pa. L. Rev.* 687, 707 (1998).

20. See Bruce L. Hay and Kathryn E. Spier, "Burdens of Proof in Civil Litigation: An Economic Perspective," 26 *J. Leg. Stud.* 413, 413 (1997) (arguing

that "[o]ptimally used, the burden of proof may minimize the expenditures devoted to gathering, presenting and processing information in litigation").

21. See Daniel M. Hausman and Michael S. McPherson, *Economic Analysis and Moral Philosophy* 30–31 (1996); see also R. Duncan Luce and Howard Raiffa, *Games and Decisions* 277–278 (1957).

22. See Frank Knight, Risk, *Uncertainty and Profit* (1921); Stephen LeRoy and Larry Singell, "Knight on Risk and Uncertainty," 95 *J. Pol. Econ.* 394 (1987).

23. For explanation of the frequentist and subjectivist (or Bayesian) approaches to probability, see Hausman and McPherson, supra note 21, at 31; see also David M. Kreps, *Notes on the Theory of Choice* 145–57 (1988); D. S. Clarke, Jr., *Practical Inferences* 125–26 (1985). What I am calling the "Bayesian" approach is most famously formulated in L. J. Savage, *The Foundations of Statistics* (1954).

24. See Milton Friedman, *Price Theory: A Provisional Text* 282 (1976).

25. For nontechnical overviews of objections to Bayesianism, see Jon Elster, *Explaining Technical Change* 185–207 (1983); David Kelsey and John Quiggin, "Theories of Choice under Ignorance and Uncertainty," 6 *J. Econ. Surveys* 133 (1992).

26. See Jon Elster, *Nuts and Bolts for the Social Sciences* 34–35 (1989).

27. See Cass R. Sunstein, "Irreversible and Catastrophic," University of Chicago Law School, Public Law and Legal Theory Working Paper No. 88 (April 2005).

28. Elster, supra note 25, at 199 (emphasis in original).

29. See Luce and Raiffa, supra note 21, at 284–285; Kreps, supra note 23, at 146 ("the principle of insufficient reason . . . says that if I have no reason to suspect that one outcome is more likely than another, then by reason of symmetry the outcomes are equally likely, and equally likely probabilities may be ascribed to them").

30. See Luce and Raiffa, supra note 21, at 284–285; Shawn Hargraves-Heap et al., *The Theory of Choice: A Critical Guide* 349 (1997). Maximin, by contrast, is not sensitive to alternative partitionings, because of the principle that identical outcome-states are simply "merged" and treated as one. See Kelsey and Quiggin, supra note 25, at 139.

31. See Elinor Mason, "Consequentialism and the Principle of Indifference," 6 *Utilitas* 316, 318–319 (2004).

32. See Elster, supra note 26, at 32–36.

33. Jon Elster, *Solomonic Judgments* 135 (1989).

34. See Luce and Raiffa, supra note 21, at 278. Two useful Some important recent expositions of maximin and related decision rules are David Kelsey, "Choice under Partial Uncertainty," 34 *Int'l Econ. Rev.* 297–308 (1993); I.

Gilboa and D. Schmeidler, "Maximin Expected Utility with a Non-unique Prior," 18 *J. Mathematical Econ.* 141–153 (1989).

35. Another possible approach, albeit one that has few supporters, is maximax: making the choice whose best possible outcome is better than the best possible outcome of any competing option. For a proof that both maximin and maximax are rational choice criteria under uncertainty, see Kenneth J. Arrow and Leonid Hurwicz, "An Optimality Criterion for Decision-Making under Ignorance," in *Uncertainty and Expectation in Economics: Essays in Honour of G. L. S. Shackle* 1 (C. F. Carter and J. L. Ford eds., 1972).

36. This is not to endorse the so-called precautionary principle, under which (in the most common version) decisionmakers should block changes from the status quo unless those changes are clearly risk-free. The conceptual error here is the unfounded assumption that the status quo is safe, while change is unsafe. See Cass R. Sunstein, *Laws of Fear: Beyond the Precautionary Principle* (2005).

37. Michael Slote, *Beyond Optimizing: A Study of Rational Choice* (1989).

38. See David Schmidtz, "Satisficing as a Humanly Rational Strategy," in *Satisficing and Maximizing: Moral Theorists and Practical Reason* 30, 39 (Michael Byron ed., 2004) [hereinafter Schmidtz, "Satisficing"].

39. See Michael Byron, "Satisficing and Optimality," 109 *Ethics* 67 (1998). On the massive computational demands imposed by standard optimal search models, see John D. Hey, "Are Optimal Search Rules Reasonable?" 2 *J. Econ. Beh. & Org.* 47–70 (1981).

40. See Herbert A. Simon, "A Behavioral Model of Rational Choice," 69 *Q. J. Econ.* 99 (1955); Herbert A. Simon, *Reason in Human Affairs* 85 (1983).

41. David A. Strauss, "Common Law Constitutional Interpretation," 63 *U. Chi. L. Rev.* 877, 913–914 (1996).

42. For the distinction between relative and absolute satisficing, see Thomas Hurka, "Two Kinds of Satisficing," 59 *Philosophical Studies* 107–111 (1990).

43. For philosophical controversy on this point, compare Slote, supra note 37, with Campbell Brown, "Consequentialise This," available at socpol.anu.edu.au/~cbrown/papers/ConsThis.pdf (June 1, 2004).

44. There are conceptual pitfalls here. As Hey puts it, once the cost of computing the optimal search strategy is taken into account, the strategy is no longer optimal; but if the optimal strategy is calculated anew, further computation costs will be incurred, and that new strategy will no longer be optimal either. See Hey, supra note 39, at 55. How can this process of recalculation ever terminate? The same problem arises in the search for new information. In what sense can one know that one has gathered a cost-justified amount of information? To know that, one must already have the information one is trying to decide whether to gather; an infinite-regress problem arises. See Matthew D. Adler, "Rational Choice, Rational Agenda-

Setting, and Constitutional Law: Does the Constitution Require (Basic or Strengthened) Public Rationality?" in *Linking Politics and Law* 109 (Christoph Engel and Adrienne Heritier eds. 2003). I argue elsewhere, however, that the infinite-regress problem is a contextual caution rather than a foundational difficulty. See Adrian Vermeule, "Three Strategies of Interpretation," 42 *San Diego L. Rev.* 607, 623 (2005).

45. See Jonathan Bendor and Sunil Kumar, "Satisficing and Optimality" (Working Paper, Graduate School of Business, Stanford University, October 4, 2003).

46. This paragraph follows the clearminded analysis in David Schmidtz, "Satisficing," supra note 38.

47. See Cass R. Sunstein and Edna Ullmann-Margalit, "Second-Order Decisions," 110 *Ethics* 46 (1999).

48. *Finley v. United States,* 490 U.S. 545, 556 (1989).

49. Letter from Oliver Wendell Holmes, Jr., to Franklin Ford (Feb. 8, 1908), in *The Essential Holmes* 201 (Richard A. Posner ed., 1992). See also *Burnet v. Coronado Oil & Gas Co.,* 285 U.S. 393, 406 (1932) (Brandeis, J., dissenting) ("in most matters it is more important that the applicable rule of law be settled than that it be settled right").

50. See Gerd Gigerenzer et al., *Simple Heuristics That Make Us Smart* (1999).

51. Id. at 81–82.

52. See id. at 119–167.

53. Sunstein and Ullmann-Margalit, supra note 47.

7. Statutory Interpretation

1. See Nicholas Quinn Rosenkranz, "Federal Rules of Statutory Interpretation," 115 *Harv. L. Rev.* 2085 (2002).

2. Compare the short list of interpretive principles, mostly banal, codified at 1 U.S.C. § 1.

3. *INS v. Cardoza-Fonseca,* 480 U.S. 421 (1987).

4. See, e.g., *Griffin v. Oceanic Contractors,* 458 U.S. 564, 571 (1982) ("There is, of course, no more persuasive evidence of the purpose of a statute than the words by which the legislature undertook to give expression to its wishes") (quoting *United States v. Am. Trucking Ass'n.,* 310 U.S. 534, 543 (1940)); Martin H. Redish and Theodore T. Chung, "Democratic Theory and the Legislative Process: Mourning the Death of Originalism in Statutory Interpretation," 68 *Tul. L. Rev.* 803, 864 (1994) ("Text is, after all, the best evidence of congressional intent").

5. *Caminetti v. United States,* 242 U.S. 470 (1917).

6. See Gerd Gigerenzer et al., *Simple Heuristics That Make Us Smart* 81–82 (1999).

7. Cf. the general finding that for a broad range of environments, "most of the potential gains from search are obtained in the first few searches . . . the marginal gains from search thereafter are relatively small." John D. Hey, "Are Optimal Search Rules Reasonable?" 2 *J. Econ. Beh. & Org.* 97, 65 (1981).

8. Richard A. Posner, "Pragmatic Adjudication," in *The Revival of Pragmatism: New Essays on Social Thought, Law, and Culture* 235, 241 (Morris Dickstein ed., 1998).

9. See Stephen Breyer, "On the Uses of Legislative History in Interpreting Statutes," 65 *S. Cal. L. Rev.* 845, 869 (1992) (referring to a "legislative history status quo" and describing critiques of legislative history as proposals for "radical change"); Cass R. Sunstein, "Justice Scalia's Democratic Formalism," 107 *Yale L.J.* 529, 540–541 (1997).

10. See Patricia M. Wald, "Some Observations on the Use of Legislative History in the 1981 Supreme Court Term," 68 *Iowa L. Rev.* 195 (1983)(finding that the Court used legislative history in almost 100 percent of its cases in the 1981 term).

11. See Thomas Merrill, "Textualism and the Future of the *Chevron* Doctrine," 72 *Wash. U. L.Q.* 351, 355 (1994).

12. See Jane S. Schacter, "The Confounding Common Law Originalism in Recent Supreme Court Statutory Interpretation: Implications for the Legislative History Debate and Beyond," 51 *Stan. L. Rev.* 1, 18 (1998).

13. William N. Eskridge, Jr., "The Dynamic Theorization of Statutory Interpretation," in *Issues in Legal Scholarship: Dynamic Statutory Interpretation* (2002): Article 16, available at www.bepress.com/ils/iss3/art16 at 24.

14. See William N. Eskridge, Jr., "Textualism, The Unknown Ideal?" 96 *Mich. L. Rev.* 1509, 1541 (1998) (noting that the "net savings in research costs" of excluding legislative history from statutory interpretation would "involve [ ] a very large number of dollars"); William N. Eskridge, Jr., "Should the Supreme Court Read The Federalist but not Statutory Legislative History?" 66 *Geo. Wash. L. Rev.* 1301, 1322 (1998) (noting, with some dubiety, that "the modern game of tracking down smoking guns in the legislative history is both widespread and expensive").

15. See William N. Eskridge, Jr., "The New Textualism," 37 *UCLA L. Rev.* 621, 685 (1990).

16. See, e.g., *Chicago, Milwaukee, St. Paul & Pac. R.R. Co. v. Acme Fast Freight,* 336 U.S. 465, 472–475 (1949) (statement of ranking minority member held to trump committee reports); *Fed. Election Comm'n v. Rose,* 806 F.2d 1081, 1089–90 (D.C. Cir. 1986) (sponsors' statements in floor debate held to trump committee report).

17. See, e.g., *United States v. Hudspeth,* 42 F.3d 1015, 1022–23 (7th Cir. 1994) (en banc) (finding statutory phrase unambiguous, but reviewing legislative history to rebut dissenting opinion).

18. Karl N. Llewellyn, "Remarks on the Theory of Appellate Decision and the Rules or Canons about How Statutes Are to Be Construed," 3 *Vand. L. Rev.* 395 (1950).

19. See Einer Elhauge, "Preference-Estimating Statutory Default Rules," 102 *Colum. L. Rev.* 2027 (2002).

20. Cass R. Sunstein, "Nondelegation Canons," 67 *U. Chi. L. Rev.* 315, 316, 333 and n.88 (2000).

21. 1 U.S.C. § 1.

22. See Richard A. Posner, *The Federal Courts: Crisis and Reform* 277 (1985).

23. See Cass R. Sunstein, *After the Rights Revolution* (1990).

24. *EEOC v. Aramco*, 499 U.S. 244 (1991).

25. *King v. St. Vincent's Hosp.*, 502 U.S. 215, 221 n.9 (1991).

26. Antonin Scalia, "Common-Law Courts in a Civil-Law System: The Role of United States Federal Courts in Interpreting the Constitution and Laws," in *A Matter of Interpretation: Federal Courts and the Law* 3, 29 (Amy Gutman ed., 1997).

27. *W. Va. Univ. Hospitals v. Casey*, 499 U.S. 83 (1991).

28. See Akhil Reed Amar, "Intratextualism," 112 *Harv. L. Rev.* 747 (1999).

29. For some mundane examples, see *McConnell v. Fed. Election Comm'n*, 124 S. Ct. 619, 724 (2003) (Scalia, J., concurring and dissenting)(saying that the Declaration of Independence's statement pledging support for the Declaration through the signers' "fortune" is proof that pooling money for expressive purposes is a form of free speech); *City of Boerne v. Flores*, 521 U.S. 507, 554 (1997)(O'Connor, J. dissenting) (saying that the language of the Northwest Ordinance supports a reading of the "free exercise" right that includes the "accommodation of religious practice").

30. The most ambitious version of holism or coherentism is Ronald Dworkin's idea of law as "integrity," on which the whole corpus of law is to be read in a coherent fashion. See Ronald Dworkin, *Law's Empire* (1986). I have confined the discussion here to holistic textualism, and Dworkin is not a textualist (at least in any ordinary sense of that term). The critique of holistic maximizing, however, could also be applied to Dworkin, with suitable modifications.

31. *Brown & Williamson v. FCC*, 533 U.S. 950 (2001); *MCI v. AT&T*, 510 U.S. 989 (1993); *Sweet Home v. Babbitt*, 515 U.S. 687 (1995).

32. Thomas Merrill, "*Chevron's* Domain," 89 *Geo. L.J.* 833 (2001).

33. *Chevron v. NRDC*, 467 U.S. 837 (1984).

34. Peter Strauss, "One Hundred Fifty Cases per Year," 87 *Colum. L. Rev.* 1093 (1987).

35. Jerry L. Mashaw, "Agency Statutory Interpretation," in *Issues in Legal Scholarship: Dynamic Statutory Interpretation* (2002), available at www.bepress.com/ils/iss3/art9.

36. See Peter L. Strauss, "When the Judge Is Not the Primary Official with Responsibility to Read: Agency Interpretation and the Problem of Legislative History," 66 *Chi.-Kent L. Rev.* 321, 332 (1990).

37. Id. at 327.

38. Dan M. Kahan, "Rethinking Federal Criminal Law: Three Conceptions of Federal Criminal-Lawmaking," 1 *Buff. Crim. L. Rev.* 5, 16 (1997).

39. *United States v. Mead,* 533 U.S. 218 (2001).

40. Id. at 236.

41. *Skidmore v. Swift & Co.,* 323 U.S. 134 (1944).

42. See *Mead,* 533 U.S. at 230–233. For later reaffirmations of this point, see *Barnhart v. Walton,* 535 U.S. 212, 222 (2002) ("the fact that the Agency previously reached its interpretation through means less formal than 'notice and comment' rulemaking . . . does not automatically deprive that interpretation of the judicial deference otherwise its due"); *Edelman v. Lynchburg Coll.,* 535 U.S. 106, 114 (2002) ("deference under *Chevron* . . . does not necessarily require an agency's exercise of express notice-and-comment rulemaking power").

43. See, e.g., *Pfau v. Trent Aluminum Co.,* 263 A.2d 129 (1970); *Phillips v. General Motors Corp.,* 995 P.2d 1002 (Mont. 2000).

44. *Fed. Election Comm'n v. Nat'l Rifle Ass'n,* 349 U.S. App. D.C. 96 (2001).

45. *United States v. McKinney,* 919 F.2d 405, 423 (7th Cir. 1990) (Posner, J., concurring).

46. *Motion Picture Ass'n of Am. v. FCC,* 353 U.S. App. D.C. 405 (2002).

47. See Lawrence C. Marshall, "Let Congress Do It: The Case for an Absolute Rule of Statutory Precedent," 88 *Mich. L. Rev.* 177, 183 (1989).

48. Oliver Wendell Homes, Jr., "Twenty Years in Retrospect," in *The Essential Holmes* 151 (Richard A. Posner ed., 1992).

49. *Neal v. United States,* 516 U.S. 284 (1996); but see *Nat'l Cable & Telecommunications Ass'n et al. v. Brand X Internet Services et al.,* U.S. Supreme Court (No. 09-277, June 27, 2005).

50. Strauss, supra note 34.

51. *K Mart Corp. v. Cartier, Inc.,* 486 U.S. 281 (1988).

52. Id. at 293.

53. Antonin Scalia, "Judicial Deference to Administrative Interpretations of Law," 1989 *Duke L.J.* 511, 521 (1989).

8. Judicial Review and Constitutional Interpretation

1. *Marbury v. Madison,* 5 U.S. (1 Cranch) 137 (1803).

2. See U.S. Const. art. VI, cl. 2 ("Laws of the United States" made "in pursuance of [the Constitution] . . . shall be the Supreme Law of the Land").

3. See Larry D. Kramer, *The People Themselves: Popular Constitutionalism and Judicial Review* (2004) [hereinafter Kramer, *The People Themselves*].

4. Larry D. Kramer, "The Supreme Court 2000 Term—Foreword: We the Court," 115 *Harv. L. Rev.* 4, 9 (2001).

5. Id.

6. See Kramer, *The People Themselves*, supra note 3, at 44.

7. Id. at 59.

8. Id. at 78.

9. Id. at 92.

10. This statement holds, at least as to national-level legislation and with various other nuances, for the United Kingdom, the Netherlands, and Switzerland. See www.concourts.net (compiled by Dr. Arne Mavcic) (discussing different types of judicial review and the countries that apply each type).

11. Matthew Adler and Michael Dorf, "Constitutional Existence Conditions and Judicial Review," 89 *Va. L. Rev.* 1105 (2003).

12. *Field v. Clark*, 143 U.S. 649 (1892).

13. *United States v. Munoz-Flores*, 495 U.S. 385 (1990).

14. See *The Federalist No. 78* (Alexander Hamilton) (Clinton Rossiter ed., 1961). Some of the discussion of Hamilton also applies to the current theorist Bruce Ackerman, whose conception of American constitutional history owes Hamilton an intellectual debt. See Bruce Ackerman, *We the People* (Vols. 1–2) (1991, 1998).

15. On the question whether elected or unelected constitutional agents will attempt to expand their power, see Daryl J. Levinson, "Empire-Building Government in Constitutional Law," 118 *Harv. L. Rev.* 915 (2005).

16. James Bradley Thayer, "American Doctrine of Constitutional Law," 7 *Harv. L. Rev.* 129 (1893) [hereinafter Thayer, "Constitutional Law"].

17. John Hart Ely, *Democracy and Distrust* Ch. 4 (1980).

18. *United States v. Carolene Products Co.*, 304 U.S. 144, 153 n.4 (1938).

19. Robert Dahl, *A Preface to Democratic Theory* (1957); Michael Klarman, "What's So Great about Constitutionalism?" 93 *Nw. U. L. Rev.* 145 (1998).

20. Stephen Holmes and Cass Sunstein, *The Cost of Rights: Why Liberty Depends on Taxes* (1999).

21. See William J. Stuntz, "The Uneasy Relationship between Criminal Procedure and Criminal Justice," 107 *Yale L.J.* 1 (1997).

22. *Dred Scott v. Sandford*, 60 U.S. 393, 19 How. 393 (1856).

23. Brief for Ronald Dworkin, Thomas Nagel, Robert Nozick, John Rawls, Thomas Scanlon, and Judith Jarvis Thompson as Amici Curiae in Support of Respondents, *Washington v. Glucksberg*, 521 U.S. 702 (1997) (No. 96–110), and *Vacco v. Quill*, 521 U.S. 793 (1997) (No. 95–1858).

24. See Cass R. Sunstein, "The Right to Die," 106 *Yale L.J.* 1123 (1997).

25. See Akhil Reed Amar, "Intratextualism," 112 *Harv. L. Rev.* 747 (1999).

26. *Griswold v. Connecticut,* 381 U.S. 479 (1965).

27. Amar, "Intratextualism," supra note 25, at 797 and n.196. In Amar's view, the key to a coherent reading of the Bill of Rights is constitutional populism, not libertarian privacy. See Akhil Reed Amar, *The Bill of Rights: Creation and Reconstruction* (1998).

28. Antonin Scalia, "Originalism: The Lesser Evil," 57 *U. Cin. L. Rev.* 849, 863 (1989).

29. Id. at 864.

30. 1 William Blackstone, *Commentaries on the Laws of England* *62.

31. Scalia, supra note 28, at 862.

32. Lawrence Lessig, "Fidelity in Translation," 71 *Tex. L. Rev.* 1165 (1993).

33. Lawrence Lessig, "Translating Federalism: *United States* v. *Lopez,*" 1995 *Sup. Ct. Rev.* 125, 192–193.

34. Daryl Levinson, "Framing Transactions in Constitutional Law," 111 *Yale L.J.* 547 (2001).

35. See *INS v. Chadha,* 462 U.S. 919, 994–995 (1983) (White, J., dissenting).

36. See Jessica Korn, *The Power of Separation: American Constitutionalism and the Myth of the Legislative Veto* 4–5 (1996).

37. See generally Stephen Breyer, *Active Liberty: Interpreting Our Democratic Constitution* (2005).

38. As Alexander and Schauer acknowledge. See Larry Alexander and Frederick Schauer, "Defending Judicial Supremacy: A Reply," 17 *Const. Comment.* 455, 477 (2000).

39. David A. Strauss, "Common Law Constitutional Interpretation," 63 *U. Chi. L. Rev.* 877 (1996).

40. Donald Horowitz, *The Courts and Social Policy* (1977).

41. Lawrence Gene Sager, "Fair Measure: The Legal Status of Underenforced Constitutional Norms," 91 *Harv. L. Rev.* 1212 (1978).

42. See Jeremy Waldron, *Law and Disagreement* (1999).

43. See Mark Tushnet, *Taking the Constitution Away from the Courts* (1999).

44. See Kramer, *The People Themselves,* supra note 3.

45. See Robert Bork, *Slouching towards Gomorrah: Modern Liberalism and American Decline* 117–18 (1996).

46. *The Federalist No. 78,* supra note 14, at 494.

47. As emphasized in Frederick Schauer, "Legislators as Law Followers and Rule-Followers," in *Legislatures and Constitutionalism: The Role of Legislatures in the Constitutional State* (forthcoming 2006), see www.law.ualberta.ca/centres/ccs (2004).

48. *United States v. Will,* 449 U.S. 200 (1980).

49. *United States v. Morrison,* 529 U.S. 598 (2000). See Judith Resnik, "Trial as

Error, Jurisdiction as Injury: Transforming the Meaning of Article III," 113 *Harv. L. Rev.* 924, 1005 n.322 (2000) (discussing judicial expression of concerns about federal civil rights legislation).

50. *Bush v. Gore,* 531 U.S. 98 (2000).

51. Klarman, supra note 19.

52. Elizabeth Garrett and Adrian Vermeule, "Institutional Design of a Thayerian Congress," 50 *Duke L.J.* 1277 (2001). See also Mark Tushnet, "Interpretation in Legislatures and Courts: Incentives and Institutional Design," in *Legislatures and Constitutionalism: The Role of Legislatures in the Constitutional State* (forthcoming 2006).

53. Garrett and Vermeule, supra note 52; Richard Fenno, *Home Style: House Members in Their Districts* (1978).

54. Scalia, supra note 28, 856–857.

55. James Thayer, *John Marshall* 107 (1901).

56. "Mere position-taking [i.e., legislative enactment of statutes that legislators anticipate will be invalidated by courts] can be particularly troublesome when the final mover takes the position that its decision should incorporate some degree of deference to prior actors, because, in circumstances of mere position-taking the final mover may be deferring to a judgment that no one ever made." Tushnet, "Institutional Design," supra note 52.

57. See Dahl, supra note 19.

58. See *Hammer v. Dagenhart,* 247 U.S. 251 (1918) (holding that Congress cannot regulate child labor under the Commerce Clause); *Baley v. Drexel Furniture Co.,* 259 U.S. 20 (1922) (striking down the Child Labor Tax Act); see also *United States v. Darby,* 312 U.S. 100 (1941) (reversing course and upholding federal statutes against child labor).

59. *Roe v. Wade,* 410 U.S. 113 (1973).

60. William Eskridge and John Ferejohn, "The Article I, Section 7 Game," 80 *Geo. L.J.* 523 (1992).

61. *The Federalist No. 62,* at 410–412 (James Madison) (Benjamin Fletcher Wright ed., 1961).

62. See Waldron, supra note 42, at 211–214.

63. See, e.g., Ran Hirschl, *Towards Juristocracy: The Origins and Consequences of the New Constitutionalism* (2004) (suggesting, on the basic of selected case studies, that judicial review promotes economic liberties but does little to better the status of disadvantaged groups); *Judicial Independence in the Age of Democracy: Critical Perspectives from around the World* (Peter H. Russell and David M. O'Brien eds., 2001).

64. See Rafael La Porta et al., "Judicial Checks and Balances," 112 *J. Pol. Econ.* 445–470 (2004).

65. Id. at 968.

66. One factor may be whether the polity's legal rules were imposed from without or developed from within. See Daniel Berkowitz, Katharina Pistor, and Jean-Francois Richard, "The Transplant Effect," 51 *Am. J. Comp. L.* 163 (2003).

67. See Jon Elster, "Arguments for Constitutional Choice," in *Constitutionalism and Democracy* 303, 307–316 (Jon Elster and Rune Slagstad eds., 1988).

68. See Richard Posner, *Frontiers of Legal Theory* 19–24 (2001).

69. Strauss, supra note 39, at 913–914.

70. *City of Boerne v. Flores*, 521 U.S. 507 (1997) (striking down the Religious Freedom Restoration Act because it extended the free exercise of religion beyond its original meaning under the First Amendment); *United States v. Lopez*, 514 U.S. 549 (1995) (striking down the Gun Free School Zone Act because it exceeded congressional commerce power); *Printz v. United States*, 521 U.S. 898 (1997) (holding that federal legislation may not constitutionally commandeer states to administer a federal regulatory program).

71. *McConnell v. Fed. Election Comm'n*, 540 U.S. 93 (2003); *Nev. Dep't of Human Res. v. Hibbs*, 538 U.S. 721 (2003).

72. Neil K. Komesar, *Imperfect Alternatives: Choosing Institutions in Law, Economics, and Public Policy* (1994).

73. See Executive Office of the President, *Budget of the United States Government: Historical Tables* (2001) and *Budget of the United States Government: Budget* (2001).

74. Congressional Research Service, *Congressional Statistics: Bills Introduced and Laws Enacted, 1947–2003* (2004) (available at www.llsdc.org/sourcebook/docs/CRS-%-727).

75. Richard A. Posner, *The Federal Courts: Challenge and Reform* 369 (1996) (urging this approach with regard to constitutional cases).

76. *Coleman v. Miller*, 307 U.S. 433 (1939) (holding that the question of ratification by state legislatures should be regarded as a political question).

77. *Field v. Clark*, 143 U.S. 649 (1892) (refusing to consider extrinsic evidence to question the enrollment of a bill). But cf. *United States v. Munoz-Flores*, 495 U.S. 385 (1990) (holding that Origination Clause issues are justiciable).

78. U.S. Const. art. I, § 5, cl. 2.

79. *Williamson v. Lee Optical*, 348 U.S. 483 (1955) (holding that economic and social regulation receives only rational basis review).

80. *United States v. Lopez*, 514 U.S. 549 (1995) (federal commerce power extends to the categories in text); *United States v. Morrison*, 529 U.S. 598 (2000) (same).

81. *Lucas v. S.C. Coastal Council*, 505 U.S. 1003 (1992) (per se taking exists only where there is a physical appropriation or a total deprivation of economic value).

82. *Home Bldg. & Loan Ass'n v. Blaisdell*, 290 U.S. 398 (1934) (allowing states to abrogate preexisting contracts).

83. *South Dakota v. Dole*, 483 U.S. 203 (1987) (applying deferential standard of review to conditions accompanying federal grants of money to subnational governments); *Frothingham v. Mellon*, 262 U.S. 447 (1923) (denying standing to citizen seeking to enjoin Secretary of the Treasury from distributing funds pursuant to the Maternity Act of 1923).

84. *Valley Forge Christian Coll. v. Americans United for Separation of Church and State, Inc.*, 454 U.S. 464 (1982) (taxpayers lack standing to challenge government's ability to give real property to religious groups).

85. *Loving v. United States*, 517 U.S. 748 (1996) (upholding delegation to the President of the power to define aggravating factors that permit imposition of statutory death penalty in military capital cases); *Am. Power & Light Co. v. SEC*, 329 U.S. 90 (1946) (upholding very broad delegation to an independent agency of authority to regulate holding companies). Some of the functions of the constitutional nondelegation doctrine have been assumed by canons of statutory construction. See Cass R. Sunstein, "Nondelegation Canons," 67 *U. Chi. L. Rev.* 315 (2000).

86. See *Lowry v. Reagan*, 676 F. Supp. 333, 340 (D.D.C. 1987) (declining to adjudicate, on political-question grounds, a claim for declaratory and injunctive relief under the War Powers Act). For an analysis of the political-question doctrine's application to foreign affairs and international relations, see Jack L. Goldsmith, "The New Formalism in Foreign Relations Law," 70 *U. Colo. L. Rev.* 1395, 1402 (1999).

87. *Gilligan v. Morgan*, 413 U.S. 1 (1973) (supervision, composition, and training of military forces are committed to the discretion of the political branches).

88. *Schlesinger v. Reservists Comm. to Stop the War*, 418 U.S. 208 (1974) (plaintiffs denied standing to claim that armed forces reserve membership of members of Congress violated the Constitution).

89. *Fiallo v. Bell*, 430 U.S. 787 (1977) (courts should not probe the justifications for legislative decision that preferential status is not warranted for illegitimate children and their natural fathers).

90. *Nixon v. United States*, 506 U.S. 224 (1993) (holding that the Senate had sole discretion to choose impeachment procedures).

91. *Luther v. Borden*, 48 U.S. 1 (1849) (Congress rather than the federal courts, is charged with enforcing the clause); *Pacific States Telephone & Telegraph Co. v. Oregon*, 223 U.S. 118 (1912) (refusing to consider republican-form-of-government challenge to the state referendum and initiative process).

92. *Nat'l Mut. Ins. Co. of D.C. v. Tidewater Transfer Co. Inc.*, 337 U.S. 582, 646–647 (1949) (Frankfurter, J., dissenting).

93. *Bush v. Gore*, 531 U.S. 98, 104 (2000).

94. Frederick Schauer, "Easy Cases," 58 *S. Cal. L. Rev.* 399 (1985).

95. *INS v. Chadha*, 462 U.S. 919 (1983).

96. *Buckley v. Vale.*, 424 U.S. 1 (1976).

97. See Strauss, supra note 39, at 906–908.

98. Larry Alexander and Frederick Schauer, "On Extrajudicial Constitutional Interpretation," 110 *Harv. L. Rev.* 1359 (1997).

99. *Abrams v. United States*, 250 U.S. 616, 629 (1919)(Holmes, J., dissenting).

100. Morton Horwitz on Frankfurter and Hand, in Morton J. Horwitz, *Transformation of American Law: The Transformation of American Law, 1870–1960: The Crisis of Legal Orthodoxy* 259–260 (1992).

101. Michael W. McConnell, "The Importance of Humility in Judicial Review: A Comment on Ronald Dworkin's 'Moral Reading' of the Constitution," 65 *Fordham L. Rev.* 1269, 1283 (1997).

102. Robert H. Bork, *The Tempting of America: The Political Seduction of the Law* 82–83 (1990).

103. *Rutan v. Republican Party of Ill.*, 497 U.S. 62, 96 (1990).

104. *Hammer v. Dagenhart*, 247 U.S. 251 (1918).

105. *Bailey v. Drexel Furniture Co.*, 259 U.S. 20 (1922).

106. *United States v. Morrison*, 529 U.S. 598 (2000).

107. Gerald N. Rosenberg, *The Hollow Hope: Can Courts Bring About Social Change?* (1991).

108. Michael Klarman, *From Jim Crow to Civil Rights: The Supreme Court and the Struggle for Racial Equality* (2004).

109. Eugene Volokh, "The Mechanisms of the Slippery Slope," 116 *Harv. L. Rev.* 1026 (2003).

110. Thayer, "Constitutional Law," supra note 16.

111. Oliver Wendell Holmes, "Law and the Court," in *Collected Legal Papers* 291, 295–296 (1920). "I do not think the United States would come to an end if we lost our power to declare an Act of Congress void. I do think the Union would be imperiled if we could not make that declaration as to the laws of the several States."

112. Evan H. Caminker, "Thayerian Deference to Congress and Supreme Court Supermajority Rule: Lessons from the Past," 78 *Ind. L.J.* 73 (2003).

113. See generally Ronald A. Heiner, "The Origin of Predictable Behavior," 73. *Am. Econ. Rev.* 560 (1983).

114. John Dinwiddy, *Bentham* 66 (1989); H. L. A. Hart, "The Demystification of the Law," in *Essays on Bentham* 2'1 (1982).

115. Peter H. Schuck, *The Limits of Law: Essays on Democratic Governance* ch. 1 (2000).

116. Jon Elster, *Alchemies of the Mind: Rationality and the Emotions* 291 n.149

(1999). For connections between the neglect of opportunity costs and status quo bias, loss aversion, and the "endowment effect," see Richard H. Thaler, *The Winner's Curse: Paradoxes and Anomalies of Economic Life* 74–77 (1992).

117. Avishai Margalit, "Ideals and Second Bests," in *Philosophy for Education* 77 (Seymour Fox ed., 1983).

Index

Abstract institutionalism, of Hart and Sacks, 64

Absurdity doctrine, Posner's defense of, 58

Active liberty, in constitutional interpretation, 248–249

ADA (Americans with Disabilities Act), 138

Adams, John, 95

ADEA (Age Discrimination in Employment Act), 138

Adjudication: Posner on, 53; with formalism, 71; legislative history and, 102–107; in *Holy Trinity*, 103–105; adjudicative error, risks of, 109; limitations of, 116

Administrative Procedure Act, 78, 207; Supreme Court instructions concerning, 120

Adversary system, learning effects and, 114

Age Discrimination in Employment Act. *See* ADEA

Agencies, 214–215; as statutory interpreters, 8, 226; costs in, 77, 214, 256–259; interpretive role of, 78, 203, 206, 213; specialized, 115; courts and, 128–129, 208–210; judicial deference to, 206, 214–215; institutional deference to, 207; law-making authority of, 216, 225–226; *Chevron* deference and, 225; common-law interpretation and, 225–226

Alder, Matthew, 236–237

Alexander, Larry, 249, 263; judicial supremacy for, 232, 252–253; on judicial review, 276–277

Alien Contract Labor Act of 1885: application of, 93; Senate debate over, 93; House proceedings of, 94; prohibitions of, 94; Supreme Court's misunderstanding of, 96; amendments to, 97; legislative history of, 98, 105, 110; structural inferences of, 100–101; statutory landscape of, 101; Chinese Exclusion Act of 1882 versus, 102

Amar, Akhil, 203; intratextualism of, 232, 252–253

American Bar Association, 48–49

American interpretive theory, after World War II, 18

American legislature, 54–55

Americans with Disabilities Act. *See* ADA

Anglo-American interpretive theory, before World War II, 15

Approximation assumption, in decisionmaking complexity, 287

Asymmetrical institutionalism, by interpretive theorists, 17. *See also* Nirvana fallacy

Authorial intentions, textual evidence of, 35–36

Authority allocation, across institutions, 253

Bailey v. Drexel Furniture Co., 281

Bayesian decision theory: use of, 51; probability assignment with, 171–172

323

Bentham, Jeremy, 21–24; legal complexity for, 286

Bias, 43

Bickel, Alexander, 254

Bill of Rights, 230–231; legislative enforcement of, 12

Blackstone and Bentham, common-law interpretation of, 18–24

Blair, Henry William, 96–98, 100

Board of Trustees v. Garrett, 138

Bolognian law, 19

Bork, Robert, 256

Bounded rationality: in interpretive choice, 157–162; satisficing in, 176–179

Brewer, David, 90, 100, 105

Breyer, Stephen: interpretive theory of, 34; purposivist judicial review and, 248

Brown v. Board of Education, 130, 231, 280–282

Buckley v. Valeo, 272–273

"Burden of proof," 226

Burger, Warren E., 88

Burger Court, 142; rule of lenity and, 135

Bush v. Gore, 258, 271

Caminetti principle, 186

Caminetti v. United States, 185–186

Caminker, Evan, 283

Canon of avoidance, 133

Canons of construction: legislative history use versus, 198; interpretation with, 198–202; usefulness of, 199; agency interpretations versus, 200

Carleone Products, 240

Case-specific consequences, systematic consequences versus, 54

Certiorari policy, 165

Chevron rule, 188; in interpretive choice, 184; as second-order default rule, 201; institutional premises of, 205–215

Chevron v. NRDC, 207, 225; evaluation of, 207–208; institutional analysis of, 211; *United States v. Mead* and, 215–223; deference test from, 216; *K Mart v. Cartier* and, 227; textualist approach to, 228

Chinese Exclusion Act of 1882, Alien Contract Labor Act of 1885 versus, 102

Civil Rights Act of 1964, 262, 281

Clean Air Act Amendments of 1990, 110

Clear statement rules, nondelegation canons and, 133

Cognitive restraints of salience, judicial preconception and, 115

Commentaries, 18, 21

A Comment on the Commentaries, 21–22

Commerce Clause: lower-court recalcitrance on, 131; judicial instability concerning, 139

Common-law constitutionalism: of Strauss, 232, 250–253; decision costs in, 260

Common-law courts: institutional considerations for, 9; administrative agencies as, 58

Common-law interpretation: of Blackstone and Bentham, 18–24; hallmarks of, 19; agencies and, 225–226

Complexity allocation, 214–215

Conceptual jurisprudence, by Supreme Court, 72

Condorcetian voting cycles, 127

Congress: statute updates by, 49; judicial oversight by, 78–79; fact finding for, 138; Supreme Court decisions overriden by, 160; interpretation rules from, 184; constitutional authority of, 268; precedential norms in, 274; constitutional rights, protection by, 282

Consequentialism: interpretation with, 6–7; formalism and, 41, 71; pragmatism and, 71, 85; Posner versus Dworkin, 83–85; value theory for, 84

Constitution: rules of interpretation from, 5, 76; Fourteenth Amendment of, 12, 230–231, 259, 272; Article I of, 30; statutory enactment in, 30; on statutory interpretation, 31; Article III of, 32; interpretive theory, 33; operating-level issues in, 33; legal supremacy commitment of, 34; First Amendment of, 243; interpretation authority concerning, 255; on constitutional review, 264; congressional authority concerning, 268; provision types of, 270–271; legislator versus lawyer updating of, 279

Constitutional adjudication, Ely representation-reinforcing view of, 239–242

Constitutional cases: decision procedure for, 12; judicial function in, 64–65, 230; rule-bound decisionmaking for, 230
Constitutional interpretation: by courts, 8; problems of, 11–12; institutional considerations for, 33, 253; democracy-forcing in, 127–143; holistic textualism in, 205; "institutional turn" for, 230; decision-procedures for, 233; Amar's textualism in, 243; Scalia's originalism, 244–246; Lessig's account of, 246–248; translation in, 246–248; "active liberty" in, 248–249; Constitution on, 264; by legislators, 275
Constitutionalism, 251–252
Constitutional jurisprudence, 242–243
Constitutional law: interpretation based on, 29; conceptualistic jurisprudence in, 72; academic theory about, 231–232
Constitutional limits, 235
Constitutional policies, legislative deliberation about, 118
Constitutional principles, "popular enforcement" of, 235
Constitutional review, political freedom from, 265
Constitutional rights, congressional protection of, 242, 282
Constitutional texts: Thayerian examples of, 270; interpretive baseline of, 272
Constitutional theory: limitations of, 33; modern, 237
Constitutional updating, 262
"Corrections Day" of House of Representatives, 75
Costs. See Decision costs; Predecision costs
Courts: interaction with legislature, 11, 109, 121–129; faithful agent of, 32; interaction with agencies, 128–129; interpretive techniques of, 213. See also Lower courts; Supreme Court
Cumulative judicial review, 276–277
Cyclical voting, 127–128

Dahl, Robert, 241
Decentralization: by judges, 164; of interpretive doctrine, 165–166
Decision costs: of judges, 166–167, 226; in interpretation, 259–260; in common-law

constitutionalism, 260; uncertainty in, 260
Decisionmaking: with rule-bound behavior, 68, 285; institutional capacities and, 68–69; with formalism, 79; techniques for, 156; "fast and frugal heuristics" for, 180–181; in Thayerism, 278
Decisionmaking complexity: cost-externalization and, 286; from self-interested motivation, 286; from opportunity cost neglect, 286–287
Decision theory: methods of, 171–172; maximin criterion in, 175–176
Declaration of Independence, 203–204
Deference: jurisprudence of, 215–216; categories of, 217, 220–221; Mead, 217, 219
Democracy: judges' intervention in, 64; judicial supremacy in, 265–266
Democracy and Distrust, 239
Democracy-forcing: interpretation and, 11, 118–120; by judges, 64, 86; institutional objections to, 118; textualism and, 120, 132, 161; division fallacy and, 121–122; judicial coordination in, 124, 223; in constitutional interpretation, 127–143; of statutory interpretation, 132–135; in rule of lenity, 133–135, 212; arguments for, 135–136; perverse results and, 135–137; for constitutional judging, 262; in Thayerism, 277–278
Distorting force of particulars: judges and, 6; second-order decision strategies for, 37–38
Division fallacy: democracy-forcing and, 121–122; of interpretive strategy, 123
Doctrine of absurdity: costs of, 38–39; Manning on, 58
Dorf, Michael, 236–237
Douglas, William, 244
Dred Scott v. Sandford, 231, 241, 281
"Due process of lawmaking," 119, 137–138, 146, 262
Dworkin, Ronald, 6, 16, 40, 45, 100, 185; Hart versus, 27; on Posner's pragmatism, 83–85; constitutional interpretation of, 232, 252–253
Dynamic interpretation: Eskridge's advocacy of, 41; nirvana fallacy of, 41; selection bias in, 43;

Dynamic interpretation (*continued*)
"countermajoritarian difficulty" of, 44;
statutory obsolescence and, 46;
justification for, 50. *See also* Dynamism
Dynamism: nirvana of, 41–46; effects on
legislative behavior, 46; institutions and,
46–49; judicial error and, 47; non-
dynamic interpretation versus, 49;
systematic effects and, 49–50

Elhauge, Einer, 18, 64, 118, 199, 240–241,
255
Elster, John, 156, 265; on insufficient
reason principle, 174–175
Ely, John Hart, 45, 239–241; legal process
theory of, 17; representation-reinforcing
view of, 232
Empiricism: judicial decisionmaking and,
61; academic versus judicial, 153–154,
163; gains from, 162; trans-science
problem in, 162
Endangered Species Act, 28, 131
Energy Policy Act of 1992, 110
"Enrolled bill rule," 236–237
Environmental Protection Agency, 208
Epstein, Richard, 59
Equal Protection Clause of Fourteenth
Amendment, 259, 279–280
Equity: Aristotelian principle of, 19;
without law, 20–21
Eskridge, William, 10, 13, 15, 17, 32, 39–
40, 46–51, 73, 120, 185, 191, 195, 206,
239; Manning versus, 31–32; on statute
interpretation, 41, 67, 225; critique of
"new textualism," 41; Posner versus, 52;
interpretive theory after, 63–64;
congressional "overrides" study of, 159–
161

"Faithful-agent" account of interpretation,
32
Fallacy of division, democracy-forcing and,
121–122
Family and Medical Leave Act, 139
"Fast and frugal heuristics" for
decisionmakers, 180–181
Federal Communications Commission,
208
*Federal Election Commission v. National
Rifle Association,* 220

Federalist 78, 238; judicial review in, 256–
257; on judicial enforcement of
Constitution, 266
First Amendment, Speech and Debate
Clause of, 243
First-best principles: rules of
interpretation, 2; second-best efforts, 2;
institutional premises and, 16; questions
about interpretive theory, 32;
conclusions from, 36; interpretive rules
from, 80–81
Fish, Stanley, 9, 34–35
Foran, Martin A., 94
Formalism: essentialist version of, 5;
justification for, 5, 45, 73; senses of, 5,
72–74; in "nature of contracts," 7;
issues in, 24; jurisprudence in, 24, 42;
failure of, 24–25; rule-bound
interpretation in, 29, 245;
consequentialist justification for, 41, 71;
democracy and, 45; adjudication with,
71; consequences of, 71–72; judicial
preference for, 72; Schauer on, 72;
alternatives to, 74; general conditions
for, 75–76; at operating level, 75–76;
institutional variables in, 76;
decisionmaking with, 79; case for, 79–
80; benefits of, 120;
"countermajoritarian" nature of, 160–
161; in judicial review, 272. *See also*
Judicial formalism; Operating-level
formalism
Fourteenth Amendment, 231, 272;
legislative enforcement of, 12; Equal
Protection Clause of, 259
Frankfurter, Felix, 12, 233–234, 270
Freedom of Access to Clinic Entrances
Act, 131
Free speech, 240
Frequentism, probability assignment with,
171

Gadamer, Hans-Georg, 42
Gadamerian theory, 42
Griswold v. Connecticut, 244

Hamilton, Alexander, 44–45; on judicial
review, 232, 252–253; defense of judicial
review, 238; on judicial enforcement of
Constitution, 266

Hammer v. Dagenhard, 281
Hand, Learned, 12, 52, 233–234
Hart, Henry, 17, 26; abstract
     institutionalism of, 64
Hart, H. L. A., 9, 18, 23; canonical
     treatment of legal interpretation, 24–26;
     Dworkin versus, 27
Holistic statutory interpretation, cost-
     benefit analysis of, 203–204
Holistic textualism, in constitutional
     interpretation, 205
Holy Trinity v. United States, 10, 86–110,
     114–117, 183, 194; legislative history of,
     87–89, 92, 105–107; overview of, 89–90;
     congressional intent in, 92; religious
     liberty and, 93; reassessment of, 93–98;
     Senate proceedings on, 95–98; Supreme
     Court's performance in, 98–105;
     statutory text in, 99–100, 185; church's
     brief in, 100; adjudicative process in,
     103–105; salience in, 104; judicial
     preconception in, 104–105;
     institutionalist lesson of, 116
Hopkins, John, 98
House of Representatives, 94; "Corrections
     Day" procedure of, 75; Committee on
     Labor, 91

Informational defects, 111
Institution(s): legal interpretation and, 1–3;
     dynamism and, 46–49
Institutional capacity: attention to, 30;
     Posner's assessment of, 55–57;
     interpretive approaches, 153
Institutionalism: interpretive theories in,
     16–18, 121; types of, 16–18;
     mechanisms of, 36–39; in legal process
     school, 63; second-best assessment of
     institutional issues, 82; value theory
     and, 83–84; as "theory of the middle
     range," 85; justice and, 156; uncertainty
     and, 158
Institutionalist dilemma: of judges, 3–4,
     149; uncertainty and, 154–155; bounded
     rationality and, 155–156
Institutionalist judges, decision costs for,
     196
Institutional review, 235–236
Institutional rules, 9
Insufficient reason, 173–175

INS v. Chadha, 272–273
Integrity: in modern era, 24–34; positivism
     versus, 27–28
Intentionalism: legal, 81; textualism versus,
     82; second-best problems of, 87; with
     legislative history, 94; irrelevance of, 115–
     117; statutory interpretation and, 144.
     See also Literary intentionalism
Interpretation: rules and standards in, 2,
     68, 76; systematic effects and, 2, 153;
     tools for interpretive choice, 4; act-
     consequentialist account of, 5; with
     consequentialism, 6–7; with
     pragmatism, 6–7; problems of, 8, 67;
     first-best accounts of, 10, 13, 80;
     institutional dimensions of, 15, 122, 153–
     154, 228–229; judicial capacities in, 18,
     22, 66, 123–129, 132, 157; formalist
     style of, 20; purposivism in, 22; "faithful-
     agent" account of, 32; literary, 34;
     political-theory analysis of, 50;
     "imaginative-reconstruction" approach
     to, 52; considerations for, 64, 68–71;
     significance of, 66; inescapability of, 67;
     agency costs in, 78, 214–215; second-
     best accounts of, 80, 116; value theory
     in, 80; theorized agreements on, 82; for
     specialized agencies versus generalist
     judges, 115; democracy-forcing, 118–120;
     distributive effects of, 145–146; variables
     for, 153; case-by-case decisionmaking
     and, 157; bounded rationality and
     interpretive choice, 157–162; uncertainty
     and interpretive choice, 157–162, 168–
     181; empirical effects of, 159–160;
     empirical determinants of, 161;
     decentralization of, 165–166; provisional
     adjudication in, 165–166; institutional
     reaction to, 167; *Chevron* rule in, 184;
     with canons of construction, 198–202;
     by agencies, 206–216; with rule of
     lenity, 211–212; courts versus agencies
     in, 213; by Supreme Court, 224; across
     institutions, 246; decision costs in, 259–
     260; complexity commitment of, 284–
     288; interim theory of, 289–290. *See
     also* Constitutional interpretation;
     Dynamic interpretation; Judicial
     interpretation; Legal interpretation;
     Statutory interpretation

Interpretive baseline, for judicial review, 272–273

Interpretive complexity, preference for, 287. *See also* Decisionmaking complexity

Interpretive formalism: second-best argument for, 22; anti-formalism versus, 37

Interpretive intentionalism: theory of, 34–35; controversy of, 35

Interpretive rules: consequences of, 53; from first-best principles, 80–81; systematic effects of, 118; coordination benefits of, 146; justification for, 146; for judges, 149; conditions of, 150

Interpretive theory: applications in, 10–12; critique in, 10–12; shortcomings of, 13; asymmetrical institutionalism in, 17; stylized institutionalism in, 17; second-best considerations in, 20; since World War II, 24; first-best questions about, 32; on Constitution, 33; literary interpretation versus, 34; institutional issues in, 36; "institutional turn" in, 63, 79; after Eskridge, 63–64; conflicts over, 82; institutionalist issues in, 121; division fallacy of, 123; history of, 125; types of, 147

Intratextualism, 232, 252–253

Judges: institutionalist dilemma of, 3–4, 149; interpretive approaches of, 4, 157; distorting force of particulars and, 6; legislative history and, 11, 30, 87, 168, 190–191; legal uncertainty and, 23; legislator treatment by, 26; role confusion by, 36; academic's criticism of, 37; competence of, 37; as agents of legislature, 42; insulation of, 48; policymaking by, 53–54, 126; democracy-forcing by, 64, 86; interpretive methodology for, 66; legislative behavior and, 70; cognitive load of, 126; noncompliance by, 126; Condorcetian voting cycles and, 127; legal process consensus and, 129; precedence theory for, 141–143, 223; interpretive rules for, 149; power limits of, 163; decentralization strategy of, 164; provisional interpretive choice by, 164;

decision costs and, 166–167, 226; statutory changes and, 168; statutory text, use by, 183–184; precedent and, 224; coordination and marginal contribution, 226; self-dealing by, 257–258; political insulation of, 279. *See also* Institutionalist judges

Judicial accuracy: on legislative intent, 103; errors of, 108–109; from legislative history, 108–109

Judicial capacity: in interpretation, 22; in Dworkin analysis, 29; Posner's view of, 56; legislative history and, 86; question of, 105; informational advantage and, 166–168

Judicial coordination: feasibility of, 122; interpretive method and, 123–129; in democracy-forcing, 124, 223; cost of, 132; on interpretive doctrine, 132; first-best, second-best and, 147

Judicial deference: to legislative interpretations, 150; to agencies, 206, 214–215; to administrative conclusions, 211

Judicial disagreement: consequences of, 125; influence of precedent on, 125

Judicial discretion: social benefits of, 54; in constitutional cases, 64; in statutory interpretation, 105–106

Judicial error: types of, 44, 108–109, 256–259; dynamism and, 47; legislative history and, 90, 111; costs of, 256–259

Judicial evaluation, 112

Judicial formalism: on legislation, 75, 192–196; cost-benefit analysis of, 192–194

Judicial institutions: collective character of, 119; structure of, 129–132

Judicial insulation, 210

Judicial interpretation: legislative preferences about, 20; risks for, 115–116; condition of, 145; errors of generalization and, 46

Judicial intervention, in constitutional adjudication, 65

Judicial power, Article III grant of, 32

Judicial preconception, in *Holy Trinity*, 104–105

Judicial resort to legislative history. *See* Legislative history

Judicial review: rule-consequentialist

critique of, 12, 280–281; democracy-promotion through, 44–45; institutional costs and benefits of, 163; Thayerian version of, 233; desirability of, 233–234; interpretive choice in, 237; Hamilton and agency in, 238–239; legislative responsibility and, 255; in *Federalist 78*, 256–257; agency costs of, 256–259; error costs of, 256–259; transition costs in, 263–264; of Constitution, 264; majoritarian tyranny and, 265; opponents' "burden of proof" concerning, 266; Strauss's defense of, 267; status quo of, 267–268; formalism in, 272; interpretive baseline for, 272–273; Alexander on, 276–277; cumulative, 276–277; Schauer on, 276–277; by Supreme Court, 280; in transitional democracies, 284

Judicial supremacy: for Alexander, 232, 252–253; for Schauer, 232, 252–253; in democracy, 265–266

Judiciary: political insulation of, 47; congressional oversight of, 78–79; coordination costs of, 119; disagreement within, 124–125

Jurisprudence, 72

Justices. *See* Judges

Kahan, Dan, 212

Kelley, William, 94–95

Kennedy, Anthony, in *K Mart v. Cartier*, 227

Kimmel v. Florida Board of Regents, 138

Klarman, Michael, 241, 259, 281

K Mart v. Cartier, 227; *Chevron* test in, 227; Scalia dissent in, 227–228

Knapp, Steven, 9, 34–35

Komesar, Neil, 18, 47, 64, 240–241, 255, 268

Kramer, Larry, 12, 235, 255

Law: agency interpretations of, 24; as integrity, 28; predecision costs in, 220; settlement function of, 249, 261

Lawmaking: due process of, 137, 279; levels of, 282–284

Legal academy, judge-centered culture of, 17

Legal form, 69–70

Legal intentionalism, literary intentionalism versus, 81

Legal interpretation: institutionalist view of, 1, 61; of statutes and Constitution, 1; normative theory of, 2; change in, 128; interim theory of, 289–290; transition period of, 290

Legal language, 16

Legal order, 21

Legal process approach: dominance of, 24; evaluation of, 27; execution of, 27; Hart and Sacks on, 27; textualism versus purposivism in, 34; institutionalism in, 63

Legal process consensus: conservative judges and, 129; Republican Party and, 129

Legal system: cognition, motivation, and agency costs, 77; formalism, antiformalism, and error, 77

Legal theory: marginal values in, 2; modern interpretive work in, 15

Legal uncertainty, 23

Legislation: aims of, 26; judges' influence on, 31; American, 54–55; judicial formalism and, 75; judicial review of, 237

Legislation dynamics, 143–145

Legislative behavior: dynamism and, 46; judges' impact on, 70; interpretive consensus and, 128

Legislative deliberation: on constitutional policy, 118; on statutory policies, 118; overbreadth and, 140–141

Legislative foresight, 24

Legislative heterogeneity, 114

Legislative history: in statutory interpretation, 8, 30–31; judges' use of, 11, 30, 87, 168, 190–191; authority of, 30; judicial recourse to, 50, 88–89, 107, 147, 190–191, 197; census for, 51; exclusion of, 70, 195–196, 225–226; judicial capacity and, 86; intent in, 87, 106; as interpretive source, 87; reliability of, 88; of *Holy Trinity*, 89; judicial error in, 90, 111; intentionalism with, 94; adjudicative process and, 102–107, 113–114; second-best thesis of, 107–115; legislative intent from, 108; judicial accuracy and, 108–109; of Alien Contract Labor Act of 1885, 110;

Legislative history (*continued*)
  statutory text versus, 110; error risks in,
  111–112; volume of, 111–112;
  accessibility of, 112; heterogeneousness
  of, 112–113; judicial preconception of,
  113–114; utility of, 116; assessment of,
  117; in statutory arena courts, 150;
  textualist critiques of, 169, 190–192;
  informational benefits of, 189; relevant
  variables in, 189–190; burden allocation
  in, 190–192; judicial formalism about,
  192–196; research cost of, 193; maximin
  approach to, 193–194; satisficing in, 194;
  accuracy of, 196–197; decision costs of,
  196–197; canons of construction versus
  use of, 199; related statutes and, 202–205
Legislative intent: judicial accuracy
  concerning, 103; from legislative history,
  108; judicial assessment of, 116;
  agencies versus courts on, 208–211;
  judicial insulation from, 210
Legislative interpretations, judicial
  deference to, 150. *See also* Interpretation
Legislative supremacy: in statutory
  interpretation, 31; Constitution's
  commitments to, 34
Legislators: judges' treatment of, 26;
  constitutional rules and, 138; power
  limits of, 163; public values and, 274
Legislature: courts' interaction with, 11,
  121–129; American, 54–55; process of,
  109; legislative responsibility, judicial
  review and, 255; self-dealing in, 257; as
  common-law constitutionalists, 278–280
Leiber, Francis, 70
Lessig, Lawrence, 239; translation theory
  of, 232, 252–253
Literary intentionalism: thesis of, 34–36;
  legal intentionalism versus, 81
Literary interpretation, interpretive theory
  versus, 34
Llewellyn, Karl, 198, 202
Lower courts: divisions within, 130;
  noncompliance by, 130; Supreme Court
  and, 139, 221

Majoritarian tyranny, 265
Manning, John, 29, 41, 73, 75–76;
  Eskridge versus, 31–32; on absurdity
  doctrine, 58

Marbury v. Madison, 232, 234–236
Marmor, Andrei, 27
Marshall, John, 244; arguments for judicial
  review, 234
Mashaw, Jerry, 106
Massachusetts v. Oakes, 140
Mead Court: on deference, 217, 219;
  objections to, 218–219; predecision costs
  from, 220
Mechanical jurisprudence. *See* Formalism
Michaels, Walter Benn, 9, 34–35
Modern constitutional theory, 237
Morgan, John Tyler, 97
*Motion Picture Association of America v.
  Federal Communications Commission,*
  221

Nagle, John, 43, 44
National Labor Relations Board, 208
"Nature of contracts," 5
Neo-Thayerianism: institutional
  justifications for, 232; institutional
  grounds of, 255
*Nevada Department of Human Resources v.
  Hibbs,* 139
"New textualism," 41
Nirvana fallacy: thesis of, 40; of dynamic
  interpretation, 41
Nondelegation canons, 133
Northwest Ordinance, 203–204

O'Connor, Sandra Day, 140
Of Laws in General, 22
O'Neill, John, 95
Operating-level formalism: justification
  for, 29; decision strategy of, 38;
  contingencies of, 76–77
Osborne v. Ohio, 141
Out-and-out philosophizing, 16

"The Philosopher's Brief," 242
Picking, with satisficing, 179–180
Policymaking discretion, 53–54, 126
Political-theory analysis: of interpretation,
  50; problem with, 51
Politics, judiciary insulation from, 47
Positivism: in modern era, 24–34; integrity
  versus, 27–28
Posner, Richard, 6–7, 10, 13, 15, 17, 39–
  40, 43, 52, 75, 199, 206, 220–221, 266;

Eskridge versus, 52; on adjudication, 53; on American appellate courts, 54, 56; institutional capacities, assessment of, 55–57; on judicial capacity, 56; on absurdity doctrine, 58; on legislatures, 65; Dworkin's criticism of, 83–85

Power limits: of judges, 163; of legislators, 163

Pragmatism: interpretation with, 6–7; statutory absurdity and, 57–59; of Posner, 58–59; consequentialism and, 71, 85; Posner versus Dworkin on, 83–85

Precedence: for judges, 141–143, 223; dilemmas from, 143; justification for, 179–180; decision costs of, 223

Predecision costs: in law, 220; from *Mead Court*, 220

Principals and agents, agency slippage between, 69

Probability assignment: with frequentism, 171; with Bayesian decision theory, 171–172; subjectivism in, 172

Prohibition Amendment of 1919, 272

Provisional interpretive choice, 164

Purposivism, 248: premise for, 22; problems of, 23; in modern era, 24–34; evaluation of, 27; textualism versus, 34; translation and, 247

Reasoning tools, 181–182

Reconstruction, in interpretive theory, 10–12

Refugee Act of 1980, 110

Rehnquist, William H., 88

Rehnquist Court, 138, 146: coordinated action by, 131; rule of lenity and, 135

Republican Party, 48–49; legal process consensus and, 129

Riggs v. Palmer, 28

Roe v. Wade, 262

Role confusion, 36

Rule-bound decisionmaking: costs of, 39; use of, 68, 285; for constitutional cases, 230

Rule-bound interpretation, in formalism, 29, 245

Rule-consequentialism: decision strategy of, 38; in judicial review, 280–281

Rule of clear mistake, in Thayerism, 270

Rule of law: formalism in, 5; court's role in, 48

Rule of lenity: democracy-forcing in, 133–135, 212; Rehnquist Court, Burger Court, and Warren Court on, 135; outcome preferences from, 145; in interpretation, 211–212

Rules and standards, 68

Rules of interpretation: from first-best conceptualism, 2; from Constitution, 76

Sacks, Albert, 17–18, 26; abstract institutionalism of, 64

Sager, Lawrence, 254

Salience: in decisionmaking, 38; distorting force of, 104; in *Holy Trinity,* 104

Satisficing: in bounded rationality, 176–179; in uncertainty, 176–179; with picking, 179–180; in legislative history, 194

Scalia, Antonin, 41, 100, 140, 179, 185, 200, 219, 221; textualism of, 134; on deference, 217–218; *K Mart v. Cartier* dissent of, 227–228; originalism of, 232, 259; judicial restraint, emphasis on, 253

Schauer, Frederick, 5, 57, 249, 263, 271; on formalism, 72; judicial supremacy for, 232, 252–253; on judicial review, 276–277

Schuck, Peter, 286

Second-best thesis, of legislative history, 107–115

Senate Committee on Education and Labor, 92, 96

Separation-of-powers objection to dynamic interpretation, 44

Separation-of-powers principle, 106

Sherman Act, 78

Skidmore v. Swift & Co., 216

Specialization, academic versus judicial, 37

Statutes: interpretive formalism for, 61; judicial updating of, 67; volume of, 110; canon of avoidance on, 133

Statutes at Large, 110

Statutory absurdity, 57–59

Statutory cases, 185–187

Statutory changes, judges and, 168

Statutory enactment, in Article I of
  Constitution, 30
Statutory enforcement, on legislative
  grounds, 20
Statutory interpretation: aim of, 2;
  institutional determinants of, 3; by
  agencies, 8, 226; by courts, 8; legislative
  history in, 8, 30–31; common-law
  approaches to, 15, 18; second-best
  justifications for, 24; in Constitution,
  31; operating-level issues about, 33;
  judicial approaches to, 49; legislative
  intent in, 90; judicial "discretion" in,
  105–106; democracy-forcing of, 132–
  135; by intentionalists, 144; statutory
  rules of, 184–185; rule-bound formalism
  in, 245. See also Holistic statutory
  interpretation
Statutory language, 28
Statutory obsolescence, problem of, 46
Statutory policies, legislative deliberation
  about, 118
Statutory precedent: application of, 11;
  Supreme Court's overruling of, 169;
  doctrine of, 183–184
Statutory system, 54–55
Statutory text: legislative history versus,
  110; judges' use of, 183–184; ambiguity,
  187; stock objections concerning, 187–
  189
Strauss, David: common-law
  constitutionalism of, 232, 250–253;
  defense of judicial review, 267;
  Thayerism versus, 272
Strauss, Peter, 208, 224
Stylized institutionalism, 17
Subjectivism, 172
Sunstein, Cass, 47–48, 82
Supremacy Clause, 234
Supreme Court: voting rules of, 9;
  conceptual jurisprudence by, 72; on
  Alien Contract Labor Act of 1885, 96;
  Holy Trinity performance of, 98–105;
  on Administrative Procedure Act, 120;
  instability within, 131; influence on
  lower courts, 139, 221; congressional
  overrides of, 160; certiorari policy of,
  165; overruling of statutory precedent,
  169; use of legislative history by, 191;

interpretation by, 224; review of
  congressional decisions by, 268; retreat
  from judicial review by, 280
Systematic effects: dynamism and, 49–
  50; mistakes and their corrections,
  78–79; decision costs and uncertainty,
  79

Taney, Robert Brooke, 231
Textualism: in modern era, 24–34; legal
  process purposivism versus, 34; new, 41;
  dynamic interpretation versus, 50;
  intentionalism versus, 82; democracy-
  forcing with, 120, 132, 161; of Scalia,
  134
Thayer, James Bradley, 12, 233, 239,
  254
Thayerism: "rule of clear mistake" in,
  254, 270; Strauss versus, 272; outcome
  of, 276; democracy-forcing in, 277–
  278; decisionmaking in, 278; in
  American law, 280; on federal versus
  state statutes, 282–283. See also Neo-
  Thayerianism
Translation: in constitutional
  interpretation, 246–248; legislative veto
  of, 248
Trans-scientific questions, 158
Treason Clause, 271, 278
Tribe, Lawrence, 102
Tushnet, Mark, 12, 254–255
TVA v. Hill, 28–29, 49

Uncertainty: in interpretive choice, 157–
  162, 168–181; allocating the burden of,
  169–170; insufficient reason in, 173–175;
  satisficing in, 176–179
United States Code, 203; as statute source,
  110
United States v. Lopez, 138–139
United States v. Mead, 215–223. See also
  Mead Court
United States v. Morrison, 138–140, 258,
  281
United States v. Will, 257–258

Value theory: background assumptions of,
  7–8; in interpretive approaches, 80;